Microsoft®

XML and SOAP

Programming for

BizTalk™ Servers

Brian E. Travis

PUBLISHED BY
Microsoft Press
A Division of Microsoft Corporation
One Microsoft Way
Redmond, Washington 98052-6399

Library of Congress Cataloging-in-Publication Data
    Travis, Brian E., 1958-
        XML and SOAP Programming for BizTalk Servers / Brian E. Travis.
            p. cm.
        ISBN 0-7356-1126-2
        1. XML (Document markup language)   I. Title.
    QA76.76.H94 T75 2000
    005.7'2--dc21   00-041582

Printed and bound in the United States of America.

    2 3 4 5 6 7 8 9   MLML   5 4 3 2 1 0

Distributed in Canada by Penguin Books Canada Limited.

A CIP catalogue record for this book is available from the British Library.

Microsoft Press books are available through booksellers and distributors worldwide. For
further information about international editions, contact your local Microsoft Corporation
office or contact Microsoft Press International directly at fax (425) 936-7329. Visit our Web
site at mspress.microsoft.com. Send comments to *mspinput@microsoft.com*.

Simple Object Access Protocol (SOAP) 1.1 copyright © 2000 DevelopMentor, International Business Machines Corporation, Lotus Development Corporation, Microsoft, UserLand Software.

BizTalk Framework 2.0 Draft: Document and Message Specification © 1999–2000, Microsoft
Corporation. All rights reserved.

Appendix A is adapted from an article written by OmniMark. Copyright © OmniMark
Technologies Corporation 1988–2000.

Acquisitions Editor: David Clark
Project Editor: Victoria Thulman
Technical Editor: Brian Johnson
Manuscript Editor: Rebecca McKay

For Miller,
who, having recently learned the rules of well-formed chess,
will go on to be a world champion.

Table of Contents

Table of Contents

Table of Contents

Acknowledgments

This book was originally my idea, but I feel like I am just a conductor of a very well-oiled publishing machine. The people at Microsoft Press really turned my idea into what I think is a book that holds together quite well and is fairly consistent from chapter to chapter.

I'd like to thank Vicky Thulman, who acted as the Hollywood producer, balancing the need for "the talent" (that would be me) to have creative control against the real-world pressures of the publishing business. Vicky kept me informed throughout production of the book, managing the editorial process and keeping me in line.

Brian Johnson, the technical editor, was fabulous at checking all of my facts and not letting me get away with glossing over a technical issue. Brian also convinced me to register the domain names mentioned in the book. Now if you go to *myduckjokes.com* or *duckbarjokes.com*, you'll know who to blame.

Becka McKay saw the manuscripts first. I wrote this book in about a dozen hotel rooms and at least as many airplane trips over several months. Consistency suffered as a result. It was Becka's job to tell you, the reader, what I actually meant. I tend to use the words "this" and "that" a lot. Becka added a lot of comments like "author is saying 'this' again. What does he mean this time?"

The team at Microsoft Press were the best an author can have. I look forward to working with them again!

The good people at OmniMark Technologies were very supportive of this book, since it showcases their great product. Chief Technical Officer John McFadden pulled out all the stops in his organization to get me a working copy of OmniMark that had world-class handling of XML documents and schemas. As always, OmniMark Technologies makes the difficult look easy. The impossible took them a little longer. Mark Baker at OmniMark worked with my last-minute deadlines on the material for Appendix A, "OmniMark for the Impatient." I left it mostly intact, only modifying it for the duck-bar theme and adding some information appropriate to the rest of the book.

There are several people at Microsoft who helped keep me in the loop about technologies in the book. Kevin McCall, the BizTalk Evangelist, never sleeps. He jets around the world telling people about BizTalk and how they can solve their B2B problems. It was Kevin who pointed out that the BizTalk Framework spec changed radically after I had shipped chapters to the publisher. Fortunately, Vicky gave me an extension to update the book to the new draft spec. John Montgomery plays a similar role for SOAP. John filled me in on the relationship between SOAP and BizTalk. Robert Coleridge is an Architect at Microsoft working on the ROPE implementation. Robert kept me in the loop as new builds came along. There are many others at Microsoft who have been a great help, and I'd like to thank them all.

Mehtap Ozkan helped with a nasty bug in ASP that caused data in a *POST* method to get lost. She worked intensely to come up with the right combination of character conversion functions to find the lost data. Mehtap also provided spiritual support during the difficult last part of the writing process.

John Iobst from the Newspaper Association of America was helpful in sorting through the history and politics of what his organization is doing with XML and standard schemas for sharing news content.

I have taught thousands of students over the past couple of years about XML and e-commerce applications. These lectures and seminars allow me to test new material and see what works and what doesn't. My students' feedback is what made the information in this book possible, and it gave me plenty of duck-bar jokes.

And I thank you for buying this book. I hope you enjoy reading it as much as I enjoyed writing it.

Introduction

The eXtensible Markup Language, or XML, is a simple technology that has taken the computer world by storm. Even before XML was formally adopted, Microsoft Chairman Bill Gates called XML a "breakthrough technology" because he saw the value of defining data transactions in an open, platform-independent way. Since then, many standards of data interchange have been built on top of XML, each with a particular purpose and all using XML's simple syntax.

BizTalk and the Simple Object Access Protocol (SOAP) are XML-based, open initiatives designed to facilitate electronic commerce between systems on the Web. Both BizTalk and SOAP use XML as their data exchange syntax, because XML enables you to specify data in a very precise way.

I've wanted to write an XML book for some time. My book, *The SGML Implementation Guide* (Springer Verlag, 1995), was a real-world hands-on guide to implementers of SGML in the mid-1990s. When XML came along, I wanted to update my first book to make it XML-compatible. This was difficult, however. Because of its simplicity, flexibility, and much smaller size, XML can do so much more than SGML. Any book that I wrote would have to be XML-specific.

I have a job that keeps me pretty busy, so I never got around to writing that XML book. Over the next year or so, there were plenty of XML books published that covered various topics, and the XML bookshelf at the local book superstore was getting pretty crowded. I didn't want my XML book to get lost on that shelf.

Then came a couple of great XML applications—BizTalk and SOAP—and I figured it was time to write my first XML book.

There are similarities between BizTalk and SOAP, but there are also differences. In this book, I will attempt to explain these differences and give examples of each.

BIZTALK

The BizTalk initiative was started by Microsoft to address the issue of moving business documents between trading partners in the e-commerce supply chain. BizTalk provides an elegant envelope for moving electronic documents around the Internet in the same way the postal service moves physical envelopes between trading partners.

BizTalk is really four different facets of a single initiative. First there is the BizTalk Framework Independent Document Specification. The BizTalk Framework is a set of tags that provides an addressing definition so that you can get your documents from one place to another and cause some kind of processing to happen at each place. The BizTalk Framework works like a virtual envelope for sending business documents to our trading partners.

Second, BizTalk.org is a Web site that provides a place to learn about e-commerce technologies—XML in general and BizTalk in particular. BizTalk.org hosts discussion groups where you can find peer support for developing your own document vocabularies, named schemas, and help in integrating your schemas into the BizTalk Framework. BizTalk.org is also a repository for schemas (definitions for XML documents) and allows you to post your schemas for others to access. This service is free.

Third, to process your BizTalk documents, you will need a BizTalk Framework Compliant (BFC) server. A BFC server is the software that reads BizTalk documents and then does something intelligent with them. The intelligent thing it does will depend on what systems you have in place and what needs to be done to process the document.

And fourth, there is Microsoft BizTalk Server 2000, which runs on Microsoft Windows 2000 Server. Because of the open nature of the BizTalk Framework specification, you can create BizTalk messages on a Linux system running a BizTalk server written in Java and read the messages on a Microsoft Windows 2000 Advanced Server using BizTalk Server 2000.

BizTalk is viewed by some as a Microsoft-specific protocol that requires Microsoft platforms. This is not the case. The first three facets of BizTalk that I've outlined here are not proprietary to Microsoft in any way. Two Java applications can pass data back and forth using BizTalk messages. Businesses that run on UNIX can use schemas published to BizTalk.org. A BizTalk server can be written in Perl or any other Internet-aware programming language.

In this book, we will write a BizTalk server using OmniMark, an internet-savvy programming language with built-in support for XML documents.

SOAP

SOAP started life as a way of invoking DCOM (Distributed COM) methods in a more loosely coupled way than regular COM method invocations. It evolved into a specification that allowed for methods to be invoked on dissimilar systems across Internet protocols (HTTP, FTP, and so on). SOAP and BizTalk are similar in their approach to interchanging information but each is optimized for different transaction types.

SOAP is at the core of a Microsoft initiative called Web Services. Web Services offers a new way of looking at the Web. By using an HTML browser to look at information, information consumers force content providers (pretty much anyone on the

Web) to "dumb down" their data so that human eyes can consume it. By removing the formatting requirements for the data, the data can be delivered in a raw format, allowing services to aggregate and process that data, ultimately offering it to users with added value. An example of such data is real-time weather. A travel site could combine its content with weather reports to provide next week's travelers with a tentative weather forecast. A Web site that provides weather as HTML pages can generate extra income by providing the raw weather data as an XML stream in response to a real-time request for weather in a particular location to parties who will pay to repackage that content.

Like the platform-independent BizTalk, you can send a SOAP method invocation to a Perl script running on Solaris, which in turn invokes a Java class to extract data from an Oracle database. The response is sent as an XML document object, which then can be used in your application. You don't need to know what platform your service is running on.

To understand BizTalk and SOAP, you need to understand the underlying syntax that makes it all possible—XML. In fact, BizTalk is an extension of SOAP, using SOAP to deliver a business document over HTTP. When you are using BizTalk, you are using SOAP and XML as well.

Part I of this book is an introduction to XML from a business and technical point of view. The purpose of this introduction is to provide a perspective for building and interchanging business information using XML structures.

This first part is really the XML book I wanted to write. Even if you don't care about BizTalk or SOAP, I hope you will find some value in the description of XML in Part I, which is aimed at the developer.

Part II of the book discusses the BizTalk Framework and shows how you can use XML and BizTalk today to create e-commerce applications. In Part III we actually build some BFC servers using various Microsoft and non-Microsoft tools.

I enjoyed writing this book because it gave me a chance to discover some great stuff happening in the B2B (business-to-business) marketplace. I think SOAP and Web Services will truly change the way people think about their jobs and even their lives. BizTalk will provide companies with a standard, cost-effective way to replace paper when doing transactions.

Now I need to concentrate on my next work, *1,001 Duck-Bar Jokes*. If we should meet, let me know your favorite Duck-bar joke and I'll buy you a beer.

About the Companion CD

The companion CD for this book contains several applications that I want readers to try out. All of these are mentioned in the book. The companion CD also includes a user interface used to browse the CD and install the sample programs, a fully searchable electronic version of the book, and a PDF version of my book, *OmniMark At Work, Volume 1: Getting Started*.

SYSTEM REQUIREMENTS

To load the samples, you must have the following software installed:

■ Microsoft Windows 98, Windows NT 4.0, or Windows 2000

To use the Microsoft Visual Basic project (poGen.vbp), you must have the following software installed:

■ Microsoft Visual Basic version 6; or Microsoft Visual Studio version 6, Professional or Enterprise Edition.

To use the OmniMark programs, you must have the following software loaded:

■ OmniMark C/VM version 6
■ OmniMark Integrated Development Environment version 2 (Optional)

To load the samples, just insert the CD into your CD drive to launch the Autorun application, StartCD.exe.

The searchable online version of this book is in the \eBook\ folder.

The electronic version of OmniMark At Work is in the \References\ folder. The file name is Oawv1.pdf.

CODE SAMPLES

The sample files for all code are installed to C:\TravisBook\ChXX\ (where XX is the chapter number) on your local drive by default. Some of the OmniMark programs on the companion CD run as CGI programs under Internet Information Services, so the OmniMark executable file needs to be mapped before these scripts can be used. See "Configuring Web Servers for OmniMark CGI" in Appendix A for specific instructions.

SOFTWARE INCLUDED ON THE CD

The following sections describe the software included on the companion CD.

Microsoft BizTalk Server 2000 Technology Preview

Microsoft BizTalk Server 2000 is due to be released in late 2000. Microsoft has provided an early release version of the product in the form of a Technology Preview. The product can be installed in client or server mode. The client contains some productivity tools for users and developers, but it does not process BizTalk transactions. The server version creates BizTalk messages and sends them to other BizTalk servers using a number of different transport protocols and methods.

The client version requires one of the following operating systems and components:

- Microsoft Windows 98
- Microsoft Windows NT Workstation 4.0
- Microsoft Windows NT Server 4.0
- Microsoft Windows 2000 Professional with the NTFS file system and Microsoft Data Access Components (MDAC) 2.5
- Microsoft Windows 2000 Server or Microsoft Windows 2000 Advanced Server with the NTFS file system, MDAC 2.5, and Distributed Component Object Model (DCOM 1.3)

The server version requires the following software:

- Microsoft Windows 2000 Server or Microsoft Windows 2000 Advanced Server with the NTFS file system
- Microsoft Data Access Components (MDAC) 2.5
- Distributed Component Object Model (DCOM) 1.3

The install program for the BizTalk Tech Preview is in the folder \Software\ BizTServ\.

SOAP Toolkit for Visual Studio 6.0

The SOAP Toolkit for Visual Studio 6.0 is a developer tool published by Microsoft. It has tools to help you create Service Description Language (SDL) files so that you can expose Web services using SOAP. It also contains the Remote Object Proxy Engine (ROPE), that provides client-side or server-side capabilities that enable you to send and receive SOAP documents.

A Microsoft manager told me, "If you can create a COM object, you can create a Web Service" using the SOAP Toolkit. He is right. This is a very powerful program. If you are a Visual Studio developer, you should get to know SOAP and the SOAP Toolkit.

The install program for the SOAP Toolkit is in the folder \Software\SOAPTK\.

Microsoft Internet Explorer 5.5

Internet Explorer 5.5 includes an XML parser that you can access programmatically from Microsoft Visual Basic or from scripting languages such as Microsoft Visual Basic, Scripting Edition (VBScript). Internet Explorer 5.5 installs on Microsoft Windows 95 or later, Microsoft Windows NT 4.0, and Microsoft Windows 2000. The installer for this program is located in the \Software\IE55\ folder on the companion CD.

Architag XRay XML Editor

The Architag XRay XML Editor, or simply XRay, is a real-time validating XML editor. By real-time, I mean that XRay checks an XML document as you type, giving you an indication of any errors in the file. XRay was developed as a learning aid for students taking Architag University (*http://architag.com/university*) courses. It's optimized for instruction, allowing you to learn XML syntax quickly with immediate feedback. The product supports well-formed XML and valid XML according to DTD schema syntax or XML Data Reduced (XDR) schema syntax, which is used by the BizTalk Initiative.

XRay can also help in debugging XML-based programs. Some applications use XML under the covers. To debug an XML-based system, you might need to take a look at the XML documents that are created. The product is called XRay because it allows you to look inside your XML documents.

XRay also has two features that we use in Architag University classes: an XSL Transformation (XSLT) window and an HTML previewer. The XSLT window allows you to transform an XML document that is in a currently open window by associating it with an XSLT style sheet. If you are transforming to HTML, the output of the transformation can be viewed instantly with the HTML preview widow.

The install program for XRay is in the \Software\Xray\ folder.

OmniMark C/VM

The OmniMark programming language is featured in this book because I really like the language for creating fast, platform-independent, scalable, network-enabled applications. The good folks at OmniMark Technologies Corporation have provided me with the latest version of their free product, OmniMark C/VM (compiler/virtual machine). OmniMark is documented throughout the book and in Appendix A.

OmniMark runs under most any popular operating system. The version on the companion CD is for Microsoft Win32 environments. You can download versions for other platforms from the OmniMark site at *http://www.omnimark.com*. OmniMark also offers a subscription service named the OmniMark Developer's Network (OMDN) that provides telephone and e-mail support, plus early access to new versions of software and peer support. If you are an OmniMark programmer, you should subscribe to this service.

The install program for OmniMark C/VM 6.0 is in the \Software\OmniMark\ folder. For OmniMark support and for the latest version of the software, go to *http://www.omnimark.com* on the World Wide Web.

OmniMark Integrated Development Environment

The OmniMark Integrated Development Environment (IDE) is a tool that you can use to develop and debug your OmniMark programs. The OmniMark virtual machine (VM) is tightly integrated with the IDE, which provides you with a set of great features including breakpoints, variable watches, and throttled execution.

The product on the CD is written for Win32 environments. It is a 10-day evaluation product. You must link to the OmniMark site to get an unlocking code for the 10-day trial. This is a great product and definitely worth installing if you are interested in developing OmniMark programs.

The install program for OmniMark IDE 2.0 is in the \Software\OmniMark\ folder.

Adobe Acrobat Reader

The Adobe Acrobat Reader is included on the companion CD to allow you to read the electronic version of my OmniMark book and some of the specifications available on the CD. You can install the Acrobat Reader from the \Software\Acrobat\ folder.

REFERENCES INCLUDED ON THE CD

The following references are included on the CD for your convenience. Keep in mind that these specifications are updated frequently and that you should refer to their respective Web sites for the latest versions. These files can be found in the \References\ folder.

Filename	*Specification*
BTF2Spec.doc	BizTalk Framework 2.0 Document and Message Specification
DOM2.pdf	Document Object Model (DOM) Level 2 Specification
SOAP.doc	Simple Object Access Protocol (SOAP) 1.1
XSLSpec.doc	Extensible Stylesheet Language (XSL) Version 1.0
XSLT.doc	XSL Transformations (XSLT) Version 1.0
Oawv1.pdf	*OmniMark at Work, Volume 1: Getting Started*

MICROSOFT PRESS SUPPORT INFORMATION

Every effort has been made to ensure the accuracy of this book and the contents of the companion CD. Microsoft Press provides corrections for books through the World Wide Web at the following address:

http://mspress.microsoft.com/support/

If you have comments, questions, or ideas regarding this book or the companion CD, please send them to Microsoft Press using either of the following methods:

Microsoft Press
Attn: XML and SOAP Programming for BizTalk Servers Editor
One Microsoft Way
Redmond, WA 98052-6399

MSPINPUT@MICROSOFT.COM

Part I

XML for E-Commerce

At its core, the eXtensible Markup Language (XML) is a simple syntax that allows you to create markup languages—called schemas—that describe your data. In practice, XML is much more than that. XML enables you to communicate with your business partners in a way that is not possible with any other technology.

To build applications that take advantage of this communication capability, you need to understand basic XML syntax and a couple of related standards. Part I of the book discusses XML from the perspective of building e-commerce transactions and covers these standards as well as well-formed XML documents, schemas, issues you need to consider when programming with the XML object model, and the importance of transforming documents from one schema to another using the Extensible Stylesheet Language (XSL) for Transformations (XSLT).

Chapter 1

The XML Business Perspective

E-commerce is huge and growing in importance every day. But what is e-commerce? For some people, it means taking credit card information on a Web site. For others, it means the presence of a shopping cart on a Web site. Everywhere I look, I see e-commerce mentioned as the present and future of human interaction.

I think most people understand that e-commerce means "electronic commerce." Commerce is, of course, the process of engaging in a business transaction—people getting together and doing what comes naturally. Adam Smith, the father of modern economic theory, said that capitalism is what people do when they are left alone (that is, left without government interference or "help"). Commerce is so natural, it would seem, that my *American Heritage Dictionary* has, as two of its definitions of commerce, the following:

2. Intellectual exchange or social interaction. 3. Sexual intercourse.

That last definition might be difficult to achieve over the Internet, but the point is that commerce is what we do when we deal with each other.

Of course, humans have engaged in commerce for thousands of years. Since the earliest days of civilization, we have conducted business with each other face to face. Only recently have we been doing commerce by technological proxy, letting a means other than face-to-face communication be instrumental in leading to a business transaction.

The wealthy elite conducted business remotely for centuries by having couriers communicate parts of a transaction. But for important or large transactions, a face-to-face meeting was almost always part of closing a deal.

In the mid-19th century, the United States benefited from a sophisticated network of mail delivery, the Pony Express. Finally, normal people could afford to do business remotely. This radically changed the way people consumed goods and made it cheaper to do business because a buyer had more choices of sellers. I guess you could say the Pony Express led to "p-commerce."

As the country developed, trains helped in the delivery of goods across the West, and a denser network of mail delivery lowered the cost even more, allowing more buyers and sellers to interact. (Hmmm, sounds like they invented the west-wide-Web.) Commerce by mail was born. Sears, Roebuck and Company made quite a few bucks taking orders by mail and shipping their products. Face-to-face interaction was not necessary once people trusted the corporate name.

Then came the telephone and 1-800-Flowers, which let you pick up a phone, pick out a flower arrangement, and make someone's day instantly, without paper. This is a business transaction that has taken place because of a system of electronics called the telephone. Isn't this e-commerce?

The book of Ecclesiastes (1:9) has a passage that comes to mind here:

What has been will be again, what has been done will be done again; there is nothing new under the sun.

Now I can go to *www.1800flowers.com* ("Flowers are just the beginning") and buy all kinds of things. I don't even need to talk to a human to show that I care. Unless you've been living in a cabin in the woods without a phone line for the past five years, the process should be familiar: Select things you want from full-color pictures viewed on your computer, and add them to your electronic shopping cart. When you finish shopping, you pay for your kindness by filling out a form that contains shipping information and asks for the all-important credit card number, and soon your joy will be spread.

I think most people would consider this to be a transaction enabled by e-commerce. But are there others? If commerce is the interaction of buyers and sellers, is a site that offers written content for a subscription price an e-commerce–enabled venture? There might be no tangible products for sale, but these sites do provide value for people who have paid money. Every time someone sees the site, a transaction is made. Wouldn't that be considered e-commerce?

What about a "free" site? I put "free" in quotes because nothing is really free. Mom always said there's no free lunch. That was a metaphor, of course. (She also said "don't take any wooden nickels." That one was a bit harder to figure out. I just had to assume there was a vast counterfeiting conspiracy that was pumping out worthless wooden nickels to ignorant kids on the streets. I'm still not sure what she meant.)

Any time someone provides you with something for free, he or she gets something in return. Take the Internet. So much information out there is free for the looking. But when you look at it, you also expose your eyes to banner ads, sponsor messages, or even the host's logo and message. Those hosts and sponsors think that your eyeballs falling on their messages is valuable enough that they pay the Web site people for the privilege of exposing themselves to you. This implicit "eyeball tax" is just as real to the advertisers as cash, so a transaction has taken place. Is this e-commerce?

BUSINESS-TO-BUSINESS E-COMMERCE

So far, the e-commerce I have mentioned is business-to-consumer, or B2C, e-commerce. This kind of e-commerce gets the attention of the popular press. When we hear about Amazon.com's problem of warehousing their previously virtual inventory, we are hearing about the new problems of B2C e-commerce. When we hear about eBay's overloaded servers shutting down when people come home from work, we are hearing about the vast potential and pent-up demand of B2C e-commerce.

But that's only part of the e-commerce story. There's also all the invisible commerce going on between the companies that make the products sold on the Web. Think about a simple ink pen. When you buy a pen from an online retailer, a single transaction is involved. If the retailer wants to save transaction costs, the retailer could make the transaction more efficient by using appropriate technologies. Let's say the online retailer shaved two cents off the cost of the transaction. That savings is respectable, but it's only a couple of pennies toward the bottom line of the pen sale.

On the other hand, it took hundreds of transactions to build the pen. The pen manufacturer had to buy steel and ink and springs and dozens of other raw materials from manufacturers. Then the pen maker had to buy production services, marketing services, and management services. Each one of these transactions has a cost. If the manufacturer of the pen could shave a couple of pennies off each transaction between its partners, all of that savings would go to the bottom line.

In this book, I will focus on this business-to-business (B2B) e-commerce, and how you can use the eXtensible Markup Language (XML) to lower transaction costs. There are a number of initiatives happening in several industries today. I'd like to mention some of these and focus on one in particular, BizTalk, so that you can see how a typical B2B transaction might work.

SEPARATION OF DATA FROM PROCESS

XML offers different cost-reducing or revenue-enhancing opportunities to a lot of people. For technical writers, XML provides a syntax that allows them to capture the meaning of their documents. For the enterprise programmer, XML provides a syntax for getting data between objects. For the programmer building systems to provide e-commerce transactions between business partners, XML provides a syntax to capture the richness of the transactions, making the transactions accurate and timely.

To all of these people, however, XML provides at least one common benefit: *XML allows them to separate their data from the processes that act on that data*. This is an important point, and you will see it repeated and illustrated throughout the book.

Separating data from the processes that act on the data is nothing new. A purchase order number that exists as a field in a relational database has a particular meaning. The number can appear in many different places: on a purchase order, on an invoice register, on an invoice, and so on. No database designer would ever think of storing that number with formatting instructions indicating how it is to be rendered on a particular form.

However, when it comes to other information types, we include formatting details quite often. Word processors are notorious for combining data and processes like well-marbled beef. Consider a chapter title that is displayed as a 24-point-Helvetica-bold-centered piece of text. A human reading a line formatted this way on a piece of paper or a computer screen can infer that the line is a chapter title. But to get a computer to look for an actual "chapter title," we need to tell the computer how a title is rendered, because a computer doesn't have a human's cognitive ability to recognize patterns. Humans' ability to deal with ambiguity is something that computers don't (yet) have. For example, we might see something in the middle of our text that we don't recognize as being written in the language we are accustomed to because the phrase is rendered in italic. We know why it is rendered in italic because of our ability to recognize patterns and figure out why distinctions in typography are used. This ability is a two-sided sword, however, because sometimes we get it wrong. And in order for a computer to distinguish between the foreign phrase and something else rendered in italic, *we* need to explicitly mark each phrase differently.

XML provides a syntax that allows you to define each information object in an unambiguous way. By doing so, you can capture the information as one object and then process it with many different applications depending upon the requirements at the time.

XML AND THREE-TIER WEB ARCHITECTURES

XML can fit into many different places on a Web site. In this section, I'll discuss a Web site that uses XML wherever appropriate, and I'll show how XML is superior to other available technologies.

A modern Web site provides personalized information to its users. Gone are the days when a company could get away with having a dozen static HTML pages to serve up to its customers or potential customers. Those companies found that a customer would visit their site initially and, after discovering nothing new in a subsequent visit, never return. The customer assumed that nothing on the site ever changed.

Today's successful site provides useful information to users, so the users come back again and again. This return traffic allows you to provide your customers with new data whenever business reasons dictate. XML can help you provide a personalized view of that data in several different ways.

Let's examine a hypothetical site that uses modern three-tier Web architecture (shown in Figure 1-1) and XML together to provide great information.

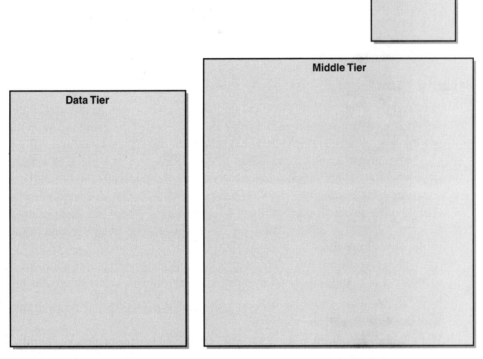

Figure 1-1. *Three-tier Web architecture showing the data, middle, and client tiers.*

To get the most out of the information in a modern Web site, we will employ a three-tier architecture. This is also called n-tier because there can be many different tiers between the two end points, depending on the task performed. Microsoft sometimes refers to this architecture as Windows Distributed interNet Architecture, or Windows DNA.

Data Tier

Data sources reside in the data tier. Notice that I did not say "databases." A database is one source of data, but there are others. In this example, we will use external sites and business partners as sources of data. When I say that data sources reside in the data tier, I don't necessarily mean that the data tier is a physical machine. It is a conceptual place where data sources are made available to processes running on another tier. Whether the data tier is a single machine, many machines, or a set of virtual HTTP connections to the Web is irrelevant to this discussion.

Client Tier

Next comes the client tier. In this example, we will rely strictly on thin clients—usually a Web browser. A thin client is called "thin" because most of the processing is done on the server and shipped to the browser for display purposes. Modern Web browsers have the ability to do more processing than they are usually called on to do; you will see that additional processing capability when you use XML to transfer data to the clients.

Middle Tier

Between the data tier and the client tier sits the middle tier. In the middle tier, business processes are applied to data from the data tier and the result is sent to the client tier. In other words, the middle tier is where the work gets done.

The most common component in the middle tier is a piece of software that responds to the client's requests to initiate a process. This software is called the HTTP server or, more commonly, the Web server. The Web server doesn't do much except receive requests and fire off middle-tier applications. These applications are written in many different computer languages and embody the business logic required to achieve a certain effect.

The example we will examine uses several server-side applications to connect to the data tier, retrieve raw data, process it according to some rules, and present it to the user.

Subscriber Profiles

When a Web browser makes a request, it sends a stream of data containing useful pieces of information to the Web server. The Web server can use this information to find out what brand of browser is making the request, what operating system it runs on, and what its display capabilities are. Some browsers can even report on the site that referred the user to our site.

On our data tier, we maintain a subscriber profile database. Figure 1-2 shows the structure of this database.

Notice that there are fields for name, e-mail address, and zip code, plus some time stamp fields that indicate when the person first visited our site and when his or her most recent visit was.

Another thing we can make use of is a cookie. We can send a cookie to a user's machine at any time. If the user accepts the cookie, the cookie stays on the user's system for a specified time period and is therefore considered a persistent object that allows us to turn a stateless protocol into a stateful protocol. Once we place a cookie on a person's machine, the machine returns it to our server whenever a request is made. For example, the VisitorID field shown in Figure 1-2 could correspond to a cookie value we place on the visitor's machine. When the server gives this cookie a new visitor, a new record is placed in the data tier database. The VisitorID then becomes a key we can use to store and retrieve subscriber information. Figure 1-3 demonstrates how these three tiers communicate.

VisitorID	Email	FirstName	LastName	Zipcode	FirstVisit	LastVisit
205757				80112	3/24/2000 5:53:23 PM	4/5/2000 5:07:49
205758				94107	3/24/2000 8:38:13 PM	3/24/2000 8:38:13
205756				60601	3/11/2000 11:33:15 AM	3/23/2000 5:11:49
205755					3/11/2000 11:33:11 AM	3/11/2000 11:33:11
205633				95402	1/17/2000 11:33:31 AM	3/7/2000 10:36:41

Record: 1 of 32138

Figure 1-2. *The subscriber profile database showing sample records, keyed by a unique VisitorID.*

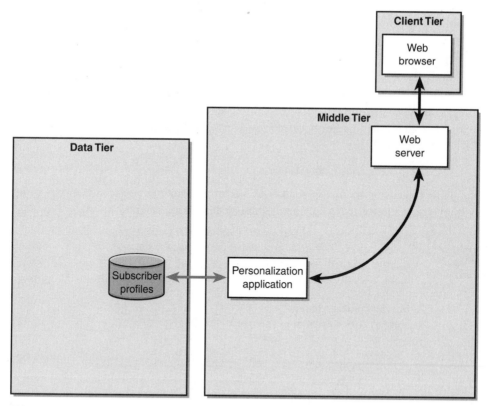

Figure 1-3. *The Web server passes HTTP header information to a personalization application, which queries a database containing subscriber information. The VisitorID field is used to access the information for each particular user.*

Now we can read the cookie and, by looking into the database, discover when the person last accessed the site. We use that information to determine what to do next. All this processing can be done without any help from the user.

SQL and XML

Structured Query Language (SQL) is a straightforward language designed to get information out of a relational database. Hundreds of thousands of programmers and database administrators use SQL. Every major relational database product supports SQL to some extent, which shows the power of standards: if an Oracle database programmer changes to a job where the database is now Microsoft SQL Server, that programmer carries an understanding of SQL to the new environment.

The open-system standards story ends there, however. Even though SQL is a standard way of sending query requests to almost any relational database, each database manufacturer has a different way of responding to that request. Responses come back in the form of a recordset, but the binary structure of this result set is different for each database.

Wouldn't it be nice to send an open standard request (SQL) to any database, and get back a standard response? (Might I suggest XML?) Several database manufacturers are working on a solution to this problem. Let's take a look at the Microsoft approach.

A Microsoft ADO (ActiveX Data Objects) Recordset object can persist a recordset as an XML stream with a fixed schema, or set of specifications. (I discuss schemas in more detail in Chapter 4.) Let's say you sent the following SQL query to an ADO-enabled database:

```
SELECT Name, Joke FROM Students
```

The following document is an XML stream returned as the result of persisting a SQL query response using Microsoft Data Access Components (MDAC).

```
<xml xmlns:s='uuid:BDC6E3F0-6DA3-11d1-A2A3-00AA00C14882'
    xmlns:dt='uuid:C2F41010-65B3-11d1-A29F-00AA00C14882'
    xmlns:rs='urn:schemas-microsoft-com:rowset'
    xmlns:z='#RowsetSchema'>

<s:Schema id='RowsetSchema'>
  <s:ElementType name='row' content='eltOnly'>
   <s:AttributeType name='Name'
     rs:number='1' rs:nullable='true' rs:write='true'>
     <s:datatype dt:type='string' rs:dbtype='str'
             dt:maxLength='50'/>
```

```
    </s:AttributeType>
    <s:AttributeType name='Joke'
      rs:number='2' rs:nullable='true' rs:write='true'>
      <s:datatype dt:type='string' rs:dbtype='str'
        dt:maxLength='2147483647' rs:long='true'/>
    </s:AttributeType>
    <s:extends type='rs:rowbase'/>
  </s:ElementType>
</s:Schema>
<rs:data>
  <z:row Name='Brian Travis' Joke='Two peanuts were walking down the
  road, and one was assaulted'/>
  <z:row Name='Ben Kinessey' Joke='A guy walks into a doctor&#x27;s office.
  The guy says,&#x22;Doc, everywhere I look I see spots&#x22;.
  The doctor says,&#x22;Have you seen a doctor?&#x22;
  The guy says ,&#x22;No, just spots.&#x22;'/>
</rs:data>
</xml>
```

Notice that the document has two main sections: one that describes the schema for the fields returned and a data section that contains the resulting rows. The schema is a fixed schema defined by the database, but it can easily be transformed into whatever schema form you need by using an Extensible Stylesheet Language (XSL) Transformations, or (XSLT) style sheet. (See Chapter 6 for a description of this style sheet.)

HTML as XML

By knowing when a visitor last accessed our site, we can look for company information that is saved in another database. This information might take the form of static HTML pages containing press releases, new product announcements, or any other type of dated material. Knowing the date the visitor last accessed the site allows us to return pages that contain only material that is new or has been updated since that date.

We query this database to find any information that is newer than the information posted on the date of our visitor's last visit to our site. In a situation like this, XML can be used as a standard syntax for returning information from a database. Figure 1-4 demonstrates a marketing application that retrieves information from the data tier and returns it to the Web server.

You will see later that HTML is *sort of like* XML. An HTML document is an XML document if it adheres to a number of rules called well-formedness constraints. This means that we can continue to use HTML in our environment for display while using XML tools to process the information.

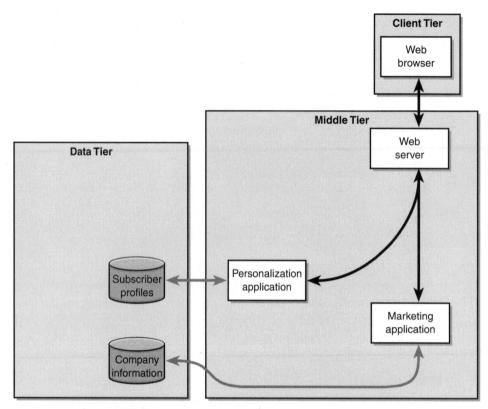

Figure 1-4. *The marketing application uses information about when the visitor last visited the site to look for new company information.*

E-Commerce Services

The whole purpose of our site is to generate business. To this end, we fire off an e-commerce application that makes a connection to a catalog of products and services our company provides. This catalog takes the form of a SQL database, shown in the data tier in Figure 1-5. In this case, the online catalog uses the personal information captured from the subscriber profile database to display a list of products or services that can be targeted to the current visitor.

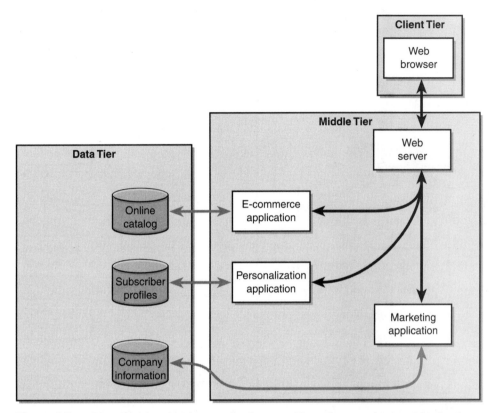

Figure 1-5. *Adding another database to the data tier. The online catalog is a SQL database, so we can use the same SQL-to-XML technique as we used with the subscriber profile.*

Content

Now we need to start giving information back to our user. If we don't personalize the site with information that is useful to our visitor, she might not bother coming back.

External sites can provide a rich source of data. These sites are not databases on our local machine, but have valuable content. We can use XML to request information and get information back as XML objects in order to process them further. Some external services, such as current weather status or traffic conditions, provide this information for a fee. These external sites give us information that we can process into a form that is useful for our visitors. Our job is to aggregate certain types of content from several sites onto our page to give our visitor what she needs. Figure 1-6 illustrates the use of external sites in our three-tier architecture.

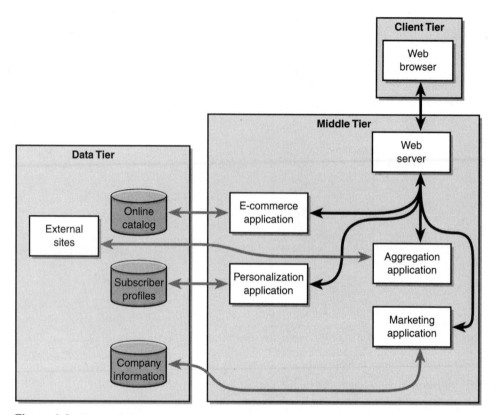

Figure 1-6. *External data sites become part of our data tier, and an aggregation application is used to integrate this new data in the middle tier.*

Suppose I wanted to add real-time weather data to my site. Current weather conditions and forecasts change on an hourly basis. I could start to gather that information myself, but setting up weather stations all over the country is a bit out of my price range and not within the scope of my business plan.

I could also get free weather information from the National Oceanic and Atmospheric Administration (NOAA), which has under its purview the National Weather Service. This organization captures weather from many reporting stations throughout the country and makes it available to qualified providers. However, the data is raw and requires interpretation to create forecasts. This is also outside the scope of my business plan.

However, there is an organization that specializes in capturing, forecasting, and providing weather data: The Weather Channel. I remember first hearing about a 24-hour channel that reported the weather back in the early 1980s when cable TV was starting to appear in more households. Of course, I thought that was quite a silly idea: an all-day television channel doing nothing but reporting weather.

Now, eating my words, I have weather.com bookmarked in my browser, I keep the current conditions synced to my Palm-size PC via AvantGo, and I frequently refer to The Weather Channel (channel 362 on DirecTV) when I want to plan a party, leave town, or am just bored with the other 499 channels showing *The Piano*.

Part of The Weather Channel's content offerings is weather.com. This site provides weather forecasting information for 25,000 zip codes around the United States. If I go to weather.com—which is shown in Figure 1-7—I can see current weather for my city by providing only the zip code.

Figure 1-7. *The Weather Channel provides real-time weather conditions and multiple-day forecasts through its weather.com Web site.*

I want to provide this information for visitors to my site. However, I don't want to link them to the weather.com site because they would leave my site. Also, I don't particularly like weather.com's format—the little sun-and-cloud icon takes up too much space. Also, I might sometimes want to provide a three-day forecast or a seven-day forecast. And finally, I want to provide the temperature in Celsius for visitors who indicate that as a preference.

So, instead of using the data as the weather.com site presents it, I decide to try to purchase the information directly from them in a way that makes it possible for me to provide extra value to my customers. I go down to The Weather Channel offices, knock on the door, and ask the staff if they are willing to work with me to leverage their content assets.

I tell them my requirements, and I suggest that whenever I need weather information from them, I send them an electronic request with the XML stream on the next page.

```
<weather_request days="5" temp="fahrenheit" wind="mph">
    <zipcode>80112</zipcode>
</weather_request>
```

In response, I would like them to send back a stream that looks like this:

```
<weather_response zipcode='80012' Updated='2000-01-07 21:49:06'>
    <location>Aurora, CO</location>
        <current>
            <condition name='temp'>28</condition>
            <condition name='wind chill'>12</condition>
            <condition name='wind'>from the Southeast at 8 mph</condition>
            <condition name='dewpoint'>18</condition>
            <condition name='relative humidity'>66%</condition>
            <condition name='visibility'>25 miles</condition>
            <condition name='barometer'>30.02 inches</condition>
            <condition name='Sunrise'>7:20 am MST</condition>
            <condition name='Sunset'>4:50 pm MST</condition>
        </current>
        <forecast>
            <day date='2000-01-08 21:49:06'
                High='49' Low='20' Sky='Partly Cloudy'/>
            <day date='2000-01-09 21:49:06'
                High='46' Low='21' Sky='Partly Cloudy'/>
            <day date='2000-01-10 21:49:06'
                High='51' Low='25' Sky='Partly Cloudy'/>
            <day date='2000-01-11 21:49:06'
                High='51' Low='19' Sky='Partly Cloudy'/>
            <day date='2000-01-12 21:49:06'
                High='53' Low='21' Sky='Partly Cloudy'/>
        </forecast>
    </weather_response>
```

Let's look at this code for a moment, before we get back to my story. This is a two-way transaction consisting of a request and a response to that request. This request-response architecture is a fundamental piece of error-free transactions. What about potential errors?

Suppose I send the following request:

```
<weather_request days="5" temp="fahrenheit" wind="mph">
    <zipcode>80000</zipcode>
</weather_request>
```

In this case, The Weather Channel doesn't understand the zip code. It can send me a response like this:

```
<weather_response zipcode='80000'/>
```

This response is an empty document, confirming that I entered a zip code. If I get a document back with this structure, I need to do something to inform my user that the zip code supplied was incorrect, and perhaps invite the user to select another zip code.

Now suppose I send a completely wrong request:

```
<weather_request days="365" temperature="f">
    <zipcode>none of your beeswax</zipcode>
</weather_request>
```

At some level, the receiving system can punt, and send back the following response:

```
<weather_response/>
```

In my meeting with The Weather Channel people, I need to deal with the transfer of data and any potential problems. This is an important part of any business-to-business transaction. Remember Ecclesiastes? There is nothing new under the sun. Even in Pony Express days a business deal required a contingency for all conceivable problems. Well-formed agreements have a way of handling even the most inconceivable of problems.

In the end, The Weather Channel agrees that providing raw weather forecast information is something it wants to do, but doing so will cost money to develop and maintain, so they want me to pay for the data.

No problem, I say, I will give The Weather Channel a half a cent every time I ask for a forecast, payable in monthly installments. Agreed, they say. The Weather Channel will develop a system to give me the information I need, and I will pay them on an ongoing basis for the content they provide.

So, what do I do with the content once I get it? The XML documents The Weather Channel sends contain just the data that I need. I can apply different processes to this data depending on the type of output that I need at any given time. I can format the weather to appear as it does on The Weather Channel site, or I can list just the current conditions in a box and have a link to a place where the five-day forecast is rendered. In other words, I can make the data look however I want it to look because I have access to that raw data. I apply the process as I deem appropriate.

SOAP

Now let's talk about how the data gets from external sites to our site. Since our data-provider partners can make their services available in a number of ways, I need to be prepared to make any type of connection required. Data might be available via an FTP connection, via an encrypted tunneling protocol, or even via e-mail. More and more, however, HTTP has been used as the preferred connection protocol. HTTP is preferable because it's a simple protocol to process and, most important, it passes through almost any firewall. These factors make it easy to build systems that communicate in a loosely coupled environment by using data as the binding layer.

How do we request this information and get a response? With the Simple Object Access Protocol, or SOAP. SOAP is an Internet Engineering Task Force (IETF) Internet draft that lets you invoke procedures on remote systems by using a standard set of XML tags. SOAP uses HTTP as its data request and response protocol, so you can deploy it quickly and efficiently to get data between you and your content-provider partners. I'll describe SOAP in detail in Chapter 8.

XML for Content Providers

A number of sites provide content on a syndicated basis. Examples of syndication partners are newspapers, traditional syndicates such as King Features or UPI, and even Web-savvy content providers reselling information gathered online.

I spent considerable time negotiating with The Weather Channel to get its content. But The Weather Channel isn't the only provider of weather data. There are Accuweather, the National Oceanic and Atmospheric Administration (NOAA), and countless re-marketers of this data. There are also providers of weather information in other countries. What if I didn't like the service I received from The Weather Channel, or they couldn't give me all of the information I needed? Or, what if I wanted to make international weather forecasts available on the site? If this were the case, I would need to go through the process of negotiating with another provider of the content we need.

From the consumer perspective, our site isn't the only site on the Web that needs to purchase weather information from providers. Many general consumer portal sites provide weather information in exchange for some marketing information about the visitor. In our scenario, each one of these portal sites would need to go to one or more of the providers of weather data and negotiate the data formats it requires.

Wouldn't it be nice if all the providers of weather information got together with all the consumers of such data and came up with a standard format for exchanging information?

Such a thing happened in the news business. Let's look at the problem the news business faced and then examine the solution they've adopted. Figure 1-8 illustrates the type of three-tier architecture that we would like to use to access news data.

Companies that supply news content, such as the members of Newspaper Association of America (NAA), realized they had a product to sell, but format differences got in the way. For example, the *New York Times* uses an editorial management and typesetting system to create its flagship product. In fact, it has many different systems, depending on what it is creating. The daily newspaper uses one system, but the Sunday magazine uses another.

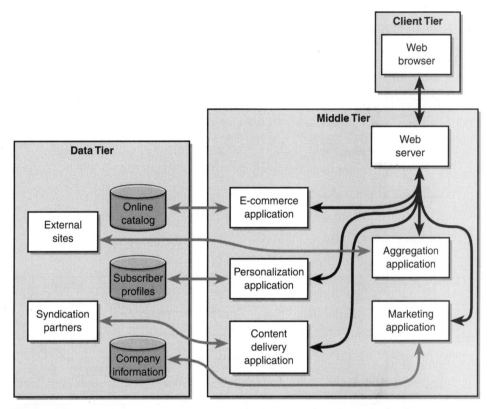

Figure 1-8. *Multiple syndication partners provide content based on standards, so we can aggregate many different sources into a single, cohesive list of articles.*

If I wanted to purchase content from the *New York Times,* I would either need to be able to accept files in the format it uses or convince the paper to convert its information to be compatible with my system. I could get national and world news from the *New York Times,* but I might also want to offer local news to my users.

If my users were only in New York, the *New York Times* would be all I needed. However, to give my users what they expect from me, I would need to contract with many different local newspapers in many different locations.

As a small Web site wanting headline news, I'd have a hard time convincing the mighty *New York Times* to convert their data for my convenience. Plus, I would need to independently approach potentially hundreds of other newspapers around the country and try to convince them to give me their content in my format. I'm not likely to convince them to do this. If I wanted to buy content from all these sites, I would more likely need to write conversion filters to translate their data into a form appropriate for my site.

Since each one of these providers of editorial content manages information in a different way, I would need to investigate all their data formats, understand them, and write conversion filters—this is time-consuming and prone to synchronization errors. The system illustrated in Figure 1-9 shows traditional newspaper providers (*New York Times* and *Denver Post*) and a new media content provider (MSNBC), as well as a provider of news in a monthly magazine format (Reason).

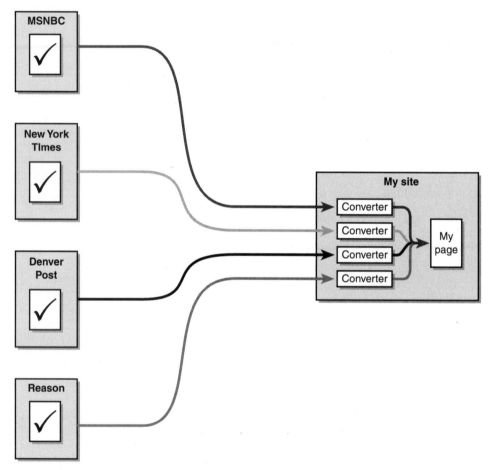

Figure 1-9. *Each syndication partner requires a specialized converter that transforms its custom structure into a form that our page can use.*

But it is even more complicated than Figure 1-9 suggests. Suppose another site wanted to buy content from the same sites I wanted to buy information from. These sites would need to write conversion filters as well. Since we are competitors, I'm not going to share my conversion programs with them. With all these different sites involved, the system really looks more like Figure 1-10.

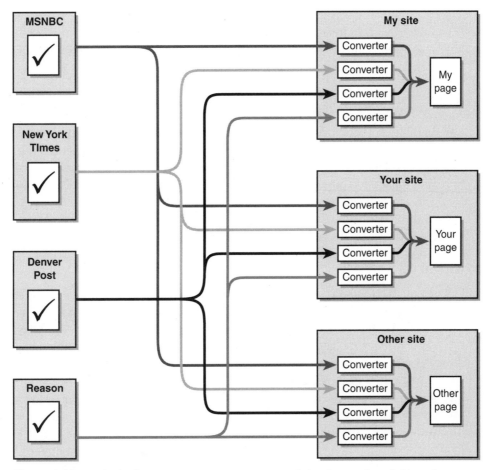

Figure 1-10. *Multiply the customer conversion approach by the number of sites using content, and the problems with individual sites are also multiplied.*

That's a whole lotta conversion going on.

And that's not the worst part. All these information sources create content for their own print newspapers and Web sites. Reporters who put these stories together often generate more information than can be printed in the paper. For example, consider the following sentence:

The Burning Man Festival is set for next June. The admission price is $150.

There is potentially useful information. We get some information about the festival that might be useful to a reader, but let's say that the news source has more information that isn't necessarily appropriate for their target audience. For example, the Burning Man Festival is an event held in the Nevada desert every year. Let's say that *our* audience wants all the details that they can get on the show. Noting the fact that the event is in June is helpful, but it would be better if we knew the exact dates.

For the purposes of brevity and journalistic style, however, putting that information in the national newspaper article would be overkill:

> *The Burning Man Festival, an event happening in the Nevada desert, is set for the week of June 12–19, 2000. The admission price, in U.S. dollars, is 150.*

Instead, the information could be captured in a form that allows the style-conscious editor to create appropriate printed material and provides the user with targeted, useful information. Wouldn't it be nice if we could use the same information for multiple audiences? If we could, our information assets would have a broader appeal and have more chance of being picked up by re-marketers who pay for that data. In other words, the more relevant our data is for the most people, the more valuable it will be for our company and investors.

Standards

When the Web gained critical momentum in the mid-1990s, many traditional providers of news realized that many sites in the world, like mine, might want to buy content but couldn't afford the cost of converting the typesetting data. If these news outlets could provide their data in some form that we small providers could use, perhaps they could create new revenue streams.

Many newspapers belong to the NAA. In the 1970s, the NAA (then called the American Newspaper Publishers Association), through its Wire Service Committee, created a specification known as ANPA 1312. The committee designed the spec to provide a way for wire services to consistently transmit stories to newspapers. The spec also ensured that the coding embedded by the wire service—boldface, spacing, typographic markup, and so on—would not only survive the trip, but actually appear correctly (as boldface or a thin space) when it got to the newspaper.

Virtually all North American wire services and all the suppliers of wire collection software adopted ANPA 1312 as the standard, though there were reports of certain wire services not completely adhering to the specification. When the ANPA turned into the NAA, ANPA 1312 became the News Industry Text Format (NITF), and the Wire Service Committee became the News Information Task Force (NITF). Get it?

In 1998, the NITF specification was reviewed and turned into an XML schema. This schema added much more to the original specification—it allowed for tags that described the data rather than the typography.

Compare Figure 1-11 with Figure 1-10 shown earlier. Using a standardized approach to news delivery requires that each provider and consumer of syndicated content create only a single converter, since all sites use the same vocabulary of elements to communicate. Figure 1-11 illustrates how data gets from a provider to a site using this standardized approach.

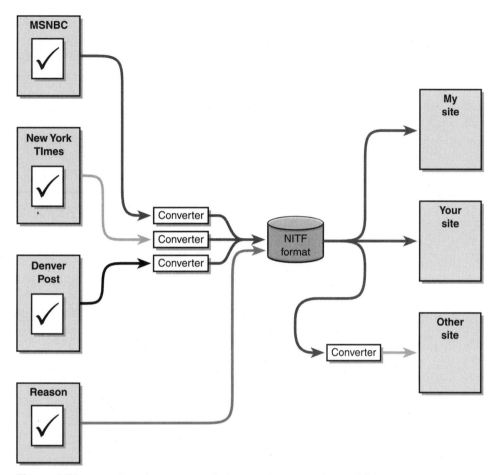

Figure 1-11. *Providing data in a single format eliminates the need for proprietary conversion software for each data provider.*

Each provider needs to create just one conversion filter, which takes content from the provider's format into the NITF format. Then sites can either take that format natively, or they can convert it to the form required for their production systems.

But that's not even the best part. Consider the Burning Man example we looked at earlier in the chapter. The basic information (event title, location, and cost) can be tagged in a way that makes more information available than what was available in the original, simple story. This extra information gives a site designer more information from which to generate content.

```
The <event><location>Nevada desert</location>Burning Man Festival
</event> is set for <chron norm="20000612">next June
</chron>. The admission price is <money unit="USD">150</money>.
```

For example, suppose that clicking on the text specified by the <event> tag brought up a list of all events happening in the Nevada desert, or clicking on "next June" brought up all events happening in that time frame. The fact that all the data in the store is tagged in a standard way allows the site designer to target information directly to users. For example, a user in Germany who has asked that all currencies be displayed in deutsch marks gets the page one way and a reader in Australia gets currencies displayed according to his personal preferences.

The NITF format provides the rich tagging of the story content, plus extra information that might be useful to consumers of this content who want to render the information in other ways.

Consider the news article from MSNBC displayed in Figure 1-12.

Figure 1-12. *A traditional newspaper article rendered as an HTML page.*

This information would appear as an NITF article with the following tagging:

```
<?xml version="1.0"?>
<nitf>
  <head>
    <title>Technology Tools and Toys</title>
  </head>
  <body>
    <body.head>
      <headline>
        <hl1>Pac-Man chomps its way toward 20</hl1>
        <hl2>Seminal video game rose from humble
```

```
      beginnings</h12>
   </headline>
   <byline>
      By<person>Steven Kent</person>
                  <bytag>MSNBC CONTRIBUTOR</bytag>
   </byline>
   <dateline>
      <location></location>
      <story.date>1999-09-03</story.date>
   </dateline>
  </body.head>
  <body.content>
      <p>He may have been a fixture in bars for
      most of the last two decades, but Pac-Man,
      one of the video game industry's greatest
      living legends, is still a bit shy of legal
      age.</p>
      ...
  </body.content>
      <body.end></body.end>
  </body>
</nitf>
```

The NITF format gives news providers a standard way to provide raw news to consumer sites. It gives consumer sites an easy way to read content sold by news providers. Now I don't need to make a separate deal with providers such as the *Denver Post* and the Reason Foundation to get news that I can read. I can just say, "Do you speak NITF?" If so, their content fits into my production system. If not, they might lose my business and should consider this industry standard.

The site we are creating is targeted to individual visitors. It is a consumer-oriented site. Using a standard like NITF lets us create specific information that's useful to the visitor. We are trying to attract customers to expose them to our products and services. In this way, our site is a B2C site.

Getting the information from the providers of information to the consumers of information requires careful coordination between sites and content-provider partners. This aspect is clearly a B2B requirement.

Building the Page

All the information we've discussed so far is captured using middle-tier applications and is generated into pages targeted to individual visitors. These pages are built specifically for users when the information is requested and are formatted according to each user's machine configuration and preferences. Our Web site builds the pages, delivers them, and waits for further requests. And XML made it all possible!

XML FOR CONTENT MANAGEMENT

The focus of this book is using XML for business-to-business e-commerce transactions. Because of XML's nature as an enabler of self-describing transactions, it is a natural fit for e-commerce. I like to think of this as an "ephemeral" form of XML—that is, you create an XML stream from scratch on one side of the transaction, and then ship it somewhere to be read, interpreted, and ultimately deleted.

XML is also an enabling technology for managing more persistent data objects, such as traditional documents. Content providers are those companies that publish information for consumption by their customers or potential customers. Publishers such as Microsoft Press, Prentice Hall, and Macmillan are content providers, but so are newspaper and magazine publishers.

Business pressures on content providers are forcing them to look at the way they maintain their information objects. In the past, it was acceptable to provide content in the form of paper documents that were physically passed to consumers of the content. This model worked for centuries.

The nice thing about paper was that you could achieve identical graphical effects on a page in many ways. Any number of word processors, typesetters, page-makeup programs—and even hot lead—could be used to achieve a similar look. You could typeset one page and then print it out a thousand times. Later, you could even copy it and pass it around easily. Paper became the universal medium for exchanging information.

However, paper, and later paper equivalents such as word processor files, Adobe Acrobat PDF files, and so on, have some problems. Think about it—a printed document is not *really* the actual information. The document is just one representation of the information, formatted for the medium of paper because paper is a convenient form of distributing content.

With the advent of the CD-ROM in the early 1990s, content providers found they had a problem with paper. They couldn't just put a paper document (or its electronic equivalent) on a CD-ROM, because people expected more from the electronic delivery of information. For example, they wanted to search the text for certain strings or keywords, or they wanted to constrain their search to certain contexts. Legal publishers found out early on that users wanted to search for certain works, but only if those works were in a treatise, or only if they were in a judge's decision. If publishers of this legal information put paper equivalents of their information on a CD-ROM, the computer had no way of knowing which piece of information was a decision, a treatise, or just a piece of emphasized text.

Freeing information locked into pages and making it more valuable to electronic-delivery customers is a difficult process. It is possible, however, and many companies who do so have earned back many times their investments.

XML FOR CONTENT AGGREGATION

The Internet has increased our expectations for information. Consumers in the past have never demanded as much from businesses in terms of information and help in making a buying decision.

Consider the world of automobiles before the Web. To buy a car, you had to spend a lot of time going from dealership to dealership to compare prices, service, and the features you wanted. This required a lot of time and expense on the part of both buyer and seller.

Now I can go to cars.com, carpoint.msn.com, or any of a dozen high-quality sites to look for cars that have the features I need. I also have access to rich content from various manufacturers' sites, so I can get technical specifications and dealer locations and even take a virtual tour of a car I might be interested in. The Internet has created a shopping environment that relieves me of the burden of driving around looking for a car in the physical world. Of course, I can't test drive a car on the Web (yet), but the information I gather will greatly reduce my time and energy in selecting the right product.

Where does XML fit into this? Consider a content aggregator such as carpoint.com, shown in Figure 1-13. This site gets information from dozens of locations and makes it available to me in a single place. Let's go through a shopping scenario and see where XML would be appropriate.

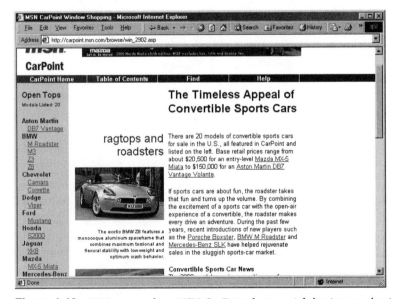

Figure 1-13. *B2C sites such as MSN CarPoint have a rich business-to-business component because consumers require information from many companies before making a buying decision.*

In this case, I'm shopping for a convertible and I want to see what's out there. The MSN CarPoint site has pointers to content on the left and featured content on the right showcasing different cars each day.

As you can see in Figure 1-14, I select the new Jaguar XK8. Nice.

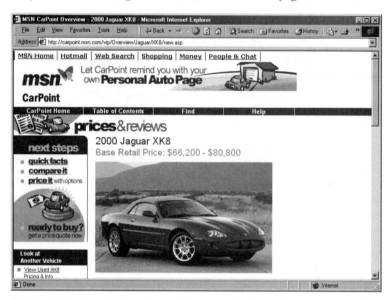

Figure 1-14. *Detailed and varied information is used to create good-looking, data-rich sites. MSN CarPoint collects the information on this page from many different places.*

On the page shown in Figure 1-15, I can see a capsule of information about the car, with links that provide deeper information. I'll select information about the engine. I live in Colorado, so I need a lot of power to make up for the thin air we have here.

There it is, the 370hp supercharged XKR configuration. Yes. Let's configure it with options and see how much it will cost, as Figure 1-16 illustrates.

I'll take the navigation system so that I won't get lost on those long trips to the store.

Then I see the damage. Let's hope that royalty check comes soon!

This is just one car out of hundreds of cars and thousands of configurations available for consumers on this site. How does all the data get there? Basically, the option information is loaded into an object on the page that communicates with the site containing configuration data and makes dynamic calculations as I enter data on the page.

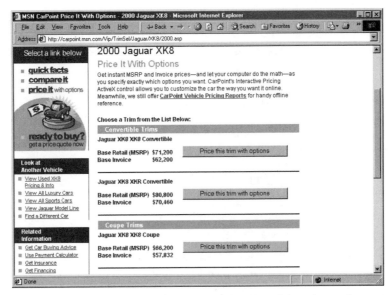

Figure 1-15. *Available configurations are displayed, based on information captured from the manufacturer.*

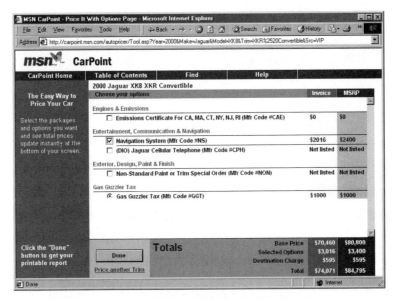

Figure 1-16. *Options available specifically for the selected car.*

Suppose we wanted to create this site. We could repeat the weather example above and go to Jaguar, and then to Honda, and then to all the other manufacturers. This would be a time-consuming process and probably not worth the trouble for the amount of revenue the site would generate.

However, we are not the only site that uses this information. As in the NITF example, there are many providers of information about cars:

■   Car manufacturers provide technical specifications and configuration options for their cars.

■   The automobile press provides critical reviews of cars their readers care about.

■   Auto enthusiasts such as local and national car clubs or collectors' societies have information about the cars they care about.

■   Insurance companies have information concerning actuarial data so that you know how much your insurance will be.

■   The Insurance Institute for Highway Safety and various national governments provide safety information from crash tests of cars.

■   Car dealers provide information about their prices and services.

To get maximum traffic and maximum advertising revenue, a Web site that wants to attract potential visitors should provide as much information as the visitors desire. Such a Web site is targeted at consumers, which means it is a B2C site. However, the information required to build such a site is highly dependent upon the site provider's ability to get the information from all the content providers in a usable way. In this way the site is a B2B site. This business-to-business transaction environment is a natural candidate for BizTalk.

THE BACKGROUND OF ELECTRONIC DOCUMENT INTERCHANGE

The granddaddy of electronic interchange is the electronic data interchange specification, or EDI. In the early 1970s, large companies such as Sears and Kmart pioneered electronic business communication. With thousands of stores and suppliers to contend with, these organizations generated and processed mountains of paper. It was obvious that all this paper was getting in the way of productivity, so methods of electronic communication began to emerge. To communicate electronically with these companies, suppliers were forced to develop and maintain a customized interface for each of their electronic business partners.

By the late 1970s, a committee composed of representatives from the transportation sector, the government, and computer manufacturers began to address developing a method of improving and standardizing electronic business communications. The American National Standards Institute (ANSI) chartered the Accredited Standards Committee (ASC) X12 in 1979. Its goal was to develop uniform standards for the electronic interchange of business transactions. X12 was the first of several standard formats for doing business electronically.

Of course, all this electronic business was done over private networks at the time. What would someday become the Internet had begun to develop but was limited to government and academic researchers.

Various X12 committees worked on standards for specific documents—mostly invoices and purchase orders. Each specification had to work for all users in all situations; standards were therefore complex and difficult to implement.

Because of the complexity of the EDI standards, some groups started to branch out and create more industry-specific standards. For example, the National Retail Merchants Association began developing a set of purchase-order message standards for EDI. However, these standards were not well defined and messages were ambiguous, so retailers and suppliers did not use them. The National Retail Merchants Association subsequently chose to support the X12 standards.

This brief history illustrates the two-sided nature of standards: they need to be general enough to be adopted, yet specific enough to be useful.

XML FOR ELECTRONIC DOCUMENT INTERCHANGE

XML is a standard created by the World Wide Web Consortium (W3C). The W3C is a consortium of companies devoted to creating and maintaining core Internet technologies. XML is a powerful syntax that allows companies to create structures for the efficient interchange of information. We'll see what XML looks like in Chapter 4.

The problems with EDI over the last quarter century (long development times, varying requirements across companies, and difficulty implementing a one-size-fits-all specification) should be a lesson to those working on interchange standards that use XML. A group called XML/EDI is working on a more open version of the EDI specifications, hoping traditional EDI users will move over to XML as their data interchange syntax. That group is not alone. Many groups are now working towards the same end—that is, to create a universal way of doing business with others by using XML as the data-definition syntax.

Another of these efforts is the ebXML Initiative. The "eb" stands for "electronic business." The United Nations /CEFACT and the Organization for the Advancement of Structured Information Standards (OASIS)—an XML industry group—are working on ebXML. The goal of ebXML is to use a standard set of XML objects to facilitate international trade. The goal of the ebXML Initiative is to develop a technical framework that will enable the use of XML in a consistent manner for the exchange of all electronic business data. The group's list of participants reads like a who's who of international trade: Ariba, Amazon.com, Bank of America, Boeing, CommerceNet, Dunn and Bradstreet, IBM, Microsoft, Oracle, Sun, and many other companies around the world. There are many specs being developed by other groups in this space. There are cXML from Ariba, CBL from CommerceOne, the RosettaNet Framework from RosettaNet, and eCo Framework from Commerce Net, to name a few.

Other industry-specific efforts include the Financial Information Exchange (FIX) spec for trading securities information, HL7 for exchanging medical records, ACORD for property and casualty insurance information, J2008 for the automotive industry, and many, many more. All these efforts use XML as their base syntax.

These specifications will probably result in a set of specifications called schemas (mentioned at the beginning of the chapter) that will describe certain business documents such as invoices, purchase orders, medical records, and securities transactions. The schema is a critical piece of the e-commerce solution. I'll discuss schemas in detail in Chapter 4.

XML and E-Commerce

So where does XML fit into all of this? Everywhere. XML is just a set of rules—a syntax—for marking up data. It is a small, standard, compact syntax, however, and that's where its value comes in. To engage in any business transaction, you must communicate clearly with your business partners. XML provides a syntax for communicating in a direct, precise way by identifying each piece of information required to complete a transaction—whether that transaction is shipping credit card information in secure packets around the Internet or serving up a free HTML page from a Web server to a 14-year-old looking for the latest MP3 tracks.

Another aspect of XML and e-commerce is trust. If you don't trust someone, you are not going to do business with him, either face to face at the town bazaar or anonymously across invisible national borders over the Web. XML can provide a level of verification because information about your transaction can be carried right along with it.

Lingua Franca

When a Japan Airlines (JAL) pilot flies a jumbo jet into Charles de Gaulle airport in Paris, he needs to communicate with the tower controller in a common language. The pilot's native language is Japanese. The tower controller's native language is French. If they choose Japanese, it would be the tower controller's responsibility to understand

Japanese. Likewise, the controller would also need to know German, Italian, English, and every other language of pilots landing at her airport.

If the pilot and controller communicated in French, it would be the pilot's job to do the translation. The pilot would also need to know German, Italian, English, and any other language spoken by native tower controllers where the pilot landed.

Either one of these scenarios would be expensive, time-consuming, and potentially dangerous. For the sake of safety and the efficiency of a transaction, the world's air traffic control system decided on a standard language to communicate between planes and ground control systems. That language is English.

When the JAL pilot wants to communicate with the tower, he must translate in his head from his native Japanese to the foreign English. He will compose a sentence in English and transmit it to the tower by speaking into a microphone. The radio sends the English sentence to the tower, where the tower controller hears it.

The tower controller translates the English sentence into French, her native language, so that she can process it in a way that is easiest for her. (Of course, professionals such as these probably speak and think in English, so they can process the information faster, but I hope I'm making my point!)

> **NOTE**   It is interesting to note that when that same pilot returns to Japan, he communicates with the tower in English because there are other planes in the area with non-Japanese-speaking pilots who might need to overhear the conversation.

In the same way, an XML document is usually created on the fly by some application. This document contains all the information necessary to effect the transaction. This recently generated document is sent to our business partner expressed in XML, a syntax foreign to the original generating application. Our partner's receiving application gets the XML stream. That stream is also foreign to this application, so it is translated by the application into a native language for processing. After it is processed on the receiving end, it is no longer an XML document. The data contained in the document has been loaded into the system, using the boundaries indicated by the XML tags to describe the data.

There's a phrase for this: lingua franca. My *American Heritage Dictionary* defines this as follows:

1. A medium of communication between peoples of different languages, and
2. A mixture of Italian with Provençal, French, Spanish, Arabic, Greek, and Turkish, formerly spoken on the eastern Mediterranean coast.

Let's forget about the second definition for now, and replace "peoples of different languages" with "computers of different configurations."

XML is thus the lingua franca of e-commerce transactions. This isn't quite accurate, because XML itself is not the vocabulary—that is the job of the schema—but

XML is the syntax used to exchange the data and make the transaction happen. (I'll include more on this when we talk about developing schemas for industry groups in Chapter 3.)

XML and Processing Languages

XML is an open standard owned not by a single company but by a consortium of highly competitive companies in many industries that have realized the great benefit to all of agreeing on a simple syntax for exchanging information.

Because of its open status, XML works on any platform with any programming language. XML really doesn't do anything—it's just a syntax that provides a way of thinking about and representing your data. The key benefit of XML is that it allows you to separate your data from the processes that act on your data.

You have probably heard a lot about XML and Java—XML for representing data and Java for processing it. The pairing of XML and Java makes a lot of sense because of the open, platform-independent nature of both. Developers can create cross-platform applications in Java and use XML to exchange data between them.

But Java isn't the only language that works well with XML. You can use Microsoft Visual Basic, Microsoft Visual C++, Perl, and even COBOL to create and read XML data. The list of languages that work with XML is as long as the list of languages. Because XML merely specifies rules for representing data, any programming language can benefit from XML's neutral data-description ability.

Unlike HTML, which has a fixed set of tags, XML gives you the flexibility of creating your own tags. You can call things whatever you want. For example, you might have tags named Title, Heading, Invoice Number, and so on. XML tags will usually represent real data.

If you move data around in text files, you have to create your own syntax and your own rules for taking a text file and getting the data out of it. If you use XML, you don't have to do that. You merely need to create an XML document that is syntactically and semantically correct and then use a parser to read the XML and extract the data from it. There are numerous XML parsers available, including the one that ships in Microsoft Internet Explorer, and they are typically free.

Chapter 2

XML Background

XML is a simple syntax to learn. The XML specification is about 30 printed pages in length, but in my lectures on XML, I manage to squeeze most of the XML syntax into two slides. Of course, that's not the whole story, but you can get a lot of useful tasks done by knowing only a couple of basic rules.

A few years ago, I taught my boy, Cooper, how to play chess. He was seven at the time, and he picked it up pretty quickly. He even got inventive when cornered in a checkmate. He utilized the vertical dimension for the king, thereby protecting himself from my bishop.

Of course, he knew his innovation was an extension to the rules, but he was able to understand the rules very quickly. Cooper will learn, however, that it takes a lifetime of working with those simple rules to become a master at chess. You need to know not only *that* you can move a piece, but also *why* you would want to and *whether* you've chosen the best of all possible moves.

XML is like that. I can show you the rules of XML syntax in a few pages of this book, but you'll need experience to know when an item should be an element or an attribute or shouldn't even exist at all. Over the years, I have found things that work and things that don't. For now, let's see what XML is by comparing it to technologies you might already know. I will try to share some of this knowledge with you as we get into the XML application.

HTML: THE GOOD STUFF

Hypertext Markup Language, or HTML, is the markup language used to build Web pages. It is by far the most widely used markup language in the universe. I've seen estimates showing that 100 billion HTML pages are on the Web. Calculating the actual number of HTML pages is impossible, because a single Perl program can create thousands of different pages depending on various inputs. Suffice it to say that HTML is unquestionably a technology that has made a difference in the world.

HTML is small and portable, it runs on millions of machines, and it's easy to learn. Many best-selling books promise to teach you HTML quickly so that you can share in the wealth of the Web. Tools that create and view HTML files are cheap and often free.

HTML employs structures for formatting and processing text in a two-dimensional space. These structures are then rendered in your Web browser. The Dynamic HTML (DHTML) model, included in Microsoft's browser and somewhat supported by other vendors, provides rich programming interfaces that extend HTML into a serious application-delivery environment. Because of differences in browsers, however, much of this functionality is not employed. HTML is used mostly to publish information in a two-dimensional way: on a Web page in a browser.

One of the best lessons Web users have learned from HTML is that hypertext really works. Anyone with access to the Internet can click on a link in a page in his browser and load a page from a Web server thousands of miles away. In the last few years, we have learned much about this universal access to information, and standards groups have invented new ways of accessing information. This ease of creating HTML pages and the ability to link them has made the Web possible. But HTML has problems.

HTML: THE BAD STUFF

The primary complaint about HTML is that it can't do certain formatting functions, such as snaked columns, tab alignment (without complex *table* elements), and precise white-space control—capabilities page designers need. Cascading style sheets (CSS) have been developed to get around some of the formatting limitations of HTML, but they are add-ons to the basic functionality of HTML, and each browser handles style attributes differently.

HTML is governed by a fairly loose set of recommendations. There are very few specific rules regarding the processing of page data, and most browsers don't enforce the rules that do exist very well. For example, including the end tag </P> for the paragraph element <P> is optional, which has implications for whether the tag is used—people don't usually indicate the ends of paragraphs. HTML programmers get comfortable with not using any end tags, their sloppiness carries over to other elements, and they end up not including end tags that actually are *required*. I once created the following tagging on an HTML page:

```
<P>To find out more, <A HREF="more.htm">Go here<A>.
```

The <A> tag is the element used to create a hyperlink. (*A* stands for anchor. Go figure.) The words "Go here" should be underlined in blue by default, and clicking the link should load the file in the browser. The tag following "here" is the end tag, and thus I should have written </A>. This is an example of poor coding. There is an official specification for HTML that, if enforced by Web browsers, would cause the browser to issue errors in cases like this and refuse to load such documents.

That doesn't happen. When I looked at the page in Microsoft Internet Explorer 4, the link looked fine, so I deployed the page to a Web site. Not long afterward, I got an e-mail addressed to the Webmaster saying that everything on the page following "Go here" was a link underlined in blue. The reader was using Netscape Navigator. The HTML parser in my Microsoft browser (the parser reads the document and determines its structure) realized that I was trying to end a link inside another link. My guess is that this had happened before, and the browser programmers put in an exception to allow this type of bad coding to get through. Netscape's HTML parser didn't pick up this particular problem, so it didn't end the link tag.

Why do browsers go through all this processing to accommodate bad code? Because no manufacturer wants its browser to get the reputation that it doesn't read everything on the Web. So browser manufacturers compete to see whose product can read the worst code! In this type of environment, programmers will continue to write bad code because there is no penalty for taking shortcuts. Therefore, bad code begets more bad code, and there is no end.

HTML is defined as a fixed set of tags optimized for delivering electronic documents. HTML has element names such as *p* (paragraph), *li* (list), and *table*, which are formatting directives. HTML does not have elements with names such as *invoice number*, *policy type*, and *blood pressure*. If you want to express that type of information, HTML is not the best choice. HTML can't be adapted directly to suit your needs.

Because of the limited number of elements available in earlier versions of the language, HTML coders use tags that don't necessarily describe the information but rather simply achieve a certain effect. For example, I've used the *dl* (definition list) element in places where no definitions could be found, just because I know that using this element creates a left indent. I've seen the *author* tag used not because the coder wants to indicate the page's author (the tag's intended purpose), but because the *author* tag creates a line break and italicizes the contained text.

The Worldwide Web Consortium (W3C), a group of companies interested in developing and maintaining core Internet technologies, is working on a standardization of HTML that will be both rigorously enforced by client software and extensible. The specification, XHTML, will solve the problem of bad code because compliant parsers will refuse to read poorly formed documents. That's fine for new documents, but a massive amount of legacy code needs to be fixed before the entire Web is properly structured. This restructuring is unlikely to happen, so parsers will have bad-code processors for the foreseeable future. Maybe this is a job for newly unemployed Y2K programmers!

SGML: THE GOOD STUFF

The International Organization for Standardization (ISO) creates and maintains standards that help the world's businesses do business. The ISO owns screw-thread standards, for example, that make it possible to order a bolt from a vendor in Luxembourg that will be compatible with a nut from a company in Taiwan.

The Standard Generalized Markup Language (SGML) is a standard owned by the ISO. SGML was created to allow the sharing of information between companies that might have different systems. IBM, DEC, and the U.S. Internal Revenue Service (IRS) were the big players when the SGML specification was being developed in the early 1980s. As the standard developed, other large industrial companies and federal government agencies became involved in the specification. One of these big players was the U.S. Department of Defense (DoD).

The DoD wanted to lower the cost of transferring contracts from an incumbent to a new contractor. The cost of converting documents from an existing contractor's system to a new contractor's system was sometimes so high that incumbents could keep underbidding new contractors—the incumbents didn't have to factor the cost of conversion into their bids. This led the DoD to look for a standard document technology, the implementation of which could be used as a condition for winning a contract. SGML became that technology. Now contractors must deliver their supporting documents as SGML. Using this standard, new contractors taking over legacy projects can easily read these supporting documents. This early adoption by the DoD and IRS led some people to call SGML the "Standard Government Markup Language." (I've also heard SGML called "Sounds good, maybe later" by people who were reluctant to implement it because of its complexity. Actual implementers claim that it stands for "Someone get my lithium.") Other industries followed suit, using SGML as a syntax for communication between players in a given industry.

SGML was the first standard technology that allowed users to separate data from the processes that acted on it. With SGML, users can go through a process called information analysis to discover the structure and content of their data. A vocabulary called a document type definition (DTD) is then developed from that analysis. The DTD defines a class of information, so each DTD is customized for each set of data. The DTD indicates the contents of objects in the information set by using a precise syntax called the content model.

Because each information set has different requirements and different objects, the DTD for describing each set is different. For example, a DTD that describes maintenance procedures for aircraft might have elements such as *access cover*, *procedure*, and *fuse*. A DTD that describes a training course will have elements such as *objectives*, *question*, and *answer*. Neither of these DTDs would have the format-oriented elements that HTML has, such as *center* and *bold*. The DTD does not contain the details about how these elements eventually appear, since that would limit a DTD's usefulness. The processing software adds only formatting and processing instructions to the information when the output method is known.

SGML gives companies the ability to leverage a single information asset by applying different processes. In this way, companies can "Create once, publish many." For example, the designer of a training course could use the same SGML source to create the student guide and instructor guide, since most of the guides' information is shared. The typesetter creating the student guide would print only the questions, but for the instructor's guide would print both the questions and answers. SGML gives companies the ability to leverage a single information asset by applying different processes. In this way, the companies can create their data once and publish it many times.

An SGML document consists of a simple ASCII stream with markup and content. A parser reads the document and determines the structure of the information by identifying markup and noting the content inside. Because an SGML document is clear ASCII, it is portable and runs on any platform that has a parser. You'll see that XML has many of these same capabilities.

Because of its status as an ISO standard, SGML is stable and difficult to change. Each ISO standard must be reviewed by the committee that created and maintains it every five years to see whether that standard is still required and, if so, whether it needs to be updated. This review process works fine for screw threads, but the business of information management changes quite a bit faster than every five years—which brings us to one of the problems with SGML that I'll discuss in the next section.

SGML: The Bad Stuff

SGML hasn't been able keep up with the Web. It was designed in an era of slow, expensive computers (by current standards). To make the most of primitive systems, the developers of SGML designed a complex set of minimization features—features designed to make files as small as possible. This minimization makes SGML complex to process and expensive to implement, and makes parsers large and slow.

To create an SGML document, a user must have in place a DTD that describes the structure of the information. This means that the user must go through an expensive information discovery process and define the information's structure in no uncertain terms before creating the first document. The user employs the DTD again and again whenever the document is processed. You will see later that it is overkill to verify that a document's structure is correct unless it or the underlying structural description (DTD) has changed.

Another problem is that SGML is owned by academics, who seem to be more interested in purity than usability. During two quinquennial (five-year) reviews in 1991 and 1996, this group had a chance to simplify SGML for the Web. Many in the industry called for "SGML Lite"—a drastically reduced syntax that would fit nicely in a Web browser. The ISO committee refused to make changes that would slim down SGML.

We needed something that was portable, cheap, fast, and easy like HTML, yet extensible like SGML. And we needed something that was compatible with what we already knew so that we could use existing techniques and tools.

WE NEED XML

With the SGML committee's reluctance to modernize the standard, a group of Internet professionals approached the W3C (a relative newcomer to the standard-setting world) and proposed a slimmed-down version of SGML that would achieve the goals of being usable on the Web while remaining compatible with HTML and SGML. The group worked mostly via e-mail through 1996 and 1997 and came up with a specification they dubbed the Xtensible Markup Language, or XML. The group designed XML with 10 goals in mind:

1. XML shall be straightforwardly usable over the Internet.

2. XML shall support a wide variety of applications.

3. XML shall be compatible with SGML.

4. It shall be easy to write programs which process XML documents.

5. The number of optional features in XML is to be kept to the absolute minimum, ideally zero.

6. XML documents should be human-legible and reasonably clear.

7. The XML design should be prepared quickly.

8. The design of XML shall be formal and concise.

9. XML documents shall be easy to create.

10. Terseness in XML markup is of minimal importance.

XML is a syntax that allows users to create markup languages. Languages that are used to create markup languages are commonly known as meta markup languages.

XML is a technical recommendation from the W3C. XML is owned by the W3C, not by any vendor, which means users aren't locked into any single platform or processing language.

XML is easy to learn and use. It is small, terse, and optimized for use on the Internet. As with SGML, XML files are sequential text files that can easily pass through firewalls and be sent over existing networks.

XML is also free. The W3C maintains a trademark on the term "XML" but provides the specification for free on their Web site at *http://www.w3c.org*. XML is just a syntax defined by the W3C specification—it doesn't actually do anything.

XML Myths

I have heard some claims about XML over the years. To explain what XML is, I find it helpful to point out what it is not—that is, to point out some commonly held misconceptions.

Myth: XML Is a Markup Language

XML is not actually a markup language, even though "markup" is part of its name. XML is a standard that specifies a syntax that allows you to create your own markup language. The markup language you create will depend on the task you are trying to accomplish.

Imagine a block of steel sitting in your driveway. It doesn't do anything sitting there in its current form. However, you can apply a process to steel and create a car. The application of these processes is unique to creating each different type of car.

You can apply a different set of processes to the same block of steel and create a bicycle. You used the same technology (steel), but a different combination of processes to achieve an alternative result. Now you have two ways to get to the store. (You can also take that same block of steel and create something else entirely—a toaster. You can't get to the store on a toaster, but you can make them fly through your screen saver.)

XML is like that block of steel. XML is the enabling technology, but it doesn't do anything by itself. HTML is a bicycle. The airline maintenance manual markup language is a car. The training course markup language is a toaster. All are applications of XML technology—just as the car, bicycle, and toaster are applications of steel technology.

Myth: XML Is Only for the Web

XML was conceived and developed as a syntax for delivering content more effectively on the Web than HTML or SGML could. In the early stages of XML development, many people thought that companies such as weapons contractors and airline manufacturers would continue to use SGML to manage their complex document assets and just translate the documents to XML to deliver the documents on the Web.

In fact, XML coeditor Tim Bray described XML as an "on-ramp" that people can use to enter the SGML highway. XML is a less threatening route than full-blown SGML and could therefore get people hooked on the joys of descriptive, hierarchical data markup. From XML, the jump to the rigors of SGML would be tolerable.

To create XML, the developers started with SGML and stripped out all the optional features. Then they made some hard decisions concerning backward compatibility with SGML so that XML users could use the tools that already existed to process SGML. And XML did start out as a proper subset of SGML. Since then, however, XML has added extensions such as namespaces and schemas that make it incompatible with SGML.

Also, since the adoption of XML, companies who use or were considering SGML found that XML does almost everything that SGML does. Most SGML users weren't using many of the optional features in SGML anyway, so the fact that those features weren't available in XML wasn't a real problem. Applications that would have been ideal for SGML are now being implemented with XML instead.

Myth: HTML Is a Subset of XML

Is a car a subset of steel? No—it is an application of steel. Similarly, HTML is not a subset of XML, but it can be a language expressed in XML syntax if it follows a set of rules called well-formedness constraints.

A couple of years ago, someone sent me an e-mail asking me to send him a list of all the XML tags. This was impossible, of course, because XML does not define a language. It defines a syntax that allows you to create your own markup language, which can describe whatever information set you want. HTML is just one of those information sets.

Myth: XML Stands for "Excellent Marketing Language"

In September 1997, Microsoft Chairman Bill Gates called XML a "breakthrough technology." The press has been all over XML ever since.

XML generates a lot of interest in the press, and putting "XML" in your press release tends to get an unexceptional release more attention than it would get otherwise. I once saw a press release excitedly announcing the release of the "Question and Answer Markup Language, QAML." It had two elements: *question* and *answer*.

Another misconception about XML is that it is a government plot to tax us more. People point out that, in Roman numerals, XML equals 1040, the despised form U.S. citizens use to report to the IRS how much of their money they need to send to the government. This Roman numeral syntax isn't quite right, but hey, I'm just reporting what I heard. I've also heard that when you ask the department of motor vehicles for the XML license plate and tell them it stands for Xtensible Markup Language, they'll send you a plate that says EML because they think you must have made a mistake.

And to clear up one last misconception: XML is not a t-shirt size.

Chapter 3

XML Standards

Standards are critical to the process of exchanging information. Without standards, we can't really do business. Take the value of a nation's currency, for example. Without a standard we all agree on, the value of the currency is arbitrary and can fluctuate. Unless currency has an established, fixed value—like a standard of measurement such as a meter or a liter—the currency can be whatever someone says it should be.

Having too many standards can be just as chaotic as having no standards. At a recent conference, someone turned to me and said, "There are so many standards for exchanging information. Just pick one!" Of course, if we all choose different standards, we can't communicate—we'd have chaos. Consider this: "You can drive on the left side of the road or the right side of the road—just pick one!"

The groups that I discuss in this chapter are committed to developing standards that everyone can agree on. They have found it helpful to bring interested parties together with the goal of creating unambiguous methods of communication.

ISO

The International Organization for Standardization (ISO), based in Geneva, Switzerland, is the world's center for diplomatic cooperation. The ISO is composed of national standards bodies that maintain thousands of specifications to enable things to work together properly. The ISO is sort of a United Nations for standards.

The American National Standards Institute (ANSI) is the U.S. member body of the ISO and sets standards for the U.S. market. Other countries have similar standards bodies. Each member body of the ISO has a single vote on ISO committees. Countries that do not have fully developed standards organizations are represented in the ISO as correspondent members. This is a nonvoting membership, but bodies from these countries are kept fully informed about the work of interest to them. Subscriber members are representatives from countries with small economies. They pay reduced fees to the ISO to maintain regular contact with the international standards community. As you learned in the previous chapter, the ISO created and maintains XML's progenitor, SGML.

OASIS

The Organization for the Advancement of Structured Information Systems (OASIS) was formed in 1993 under the name SGML Open. The group changed its name in 1998 to reflect support for XML and CGM, the Computer Graphics Metafile standard.

OASIS was formed with two general goals. First, the group strives to further the adoption of product-independent structured information systems by publishing marketing information and acting as a clearinghouse for information about structured information systems. OASIS is active at many different conferences—such as the Graphic Communications Association's SGML/XML series, Documation, and Seybold—spreading the word.

The group's second goal is to create standards that provide guidance to companies that implement products to support structured information systems. Whenever a member suggests a standard to implement, OASIS will form a technical committee. For example, an OASIS technical committee developed a standard for registering schemas and storing them in a public repository. OASIS has developed several such standards over the years, and makes them available to the public. OASIS standards information is available from its Web site at *http://www.oasis-open.org/*.

W3C

The World Wide Web Consortium (W3C), based in Cambridge, Massachusetts, is an international association of companies interested in maintaining standards for the World Wide Web. (You learned a little about the W3C in Chapter 2.)

W3C standards are the result of global input refined through an extensive process that eventually leads to consensus. The steps in the W3C specification approval process include the following:

1. A member of the W3C sends a Submission to the consortium. The consortium considers whether the submission is within the W3C charter, and whether the consortium should expend the energy necessary to refine the submission into a recommendation. Some member companies make submissions to the W3C just to get a jump on the competition or to say they are implementing a "W3C Submission." It is important to note that any W3C member can submit a spec. Simply submitting a spec, however, does not mean that the W3C will accept the spec's viability.

2. Sometimes, submissions become Notes. A Note is a dated public record of an idea, a comment, or a document. Once the W3C reviews a Note, the Note becomes an Acknowledged Submission. A Note does not represent a commitment by the W3C to pursue work related to the Note. Members who want to have their ideas published on the W3C site as Notes follow a formal submission process.

3. Once a submission becomes acknowledged, a Working Group forms. This group usually consists of a representative from the member group that submitted the draft, plus other representatives from interested parties. Every so often, the Working Group issues a Working Draft that represents work in progress and a commitment by the W3C to pursue work in this area. A Working Draft does not imply consensus by a group or the W3C. Working Drafts are usually posted on the W3C Web site, along with an invitation for comments from the public. These Working Drafts are sometimes implemented by software vendors, who are eager to see whether the specification is usable. Input from these vendors is valuable to the Working Group, but the implementing companies understand that the spec might change considerably, rendering their work obsolete.

4. Once the Working Group is comfortable that its work is ready to finalize, it will issue a Proposed Recommendation, which represents the group's consensus. The Working Group sends the Proposed Recommendation to an Advisory Committee for review.

5. A Recommendation represents consensus within the W3C and has the W3C Director's stamp of approval. The W3C considers whether the ideas or technology specified by a Proposed Recommendation are appropriate for widespread deployment and whether they promote the W3C's mission.

6. Complex specifications might require more input for final consideration. If this is the case, the committee will issue a Candidate Recommendation, which is designed to tell the world that the Working Group thinks that the specification is mostly complete and stable, and that it is safe to spend resources to implement software for the specification. The Working Group invites feedback from implementers to gauge how their Recommendation can be implemented. However, a Candidate Recommendation might change based on the input the Working Group receives when the group releases the final Recommendation.

W3C Standards

The W3C has created many Recommendations during its lifetime. HTML and CSS are two of the most widely used. In 1996, a group of Web-savvy SGML gurus submitted an idea to the W3C for a slimmed-down version of SGML that would fit easily into Web browsers or server-side applications. This effort became known as XML.

XML 1.0 was formally adopted as a W3C Recommendation in February 1998. To create the XML Recommendation, the W3C XML Working Group started with SGML, removed all the optional features, and streamlined the syntax. This resulted in a small, terse syntax that small, fast parsers can process. As you learned in earlier chapters, XML provides only a way of describing your data; it doesn't have features for processing the data. XML is small, and it will stay that way. However, many users have found the need to do certain common types of processing, so the W3C is working on standards to use with XML to provide more processing functionality.

In this section, we'll look at the standards established by the W3C that support XML and make programming it more efficient. Figure 3-1 illustrates how these various standards are related.

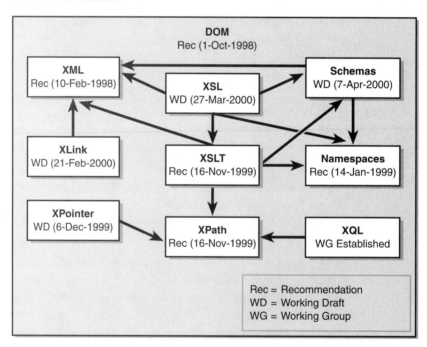

Figure 3-1. *The W3C publishes a rich set of standards that support XML. By plugging into the base spec (DOM), an implementer can select specific technologies for a particular task.*

XLink and XPointer

An example of a standard that addresses the need for better processing functionality is one that deals with linking. XML expresses information in terms of hierarchical relationships. An element can have children, which, in turn, can have their own children. The structure of an XML document describes only this model. Some data structures, however, have nonhierarchical relationships; an object might have a relationship with another object in a different location. This type of relationship must be expressed in terms of a link rather than as a parent-child relationship.

Two W3C Working Drafts provide a standard way of representing linking: XLink and XPointer. I can best illustrate these specifications with an example. Consider the HTML anchor element, <A>. The element's form looks like this:

```
<A HREF=
"http://architag.com/solutions/senior.html#btravis">
Brian Travis</A>
```

This element consists of two distinct pieces:

- **The <A> tag, which indicates the semantics, or processing characteristics, of the link** The HTML parser looks at the <A> element and extracts the string in the *HREF* attribute. The text between the <A> tag and the closing </A> tag is usually underlined in the browser. The browser does not display the address contained in the *HREF* string.

- **The *HREF* attribute, which indicates the location of the hypertext link** The string in the *HREF* attribute consists of a filename (usually an HTML file), with an optional domain name and path in front of it and an optional hash sublocation. In our example, *HREF* tells the *A*-element processor to grab the file senior.html in the solutions directory from the site *http://architag.com* by using the HTTP *get* method, and then to scroll down to the marker in that file indicated with the name *btravis*.

What if we want to indicate a different processing semantic to our own links? For example, what if I want to create a link that allows a user to select one destination from a number of different destinations? A link in a document that refers to Beethoven might lead to different places, depending on what the user wants to see. It could lead to a biography of the composer Ludwig van Beethoven, a symphony score by the composer, or a showing of *Beethoven*, the movie about a slobbering dog.

If I want to include such a link on my page, I need to create a script that shows a pop-up window, allows the user to select an option, and then goes to the selected destination. XLink provides this functionality. A browser that supports XLink can do such one-to-many links declaratively, without requiring special scripting.

XLink also allows inline links. What if I want to include bits and pieces of many different documents in my document? Inline links allow me to grab several documents from different locations and include them all on the same page. In this way, I can have a page consisting of only a set of links. I think XLink offers the <A> tag on steroids.

By the same token, XPointer works like the *HREF* attribute on steroids. In the previous example, the URL points to a location inside the document referenced. This bookmark pointer simply causes the browser to scroll to a marked location after the page is loaded.

But what if I don't want to see the whole page? What if I want to include only the paragraphs concerning btravis and not the rest of the document? The XPointer syntax allows you to target a portion of a page with more granularity than the *HREF* can. For example, you can present an XPointer string to tell an XLink tag that you want to include only the third through the sixth paragraphs of a section with an identifier of chapter2.

Schemas

A schema describes the structure of an information set. XML 1.0 specifies a schema syntax named a document type definition (DTD). The DTD is a relic of SGML and as such does not have modern data processing capabilities built in. The DTD is great for expressing textual documents such as technical manuals, business plans, and training guides. However, the DTD schema syntax has some limitations when XML is used to transmit real-time database data and business documents between trading partners in an e-commerce environment.

Shortly after the W3C XML Working Group finalized the XML 1.0 Recommendation, several groups made formal submissions to the W3C for a schema syntax that extends the capabilities of the DTD. These were XML Data, Document Definition Markup Language (DDML), Schema for Object-oriented XML (SOX), and Document Content Description for XML (DCD). I discuss XML schemas in depth in Chapter 4.

Namespaces

Namespaces indicate to the XML processor where to find the structural rules (the schema) to apply to a document. A namespace declaration points to a resource containing the schema that describes the document.

Let's look at how a namespace works in practice. In the preceding XLink and XPointer discussion, I mentioned that you can link to pages in a more granular way. Suppose I pull in several different fragments from various XML documents on the Web. Each of these documents might use the same element name, but each element name might imply something different to each particular document creator. For example, I want to grab three paragraphs from George's document and four paragraphs from Martha's document and make them all appear on a single page. I'll then write a style sheet that formats the finished page to make it presentable in the browser.

Well, George has an element named *date* that represents a day of the week:

```
<date>Feb 13, 2000</date>
```

Martha also has a *date* element, but Martha thinks a date is a night on the town with George:

```
<date>Dinner, then a movie</date>
```

If I include both these elements in the same virtual document, I'll have what is called a namespace collision.

Namespaces provide a way of differentiating elements in a single document. To prevent a namespace collision, I declare two namespaces that point to the two schemas that describe the structure of the two documents. Then I prefix each element with the appropriate namespace prefix:

```
<document
    xmlns:george="http://no1prez.com/schemas/schema1.xdr"
    xmlns:martha="http://schemas.martha.com/funstuff.xdr">
    ...
    <george:date>Feb 13, 2000</george:date>
    ...
    <martha:date>Dinner, then a movie</martha:date>
    ...
</document>
```

I've thereby eliminated the identical element names. Once I prefix these elements, I can use a style sheet to create two rules to identify the elements independently, and an application can process each element separately. I'll discuss namespaces further in Chapter 5.

XSL, XSLT, and XPath

It's important to note that the XML 1.0 Recommendation doesn't provide any standard way of formatting the content in XML documents. Enter XSL, the Extensible Stylesheet Language. The W3C XSL Working Group was formed by some of the same people who worked on the Document Style Semantic Specification Language (DSSSL). DSSSL is an ISO standard that provides a syntax for adding style semantics to an SGML document. DSSSL is terribly complex because of the intricate page-definition tasks it must perform. The XSL Working Group used DSSSL as a starting point for adding semantics but quickly decided that DSSSL would need to change too much, so the group redirected its focus.

To that end, XSL consists of two main functions: XML document transformation and formatting object interpretation. The main purpose of XSL is to convert XML documents into some formatted representation. The latter function—interpreting the formatting object string—is really only necessary if you are creating printed documents. (By printed, I mean on paper or a paper equivalent, such as a Web site or a CD-ROM image.)

As the XSL standard progressed, the Working Group realized that document transformation could have a lot of value even if an XML document was never rendered for human consumption. The XSL committee extracted the transformation part from XSL and created a new standard, XSL Transformations (XSLT). XSLT is a W3C

Recommendation, and several software vendors have created XSLT processors to work with the spec. XSLT is a general-purpose transformation engine that you can use in many places. You should learn XSLT if you use XML in any serious way.

The W3C extracted the pattern-matching syntax from XSL and created the XPath specification. XPath provides a way to describe the structure of a source document so that you can transform the document. I discuss both XSLT and XPath in depth in Chapter 6.

XQL

Many people in the XML community felt the need for a standard way to query a set of XML documents. This standard would be equivalent to the Structured Query Language (SQL) used to query relational databases from many different vendors.

Currently, there is no standard way of querying the contents of a collection of XML documents. The XML Query Language (XQL) Working Group is currently working on a specification to do just that: provide a standardized syntax that looks into the structure of a database of XML documents and returns a result set that can be processed in a standard way.

DOM

All the specifications I've mentioned so far can be included in an implementation that processes XML documents. The W3C formed a committee to work on a model that described an XML document for the purpose of developing standardized applications. The Document Object Model (DOM) specification is the result of that committee's work.

The DOM provides a standard set of interfaces that expose the properties and methods of XML and HTML documents. Although the W3C DOM is an agreed-upon standard, the developers left out implementation specifics, preferring that individual implementers do the heavy lifting. I'll discuss the DOM in Chapter 5.

IETF

The Internet Engineering Task Force (IETF) is a large, open, international community of network designers, operators, vendors, and researchers concerned with the evolution of Internet architecture and the smooth operation of the Internet. The IETF is open to any interested individual. It owns HTTP, FTP, NNTP, and other transport protocols.

The IETF works in much the same way as the other standards groups I've mentioned. The actual technical work of the IETF takes place in its working groups, which are organized by topic into several areas (for example, routing, transport, and security). These working groups handle much of their work via mailing lists. The IETF holds meetings three times each year.

For a specification to become an IETF standard, it must undergo a period of development and several iterations of review by the Internet community. It then undergoes revisions based on comments. After this process, the appropriate body within the IETF adopts the specification as a standard and publishes it. One of the standards the IETF owns is SOAP. I'll discuss SOAP in depth in Chapter 8.

Standards by Convention

In addition to standards that develop by consensus of the players in a given community, useful standards have been widely adopted simply because they work well and people agree to use them. Just because a standard hasn't been adopted by a national or international organization or industry group doesn't mean we cannot or should not use it.

Adobe PostScript is a great example of a *de facto* standard. Adobe created PostScript as a way to describe the layout of printed text on paper so that the page can be faithfully rendered after being transmitted electronically. PostScript is an extremely useful "standard" that has withstood the test of time. Adobe put the language in the public domain, and other companies created PostScript interpreters that could read PostScript documents created on any machine.

Some of Adobe's competitors believed that a standardized page description language (PDL) was necessary to keep this important specification open. In the early 1990s, the ISO embarked on a plan to create a standardized PDL that would be vendor-neutral and therefore, the submitters thought, widely adopted.

After a couple of years of experimentation, the group created the Standard Page Description Language (SPDL). SPDL is essentially PostScript out of the box, with a page-boundary indicator. Although hundreds of printer manufacturers have adopted PostScript as a PDL, and millions of people create and use PostScript documents every day, I don't know of a single implementation of SPDL.

The BizTalk Open Document Specification is another standard developed by interested parties outside of the "standards industry." The BizTalk spec is available to the public on the BizTalk Web site at *http://www.biztalk.org* (more about BizTalk in Part II of this book).

Developing Industry Schemas

To successfully exchange data with your trading partners, you need to come up with a common vocabulary. In an XML-powered e-commerce environment, these vocabularies take the form of XML schemas.

Who creates these schemas? At a recent conference, I spoke about schemas and the importance of building vocabularies for interchanging information between business partners. At the break, a rather imposing man came up to me and asked, "Brian, who does schemas for the auto repossession industry?" The repo man standing in front of me needed to come up with a vocabulary so that his customers (banks and finance companies) could·communicate requests for his services. He hoped there would be a centralized committee that would develop a formalized vocabulary for his industry. Before I tell you about the answer I gave him, let me explain the situation that probably led to this question.

Most industries have associations that represent their interests. These associations represent industries in legislative matters, standards setting bodies, and to the public. For example, most commercial airlines and makers of aircraft belong to the Air Transport Association (ATA). Even with the fierce competition between the makers of jets (Boeing, Airbus, Bombardier, and so on) and between commercial airlines (such as United, American, and Northwest), it is in the best interest of all parties to belong to a common association that represents all members and supports them in common issues.

Many years ago, the ATA published Appendix 100 (ATA-100) of their specification for maintaining aircraft. Most aircraft, no matter how different they look on the outside, have similar components. Members of the ATA from both sides of the industry (airframe manufacturers and aircraft operators) came up with a rigorous specification called the Airline Maintenance Manual (AMM). The AMM contained standardized structures to describe the maintenance of common pieces of any aircraft, with chapters on electronics, engines, fuel, hydraulics, and so on. When an airline purchased an aircraft, the airline's representatives could point to ATA-100 in their contract and know they would get documents containing similar structures from all manufacturers.

In the 1980s and 1990s, the ATA embarked on a project to turn that paper-based specification into an electronic one. The resulting specification, ATA-2100, was a set of schemas (using DTD syntax) that described the maintenance procedures for aircraft. The Boeing 777 was the first aircraft delivered (in this case to United Airlines) without any paper documentation. A set of electronic media contained all maintenance information for the aircraft.

NOTE The ATA-2100 spec is actually defined using SGML syntax, but the concepts are the same as if the spec used XML syntax.

United Airlines buys planes from manufacturers other than Boeing, and requires that all vendors provide documentation that adheres to a common structure. The big win here is that all maintenance data comes from all suppliers in this same format, which United can easily integrate into a single maintenance system. Other airlines followed suit, and now most airframe manufacturers send documents to their airline customers in this open format.

This process has been repeated in many different industry groups. The Independent Insurance Agents of America's Agents Council for Technology (ACT) and the Agency Company Organization for Research and Development (ACORD) have developed a set of schemas that describe forms for submitting life insurance claims, property and casualty information, and other data traditionally communicated in paper forms.

The automotive industry and the U.S. Environmental Protection Administration (EPA) developed J2008, a schema for transmitting emission and repair information between manufacturers and government regulators. Auto parts suppliers and auto manufacturers also use the J2008 spec to communicate with each other. The trucking industry took J2008 and adapted it into T2008, which provides a similar functionality for their hardware.

So the answer I gave the repo man when he asked, "Who creates schemas for the auto repossession industry?" was, "You do." No one knows the terminology and the structure of information of a particular community better than the members of that community. The repo man could hire a specialist in XML syntax. That specialist could facilitate a meeting to help participants look for the data they want to express, and help finalize the vocabulary into one or more schemas. But first the repo man needs to get together with representatives from his community and learn what those information objects are.

Chapter 4

XML Syntax

The syntax of XML is rather straightforward, with only a few simple rules to follow. Some of these rules are a little more complex than others but are still much easier to understand than most Internet technologies out there.

An XML document can be either well-formed or valid. A well-formed document adheres to a number of well-formedness constraints detailed in the XML specification. And an XML document is valid if, to quote the XML specification, "… it has an associated document type declaration and if the document complies with the constraints expressed in it." You'll learn about document type declarations and valid XML documents later in the chapter.

THE WELL-FORMED XML DOCUMENT

For the impatient, here are the most common rules for well-formed XML documents. I'll explain these rules in detail in the next section.

- Every element must have a start tag and an end tag.

- A document must have a single, unique root element.

- Element and attribute names are case-sensitive.

- Elements must be properly nested. (They cannot have structural overlaps.)

- Certain characters must be escaped, or represented by a combination of characters.

- Attribute values must be in quotes.

- Empty elements have a special form that they must adhere to.

The XML Declaration

A well-formed XML document starts with an optional XML declaration. The declaration defines the document as XML for the XML parser. The declaration can also provide the parser with useful information about the stream. The XML declaration looks like this:

```
<?xml version="1.0"?>
```

XML 1.0 is currently the only version of XML, but the version attribute is still required. Notice that the attribute value, *1.0*, is in quotes. You can use either single quotes or double quotes.

The encoding declaration follows the version attribute. It looks like this:

```
encoding="SHIFT_JIS"
```

The encoding declaration indicates the character set used to create the document. By default, XML documents are encoded in Unicode, either 8-bit (UTF-8) or 16-bit (UTF-16). If you use either of these encodings, you don't need to specify the encoding attribute.

The stand-alone document declaration follows the encoding declaration. It looks like this:

```
standalone="yes"
```

The value of the stand-alone declaration can be either *yes* or *no*. A value of *yes* tells the parser that everything it needs to know about the document is contained in the stream that follows. That is, no external pieces (entities) are specified, and no defaulted attribute values are specified by an external schema. A value of *no* tells the application that it might need to go outside and get some more information to complete parsing.

Both the encoding declaration and the stand-alone document declaration must appear inside the XML declaration. Combining them all gives us an XML declaration that looks like this:

```
<?xml version="1.0" encoding="EBCDIC" standalone="no"?>
```

The XML declaration must come first in the well-formed document and, like the rest of XML, it is case-sensitive.

Start Tags and End Tags

A document consists of text and markup. Markup indicates the structure of the document to the application that processes the document. Markup consists of delimiting tags that are used to describe the data within a document. A tag is a markup construction that is set off from the content of a document by the left and right angle brackets (<>). Tag pairs are used to delimit data.

An element is a particular data object that you need to identify. An element has properties, the most important of which is the element name. (An element name is a descriptive name given to a piece or type of data.) You use tags to indicate the start and end of an element. Each element in an XML document must start with an indicator called a start tag and end with a complementary end tag. The end tag looks like the start tag, except that the end tag includes a slash (/) before the element name. The data between the start and end tags is the content of the element. Content can be text or even other elements with their own tags. Here's an example of an element:

```
<prologue>We the people</prologue>
```

The start tag is <prologue>. The content is "We the people." The end tag is </prologue>. All three parts taken together constitute an element.

Element names must begin with a letter or an underscore. Following the first character are zero or more letters, numbers, underscores, or hyphens.

> **NOTE**   Many XML 1.0 parsers will let you use a colon in your element names, but you shouldn't—colons are reserved for a W3C Recommendation called "Namespaces in XML" that was adopted after the XML 1.0 Recommendation. I will talk about namespaces later in this chapter.

Root Elements

An XML document must have a single, unique root element: an element that has a start tag at the top of the document and an end tag at the bottom of the document. The first start tag that is encountered is considered the root element. As soon as the end tag for this element is encountered, the document is finished. If the parser encounters another start tag after this, it will issue an error, because that new start tag will be at the root level, and only one element is allowed at the root level.

Case Sensitivity

In HTML, element and attribute names are not case-sensitive. That is, you can create a table with any of these tags: <TABLE>, <table>, or even <TaBlE>. The HTML parser considers them all equivalent.

All XML element and attribute names are case-sensitive. If you start an element with the <List-item> tag, you must end it with the </List-item> end tag—not the </LIST-ITEM> end tag, the </list-item> end tag, or any other variation.

Proper Nesting

Elements in a well-formed document must have a proper tree structure. The end tag for an element contained inside another element must come before the end tag of the parent. Most HTML browsers overlook this rule. For example, on an HTML page, you could write code that looks like the code at the top of the next page.

```
<P>The rights <B>of the <I>individual person</B>
outweigh</I> the rights of the collective.
```

Notice that the *B* element starts, and then the *I* element starts. But the *B* element ends before the *I* element ends. A browser would render this code as follows:

The rights **of the *individual person* outweigh** the rights of the collective.

This is not proper nesting. XML that is formatted this way is rejected outright by the parser. To achieve the same effect with properly nested XML, the code would look like this:

```
<P>The rights <B>of the <I>individual person</I></B>
<I>outweigh</I> the rights of the collective.</P>
```

Special Characters

The parser depends on a small number of characters to determine which parts of an XML document are content and which parts are markup. To differentiate content from markup, the parser continually looks for special characters. We've used three such characters in this chapter so far—the left and right angle brackets (<>) and the slash (/). If you want to use special characters in your XML content and you don't want the parser to see them as markup, you must use entity references. An entity reference is a string of characters that are read by the parser and translated into another character. For example, if you place a left angle bracket somewhere in the data in a well-formed XML document, you'll get an error because the parser will be confused. Upon seeing the left angle bracket, the parser begins to turn what it's parsing into either a new tag or a closing tag. Consider the following markup:

```
<P>Paul used the calculation A<B, but I don't agree.</P>
```

You, Paul, and I see a calculation here, because we read the sentence with human cognitive powers. The parser, however, will infer from the left angle bracket before the *B* that a tag is coming up. The parser will find the *B*, which is a valid start character for an element name, and then it will find the comma and throw an error, because the comma is not a valid character inside of a name.

If you want a literal left angle bracket to appear in your document (as a less-than character, for example), you must use the *<* entity reference:

```
<P>Paul used the calculation A&lt;B, but I don't agree.</P>
```

Another character to watch out for is the ampersand. Notice that the entity reference starts with the ampersand character. If you want to store a literal ampersand, you must use the *&* entity reference, as shown here:

```
<P>My AT&amp;T mobile phone is working much better now that
    they put the cell antenna on my neighbor's birdhouse.</P>
```

A well-formed parser recognizes five entity references:

Entity Reference	Meaning
&lt;	< (less than)
&gt;	> (greater than)
&amp;	& (ampersand)
&apos;	' (apostrophe or single quote)
&quot;	" (double quote)

Attributes

Sometimes, just naming an element isn't enough. You can qualify or describe XML elements using attributes. Attributes contain additional information about the element. Attributes appear as name-value pairs in the start tag of an element:

```
<insuranceClaim dateFiled="2000-06-24">
```

The attribute name is *dateFiled*. The attribute value is *2000-06-24*. Notice that an equal sign separates the name from the value. You can have white space on either side or both sides of the equal sign—that's up to you.

Notice, also, that the value is in quotes. In HTML, attribute values don't need quotes if the value is a single word. In XML, all attribute values must be in quotes, even if the attribute is a single word. You can use either single quotes or double quotes, as long as you use them in pairs (not one of each).

You must escape certain characters if they appear in an attribute value. If you use single quotes to delimit your attribute value, you can use the double quote as a literal. Likewise, if you use double quotes to delimit your value, you can use a single quote inside:

```
<driveway length="350'">
<gangster name='Wally "Fingers" Gambino'>
```

What if you need to use both single and double quotes inside an attribute value? Use the *'* or *"* entity references:

```
<irish-gangster name='Shawn "Lefty" O&apos;Doull'>
```

You must also escape the left angle bracket:

```
<math calculation="A&lt;B">
```

You cannot place attributes in the end tag.

Over the years, XML programmers (and SGML programmers before that) have debated whether to specify a certain piece of information as content inside an element or as the value of an attribute. On the next page are some factors to consider when deciding which form is appropriate.

- Whereas elements indicate objects such as purchase orders, line items, and part numbers, I like to think of attributes as specifying properties, such as date-last-modified, author, or currency-type. In other words, think of an attribute as a modifier of an element, just as an adjective modifies a noun.

- Attributes are slightly more efficient in syntax. The smallest element has a seven-character overhead, whereas the smallest attribute has a five-character overhead. The difference becomes more dramatic when the attributes or elements have longer names.

- Attributes are easier to access than elements in the W3C Document Object Model (DOM), but elements and attributes are equally easy to access in XSL.

- Attributes cannot have element structure. If an object has child objects, make it an element, not an attribute.

But don't come to blows over these decisions. Let me make it easy for you: if you can't decide, make the information piece an element. And move on.

Empty Elements

Earlier I mentioned that elements have a start tag, an end tag, and content. Sometimes you might have an element that doesn't have any content. Why bother? Why would you create an element without any content? Consider the horizontal rule tag in HTML. You use it to draw a rule across the page, indicating some kind of break. A horizontal rule element has no content. Since it has no content, you have no need for an end tag to delimit the end of the element. In HTML, the horizontal rule tag looks like this:

```
<HR>
```

In a well-formed XML document, that horizontal rule tag would work fine, except that the parser would look for the *HR* element's end tag—and wouldn't find it. You could use the following code to create a well-formed <HR> tag:

```
<HR></HR>
```

But that would be a silly tag because it really doesn't indicate the purpose of the element. To solve this problem, the developers of the XML Recommendation used an obscure SGML feature that combines the start tag and the end tag into a single tag—the empty element tag. The empty element tag starts like a start tag and ends with a slash. For our horizontal rule element, the tag looks like this:

```
<HR/>
```

When the XML parser sees this tag, it knows not to look for a corresponding end tag.

An empty element can have attributes. Consider the HTML element that inserts an image into a page: *IMG*. Although the element *IMG* uses the *SRC* attribute to point to an image, it's still an empty element. To be well formed, the image element must look like this:

```
<IMG SRC="/images/hookah.gif"/>
```

Notice that the tag ends with a slash-right-angle bracket combination (/>). The slash and right angle bracket characters must be together, without any characters or white space between them.

Comments

Comments can appear almost anywhere in an XML document. Comments look like this:

```
<!-- Better check these figures before sending the file -->
```

The parser ignores comments; they will not be sent to the application. Comments provide a good way to hide information in the source document.

Examples of Well-Formed Documents

This section offers some examples of well-formed documents. The first example, which follows, describes a configuration entry for a piece of computer hardware. Based on the element names, you can probably see what it describes. That's the power of descriptive markup!

```
<configuration type="printer">
    <parm name="port">/usr/lpr</parm>
    <parm name="driver">/usr/drivers/HP5SIPS</parm>
    <parm name="option">sheet feeder</parm>
    <configured/>
    <online/>
</configuration>
```

Notice that the preceding example has no XML declaration. As you learned earlier in the chapter, the XML declaration is optional.

The next example shows a valuable piece of information:

```
<?xml version="1.0"?>
<Joke author="Groucho Marx">
    <Setup>Outside of a dog, a book is man's best
    friend.</Setup>
    <Punchline>Inside of a dog, it's too dark to
    read.</Punchline>
</Joke>
```

Take a look at the XML declaration at the top. Notice also that the case of each start tag and end tag matches.

THE VALID XML DOCUMENT

Let's say I ask you to give me a well-formed document that describes your favorite jokes. You give me two documents, a short joke and a long one.

```
<?xml version="1.0"?>
<favorite-joke author="Pate">
    <one-liner>A duck walks into a bar and says to the
    bartender, "Gimme a shot of whisky and put it on
    my bill."</one-liner>
</favorite-joke>
```

The long joke has a more complex format than the first.

```
<?xml version="1.0"?>
<duck_joke>
    <scene number="1">
        A duck walks into a bar, goes up to the bartender,
        and says, "Do you have any grapes?" The
        bartender says, "No, this is a bar, of course
        we don't have any grapes."
    </scene>
    <scene number="2">
        The next day, the duck walks into the bar, goes
        up to the bartender, and says, "Do you have any
        grapes?" The bartender says, "No, like I told
        you yesterday, we don't have any grapes.
        If you come in here one more time asking for
        grapes, I'm going to nail your webbed feet to
        that bar!"
    </scene>
    <scene number="3">
        The next day, the duck walks into the bar, goes
        up to the bartender, and asks, "Do you have any
        nails?" The bartender says, "No, this is a bar,
        of course we don't have any nails." Then the
        duck says, "Do you have any grapes?"
    </scene>
</duck_joke>
```

Both of these documents contain enough information for a human to figure out the meaning of each element. The first document is clearly the author's favorite joke, and it is clearly a one-liner. We can see that the second document is a duck joke with three scenes. Both documents are well-formed, and an XML parser will not issue any errors when it reads them.

But what if I want to gather many documents like these together and write a program to load jokes into a database? The two documents here—and whatever documents I get from other people—are entirely useless to me. Why? Because there is no standard structure. There's no way to predict how the data will be arranged or even how a submitter will format their tags. Therefore, I can't write a program that can reliably interpret all the different jokes that might come in.

Even though the documents here are self-describing to a human, computers aren't as smart as we are. They need some help in understanding the data before they can process it. Without a predefined formal structural definition, an XML document is only a text file.

To help the computer interpret these documents, I can create a predefined structure for the information and give that to you. A computer on your end can use that structural definition to guide your document creation. You then give me an XML document that is compatible with my database-loading program. This definition becomes a style guide for structure.

Style guides are not a new invention. Every journalist in the field gets a style guide that he uses to ensure that he follows the rules of the newspaper. This style guide will probably have policies for grammatical style, libel avoidance, and the overall tone of an article. A style guide will also indicate the desired structure for an article submission. For example, it might indicate that an article must consist of a headline, followed by a byline, followed by a dateline, an abstract, and an article body. The body, in turn, must consist of one or more paragraphs.

The journalist puts a piece of paper in the typewriter and starts typing his article. He types the headline, byline, and abstract, and then he starts writing paragraphs. He removes the paper from the typewriter and sends it downstairs to the copy editor.

The copy editor notices that the journalist forgot the dateline. She sends the paper back upstairs. What happened here? Two humans were involved in this error, an expensive proposition. If only this journalist had a guardian angel to watch over the keyboard, help him create the document to spec, and keep him from removing the paper until he follows all the rules. For implementers of XML, that guardian angel is valid XML, and the set of rules is the schema.

The Document Type Definition

As you learned in the beginning of this chapter, the XML spec defines a valid XML document thusly:

An XML document is valid if it has an associated document type declaration and if the document complies with the constraints expressed in it.

So, what's a document type declaration?

The document type declaration tells the XML parser where to find a set of rules against which a document can be checked. Where does this set of rules come from? Someone determines the structure of the members of a particular class of documents and makes that structural description available to the parser. The parser reads the structural description, and then parses the document to determine whether it is well-formed. In XML 1.0, the set of rules pointed to by the document type declaration (DOCTYPE) is called the document type definition (DTD).

The well-formed document now has an extra burden: not only must it adhere to the well-formedness constraints that I listed previously, but it also must be structured according to this user-created structural description.

This structural description is called a schema. In XML 1.0, the only type of schema allowed is the DTD. The DTD was taken straight from SGML and slimmed down to get rid of some optional features and hard-to-implement bits.

A DTD for the first Joke document looks like this:

```
<!ELEMENT Joke      (Setup, Punchline)          >
<!ATTLIST Joke      author    CDATA  #REQUIRED
                    firstTold CDATA  #IMPLIED   >
<!ELEMENT Setup     (#PCDATA)                   >
<!ELEMENT Punchline (#PCDATA)                   >
```

To create a valid XML document, I place the document type declaration on top of the document to indicate that the physical file containing the DTD—named Joke.DTD—should be read first, and that the Joke document should be validated according to that structure.

```
<?xml version="1.0"?>
<!DOCTYPE Joke SYSTEM "Joke.dtd">
<Joke author="Groucho Marx">
    <Setup>Outside of a dog, a book is man's
    best friend</Setup>
    <Punchline>Inside of a dog, it's too dark
    to read.</Punchline>
</Joke>
```

This book is probably the only XML book on the shelf that will not attempt to teach you the DTD. Many XML resources are available to teach you the syntax and meaning of the various parts of the DTD.

The DTD was designed to describe legacy document information. We have 15 years of experience in SGML and XML indicating that the DTD works as designed. However, several factors limit the DTD's applicability in e-business transactions.

First, DTD is not written using XML syntax. As you can see from the preceding example, the DTD uses a terse syntax with strange words such as #PCDATA and ATTLIST. Such syntax is not consistent with the sixth XML design goal: "XML documents should be human-legible and reasonably clear."

Another problem is that the DTD has just a single useful data type: TEXT. We can define an element as containing other elements or text. What if we want to validate that the contents of a document form a valid number or a valid date? The parser verifies only that an element contains characters. It's the application's job to verify that a particular string of characters forms a valid date.

But remember that one of the advantages of an XML document is that XML separates data from the processes that act on the data. Thus, several different applications might process the same XML document. Each application that touches the document bears the burden for verifying that a particular element content or attribute value contains a particular data type. Wouldn't it be better if the parser verified the correctness of the data types before the application got the document?

The last major problem with the DTD is that a document can have only one document type to describe the entire document, making it fairly inflexible. The DTD was created in the days of top-down bureaucratic document management. This is good when you need to make sure that documents conform to very rigid standards. For example, all aircraft maintenance manuals must have the same predictable structure because safety is at stake. Safety engineers, maintenance personnel, and even legal departments had a say in this structure's design. Failure to adhere to the approved structure could have disastrous consequences.

The top-down design approach doesn't work quite so well for a business document such as an invoice or medical record though. Consider an invoice, such as the one shown in Figure 4-1. A typical invoice has some header information such as invoice number, date, and customer number. Then there's a place for the address of the vendor, followed by an area that describes the items ordered.

We can use this invoice to bill customers all over the world. Part of the invoice will be the same no matter where we send it. The customer number, invoice number, and line items are all objects common to all vendors. However, what if we do business with a company in the United States? In the United States we use a street address structure that has a city, state, and zip code. The Canadian structure uses a city, province, and postal code. Japan, Germany, and France all have different addressing standards. If we were forced to define our invoice using the all-inclusive, top-down approach that the DTD requires, the invoice would be overly complex.

Wouldn't it be nice to describe an invoice with a single schema, and then "plug in" a second schema from a collection of schemas that describe address blocks? We can do exactly that with the new XML schema syntax and namespaces.

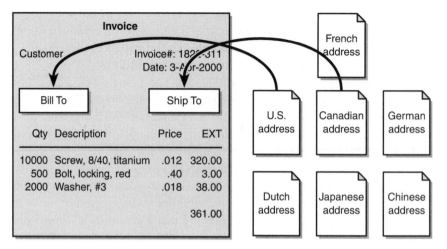

Figure 4-1. *A business document can include other documents. This invoice can be sent to many different countries, each of which has a different way of specifying physical address information.*

NAMESPACES

Before I talk more about schemas, I need to cover a W3C Recommendation called "Namespaces in XML," which you can find at *http://www.w3.org/TR/REC-xml-names/*.

Namespaces have two basic purposes: to enable the sharing of schema structures and datatypes and to uniquely qualify element names in a multischema environment. Namespaces are designed to solve the problem of data sources having elements with the same name but different meanings.

Namespaces point to schemas that contain information about the document you are using. You access this functionality by declaring a namespace and providing information that allows the parser to access the resource where it lives.

Consider the invoice example shown in Listing 4-1. Since the invoice is for books, one of the elements in the body of the invoice is *title*, meaning the title of a book. However, in the schema that contains the address block, the element *title* means the salutatory title of the person ordering the book (Ms., Mr., Dr., Esq., Potentate, and so on). These two *title* elements have distinct meanings, yet they both have the same element name. We want to process them in different ways, but we run the risk of confusing one element with the other.

Invoice.xml

```
<invoice>
    <number>A-99-1443</number>
    <customer>RA-81122</customer>
    <billto>
        <company></company>
        <contact>
            <title>Mr.</title>
            <name>Barnes</name>
        </contact>
        <street1></street1>
        <street2></street2>
        <city></city>
        <state></state>
        <zip></zip>
    </billto>
    <body>
        <line>
            <title>The Fountainhead</title>
            <quantity>600</quantity>
            <price>4.12</price>
        </line>
        <line>
            <title>XML Programming for BizTalk Servers </title>
            <quantity>1000</quantity>
            <price>49.99</price>
        </line>
        <line>
            <title>1001 Duck-Bar Jokes</title>
            <quantity>1000</quantity>
            <price>6.34</price>
        </line>
    </body>
</invoice>
```

Listing 4-1. *Namespace collision results in an ambiguous situation because two elements with different meanings have the same name. In this case, a person's salutatory title and the title of a book.*

We need some way of addressing each element individually and processing it properly, without the ambiguity of namespace collision, so we use namespace declarations. A namespace declaration must appear before or in the first element that comes from that namespace. The namespace declaration looks like an attribute on a start tag. All namespace declarations begin with *xmlns*, followed by an optional local space name (more on space names later).

The value of the namespace declaration attribute is a URL that points to a schema that defines the document.

> **NOTE**   The W3C namespace specification notes that "The namespace name, to serve its intended purpose, should have the characteristics of uniqueness and persistence. It is not a goal that it be directly usable for retrieval of a schema (if any exists). An example of a syntax that is designed with these goals in mind is that for Uniform Resource Names [RFC2141]. However, it should be noted that ordinary URLs can be managed in such a way as to achieve these same goals."

The following invoice start tag contains an example of a namespace for our invoice:

```
<invoice xmlns="http://architag.com/schemas/invoice.xdr">
```

The application that reads the invoice document can then go to the resource listed, retrieve the schema, and validate the structure of the document according to the rules therein. Since this namespace declaration is on the root element of the document, it remains active for the entire scope of the document—unless another namespace overrides it. (I'll explain that later.)

The namespace declaration applies to the element in which it is declared as well as to all child elements of that element. Thus we can have as many namespaces in a document as we want, but only the most recently declared namespace will be current.

What do I mean by most recently declared? Remember that XML is a hierarchical syntax. All elements in a document are descendants of the root element. Elements inside the root relate to each other through a hierarchical structure. A namespace applies to all elements inside the parent, unless another namespace declaration overrides it. That overriding declaration lives for as long as the element in which it is declared remains open.

Consider our invoice. We defined an invoice with a hole into which we can later drop an address block. This kind of structure is called an open content model because it is open for the implementer to fill later. The following document is an example of the namespace scoping in effect:

Nsinvoice.xml

```xml
<?xml version="1.0"?>
<invoice xmlns="http://architag.com/schemas/invoice.xdr">
    <number>21153</number>
    <customer>SY221-00</customer>
    <date>2000-01-24</date>
    <address xmlns="http://xml.org/schemas/us-address.xdr">
        <street>750 Davis Street</street>
        <city>San Francisco</city>
        <state>CA</state>
        <zipcode>94107</zipcode>
    </address>
    <body>
        <item num="YI-2289" qty="100"   price="23.11"/>
        <item num="WD-7198" qty="35000" price=".137"/>
        <item num="ER-3211" qty="120"   price="112.00"/>
    </body>
</invoice>
```

Listing 4-2. *An invoice that uses namespaces to "plug-in" an address block at the appropriate place.*

Notice in Listing 4-2 that the root element, *invoice*, contains a namespace attribute and that the child element *address* contains its own namespace attribute. If you go to the xmlns document, you'll find that the *invoice* namespace defines elements like *number*, *customer*, and *date*. If you look at the *address* namespace, you'll find elements like *street*, *city*, *state*, and *zipcode* defined.

Any time you declare a namespace, the child elements within the scope of the parent become part of that namespace. This is called the default namespace. But what if you want to mix namespaces within an element scope? What if, for example, you want the *date* element inside the *invoice* element to have a data type declared somewhere else?

In that case, you can declare another namespace in the *invoice* element's start tag. Since you can declare only one default namespace at a time, the second namespace must indicate the namespace prefix. You append this prefix to the element names in the start tags and end tags of the elements that are part of that namespace.

Listing 4-3 shows the same invoice with multiple namespace prefixes. The two namespaces indicate where to find element descriptions (schema).

Mnsinvoice.xml

```
<?xml version="1.0"?>
<invoice xmlns="http://architag.com/schemas/invoice.xdr"
    xmlns:dt="http://schemas.com/schemas/datatypes.xdr">
    <number>21153</number>
    <customer>SY221-00</customer>
    <date dt:type="date">2000-01-24</date>
    <address xmlns="http://xml.org/schemas/us-address.xdr">
        <street>750 Davis Street</street>
        <city>San Francisco</city>
        <state>CA</state>
        <zipcode>94107</zipcode>
    </address>
    <body>
        <item num="YI-2289" dt:qty="100"   dt:price="23.11"/>
        <item num="WD-7198" dt:qty="35000" dt:price=".137"/>
        <item num="ER-3211" dt:qty="120"   dt:price="112.00"/>
    </body>
</invoice>
```

Listing 4-3. *An invoice that uses multiple name spaces.*

Notice the second namespace declaration on line 3. This declares a namespace that you can use anywhere within the scope of the *invoice* element, but you must explicitly indicate the namespace on the element's start tags and end tags or attribute names. On line 6, an attribute on the *date* element uses the *dt* namespace. In this case, the type attribute in the datatype schema is set to *date*. Notice that the *dt* namespace is also used on attributes in the body element on lines 14 through 16.

Another way to specify the namespace is to use the namespace prefix on all elements. That is, get rid of the default namespaces all together, as shown in listing 4-4.

Prefixns.xml

```
<?xml version="1.0"?>
<inv:invoice xmlns:inv="http://architag.com/schemas/invoice.xdr"
    xmlns:dt="http://schemas.com/schemas/datatypes.xdr">
    <inv:number>21153</inv:number>
    <inv:customer>SY221-00</inv:customer>
    <inv:date dt:type="date">2000-01-24</inv:date>
    <addr:address
        xmlns:addr="http://xml.org/schemas/us-address.xdr">
        <addr:street>750 Davis Street</addr:street>
        <addr:city>San Francisco</addr:city>
```

Listing 4-4. *The namespace prefix can be used in front of any element. This shows which elements belong to which namespaces, but the coding is quite ungainly.*

```
        <addr:state>CA</addr:state>
        <addr:zipcode>94107</addr:zipcode>
    </addr:address>
    <inv:body>
        <inv:item inv:num="YI-2289"
            dt:qty="100"    dt:price="23.11"/>
        <inv:item inv:num="WD-7198"
            dt:qty="35000" dt:price=".137"/>
        <inv:item inv:num="ER-3211"
            dt:qty="120"    dt:price="112.00"/>
    </inv:body>
</inv:invoice>
```

SCHEMAS

Since the XML 1.0 Recommendation came out in February 1998, the W3C has been working on an alternative specification to replace the DTD for describing schemas. As I write this, the XML Schema work is in its final stages, and should be out as a Candidate Recommendation in the first half of 2000.

The W3C XML Schema Working Group is focusing on three improvement areas:

■ They want to see schemas written using XML syntax, thereby allowing us to use the same tools we use to process our XML documents.

■ They want the new schema standard to support common data types such as number, date, and currency, as well as user-defined data types. This kind of support would move the validation of the data from the application down to the XML parser, where data is accessible by all programs reading the XML document.

■ They want the XML Schema to have open content models. Think of our invoice that required flexible address information. An XML Schema would allow us to define one schema for the invoice information, with a "hole" for an address block. We could then use any schema that describes the required addressing convention and plug that schema into the invoice schema.

NOTE The W3C is working on a specification called Datatypes for DTDs (DT4DTD) that will add data type support to the DTD. This is a patch to the DTD syntax, but will allow users who want to continue to use the DTD to have access to rich data types. Of course, XML parsers must support the standard for it to be useful.

The W3C schema has other features that are lacking in the DTD.

XML Data Reduced

Microsoft was an early proponent of XML and has been involved in the W3C's work on XML standards by submitting specifications for technical review or participating in the many XML-related committees. In January 1998, Microsoft, DataChannel, ArborText, and Inso submitted an alternative schema syntax called XML Data. This syntax achieved the three goals I listed at the end of the previous section, along with a couple of new items.

In December 1998, Microsoft released Internet Explorer 5, which shipped with a parser implemented as a COM object called MSXML. MSXML contains a reduced version of XML Data called XML Data Reduced, or XDR.

Since the W3C XML Schema Working Group is still working on their official schema, Microsoft recommended XDR as the schema syntax for BizTalk. Microsoft has, however, committed to implementing the W3C Schema syntax (dubbed XSD) once it is a final Recommendation.

Should you use XML Data knowing that a schema standard is months away? If you write applications using BizTalk and XML Data today, won't you have to rewrite those applications tomorrow? The answer is no. Microsoft and other vendors will provide tools to convert XDR syntax to XSD. Since the two syntaxes have identical goals, a machine translation of one syntax to another is trivial. Since all syntaxes are in XML syntax, XSL (the Extensible Stylesheet Language) can be used to convert from one schema syntax to another.

A tool available from Extensibility, Inc., named XML Authority (*http://www.extensibility.com*), also allows you to create and maintain schemas. With this product, you can create a schema in a graphical way without worrying about how the syntax will eventually look. I like the product because it stresses what is important, that is, defining a logical hierarchical representation of your data. The product can write to any of a number of schema syntaxes. It can even read one syntax and save as another. Figure 4-2 shows the tool in action.

You can also create an example of a well-formed document, and XML Authority will create a schema from it. It will also create schemas from COM objects, Java Classes, and ODBC data sources.

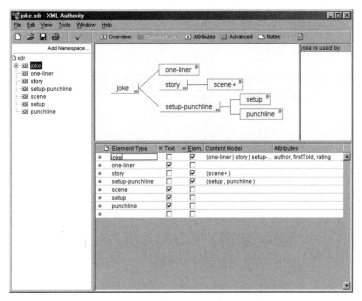

Figure 4-2. *XML Authority, a tool from Extensibility, Inc.*

The XML Data Reduced syntax is documented on the Microsoft XML Developer Center, *http://msdn.microsoft.com/xml*. Listing 4-5 shows an example XDR schema.

Joke.xdr

```
 1 <?xml version ="1.0"?>
 2 <Schema name="Joke.xdr"
 3     xmlns="urn:schemas-microsoft-com:xml-data"
 4     xmlns:dt="urn:schemas-microsoft-com:datatypes">
 5     <ElementType name="joke" content="eltOnly" order="one">
 6         <AttributeType name="author" dt:type="string"
 7             required="yes"/>
 8         <AttributeType name="firstTold" dt:type="dateTime.tz"/>
 9         <AttributeType name="rating" dt:type="enumeration"
10             dt:values="G PG R NC-17" required="yes"/>
11         <attribute type="author"/>
12         <attribute type="firstTold"/>
13         <attribute type="rating"/>
14         <element type="one-liner"/>
15         <element type="story"/>
```

Listing 4-5. *Sample XML Data Reduced (XDR) schema.*   *(continued)*

Listing 4-5. *continued*

```
16          <element type="setup-punchline"/>
17      </ElementType>
18
19      <ElementType name="one-liner" content="textOnly"/>
20      <ElementType name="story" content="eltOnly" order="seq">
21          <element type="scene" minOccurs="1" maxOccurs="*"/>
22      </ElementType>
23
24      <ElementType name="setup-punchline" content="eltOnly"
25          order="seq">
26          <element type="setup"/>
27          <element type="punchline"/>
28      </ElementType>
29
30      <ElementType name="scene" content="textOnly"/>
31      <ElementType name="setup" content="textOnly"/>
32      <ElementType name="punchline" content="textOnly"/>
33 </Schema>
```

Table 4-1 describes the schema in Listing 4-5.

Line	Description
1	The schema is an XML document.
2	The *Schema* start tag indicates the root element. The name of the schema is contained in the *name* attribute.
3–4	The XDR schema specification includes two namespaces: one for structures and the other that defines the datatypes used in the schema.
5–17	The *ElementType* element declares an element and indicates its contents. In this case, we are declaring the *joke* element. Attributes indicate that the joke element contains only elements (*content="eltOnly"*), and that this element can contain only one of the subelements listed (*order="one"*).
6–7	Attributes are declared with the *AttributeType* element. Here, the *author* attribute is declared as having a string data type (*dt:type="string"*). When the *joke* element is started, the *author* attribute is required (*required="yes"*).

Table 4-1. *Description of the schema in Listing 4-5.*

Line	*Description*
8	The *firstTold* attribute is declared as containing a valid date. The *dateTime.tz* datatype is defined by the XDR specification as being a subset of the ISO 8601 standard for specifying date, time, and time zone. The syntax looks like this: 2000-04-25T09:00-08:00. It indicates 9:00 a.m. on April 25, 2000, offset 8 hours behind Greenwich Mean Time. The *firstTold* attribute is not required.
9–10	The *rating* attribute has a datatype of *enumerated*. That means it can only be one of a list of values indicated in the *dt:values* attribute. In this case, the value can only be "G", "PG", "R", or "NC-17". The *rating* attribute is required.
11–13	After attributes are declared for each element, they must be placed using the *attribute* element.
14–16	The *element* element indicates the elements that can be placed inside the *joke* element. Remember that the *content* attribute of the *ElementType* element indicated that only one of these three elements can be contained inside the parent element. Each one of these elements must be declared with its own *ElementType* element.
24–28	The *setup-punchline* element is declared here. The attribute, *order="seq"*, indicates that the elements listed here must appear in the order in which they are placed in the declaration. The elements listed are *setup* and *punchline*. So in the document, the *setup-punchline* element must consist of a single *setup* element followed by a single *punchline* element.
30–32	The three elements here consist only of text.

The W3C XML Schema Working Group continues to work on the XML Schema syntax. As of April 2000, Working Drafts of XML Schema Parts 1, 2, and 3 have been released. XML Schema provides a superset of the capabilities found in XML 1.0 DTDs. The BizTalk initiative uses XDR as its syntax for describing XML documents.

The main difference between XSD and XDR is the actual syntax of the schema documents. However, there really isn't a conceptual difference between the two. Microsoft has committed to implementing XSD as soon as it is available, either as a Candidate or final Recommendation.

Chapter 5

The XML Application

Now that you've seen an XML document and a schema to describe its structure, let's create an application to use the data. I'll walk you through the two basic ways to deal with an XML document: as an in-memory tree object and as an object that generates events as it is processed by the parser and any attached applications.

THE DOCUMENT OBJECT MODEL

The Document Object Model, or DOM, exposes an XML document as a tree structure in memory and provides an easy-to-use environment for the programmer. The DOM provides an accessible object that you can interrogate and manipulate like any other object in modern-day programming languages.

The DOM defines a standard set of objects and interfaces that you can use to manipulate XML, providing access to documents, elements, and attributes. The DOM lets you express an XML document as an object, so you can work with it as you can any other object on your system—by using a well-documented application programming interface (API) with useful properties and methods.

As you learned in earlier chapters, the DOM is a World Wide Web Consortium (W3C) Recommendation. Because the DOM is a large project, the W3C DOM Working Group faced and still faces a daunting task. To better manage the project, the group broke up the work into multiple parts, adopting the first part in October 1998; I expect that the second part will be complete in the first half of 2000.

The W3C recommendation is useful as a blueprint for a common object model, but it does not go far enough in defining a specific implementation of the DOM. Each implementation of the DOM, therefore, will probably consist of a different view of the document object. For example, there are some key interfaces missing from the

W3C version of the DOM that Microsoft felt were important to include. I use two methods, *selectNodes* and *selectSingleNode*, that are not in the W3C specification. Several parser providers offer implementations of the DOM in their products. Because the environment in which you implement each parser has different requirements, each of these implementations is different.

Now I will describe the Microsoft implementation of the DOM, since it has by far the best documentation and support. The Microsoft DOM is part of the Microsoft XML parser object. Microsoft includes the Microsoft XML DOM object in Microsoft Internet Explorer 5, Microsoft Office 2000, and Microsoft Windows 2000. The XML DOM object is also a redeployable object that you can include in your own applications. The DOM's filename is msxml2.dll (see the sidebar), and it is registered as a COM object with the name MSXML2.DOMDocument. Since the DOM is a COM object, you can invoke it wherever you would invoke a COM object in any COM-enabled application. You can access it as an ActiveX control in scripting using Microsoft.XMLDOM.

XMLDOM VERSIONS

Because development of the XML DOM is ongoing, you might find a number of versions of xmldom.dll on your machine. If you program to *MSXML.DOMDocument*, you are accessing version 2.5 of the DLL. Using *MSXML2.DOMDocument* lets you access version 2.6 of the DLL, and *MSXML.DOMDocument30* gives you access to version 3 of the DLL. You can run the file xmlinst.exe after installing the latest version of MSXML to point all of your registry entries to the latest version of the file. In this chapter we'll program to MSXML2.DOMDocument.

The DOM in Action

Think of the DOM as a dynamic hierarchical object with a set of interfaces, properties, and methods. It is important to note that the computer sees the object we call an XML document as just a serial collection of bytes. Because this collection of bytes takes the form of plain text, it's easy to read and easy to move around our networks and over the Internet.

However, for the computer to interrogate and manipulate the information in an XML document, you must turn the document into an in-memory object that is better suited for treatment by high-level programming languages. You do this by instantiating a copy of the DOM, which invokes a parser to break up the XML document into pieces. Figure 5-1 shows the operation of the parser in creating the DOM object.

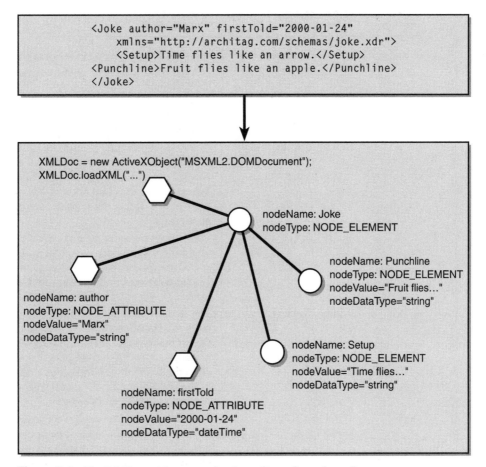

Figure 5-1. *The DOM provides a standard set of interfaces that allows a programmer to access the hierarchical objects represented by an XML stream.*

At the top of Figure 5-1 is a small XML document representing a joke. You can see elements for *Joke, Setup,* and *Punchline,* and attributes for *author* and *firstTold.* The XML parser reads this document one character at a time, determining which characters are markup and which are content. If the parser doesn't find a schema, it follows the rules of well-formed XML. If the parser does find a schema, it reads the schema and then ensures that the document adheres to the structure described by the schema.

Once the parser is satisfied that the document is properly defined, it creates a set of nodes that have certain properties. (I discussed XML nodes in Chapter 4.) Table 5-1 lists the 12 node types in the Microsoft DOM implementation.

Value	Name	Description
1	NODE_ELEMENT	The node represents an element. An element node can have the following child node types: Element, Text, Comment, ProcessingInstruction, CDATA-Section, and EntityReference. An element node can be the child of the Document, Document-Fragment, EntityReference, and Element nodes.
2	NODE_ATTRIBUTE	The node represents an attribute of an element. An attribute node can have the following child node types: Text and EntityReference. The attribute does not appear as the child node of any other node type; note that it is not considered a child node of an element.
3	NODE_TEXT	The node represents the text content of a tag. A text node cannot have any child nodes. The text node can appear as the child node of the Attribute, DocumentFragment, Element, and EntityReference nodes.
4	NODE_CDATA_SECTION	The node represents a CDATA section in the XML source. CDATA sections are used to escape blocks of text that would otherwise be recognized as markup. A CDATA section node cannot have any child nodes. The CDATA section node can appear as the child of the DocumentFragment, Entity-Reference, and Element nodes.
5	NODE_ENTITY_REFERENCE	The node represents a reference to an entity in the XML document. This node type applies to all entities, including character entity references. An entity reference node can have the following child node types: Element, ProcessingInstruction, Comment, Text, CDATASection, and EntityReference. The entity reference node can appear as the child of the Attribute, DocumentFragment, Element, and EntityReference nodes.
6	NODE_ENTITY	The node represents an expanded entity. An entity node can have child nodes that represent the expanded entity (for example, Text and Entity-Reference nodes). The entity node can appear as the child of the DocumentType node.
7	NODE_PROCESSING_INSTRUCTION	The node represents a processing instruction (PI) from the XML document. A PI node cannot have any child nodes. The PI node can appear as the child of the Document, DocumentFragment, Element, and EntityReference nodes.

Table 5-1. *Node types defined by the Microsoft implementation of the W3C DOM.*

Value	Name	Description
8	NODE_COMMENT	The node represents a comment in the XML document. A comment node cannot have any child nodes. The comment node can appear as the child of the Document, DocumentFragment, Element, and EntityReference nodes.
9	NODE_DOCUMENT	The node represents a document object, which, as the root of the document tree, provides access to the entire XML document. It is created by using the ProgID "MSXML2.DOMDocument", or through a data island using <SCRIPT LANGUAGE=XML> or <XML>. The document node can have the following child node types: Element (maximum of one), Processing Instruction, Comment, and Document-Type. The document node cannot appear as the child of any node types.
10	NODE_ DOCUMENT_TYPE	The node represents the document type declaration, indicated by the <!DOCTYPE> tag. The document type node can have the following child node types: Notation and Entity. The document type node can appear as the child of the Document node.
11	NODE_DOCUMENT_ FRAGMENT	The node represents a document fragment. The document fragment node associates a node or subtree with a document without actually being contained within the document. The document fragment node can have the following child node types: Element, ProcessingInstruction, Comment, Text, CDATASection, and EntityReference. The DocumentFragment node cannot appear as the child of any node types.
12	NODE_NOTATION	A node represents a notation in the document type declaration. The notation node cannot have any child nodes. The notation node can appear as the child of the DocumentType node.

The properties and methods available for each node depend on the type of node it is. For example, you can load a document node with a serialized (raw text) XML document, but you can't load an element or attribute node directly. To access an element node, you must first successfully read the document into a document node.

In Figure 5-1, Joke has four nodes. The first two are the element nodes Setup and Punchline. The second two nodes are the attribute nodes *author* and *firstTold*. In the <Joke> start tag, a namespace points to a schema on an external site. This schema is specified using XML Data Reduced (XDR) syntax. Notice the *nodeDataType* property of each node. All are strings except for the *firstTold* attribute, which has been declared a *dateTime* data type. If you don't specify a namespace, all *nodeDataType* properties are strings. By accessing the *typedValue* property of *nodeDataType*, the object will return the value of the date as a date variant, so your application does not need to validate the data type or convert the value for processing.

You'll find the full Microsoft DOM API at http://msdn.microsoft.com. Like most APIs, the DOM API is rich, allowing you to do a number of things including loading and saving, creating elements and nodes, and of course, parsing XML documents. And as with most APIs, the DOM API has only a couple of methods and properties that you will use in your day-to-day work. Let's see how to use some of these more common properties and methods.

Creating a DOM Object

The first requirement when you work with the DOM is to instantiate a copy of the XML parser/DOM object in your application. In JavaScript, you use the *ActiveXObject* function to create the object, as shown in the following code:

```
var objDocument = new ActiveXObject("MSXML2.DOMDocument");
objDocument.async = false;
```

The first line instantiates the object and creates a variant called *objDocument*. This object will contain the document node after you've loaded the document. You can test this by accessing the value of the *objDocument.nodeType* property. In this case, the property contains the value *9*, which maps to the NODE_DOCUMENT node type in Table 5-1.

The *async* property indicates whether the parser should load the entire document before making it available to the programmer. Setting the *async* property to *false* ensures that no actions will be taken against a document that is not fully loaded. This is the safe and easy way to program, but it might make your application work more slowly. When set to *true* (the default setting), the control returns to the caller before the download is finished. You can then use the *readyState* property to check the status of the download. You can also attach an *onreadystatechange* handler or connect to the *onreadystatechange* event to notify you when the ready state changes and the download are complete.

For loading large documents, you will probably want to set the *async* property to *true* so that you can continue to do other processing while the object loads. In effect, the load is spun off as a separate thread. If you do set the *async* property to *true*, you should check the value of the *readyState* property before you try to access the document. Table 5-2 describes the values of *readyState*.

Table 5-3 describes the two ways to load a stream of XML text into the object.

Value	State	Description
1	LOADING	The object is bootstrapping, which means it is reading any persisted properties, not parsing data.
2	LOADED	The object is finished bootstrapping and is beginning to read and parse data.
3	INTERACTIVE	Some data has been read and parsed, and the object model is now available on the partially retrieved data set.
4	COMPLETED	The document has been loaded, successfully or unsuccessfully.

Table 5-2. *Values returned by the* readyState *property.*

Method	Description
load(url)	This method loads an XML document from the location specified by the URL. If the URL cannot be resolved or accessed or does not reference an XML document, the *documentElement* property is set to null and an error is returned.
loadXML(xmlString)	This method loads an XML document using the supplied string. The *xmlString* argument can be a well-formed or valid document. If the XML within *xlmString* cannot be loaded (because of parsing errors), the *documentElement* property is set to *null* and an error is returned.

Table 5-3. *Methods for loading an XML document into a DOM object.*

The following code loads an XML string into a DOM object:

```
objDocument.loadXML("<fact verified='2000-01-24'>Movies are " +
                "better than books because you can't " +
                "spill coffee on them.</fact>");
```

Once the object is loaded, the *parseError* object should be checked. A correctly parsed object will return *0*, as in this example:

```
if (objDocument.parseError.errorCode != 0)
    {
    alert("Error: " + objDocument.parseError.reason +
        " on line " + objDocument.parseError.line);
    }
```

Table 5-4 describes the properties of this read-only *parseError* object.

Property	Description
errorCode	The error code number in decimal format
url	The URL of the XML file containing the error
reason	The reason for the error in human-readable form
srcText	The full text of the line containing the error
line	The number of the line containing the error (Note that the line number is relative to the top of the document, so if you have a document type definition (DTD), the numbering will start counting at the point immediately following the DTD, not necessarily at the first line of the document content.)
linepos	The character position within the line where the error occurred
filepos	The absolute character position in the file where the error occurred

Table 5-4. *Properties of the* parseError *object.*

Accessing the *documentElement*

Once we are satisfied that the document has been loaded properly, we can start to access the contents of the object. We have many ways to do this. The easiest approach is to access the properties of the document element. The following code adds the *documentElement.nodeName* and the *documentElement.text* properties to the result string:

```
result += "objDocument.parseError.errorCode: "
    + objDocument.parseError.errorCode + "\n";

result += "objDocument.documentElement.nodeName: "
    + objDocument.documentElement.nodeName + "\n";

result += "objDocument.documentElement.text: "
    + objDocument.documentElement.text + "\n";

alert (result);
```

The *nodeName* and *text* properties work on any element node. The *objDocument* object is a document node. The *documentElement* property of this node gives us the element node. We can set a variant to this element to make our coding a little simpler:

```
var rootElem = objDocument.documentElement;
```

Attributes are contained in the *XMLDOMElement* object as a collection of named items. This collection belongs to the element in which the attributes are specified.

You can think of the *attributes* collection as an associative array—that is, a collection of like objects, each keyed by a string rather than an offset index. To access the value of the *verified* attribute, you need to use the *getNamedItem* method:

```
result += "rootElem.attributes.getNamedItem('verified').nodeValue: "
    + rootElem.attributes.getNamedItem("verified").nodeValue + "\n";
```

It's easy to access the properties of the document element, but what about other elements in the document? They are a bit harder to access, but in the next section I'll show you some methods that help you access elements directly.

Getting Items in the Document

Let's load a more complex document. How about our favorite duck-bar joke from Chapter 4.

```
<?xml version="1.0"?>
<joke type="story" keywords="duck bar grapes nails">
    <scene number="1">
        A duck walks into a bar, goes to the bartender,
        and says, "Do you have any grapes?" The
        bartender says, "No, this is a bar, of course
        we don't have any grapes."
    </scene>
    <scene number="2">
        The next day, the duck walks into the bar, goes
        up to the bartender, and says, "Do you have any
        grapes?" The bartender says, "I told you
        yesterday, 'no, we don't have any grapes.'
        If you come in here one more time asking for
        grapes, I'm going to nail your beak to that bar!"
    </scene>
    <scene number="3">
        The next day, the duck walks into the bar, goes
        up to the bartender, and asks, "Do you have any
        nails?" The bartender says, "No, this is a bar,
        of course we don't have any nails." Then the
        duck says, "Do you have any grapes?"
    </scene>
</joke>
```

Assume this document is loaded into our object and the parser returns an *errorCode* of *0*. We can easily access the element and attributes of any element node, as you learned in the previous section, but what about the *scene* elements? To get them, we can use the *childNodes* property. Then we can interrogate the *scene* elements to get the information we need:

```
result += " rootElem.childNodes.item(1).text: "
    + rootElem.childNodes.item(1).text + "\n"
```

The *item* property returns the child node. The collection of nodes returned from the *childNodes* method is zero-based, so the example here returns the text of the second scene in which the bartender threatens our little hero with physical violence.

You can access an array of child nodes through the *XMLDOMNodeList* object. Table 5-5 lists the properties and methods available.

Property	Description
length	Returns the number of nodes in the node list. The length of the list will change dynamically as children or attributes are added and deleted from the parent element.
Method	
item(index)	Returns the node in the node list with the specified index. Index is zero-based.
nextNode	Returns the next node in the node list based on the current node.
reset	Returns the iterator to the uninstantiated state; that is, before the first node in the node list.

Table 5-5. *The* XMLDOMNodeList *interface exposes these properties and methods.*

We can use the *length* property to iterate through the collection one member at a time:

```
for (i = 0; i < rootElem.childNodes.length; i++)
    {
    result += " rootElem.childNodes.item(" + i + ").text: "
        + rootElem.childNodes.item(i).text + "\n";
    }
```

To make the preceding code more readable, we can create a new variant that contains the collection of items:

```
var colScenes = rootElem.childNodes;
for (i = 0; i < colScenes.length; i++)
    {
    result += "colScenes.item(" + i + ").text: "
        + colScenes.item(i).text + "\n";
    }
```

The *colScenes* variant is a DOM *NodeList* object containing all the direct child elements of the root element *joke*. Using this object makes accessing elements in the DOM very straightforward.

What if you want to access one of the scenes, but only if its attribute is a certain value? Here's one approach:

```
var colScenes = rootElem.childNodes
for (i = 0; i < colScenes.length; i++)
    {
    if (colScenes.item(i).attributes.getNamedItem("number").nodeValue == "1")
        {
        result += "colScenes.item(" + i + ").text: "
            + colScenes.item(i).text + "\n"
        }
    }
```

It works, but it's pretty clumsy. Let's take a look at an alternative approach for accessing nodes, and then I'll show you an easy way to get a particular node. The Microsoft DOM implements two handy methods for accessing exactly what you want: *selectNodes(query)* and *selectSingleNode(query)*. These methods are described in Table 5-6.

Method	*Description*
*selectNodes(*query*)*	Returns a node list containing the results of the query indicated by the *query* string by using the current node as the query context. If no nodes match the query, an empty node list is returned. If the *query* string has an error, DOM error reporting is used.
*selectSingleNode(*query*)*	Returns a single node that is the first node the node list returned from the query, using the current node as the query context. If no nodes match the *query* string, null is returned. If the *query* string has an error, an error is returned.

Table 5-6. *You can access an element or set of elements by using the* selectNodes *and* selectSingleNode *methods in the Microsoft DOM implementation. The query argument contains a pattern defined by the W3C XPath specification.*

The query strings passed to the methods in Table 5-6 are Extensible Stylesheet Language (XSL) patterns. I'll discuss XSL patterns in Chapter 6. For now, to access our document, let's take a look at the *selectNodes* method as an alternative to *childNodes*:

```
var colScenes = rootElem.selectNodes("scene")
for (i = 0; i < colScenes.length; i++)
    {
    result += "colScenes.item(" + i + ").text: "
        + colScenes.item(i).text + "\n"
    }
```

Using the *selectNodes* method is a little bit of an improvement over using the *childNodes* method, and it is clearly more self-explanatory. The advantages of the *selectNodes* method become more obvious once you start delving deeper into a complex document. For example, you can easily access a collection of line items deep in an invoice document by using a complex XSL query pattern such as the following:

```
selectNodes("/invoice/body/items/item")
```

Accessing an item using the *childNodes* method to drill down through the hierarchy would require quite a bit of code. We would need to iterate through our node list a number of times to select the nodes that we want. To eliminate most of that code, you can use the *selectSingleNode* method:

```
result += rootElem.selectSingleNode("scene[@number='2']").text;
```

The XSL pattern here returns the first scene, which has an attribute (@) named *number* that has a value of *2*.

Now you have enough practical knowledge of the DOM to create an application that produces actual results.

EXERCISE: USING THE DOM IN VISUAL BASIC

The DOM provides an interface into an XML document, allowing you to access the document's contents. Because the Microsoft XML processor is a COM object and contains support for the W3C DOM, you can instantiate it in any tool that can use COM objects. Thus you can use the XML processor in Microsoft Visual Basic, as in the this exercise, and you can use it in a Web browser function written in JavaScript, in a C++ program, or even in a Java application.

In this section, you will build a Visual Basic program that uses the DOM to access the contents of an XML document. The program instantiates a DOM object, loads an XML document into the object, creates a collection of elements, and iterates through the collection. You'll find all files—including the Architag XRay XML Editor—on the companion CD. Before you begin this exercise, install the editor from the XRaySetup.exe file.

The Microsoft implementation of the W3C DOM is contained in a DLL named msxml2.dll. This object is registered as a COM object as *MSXML2.DOMDocument*. You can use it wherever you can instantiate a COM object.

1. Load mvp.xml document into the XRay XML Editor. You'll find this file in the \Samples\Ch05\ directory on the companion CD. You'll see the screen shown in Figure 5-2.

    Notice that Figure 5-2 is a well-formed XML document containing more than 150 entries. There is one entry for each baseball player who has won baseball's Most Valuable Player award. (For those of you who are counting, there have been three such awards: the Chalmers Award, given from 1911–1914; the League Award, given from 1922–1929; and finally the Baseball Writer's Award, also known as the MVP Award, first given in 1931.) Each entry in this example has a unique identifier on the entry element and seven elements describing the player. Our task is to calculate the batting average of each player that year and display the best and worst averages in a window.

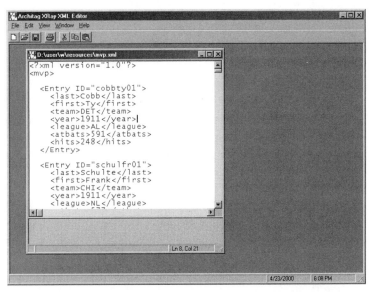

Figure 5-2. *The file mvp.xml in the Architag XRay XML Editor.*

2. Start Visual Basic as shown in Figure 5-3, click on Standard EXE, and then click Open.

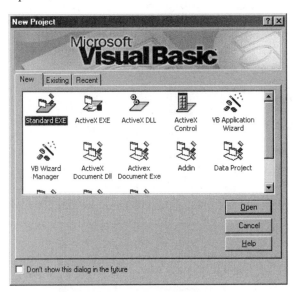

Figure 5-3. *Microsoft Visual Basic 6.0.*

3. Select Form1 from the Project Explorer window as shown in Figure 5-4. From the Project menu, choose Remove Form1.

Figure 5-4. *The Project Explorer window.*

4. Add the DOM form to the project by selecting Project, choosing Add File, and then choosing \Samples\Ch05\DOM.frm.

5. Open the form by clicking the plus sign in the Project window. Double-click on the BaseballStats form, as shown in Figure 5-5.

Figure 5-5. *Getting to the BaseballStats form.*

6. Make this form the startup form by selecting Project1 Properties from the Project menu. Choose BaseballStats from the Startup Object pull-down menu, as shown in Figure 5-6. Click OK.

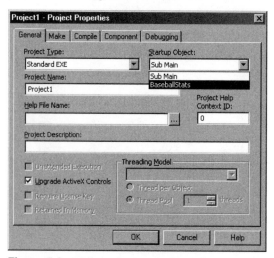

Figure 5-6. *Making the BaseballStats form your startup form.*

7. From the Project menu, choose References. Add the MSXML parser to the project by choosing Microsoft XML, v3.0 from the Available References list, as shown in Figure 5-7. Click OK.

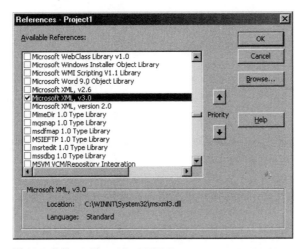

Figure 5-7. *Adding the MSXML parser to your project.*

You should see an environment that looks like Figure 5-8.

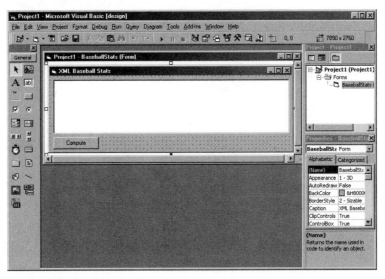

Figure 5-8. *The BaseballStats form.*

8. Double-click the form just to the right of the Compute button. This will bring up the *Form Load* subroutine. There are two lines missing. Enter them as follows:

```
Set oXMLDoc = CreateObject("MSXML2.DOMDocument")
oXMLDoc.Load ("c:\mvp.xml")
```

Replace the path c:\ with the path to the mvp.xml file on your machine.

Notice that the IntelliSense processor pops up all the available properties and methods when you key in the second line, as shown in Figure 5-9.

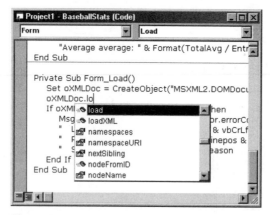

Figure 5-9. *The IntelliSense processor shows all available properties and methods in a pop-up menu.*

Your subroutine should look like Figure 5-10 when you are finished.

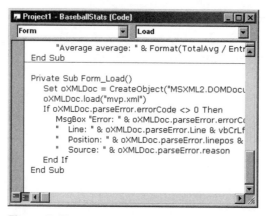

Figure 5-10. *The* Form_Load *subroutine.*

The first line creates an instance of the Microsoft XML parser, "Microsoft.XMLDOM". This parser is a COM object that you can use in any program. Think of XML's processing capabilities as a part of the operating system.

The second line loads the MVP document into the object to make it available for scripting.

9. Notice that at the top of the BaseballStats(Code) window there is a drop-down list box that displays Form. Click this, and select Compute. Doing so reveals the subroutine shown in Figure 5-11. This is the subroutine that will execute when the user clicks the Compute button.

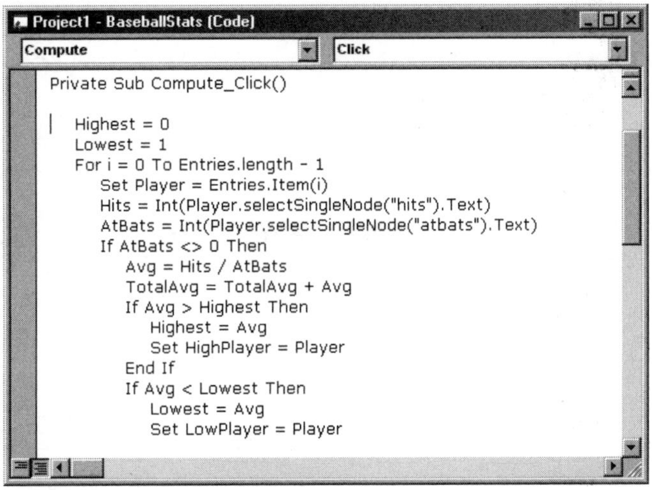

```
Project1 - BaseballStats [Code]
[Compute ▼]   [Click ▼]

Private Sub Compute_Click()

    Highest = 0
    Lowest = 1
    For i = 0 To Entries.length - 1
        Set Player = Entries.Item(i)
        Hits = Int(Player.selectSingleNode("hits").Text)
        AtBats = Int(Player.selectSingleNode("atbats").Text)
        If AtBats <> 0 Then
            Avg = Hits / AtBats
            TotalAvg = TotalAvg + Avg
            If Avg > Highest Then
                Highest = Avg
                Set HighPlayer = Player
            End If
            If Avg < Lowest Then
                Lowest = Avg
                Set LowPlayer = Player
```

Figure 5-11. *The* Compute_Click *subroutine.*

10. Notice the blank line as the first line in the subroutine. Enter the following code:

```
Set Entries = oXMLDoc.selectNodes("//Entry")
```

As you enter code, you will see that the IntelliSense processor is helping you, as shown in Figure 5-12.

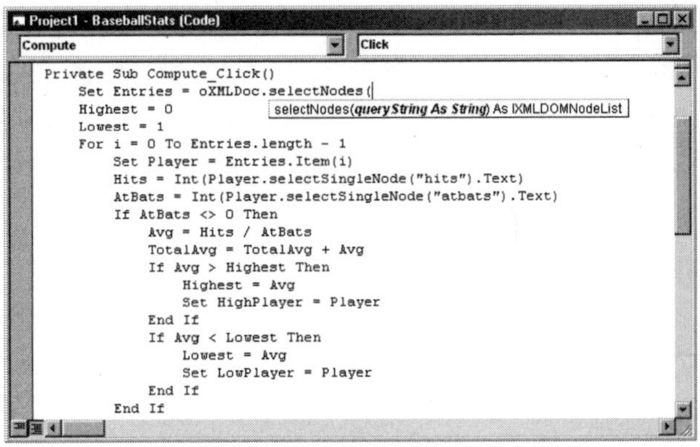

```
Project1 - BaseballStats [Code]
[Compute ▼]   [Click ▼]

Private Sub Compute_Click()
    Set Entries = oXMLDoc.selectNodes (|
    Highest = 0         [selectNodes(queryString As String) As IXMLDOMNodeList]
    Lowest = 1
    For i = 0 To Entries.length - 1
        Set Player = Entries.Item(i)
        Hits = Int(Player.selectSingleNode("hits").Text)
        AtBats = Int(Player.selectSingleNode("atbats").Text)
        If AtBats <> 0 Then
            Avg = Hits / AtBats
            TotalAvg = TotalAvg + Avg
            If Avg > Highest Then
                Highest = Avg
                Set HighPlayer = Player
            End If
            If Avg < Lowest Then
                Lowest = Avg
                Set LowPlayer = Player
            End If
        End If
```

Figure 5-12. *The IntelliSense processor helps determine the parameters of the* selectNode *method.*

The *Compute_Click* subroutine creates a collection of element nodes containing all 154 baseball player entries. Now we can access this collection one player at a time to find which players have the highest and lowest averages.

Once we find the highest and lowest averages, the *HighPlayer* and *LowPlayer* objects contain the entire entries for the appropriate players. These objects are interrogated at the end of the subroutine and presented in the text box of the application.

11. Start the program by pressing F5. You should see the window shown in Figure 5-13.

Figure 5-13. *The main window of the MVP program.*

12. Click the Compute button, and see your beautiful results, shown in Figure 5-14.

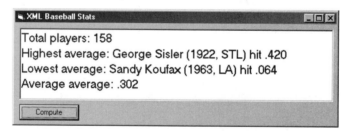

Figure 5-14. *The results of the MVP program.*

13. Close this window, and save the project as DOM.vbp.

WRITING TO THE DOM

In addition to accessing the values of certain properties in the DOM, you can also add nodes, prune nodes, and perform other manipulations while the document object is in memory. Let's say we want to create an XML document that has the following structure:

ToyCarPO.xml

```
<?xml version="1.0"?>
<ToyCarPO_1.0
    poNum = "18892"
    poDate="2000-02-21">
    <header>
        <vendorNum>76671</vendorNum>
        <terms>1/10 net 30</terms>
        <shipTo>shipto</shipTo>
        <billTo>billto</billTo>
    </header>
    <body>
        <item needBefore="2000-02-29" needAfter="2000-02-22">
            <partNum>SY120</partNum>
            <qty>10</qty>
            <price>12.43</price>
        </item>
        <item needBefore="2000-03-01" needAfter="2000-02-23">
            <partNum>TQ331</partNum>
            <qty>100</qty>
            <price>0.443</price>
        </item>
    </body>
</ToyCarPO_1.0>
```

Listing 5-1. *The desired structure for a particular XML document.*

We could create each element using a technique called concatenation in which we link together strings inside our program by building them up with the string-handling features of our programming language. This would require parsing the XML document ourselves. This would be a lot of work. We can save ourselves some effort by taking advantage of the functionality written into the Microsoft DOM object.

In this example, we will create an empty invoice document and use the DOM to add items under program control. Let's use Visual Basic to create the document. This is a fairly simple Visual Basic program. It runs when the form is loaded and opens message boxes that display the output. You can find this project on the companion CD in \Samples\Ch05\Struct.vbp.

First we need to instantiate a copy of the XML document object and load it with the root element. Table 5-7 describes the code in Listing 5-2 line by line.

Once we've instantiated and seeded the document, we can start to add elements and attributes. First let's add a couple of attributes to the root element. These attributes are detailed in Table 5-8.

buildXML.frm

```
1  Dim oXMLDoc As MSXML2.DOMDocument30
2  Dim rootElement
3
4  Set oXMLDoc = CreateObject("MSXML2.DOMDocument")
5  oXMLDoc.loadXML ("<ToyCarPO_1.0></ToyCarPO_1.0>")
6  set rootElement = oXMLDoc.documentElemen
```

Listing 5-2. *Using* loadXML *to load a line of XML code.*

Line	Description
1–2	Declare the oXMLDoc and rootElementobjects.
4	Create an instance of the oXMLDoc document object.
5	Load the root element into the object, creating a single node that we can use as an anchor to add other nodes.
6	We could refer to the root element as *oXMLDoc.documentElement* for the rest of the program, but it is easier to create a new object as a reference point, so we instantiate rootElement.

Table 5-7. *Creating the objects needed for our program.*

buildXML.frm

```
1  Dim namedNodeMap
2  Set namedNodeMap = rootElement.Attributes
3  Dim newAtt
4  Set newAtt = oXMLDoc.createAttribute("poNum")
5  newAtt.Value = "19982"
6  namedNodeMap.setNamedItem newAtt
```

Listing 5-3. *Adding elements to a document object by using* createAttribute.

Line	Description
1–2	Create a node that will contain all the attributes. This *namedNodeMap* is an object that will contain all the attribute objects, each of which has a name and a value.
3–5	Create an attribute object, and give it a name. In this case, we are creating an attribute named *poNum* with a value of 19982. This is the name-value pair necessary to create an attribute.
6	The *setNamedItem* method adds a member to the named node map.

Table 5-8. *Adding attributes to the root element.*

If we were to serialize (output to text) our XML document now, it would look like this:

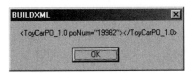

We'll be creating a lot of attributes, so let's put the logic inside a reusable function:

```
Public Function addAttribute(oDoc, nodeMap, attrName, attrValue)
    Dim newAtt
    Set newAtt = oDoc.createAttribute(attrName)
    newAtt.Value = attrValue
    nodeMap.setNamedItem newAtt
End Function
```

The *addAttribute* function is called from the application whenever we need to create an attribute with a name and value:

```
addAttribute oXMLDoc, namedNodeMap, "poNum", "19982"
addAttribute oXMLDoc, namedNodeMap, "poDate", Now()
```

Our XML document now looks like this:

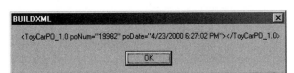

Now let's add some elements to our document. We create elements by using the *createElement* method, which creates an element node that stands by itself. We can then use the *appendChild* method to place that node into our document:

```
Dim headerNode
Set headerNode = oXMLDoc.createElement("header")
rootElement.appendChild (headerNode)
```

Now we have the following document:

Notice that once we create an element, we must fill it with content or it will be an empty element. We need to add some subelements to the header element and fill them with text content.

```
Dim headerNode
Set headerNode = oXMLDoc.createElement("header")
    Dim newChild
    Set newChild = oXMLDoc.createElement("vendorNum")
    newChild.Text = "76671"
    headerNode.appendChild (newChild)
    rootElement.appendChild (headerNode)
```

The *newChild* object is created just like the *headerNode* element. It is an element node that is given a name (*vendorNum*) and a value (*76671*). The *appendChild* method adds the node to the *headerNode* object. This object is then grafted to the *rootElement* object with another *appendChild* method. The resulting XML looks like this:

We will be adding many elements with content, so let's place this code into a function:

```
Public Function addElement(oDoc, node, elementName, elementValue)
    Dim newChild
    Set newChild = oDoc.createElement(elementName)
    newChild.Text = elementValue
    node.appendChild (newChild)
End Function
```

The function is called once for each element in the header element:

```
addElement oXMLDoc, headerNode, "vendorNum", "76671"
addElement oXMLDoc, headerNode, "terms", "1/10 net 30"
addElement oXMLDoc, headerNode, "shipTo", "Shipto address"
addElement oXMLDoc, headerNode, "billTo", "Billto address"
```

We follow the same procedure to create the *body* element and its child elements. Table 5-9 walks you through the code line by line.

buildXML.frm

```
1    Dim bodyNode
2    Dim itemNode
3    Set bodyNode = oXMLDoc.createElement("body")
4        Set itemNode = oXMLDoc.createElement("item")
5            ' set attributes on item
6            Set namedNodeMap = itemNode.Attributes
7            addAttribute oXMLDoc, namedNodeMap, "needBefore", Now() + 8
```

Listing 5-4. *Building the body using the* createElement *method.*

```
8        addAttribute oXMLDoc, namedNodeMap, "needAfter", Now() + 14
9        ' set children of item
10       addElement oXMLDoc, itemNode, "partNum", "SY120"
11       addElement oXMLDoc, itemNode, "qty", "10"
12       addElement oXMLDoc, itemNode, "price", "12.43"
13   bodyNode.appendChild (itemNode)
14
15   Set itemNode = oXMLDoc.createElement("item")
16       ' set attributes on item
17       Set namedNodeMap = itemNode.Attributes
18       addAttribute oXMLDoc, namedNodeMap, "needBefore", Now() + 7
19       addAttribute oXMLDoc, namedNodeMap, "needAfter", Now() + 21
20       ' set children of item
21       addElement oXMLDoc, itemNode, "partNum", "TQ331"
22       addElement oXMLDoc, itemNode, "qty", "100"
23       addElement oXMLDoc, itemNode, "price", "0,443"
24   bodyNode.appendChild (itemNode)
25  rootElement.appendChild (bodyNode)
```

Line	Description
1–2	The *bodyNode* and *itemNode* objects are declared. These objects will hold the element objects as we create them.
3–4	Instantiate copies of the nodes and use the *createElement* method to give them names.
7–8	Add attributes to the *item* element. Notice that we use the *Attributes* property to create *namedNodeMap* as part of the *itemNode* object. All attributes that we add by using the *addAttribute* function get attached to that node map.
10–12	The *addElement* function adds children to the *itemNode* element and gives them names and values.
13	Finally, we use the *appendChild* method to add the item node and its three child nodes (*partNum*, *qty*, and *price*) to the body node.
15–24	We use the same techniques described in this table to add another *item*.
25	We use the *appendChild* method to add the body node we built to the root element.

Table 5-9. *A description of Listing 5-4, in which we create the* body *element and its child elements.*

Now you can see that the document is complete:

Listing 5-5 shows the entire Visual Basic program:

buildXML.frm

```
Option Explicit
Public Function addAttribute(oDoc, nodeMap, attrName, attrValue)
    Dim newAtt
    Set newAtt = oDoc.createAttribute(attrName)
    newAtt.Value = attrValue
    nodeMap.setNamedItem newAtt
End Function
Public Function addElement(oDoc, node, elementName, elementValue)
    Dim newChild
    Set newChild = oDoc.createElement(elementName)
    newChild.Text = elementValue
    node.appendChild (newChild)
End Function

Private Sub Form_Load()
    Dim oXMLDoc As MSXML2.DOMDocument30
    Dim rootElement

    Set oXMLDoc = CreateObject("MSXML2.DOMDocument")
    oXMLDoc.loadXML ("<ToyCarPO_1.0></ToyCarPO_1.0>")
    Set rootElement = oXMLDoc.documentElement

    Dim namedNodeMap
    Set namedNodeMap = rootElement.Attributes
        addAttribute oXMLDoc, namedNodeMap, "poNum", "19982"
        addAttribute oXMLDoc, namedNodeMap, "poDate", Now()

    Dim headerNode
    Set headerNode = oXMLDoc.createElement("header")
        addElement oXMLDoc, headerNode, "vendorNum", "76671"
        addElement oXMLDoc, headerNode, "terms", "1/10 net 30"
        addElement oXMLDoc, headerNode, "shipTo", "Shipto address"
        addElement oXMLDoc, headerNode, "billTo", "Billto address"
    rootElement.appendChild (headerNode)
        MsgBox (rootElement.xml)

    Dim bodyNode
    Dim itemNode
    Set bodyNode = oXMLDoc.createElement("body")
        Set itemNode = oXMLDoc.createElement("item")
            ' set attributes on item
            Set namedNodeMap = itemNode.Attributes
```

Listing 5-5. *An XML document built by using the DOM interfaces and Visual Basic.*

```
            addAttribute oXMLDoc, namedNodeMap, "needBefore", Now() + 8
            addAttribute oXMLDoc, namedNodeMap, "needAfter", Now() + 14
            ' set children of item
            addElement oXMLDoc, itemNode, "partNum", "SY120"
            addElement oXMLDoc, itemNode, "qty", "10"
            addElement oXMLDoc, itemNode, "price", "12.43"
        bodyNode.appendChild (itemNode)

        Set itemNode = oXMLDoc.createElement("item")
            ' set attributes on item
            Set namedNodeMap = itemNode.Attributes
            addAttribute oXMLDoc, namedNodeMap, "needBefore", Now() + 7
            addAttribute oXMLDoc, namedNodeMap, "needAfter", Now() + 21
            ' set children of item
            addElement oXMLDoc, itemNode, "partNum", "TQ331"
            addElement oXMLDoc, itemNode, "qty", "100"
            addElement oXMLDoc, itemNode, "price", "0.443"
        bodyNode.appendChild (itemNode)
    rootElement.appendChild (bodyNode)

    MsgBox (rootElement.xml)
    End
End Sub
```

EVENT-DRIVEN MODELS

The DOM provides a compact, easy-to-use set of interfaces for processing the contents of an XML document. However, sometimes using the DOM API is not the best approach. Suppose, for example, that you have a huge XML document to process. Because the DOM is a tree-based API, it does not allow you to process any of the document until the entire document is read successfully into the object. Event-driven APIs can report parsing events directly to the calling application, which can save a lot of processing time on large documents.

For example, suppose you need to get just the first few elements at the top of a document. Loading the entire document if you want to process only the first few elements wastes cycles. The event-driven model allows you to access the elements as the parser encounters them during processing. You can access an element in this manner whether or not an error lurks below. Remember that with the in-memory DOM API, an error in the last element of the document will render the entire document in error.

The tools that use this approach generate events that can be captured by rules. These rules then process the elements as they are encountered in the document.

One event-driven model that has been competing for the attention of developers is SAX, the Simple API for XML. SAX was developed by members of the XML-DEV mailing list, hosted by OASIS. In some ways, SAX is considered a competitor of DOM. However, I don't see it that way. Sometimes the DOM is more appropriate for a given situation, and sometimes SAX is more appropriate. In fact, Microsoft has begun to implement some features of SAX in the Microsoft XML Parser (MSXML). You can find out more about SAX at *http://www.megginson.com/SAX/.*

SAX is a great interface, but I want to concentrate on OmniMark, which is a more mature, event-driven, object model programming language. I'll describe OmniMark in detail in Appendix A.

Chapter 6

XSL

The Extensible Stylesheet Language, or XSL, is a general-purpose resource used to transform and format XML documents. Transform refers to changing one XML document into another document. Format refers to the visual display or rendering of the XML document. You can use an XSL style sheet to transform XML into HTML for display, or one XML structure into another. Transformation is useful if your company uses one schema internally and your suppliers use a different schema: You can employ XSL to translate an XML document that uses one schema into an XML document that uses another schema. The data in each document usually remains the same, but you can also transform it using scripting.

XSL: THE BACKGROUND

Let me provide a little history lesson. You can skip this if you just want to get straight to the code, but you might find the evolution of XSL interesting.

As you learned in earlier chapters, in 1986, the International Organization for Standardization (ISO) adopted the Standard Generalized Markup Language (SGML). Like XML, SGML allows implementers to express the structure—but not the formatting—of their information. Soon after the adoption of SGML, some members of the SGML committee formed a new committee to work on a standard language for expressing the formatting characteristics of an SGML document. This language was called the Document Style Semantics and Specification Language (DSSSL). DSSSL took 10 years to complete because of the difficulty of designing a single syntax to express all formatting information for all documents and all devices.

The DSSSL spec was finally adopted as an ISO standard in 1996. Unfortunately for DSSSL, that was about the time XML was being developed, and potential DSSSL implementers took a wait-and-see attitude toward the DSSSL spec. To this day, I don't know of a single serious implementation of DSSSL.

In 1998, some members from the DSSSL committee formed a working group under the auspices of the World Wide Web Consortium (W3C) to create a standard for rendering XML documents (the way DSSSL was supposed to create a standard for SGML documents). Because this group had already worked for 10 years to understand how documents could be rendered, members got off to a quick start and ultimately developed XSL.

HOW DOES XSL WORK?

W3C XSL has two major purposes: formatting objects and transforming XML documents. To format a document, XSL reads an XML document and applies a set of transformation processes to create another XML document, called a result tree. This result tree adheres to the formatting object namespace, which contains hundreds of elements and attributes that describe the presentation of the XML document. For example, the result tree indicates whether a particular textual object will be bold or italic, red or salmon, inline or blocking. The result tree does not have any instructions for a particular typesetting language. Instructions are applied in the next step of the XSL process: formatting object interpretation.

This result tree is read into a formatting object interpreter, which interprets the formatting object elements and attributes and outputs typesetting codes for a particular typesetter. Figure 6-1 illustrates this process.

In this example, if a designer wants to display a particular piece of text in green italics, all she needs to do is indicate those requirements in generic terms. The font style and color attributes are in the schema referenced by the formatting object namespace. These attributes are set to *italic* and *green*. This declarative way of indicating output transcends any particular output medium, which means that the designer needn't worry about particular typesetting codes.

Let's use HTML to show how the XSL formatting works. In HTML, inline cascading style sheet (CSS) styles indicate font style and color. The formatting object interpreter for HTML renders the green italic object as *STYLE="font-style:italic;color:green"*. This string is readable by an HTML typesetter (a Web browser). The final paragraph tag looks like this:

```
<P STYLE="font-style:italic;color:green;">December 3, 1997</P>
```

Suppose you want a paper (rather than an HTML) document. To render our document on paper, we could use a formatting object interpreter that understands the rich text format, or RTF. (Microsoft created RTF syntax in the mid-1980s as a 7-bit ASCII representation of richly formatted word-processing documents. Because RTF was plain text, it was easy to transmit over e-mail and other early transport protocols.) Our example's formatting object interpreter transforms the *font-style="italic"* command into \i, which turns the text that follows the command into italics. The *color="green"* command is transformed into \c6, indicating that the color is found in the sixth entry of the color table at the top of the RTF document. The resulting RTF document fragment might look something like this:

```
{\c6\i December 3, 1997\par}
```

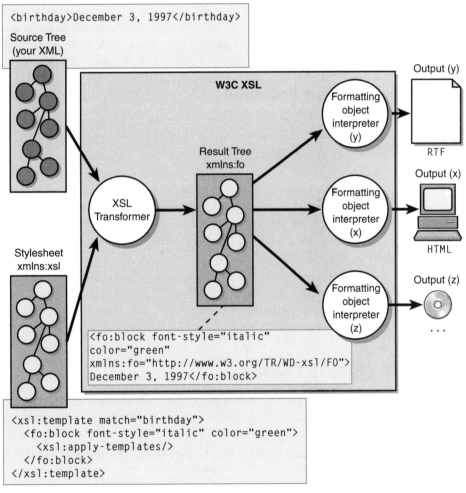

Figure 6-1. *The two parts of the W3C XSL presentation process: First the input XML document is transformed into a result tree, and then the result tree is interpreted by a formatting object interpreter optimized for a particular output.*

The XSL presentation process provides a powerful model because it allows an organization to get any number of outputs from the same XML inputs and style sheets. Of course, this model is advantageous only if you have support for a formatting object interpreter for the types of outputs you are considering.

Microsoft's Implementation of XSL

As of this writing, the XSL specification is still under development. The formatting object libraries are complex, and many outstanding issues still need resolution.

In 1998, Microsoft felt that the transformation piece of XSL was stable enough and implemented only the transformation part of XSL from a working draft of the XSL specification. Microsoft introduced this part of XSL in the MSXML parser, which shipped with Microsoft Internet Explorer 5. This gave developers access to a mechanism that allowed general-purpose, XML-to-XML transformation.

XSLT and XPath Breakout

Although some people criticized the Microsoft XSL implementation as an incomplete part of a W3C specification, many other people used the implementation to understand the power of a declarative transformation language. As a result of this wide understanding, the W3C XSL Working Group extracted the transformation part from XSL and created a new W3C Recommendation, XSL Transformations (XSLT) Version 1.0. While XSL now points to XSLT as its transformation engine, XSL still contains all the formatting object support.

XSLT requires a syntax that enables the selection of certain parts of an XML document. For example, to render a chapter title one way and a section title another way, two rules must be able to specify a path to the appropriate objects in a particular context. Because XSLT is not the only W3C standard that requires this syntax, the XML Path Language (XPath)—was extracted from the XSLT specification. The W3C adopted both XPath and XSLT as Recommendations in November 1999.

XSLT OPERATION

XSLT is a rules-based, event-driven programming language. It is not a procedural language. Think of XSLT as a clerk who's in charge of a room filled with boxes. Each box does something useful. Figure 6-2 shows a template rule—which is a stand-alone object—waiting for an event defined by the *match* attribute. Once the rule receives an event, the rule can expose the content to other rules *(apply-templates)* or can output directly *(value-of)*.

When an element comes along, the clerk selects a box based on certain criteria (usually events happening in the XML input document) and drops the result of those events into the box. Figure 6-3 illustrates this step.

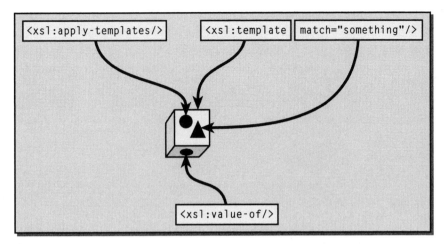

Figure 6-2. *An XML template rule encapsulates processing details, allowing the programmer to focus on input and output.*

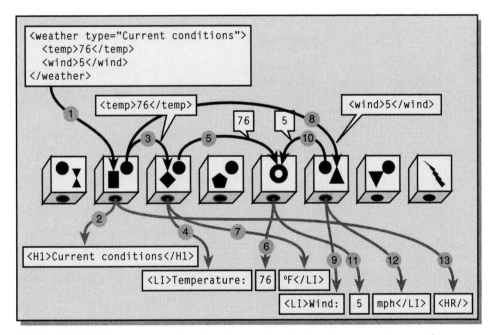

Figure 6-3. *XSLT is analogous to a set of boxes that do mysterious processing inside. Depending on the processing, a box might output something for other boxes to process, something that is directly sent to the output, or nothing at all. Table 6-1 describes this processing in detail.*

The processing happens in a box. Most of the time something comes out of that box. Depending on what the box does, this output might be static text, the result of calculations, or an element structure. The result that comes out will either go directly to the output or will be exposed to other boxes, which will process it further. I will show later how this process is done using the XSL transformation engine. In the following example, I'll walk you through the processing illustrated in Figure 6-3 with the simple XML document Curcon.xml:

```
<?xml version="1.0"?>
<weather type="Current conditions">
    <temp>76</temp>
    <wind>5</wind>
</weather>
```

I'll also use the XSL style sheet Weathersheet.xsl, shown in Listing 6-1.

Weathersheet.xsl

```
1   <?xml version="1.0"?>
2   <xsl:stylesheet
3       version="1.0"
4       xmlns:xsl="http://www.w3.org/1999/XSL/Transform">
5
6       <xsl:template match="weather">
7           <H1><xsl:value-of select="@type"/></H1>
8           <xsl:apply-templates/>
9               <HR/>
10      </xsl:template>
11
12      <xsl:template match="temp">
13          <LI>Temperature <xsl:apply-templates/>&#x00B0;F</LI>
14      </xsl:template>
15
16      <xsl:template match="wind">
17          <LI>Wind <xsl:apply-templates/>mph</LI>
18      </xsl:template>
19
20      <xsl:template match="text()">
21          <xsl:value-of select="."/>
22      </xsl:template>
23
24  </xsl:stylesheet>
```

Listing 6-1. *Weathersheet.xsl, an XSL style sheet that formats weather data.*

Table 6-1 describes the processing illustrated in Figure 6-3. You'll find the corresponding line numbers from Listing 6-1 in the description section of the table. Read through the description and see how each step is implemented in code.

Step in Figure	*Description*
1	One of the boxes is designed to process the *weather* element in the XML document. Since the *weather* element is the root element, the *weather* element *and all of its descendants* (an important fact to remember) are stuffed into the box. This box, with a square hole (as shown in Figure 6-3), is defined in the template rule on lines 6–10.
2	The first thing the box produces is some output. Using the <xsl:value-of/> element creates the text contents of the object in the *select* attribute. In this case, the content of the *type* attribute (@*type*) are sent out inside an HTML <H1> element. The XSL processor processes any element with the *xsl:* namespace prefix. Anything without the *xsl:* namespace prefix is sent verbatim to the output. The next command, <xsl:apply-templates/>, spits out the content of the *weather* element so that other boxes in the room can process it.
3	The first item contained inside *weather* is <temp>76</temp>. This is an element, and a box is waiting to process it—the one with a diamond-shaped hole. This box maps to the template rule on lines 12–14.
4	The HTML list item (<LI>) element start tag and the literal text "Temperature" do not have the *xsl:* namespace prefix, so they are sent directly to the output.
5	Now the box notices the <xsl:apply-templates/> element and, as with the *weather* element, spits out the content of the *temp* element, "76". This content can now be processed by another box.
6	The box with a donut hole is waiting. This box processes all text exposed by the other boxes. It is the template rule on lines 20–22. The single <xsl:value-of/> element will send the textual content of the thing that was captured (which can only be a textual element) directly to the output, which is indicated by the round hole in the front of the box.
7	After the text is processed, control returns to the "temp" rule, which outputs the end tag for the list item element. Once the *temperature* element has been processed, control reverts back to the weather template rule, where it waits to process the next child.
8–12	The *wind* element is that child, so the weather box spits out the *wind* element just like it spat out the *temperature* element, exposing the element to the boxes in the room.
13	After all children of the *weather* element have been processed, the <xsl:apply-templates/> element is finished and the rule continues to process the commands following it. In this case, there is a single HTML horizontal rule tag. It is sent to the output and processing terminates.

Table 6-1. *A step-by-step breakdown of the XSLT processing illustrated in Figure 6-3.*

Notice the syntax of the HTML horizontal rule tag in line 9. Remember that an XSL style sheet is a well-formed XML document. That means that it must adhere to the well-formedness constraints described in Chapter 4. Normally, the tag looks like this: <HR>. However, the horizontal rule tag is an empty element. Since the horizontal rule tag is included in line with the other XSL elements, it must also be well-formed, so it takes a slightly different form: <HR/>.

Recursive Processing

It is important to note that when a box spits out the content of an element for which it finds a match, the content is exposed to all the template rules, including the rule that created it. I'll demonstrate this with the short XSL program Generic.xsl, shown in Listing 6-2.

Generic.xsl

```
1   <?xml version="1.0" ?>
2   <xsl:stylesheet
3       version="1.0"
4       xml:space="default"
5       xmlns:xsl="http://www.w3.org/1999/XSL/Transform">
6
7       <xsl:template match="node()">
8           <DIV STYLE="margin-left:12pt;">
9               [start <xsl:value-of select="name()"/>]
10              <xsl:apply-templates select="@*"/>
11              <xsl:apply-templates/>
12              [end <xsl:value-of select="name()"/>]
13          </DIV>
14      </xsl:template>
15
16      <xsl:template match="@*">
17          [attr <xsl:value-of select="name()"/>:
18          <xsl:value-of select="."/>]
19      </xsl:template>
20
21      <xsl:template match="text()">
22          <xsl:value-of select="."/>
23      </xsl:template>
24
25  </xsl:stylesheet>
```

Listing 6-2. *Generic.xsl, an XSL style sheet for generically processing any XML document to create a hierarchical view.*

Notice that the style sheet in Listing 6-2 has no hard-coded element or attribute names. All elements are processed anonymously, according to their position in the document. We'll need ways to find out the names and types of each node that comes along, so we must build those capabilities into our style sheet that processes the document. Listing 6-3 shows the XML document 80112.xml, which I'm going to process.

80112.xml

```
<weather zipcode="80112">
    <location>Englewood, CO </location>
        <current>
            <condition name="temp">32</condition>
            <condition name="wind chill">20</condition>
            <condition name="wind">from the South at
                7 mph</condition>
            <condition name="dewpoint">16 </condition>
            <condition name="relative humidity">51%</condition>
            <condition name="visibility">10 miles</condition>
            <condition name="barometer">30.01 inches</condition>
            <condition name="sunrise">7:20 am MST</condition>
            <condition name="sunset">4:51 pm MST</condition>
        </current>
    <forecast updated="2000-03-21T15:03:27-07:00">
        <day date="2000-03-22T15:03:28-07:00" high="46" low="21"
            sky="Partly Cloudy"/>
        <day date="2000-03-23T15:03:28-07:00" high="51" low="25"
            sky="Partly Cloudy"/>
        <day date="2000-03-24T15:03:28-07:00" high="51" low="19"
            sky="Partly Cloudy"/>
        <day date="2000-03-25T15:03:28-07:00" high="53" low="21"
            sky="Partly Cloudy"/>
        <day date="2000-03-26T15:03:28-07:00" high="49" low="20"
            sky="Partly Cloudy"/>
    </forecast>
</weather>
```

Listing 6-3. *80112.xml, an XML document for our generic processing example.*

Table 6-2 gives you a play-by-play of what happens when the style sheet in Listing 6-2 processes the XML document in Listing 6-3.

Line	Description
7	The *match="node()"* rule will match just about any node that comes along. We are mostly interested in processing the element nodes, so *node* is a good choice.
8	The first line of the *match* rule (line 8) has an HTML <DIV> element. A <DIV> is a breaking container that we can use to hold each element. Notice that <DIV> does not have an *xsl:* namespace declaration, so the <DIV> element will be sent directly to the output, along with its attributes. The *STYLE* attribute is an inline CSS style indicating the left margin of the <DIV>.
9	The literal string *[start* does not have the *xsl:* namespace prefix, so it is sent to the output. Then the name of the element is *output*. By using the name node text inside the *select* attribute of the <xsl:value-of/> element, we are asking the node for its name—just as we ask it for its value when we use *select="."*. A literal *]* follows the name of the element.
	The resulting output from this line takes the following form:
	`[start weather]`
10	Until now, we have used only the <xsl:apply-templates/> element used by itself. Notice the *select* attribute on the *apply-templates* element. By default, the *select* attribute will select all nodes and expose them to all the templates in the style sheet. However, if we change the *select* attribute, we can restrict the kinds of nodes that we process. In this example, we want to process only attribute nodes. The pattern for selecting all attributes is "@*".
16	Since our first element has an attribute (*zipcode*), this template rule in this line will catch it.
17–18	The *select="name()"* node test returns the name of the attribute that was matched by the parser. In this template, an attribute was matched, so *name* returns the name of the attribute. The value of the attribute is processed the same way as the text value of an element node.
	The resulting output from this line takes the following form:
	`[attr zipcode: 80112]`
11	When the attributes finish processing, control returns to the line following the *apply-templates* element that exposed the attributes (line 11). This line is the un-qualified *apply-templates* element, which will expose all the element children to all the template rules.
7	Surprise! The first element in the <weather> element is <location>. The same rule that caught the root element <weather> will catch and process the <location> element also.
8	Just as with the parent element, a <DIV> is generated with a cascading style of a 12-point left indent. Remember that when the <weather> element was processed, a 12-point left-indenting <DIV> appeared, but that <DIV> was not yet closed. The <DIV> for our <location> element is inside the <weather> <DIV>. One nice feature of cascading style sheets is (of course) that they cascade, which in this case means that everything inside the <location> element is indented 12 more points, to result in a 24-point indent.

Table 6-2. *A line-by-line breakdown describing the XSLT processing of the file 80122.xml using the Generic.xsl stylesheet.*

Line	Description
11	The content of the <location> element is processed on this line. A single text node is inside of this element, and that text node is caught by the rule that matches text in line 21.
21	In the same way that the node test matches any element node, the text node test captures any contiguous string of text.
22	The value of the text captured is output to the browser. Control returns to line 11, where parsing continues.
12	After the content of each element is processed, we want to indicate some kind of ending notification. This line will output the name of the element that is currently being processed inside square brackets.
13	The closing </DIV> tag marks the end of this 12-point indent. The indent level reverts back to where it was before the element was processed.
7–14	This template rule will be called recursively (meaning it calls itself) for each element in the XML file until the entire document is processed.

When we pop the resulting HTML output into our favorite Web browser, we can see that there is a nested representation of the information, as shown in Figure 6-4. The file in Figure 6-4 was created by using the *transformNode()* method of the Microsoft XML DOM implementation. We will see several different ways to use this method later.

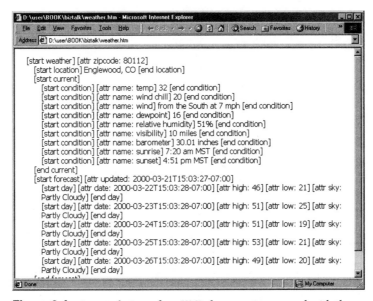

Figure 6-4. *A nested view of an XML document processed with the generic style sheet.*

XSLT by Example

Let's try some other XSLT elements. Keep in mind the recursive nature symbolized by the room full of boxes. Consider the XML document Duckone.xml in Listing 6-4.

```
Duckone.xml

<?xml version="1.0"?>
<?xml-stylesheet type="text/xsl" href="joke.xsl"?>
<Jokes xml:space="default">

    <Joke type="one-liner" author="Brian">A duck
        walks into a bar and says,<quote>Gimme
        a beer and put it on my bill</quote>.
    </Joke>

    <Joke type="story" author="Monty">
        <Scene num="1">My dog has no nose</Scene>
        <Scene num="2">How does he smell?</Scene>
        <Scene num="3">Terrible!</Scene>
    </Joke>

    <Joke type="knock-knock" author="Miller">
        <Line>Knock-knock</Line>
        <Line>Who's there?</Line>
        <Line>Boo</Line>
        <Line>Boo who?</Line>
        <Line>It's just a joke, you don't have to
        cry about it.</Line>
    </Joke>

</Jokes>
```

Listing 6-4. *The Duckone.xml XML document used in the XSLT demonstration.*

This document contains three elements named *Joke*. Each has a different value for the *type* attribute. Rules in the XSLT document Joke.xsl will individually process each element. Listing 6-5 contains the XSLT style sheet for this example.

```
Joke.xsl

1  <?xml version="1.0"?>
2  <xsl:stylesheet
3      version="1.0"
4      xmlns:msxsl="urn:schemas-microsoft-com:xslt"
5      xmlns:scripts="http://architag.com/scripts"
```

Listing 6-5. *The XSL style sheet Joke.xsl transforms an XML document for HTML output in the browser.*

```
6      xmlns:xsl="http://www.w3.org/1999/XSL/Transform">
7
8      <xsl:output method="html" version="4.0"/>
9
10     <msxsl:script implements-prefix="scripts">
11         <![CDATA[
12         function showXML(nodelist)
13             {
14             txtResult = "<SPAN "+
15                 "STYLE='background-color:lightyellow;" +
16                 "cursor:hand;font-size:8pt;' " +
17                 "TITLE='"
18             replaceText = nodelist.nextNode().xml
19             replaceText = replaceText.replace(/&/g, '&amp;')
20             replaceText = replaceText.replace(/</g, '&lt;')
21             replaceText = replaceText.replace(/>/g, '&gt;')
22             replaceText = replaceText.replace(/'/g, '&rsquo;')
23             txtResult += replaceText
24             txtResult += "'>(show xml)</SPAN>"
25             return txtResult;
26             }
27         ]]>
28     </msxsl:script>
29
30     <xsl:template match="Jokes">
31         <HTML>
32             <HEAD>
33                 <TITLE>XSL Demonstration</TITLE>
34                 <STYLE>
35                 P, UL {margin-top:2pt;margin-bottom;2pt;}
36                 H1, H2, H4 {margin-top:2pt;margin-bottom:2pt;}
37                 </STYLE>
38             </HEAD>
39             <BODY STYLE="font-family:Verdana;">
40                 <xsl:value-of select="scripts:showXML(.)"
41                     disable-output-escaping="yes"/>
42                 <H1>World's Funniest Jokes</H1>
43                     <DIV STYLE=
44                         "border:1px solid black;padding:3pt;">
45                     <H4>Table of Contents</H4>
46                     <xsl:for-each select="Joke">
47                         <A>
48                             <xsl:attribute
49                                 name="HREF">#<xsl:value-of
50                                 select="generate-id()"/>
51                             </xsl:attribute>
52                             <xsl:value-of select="@type"/>
```

(continued)

Joke.xsl *continued*

```
53                        </A><BR/>
54                    </xsl:for-each>
55                </DIV>
56                <xsl:apply-templates/>
57            </BODY>
58        </HTML>
59
60    </xsl:template>
61    <xsl:template name="email-author">
62        <xsl:param name="author-alias"/>
63        Author: <xsl:element name="A">
64            <xsl:attribute
65                name="HREF">mailto:<xsl:value-of
66                select="$author-alias"/>@jokes.architag.com
67            </xsl:attribute>
68            <xsl:value-of select="$author-alias"/>
69        </xsl:element><BR/>
70    </xsl:template>
71
72    <xsl:template name="set-name">
73        <A>
74            <xsl:attribute name="NAME">
75                <xsl:value-of select="generate-id()"/>
76            </xsl:attribute>
77        </A>
78    </xsl:template>
79
80    <xsl:template match="Joke[@type='story']">
81        <xsl:call-template name="set-name"/>
82        <H2>Story Joke
83        <xsl:value-of select="scripts:showXML(.)"
84            disable-output-escaping="yes"/>
85        </H2>
86        <xsl:call-template name="email-author">
87            <xsl:with-param name="author-alias">
88                <xsl:value-of select="@author"/>
89            </xsl:with-param>
90        </xsl:call-template>
91        <P>
92        <xsl:for-each select="Scene">
93            <B>Scene <xsl:value-of select="@num"/>: </B>
94            <xsl:value-of select="."/><BR/>
95        </xsl:for-each>
96        <I><xsl:value-of select="$laughtrack"/></I></P>
97    </xsl:template>
```

```
98     <xsl:template match="Joke[@type='knock-knock']">
99         <xsl:call-template name="set-name"/>
100        <H2>Knock-knock
101        <xsl:value-of select="scripts:showXML(.)"
102            disable-output-escaping="yes" />
103        </H2>
104        <xsl:call-template name="email-author">
105            <xsl:with-param name="author-alias">
106                <xsl:value-of select="@author"/>
107            </xsl:with-param>
108        </xsl:call-template>
109        <UL>
110            <xsl:apply-templates/>
111        </UL>
112        <I><xsl:value-of select="$laughtrack"/></I>
113    </xsl:template>
114
115    <xsl:template match="Joke[@type='one-liner']">
116        <xsl:call-template name="set-name"/>
117        <H2>One-liner
118        <xsl:value-of select="scripts:showXML(.)"
119            disable-output-escaping="yes"/>
120        </H2>
121        <xsl:call-template name="email-author">
123            <xsl:with-param name="author-alias">
124                <xsl:value-of select="@author"/>
125            </xsl:with-param>
126        </xsl:call-template>
127        <P><xsl:apply-templates/><BR/>
128        <I><xsl:value-of select="$laughtrack"/></I></P>
129    </xsl:template>
130
131    <xsl:template match="Joke[@type='knock-knock']/Line">
132        <LI><xsl:apply-templates/></LI>
133    </xsl:template>
134
135    <xsl:template match="quote">
136        "<xsl:apply-templates/>"
137    </xsl:template>
138
139    <xsl:variable name="laughtrack">(laugh track)</xsl:variable>
140
141 </xsl:stylesheet>
```

Table 6-3 provides a line-by-line description of the transformation implemented in the Joke.xml file in Listing 6-4.

Line	Description
4–6	This XSLT program requires three namespaces. The first namespace contains Microsoft extensions to the XSLT language. The next namespace is required by the *script* element, as you'll see later. The XSLT processor requires the third namespace to know which version of XSLT to use. In this case, the processor will use the final XSLT Recommendation approved by the W3C in November 1999.
8	The *xsl:output* element declares the type of output desired. In this case, we want the output to adhere to the HTML version 4.0 specification.
10–28	This block of code is an example of script. The XSLT specification does not include a built-in scripting interface. Each implementer of the spec is responsible for designing a script interface if one is required. The Microsoft implementation offers a number of scripting options. In this case we're using Microsoft JScript.
	We'll use this script to create a string of HTML that represents the structure of an XML node.
30–59	When the XML document is loaded, the XML parser reads the document into the document object model tree and starts navigating the tree from the root. The root element, *Jokes*, will be processed first, and then the rest is processed. The first template matched will be for the first event generated. In this case, the template is the root element, *Jokes*. This rule defines the structure of the HTML document, including a CSS element.
40	The *xsl:value-of* element can call on a script defined by the XSLT implementation. In this case, the *ShowXML* function defined in line 12 is called, causing the text "Show XML" to be put inside of a span, with the contents of the current element (the argument, ".", passed to the function) put in the *TITLE* attribute. The net result is to create a string of text that has other text "behind" it—that is, when the user hovers the mouse pointer over the text "Show XML", the actual text of the element appears in a yellow pop-up window.
41	By default, the *value-of* element escapes the content it processes, meaning that all markup characters turn into their entity reference equivalents. For example, if a left angle bracket (<) is encountered, it is replaced with the entity reference for a left angle bracket, *<*. This replacement protects the XML output from interpreting literal characters in the text as markup.
	In our example, we don't want to use this kind of escaping, so we use the *disable-output-escaping* attribute to override the default behavior.
45–54	This section generates a table of contents based on the content of the document.
46	The *xsl:for-each* element establishes a collection of elements according to the *select* attribute. In this case, it will create a three-member collection of *Joke* element nodes. These members are processed by the content of the *xsl:for-each* element one member at a time.
47–53	In this section, the HTML *A* element encloses each item.

Table 6-3. *A line-by-line description of the transformation defined by the XSLT Joke.xsl.*

Line	*Description*
48	The *xsl:attribute* element adds an element to the currently open element. In this case, the element is *A*. The *HREF* attribute will be added with a value of a hash mark (#) and...
49	...the unique identifier of the member of the collection. The Microsoft XML parser assigns a locally unique identifier to each element in the document. You can access this unique identifier with the *generate-id* function.
52	The value of the *type* attribute on the *Joke* element is processed here. This value will be listed inside the <A> tag.
53	Notice the strange form of the HTML break tag ( ). Remember that an XSLT style sheet is a well-formed XML document and thus must adhere to a number of well-formedness constraints defined by the XML spec. The HTML break tag, , is an empty element, and the HTML processor will interpret it properly if it looks like a normal start tag. However, because we are creating well-formed HTML, empty elements have a special form. In this case, the break tag appears as .
56	The content of the node captured by the *template* element in the *match* attribute are exposed to all of the templates in the style sheet by this *xsl:apply-templates* element. This element will force document processing at this point.
57–58	Once the children are processed, the HTML *BODY* and *HTML* tags are closed.
61–70	Until this point, we have seen templates that sit around until an event in the input fires them. You can also create templates that act as subroutines that are called by other templates. Notice that this particular template does not have a *match* attribute. This kind of template is called a named template; it will be called by name from somewhere else. Named templates are similar to subroutines in any other language: you use named templates when you have a certain amount of processing to do and you don't want to repeat code in all the places that require the processing.
62	Named templates can interpret parameters passed from the calling rule. In this case, a parameter called *author-alias* is passed.
66	The *author-alias* parameter is put inside the HREF attribute of the HTML *A* element.
68	The *author-alias* value is repeated in this section.
72–78	The template *set-name* is another named template, but it does not require a parameter. This template will be called from somewhere else, and the required values are calculated internally within the template rather than being passed from an external call.
80	This template matches a joke, but only if it has an attribute named *type* that has a value of *story*. The string adheres to the XPath abbreviated form.
81	The named template on lines 72–78 is called here, causing any output produced by the named template to be output at this point.

(continued)

Table 6-3. *continued*

Line	Description
83	Again, the *showXML* function is called, passing the content of the current element ".".
86–90	We invoke named templates with the *xsl:call-template* element. This element calls the *email-author* named template and passes the *author-alias* parameter equal to the value of the *author* attribute of the *Joke* element.
92–95	This particular type of *Joke* (*type='story'*) contains a number of scenes, which the *xsl:for-each* element processes in order.
93	The literal text *"Scene"* is followed by the value of the *number* attribute and appears in bold.
94	The *xsl:value-of* element outputs the text content of the scene by using the *select="."* attribute, followed by a well-formed HTML break tag.
139	XSLT allows you to assign variable names to constant values. The *xsl:variable* element sets the value of the *laughtrack* variable.
96	The *xsl:value-of* element can output the content of predefined variables. In this case, the value of the *laughtrack* variable is output in italics following the story.
99	The next type of joke, *knock-knock*, is processed here. The processing is similar to the *story* joke.
116	The processing that occurred with the previous jokes occurs with a *one-liner* joke.
131–133	A *knock-knock* joke contains a number of lines—a structure similar to that of the *story* joke. In the *story* joke, however, we used the *xsl:for-each* structure to process the children. For *knock-knock* jokes, the content of the joke is processed on line 111. At that point, the template on line 131 is called.
131	Notice the *match* attribute. This returns a *Line* element, but only if the *Line* element is a direct child (indicated by the / separator) of a *Joke* element, and only if the *Joke* element has an attribute *type* with a value of *knock-knock*. As you can see, XPath patterns can get pretty detailed.
135–137	This section contains one last template to process quotes inside literal quotation marks.

Transforming the XML document in Listing 6-4 with the XSL document in Listing 6-5 results in the HTML in Listing 6-6.

Joketrans.htm

```
<HTML>
<HEAD>
<META http-equiv="Content-Type" content="text/html;
```

Listing 6-6. *HTML output from the transformation of XML in Listing 6-4 with XSL in Listing 6-5.*

```
charset=UTF-16">
<TITLE>XSL Demonstration</TITLE>
<STYLE>
    P, UL {margin-top:2pt;margin-bottom:2pt;}
    H1, H2, H4 {margin-top:2pt;margin-bottom;2pt;}
</STYLE>
</HEAD>
<BODY STYLE="font-family:Verdana;">
    <SPAN STYLE='background-color:lightyellow;cursor:hand;
            font-size:8pt;'
        TITLE='&lt;Jokes xml:space="default"&gt;
    &lt;Joke type="one-liner" author="Brian"&gt;A duck
        walks into a bar and says,&lt;quote&gt;Gimme
        a beer and put it on my bill&lt;/quote&gt;.
    &lt;/Joke&gt;
    &lt;Joke type="story" author="Monty"&gt;
        &lt;Scene num="1"&gt;My dog has no nose&lt;/Scene&gt;
        &lt;Scene num="2"&gt;How does he smell?&lt;/Scene&gt;
        &lt;Scene num="3"&gt;Terrible!&lt;/Scene&gt;
    &lt;/Joke&gt;
    &lt;Joke type="knock-knock" author="Miller"&gt;
        &lt;Line&gt;Knock-knock&lt;/Line&gt;
        &lt;Line&gt;Who&rsquo;s there?&lt;/Line&gt;
        &lt;Line&gt;Boo&lt;/Line&gt;
        &lt;Line&gt;Boo who?&lt;/Line&gt;
        &lt;Line&gt;It&rsquo;s just a joke, you don&rsquo;t
        have to cry about it.&lt;/Line&gt;
    &lt;/Joke&gt;
&lt;/Jokes&gt;'>(show xml)</SPAN>
<H1>World's Funniest Jokes</H1>
<DIV STYLE="border:1px solid black;padding:3pt;">
<H4>Table of Contents</H4>
<A HREF="#ID0JNN2">one-liner</A><BR>
<A HREF="#IDwONN2">story</A><BR>
<A HREF="#ID0VNN2">knock-knock</A><BR>
</DIV>
<A NAME="ID0JNN2"/>
<H2>One-liner
        <SPAN STYLE='background-color:lightyellow;cursor:
            hand;font-size:8pt;'
            TITLE='&lt;Joke type="one-liner"
            author="Brian"&gt;A duck
        walks into a bar and says,&lt;quote&gt;Gimme
        a beer and put it on my bill&lt;/quote&gt;.
    &lt;/Joke&gt;'>(show xml)</SPAN></H2>
        Author: <A
                HREF="mailto:Brian@jokes.architag.com">Brian</A><BR>
```

(continued)

Joketrans.htm *continued*

```
<P>A duck
        walks into a bar and says,
        "Gimme
        a beer and put it on my bill"
    .
    <BR><I>(laugh track)</I></P>
<A NAME="IDwONN2"/>
<H2>Story Joke
        <SPAN STYLE='background-color:lightyellow;
            cursor:hand;font-size:8pt;'
            TITLE='&lt;Joke type="story" author="Monty"&gt;
    &lt;Scene num="1"&gt;My dog has no nose&lt;/Scene&gt;
    &lt;Scene num="2"&gt;How does he smell?&lt;/Scene&gt;
    &lt;Scene num="3"&gt;Terrible!&lt;/Scene&gt;
&lt;/Joke&gt;'>(show xml)</SPAN></H2>
        Author: <A
                HREF="mailto:Monty@jokes.architag.com">Monty</A><BR>
<P>
<B>Scene 1: </B>My dog has no nose<BR><B>Scene 2: </B>
How does he smell?<BR><B>Scene 3: </B>Terrible!<BR>
<I>(laugh track)</I></P>
<A NAME="ID0VNN2"/>
<H2>Knock-knock
        <SPAN STYLE='background-color:lightyellow;cursor:hand;
            font-size:8pt;'
            TITLE='&lt;Joke type="knock-knock"
            author="Miller"&gt;
    &lt;Line&gt;Knock-knock&lt;/Line&gt;
    &lt;Line&gt;Who&rsquo;s there?&lt;/Line&gt;
    &lt;Line&gt;Boo&lt;/Line&gt;
    &lt;Line&gt;Boo who?&lt;/Line&gt;
    &lt;Line&gt;It&rsquo;s just a joke, you don&rsquo;t
        have to cry about it.&lt;/Line&gt;
&lt;/Joke&gt;'>(show xml)</SPAN></H2>
        Author: <A
                HREF="mailto:Miller@jokes.architag.com">Miller</A><BR>
<UL>
<LI>Knock-knock</LI>
<LI>Who's there?</LI>
<LI>Boo</LI>
<LI>Boo who?</LI>
<LI>It's just a joke, you don't have to
    cry about it.</LI>
</UL>
<I>(laugh track)</I>
</BODY>
</HTML>
```

Figure 6-5 shows the HTML output produced by the transformation. This output was created using the XSL transformation engine in XRay. The workspace is available on the companion CD at \Samples\Ch06\Chapter6.xrw. This will load the XML document, the XSL stylesheet, the transformation window, and an HTML browser window. We will use XRay to do this in the next section.

Figure 6-5. *The resulting output of Listing 6-6, as seen in a Web browser. This figure shows both the XML document and the XSL style sheet in XRay, along with the resulting HTML and an example in the browser window. This example shows a pop-up window containing the source XML document, as contained in the* TITLE *attribute of the HTML* SPAN *element.*

EXERCISE: BUSINESS DOCUMENT TRANSFORMATION

In this exercise, you will use XSL to transform a purchase order from one structure to another—more specifically, you'll create an XSL transformation to transform a purchase order from one schema to another. The companion CD contains all the files in the exercise at \Samples\Ch06\Workshop\. You'll perform the transformation with the XSL processing engine built into XRay.

The kind of transformation we're going to do in this exercise is necessary in many different situations. Let's say your company has an XML-enabled back end from which you can accept XML documents adhering to certain schemas. You ask your trading partners to give you purchase orders that look like the example in Listing 6-7.

POReq.xml

```
<PurchaseOrder customer="H1553-7" PODate="12-Oct-1999">
    <LineItem>
        <Quantity>100</Quantity>
        <Item>SY120</Item>
    </LineItem>
    <LineItem>
        <Quantity>50</Quantity>
        <Item>SY100</Item>
    </LineItem>
    <LineItem>
        <Quantity>125</Quantity>
        <Item>AR238</Item>
    </LineItem>
    <LineItem>
        <Quantity>100</Quantity>
        <Item>JH877</Item>
    </LineItem>
</PurchaseOrder>
```

Listing 6-7. *An XML document that expresses a purchase order.*

However, one of your large customers who also has an XML-based purchase order system is equipped to provide the same information, but according to a different schema. Listing 6-8 shows an example of the customer's document.

POIn.xml

```
<PO date="12-Oct-1999">
    <Customer>H1553-7</Customer>
    <Item qty="100">SY120</Item>
    <Item qty="50">SY100</Item>
    <Item qty="125">AR238</Item>
    <Item qty="100">JH877</Item>
</PO>
```

Listing 6-8. *An XML document as it comes from a customer.*

You could write a traditional program with C++, BASIC, Perl, or any language that processes text, but there is a better way: XSLT. Listing 6-9 shows a simple XSL style sheet that can transform the information in the XML document in Listing 6-8 into the XML document in Listing 6-7.

POTrans.xsl

```
1    <?xml version="1.0"?>
2    <xsl:stylesheet
3        version="1.0"
4        xmlns:xsl="http://www.w3.org/1999/XSL/Transform"
5        xml:space="default">
6
7        <xsl:template match="PO">
8            <PurchaseOrder>
9                <xsl:attribute name="customer">
10                   <xsl:value-of select="Customer"/>
11               </xsl:attribute>
12               <xsl:attribute name="PODate">
13                   <xsl:value-of select="@date"/>
14               </xsl:attribute>
15               <xsl:apply-templates/>
16           </PurchaseOrder>
17       </xsl:template>
18
19       <xsl:template match="Item">
20           <LineItem>
21               <Quantity>
22                   <xsl:value-of select="@qty"/>
23               </Quantity>
24               <Item>
25                   <xsl:value-of select="text()"/>
26               </Item>
27           </LineItem>
28       </xsl:template>
29
30       <xsl:template match="Customer"/>
31
32   </xsl:stylesheet>
```

Listing 6-9. *The XSL transformation that can convert the XML document in Listing 6-8 to the XML document in Listing 6-7.*

The code description in Table 6-4—and the step-by-step instructions that follow the table—break down the transformation process line by line.

Line	Description
7	Two elements must be matched in the input: *PO* and *Item*. The *PO* element is captured by the *match="PO"* rule.
8	The <PO> element from the input file is transformed into a <PurchaseOrder> element on the output. First a <Purchase-Order> start tag is output. Remember that the XSL processor processes anything in the XSL document with the *xsl:* namespace prefix. Everything else is sent verbatim to the output. In this case, the <PurchaseOrder> start tag does not have the *xsl:* namespace prefix, so the processor sends it directly to output.
9–11	The *PurchaseOrder* element has two attributes that must be output. The *xsl:attribute* element adds an attribute name and value to the currently open element. In this case, a *customer* attribute is added to the *PurchaseOrder* element with a value equal to the content of the <Customer> element on the input.
12–14	Another attribute, *PODate*, is added to the <PurchaseOrder> element. The *PODate* attribute has a value equal to the value of the *date* attribute on the input.
15	The content of the element matched in the *match="PO"* rule is exposed to the template rules in the XSL program by using the <*xsl:apply-templates/*> element, thereby exposing the content to the *Item* template rule.
16	After the content is processed, the *PurchaseOrder* element is ended.
19	The *match="Item"* rule finds each <Item> element in the input file. It's then transformed into a <LineItem> element.
20	The <LineItem> element has two subelements: *Quantity* and *Item*.
21–23	The *Quantity* element contains the value of the *qty* attribute on the input.
24–26	The *Item* element contains the text content of the *Item* element on the input.

Table 6-4. *A line-by-line breakdown of the transformation process in Listing 6-9.*

Now let's look at the step-by-step instructions for the XSL transformation.

1. Load XRay by selecting Start, Programs, Architag XRay XML Editor, and then XRay XML Editor. You will be presented with an empty workspace.

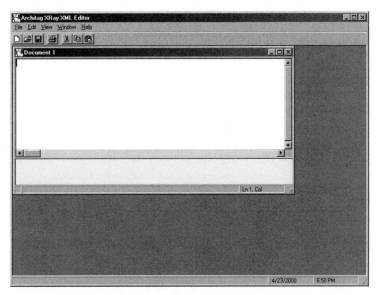

2. Load the XML document: Click on File, Open, and \Samples\Ch06\ Workshop\POIn.xml. The document appears in the document window.

3. Load the XSL style sheet: Select File, Open, and \Samples\Ch06\ Workshop\POTrans.xsl. You will see the XSL style sheet in the editor window, as shown in the following screen shot.

```
D:\Samples\Ch06\Workshop\POTrans.xsl                    _ □ ×
<?xml version="1.0"?>
<xsl:stylesheet
  version="1.0"
  xmlns:xsl="http://www.w3.org/1999/XSL/Transform"
  xml:space="default">

    <xsl:template match="PO">
        <PurchaseOrder>
            <xsl:attribute name="customer">
                <xsl:value-of select="Customer"/>
            </xsl:attribute>
            <xsl:attribute name="PODate">
                <xsl:value-of select="@date"/>
            </xsl:attribute>
            <xsl:apply-templates/>
        </PurchaseOrder>
    </xsl:template>

    <xsl:template match="Item">
        <LineItem>
            <Quantity>
                <xsl:value-of select="@qty"/>
                                                    Ln 1, Col 0
```

4. Load a new transformation window: Click on File, and select New XSL Transform. Choose POIn.xml from the XML Document drop-down list box, and then choose POTrans.xsl from the XSL Stylesheet drop-down list box.

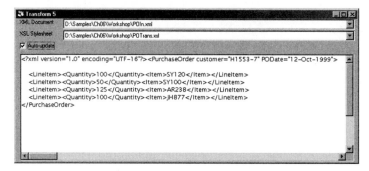

```
Transform 5                                                  _ □ ×
XML Document    D:\Samples\Ch06\Workshop\POIn.xml                    ▼
XSL Stylesheet  D:\Samples\Ch06\Workshop\POTrans.xsl                 ▼
☑ Auto-update
<?xml version="1.0" encoding="UTF-16"?><PurchaseOrder customer="H1553-7" PODate="12-Oct-1999">

    <LineItem><Quantity>100</Quantity><Item>SY120</Item></LineItem>
    <LineItem><Quantity>50</Quantity><Item>SY100</Item></LineItem>
    <LineItem><Quantity>125</Quantity><Item>AR238</Item></LineItem>
    <LineItem><Quantity>100</Quantity><Item>JH877</Item></LineItem>
</PurchaseOrder>
```

This window shows the document that results from the transformation process. Notice that this document is also an XML document.

You can experiment with the template rules and match statements in the XSLT document to see what effect those changes have on the output. If you click the Auto-Update button, the transformation will be performed whenever you focus on the transformation window. This implementation of XSLT is very unforgiving. Everything must be exactly right in order to do any processing. If you make a change and nothing shows up in the window, you did something wrong and the transformation did not complete.

The transformation functionality of the XSL standard is a powerful tool, allowing you to easily change XML from one structure to another. The Microsoft BizTalk Server has a tool, the Microsoft BizTalk Mapper, that simplifies the creation of XSLT style sheets to perform these transformations automatically when you receive documents from various trading partners and when you send documents to partners from your own system. We will create a stylesheet that does a transformation similar to this one using the BizTalk Mapper in Chapter 12.

Part II

XML
Messaging

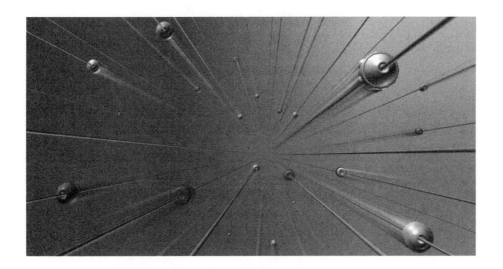

XML messaging refers to the sending of messages between computers. An XML message can take the form of a package containing business data, such as an invoice, purchase order, or medical record; or it can take the form of a request for some kind of service from a remote machine. XML messaging is ideal for sending messages because it uses XML to create a structure for passing information from one place to another as platform-independent messages. It does not rely on platform-specific data structures and object invocation calls.

In this part, you will learn about two XML messaging standards: SOAP, the Simple Object Access Protocol; and BizTalk, the universal language for business document interchange.

Chapter 7

Web Services

The Web as we know it today is built on a series of innovations driven by technology standards created over the past decade or so. As Figure 7-1 illustrates, each innovation built on the successes of the previous one, leading up to the current ability to write network programs that take advantage of data and processes all over the network.

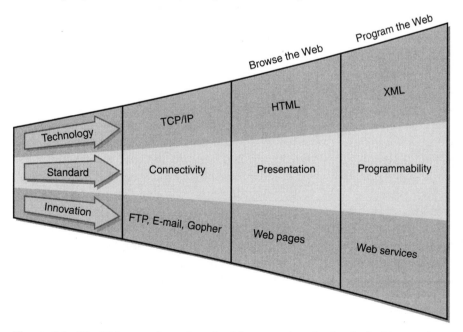

Figure 7-1. *The Web as we know it evolved from a series of technological innovations.*

In the 1980s, the U.S. Department of Defense (DoD) developed TCP/IP (Transmission Control Protocol/Internet Protocol). TCP/IP is a simple protocol that gave us physical connectivity between proprietary networks by sending packets over a public network. Once networked computers could be connected to each other, applications emerged to take advantage of that capability. The first technologies, File Transfer Protocol (FTP) and e-mail, sit on top of TCP/IP to allow people to communicate. This revolutionized the way we do business.

As good as FTP and e-mail were, they did not provide a way to look at information in a consistent manner with a consistent interface. HTML was designed as a simple tagging structure for creating a pleasing way for users to view information in what we now know as a Web browser. One of the tags in HTML—the "link" tag—created a way to take advantage of the new interconnected network by providing a means of jumping to another point on the page or to another page entirely.

Sharing hyperlinked documents over a public network revolutionized the way we look at information because users could share information in a standard way no matter what operating system platform or software version they used. Now anyone can browse the entire network from a single application.

HTML is an integral technology for communicating information to humans, but it falls short when we want our computers to talk to each other. First of all, HTML is designed to create a two-dimensional presentation of document information for consumption by eyeballs. Computers don't have eyeballs yet, so HTML doesn't do computers much good. HTML forces us to flatten our information to fit on a screen, and it also forces us to leave much interpretation up to our cognitive ability to understand ambiguity.

Think about a travel agent. Her job is to interpret what her clients want to do and come up with a travel package that they will buy. If I ask my travel agent to find me a vacation spot that's "cheap, warm, and for families," she's got enough information to get started. She knows what "warm" means, because that's a pretty standard term, although she might ask me to clarify: Do I want Death Valley warm or Orlando warm? I'll also probably clarify what "cheap" means (to make sure she finds us a place with indoor plumbing!). She would also ask what my "family" consists of—teenagers or toddlers, for example—and then she would go to work.

First, she researches places around the world that will be warm at the time of year I want to take my vacation. Then she looks at airfare, hotels, car rentals, and a dozen other factors that influence price. She might use printed travel brochures provided by hotels and vacation packagers, or she might consult any of hundreds of Web sites for the information she needs.

As Figure 7-2 illustrates, my travel agent becomes an information aggregator, looking for a combination of services that fit my needs. She is at the center of an information universe.

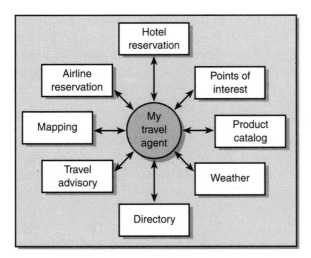

Figure 7-2. *A travel agent is an information aggregator, relying on many different information sources to create a travel package for her customers.*

After researching various information sources, my travel agent starts making decisions. For example, the temperature might be 85 degrees in Grand Cayman Island, but hotels are expensive and limited flights are available from Denver. St. Thomas is only 82 degrees, but also much cheaper and more easily accessible. However, St. Thomas doesn't have a lot for kids to do. The Bahamas are a little more expensive and not quite as warm, but have plenty of activities for kids. In other words, I'll need to make some trade-offs to accommodate all of my requirements. Finally, she comes up with a couple of plans and runs them past me.

My travel agent is human and can do only a couple of things at once. Plus, she has other customers; she can't spend all year on my project. Because of these limitations, my travel agent can consider only a small number of alternatives before proposing one or two to me. It is conceivable that a small, warm, family-friendly island is out there somewhere, and maybe the locals are cutting prices to attract more tourists. If that information doesn't get to my overloaded travel agent, she can't consider it and I've lost an opportunity.

Wouldn't it be nice if computers could help to broaden my travel agent's effectiveness by allowing her to consider more alternatives? Nice fantasy, but not very workable. The problem is the format of the available data.

If my travel agent gets information from the Web, that information is probably delivered using HTML and viewed by her eyeballs in a Web browser. Many of the HTML pages she views were created on the fly by the site's middle-tier applications. When my travel agent visits a hotel's Web site looking for room availability, some program at the hotel's Web operation queries a database containing room information and then creates a page for her.

If I were to create a computer program that could access this information in the same way as my travel agent, the computer would have trouble. It would look at an HTML page as a one-dimensional string of markup characters, not as a two-dimensional photograph or text conveying certain information. For example, when you see the text "76°F", you recognize that it means seventy-six degrees Fahrenheit, and that many people would consider that a pleasant, warm temperature. But the computer sees four ASCII characters and can't interpret them as humans do.

Take the example of the hotel page. We know valuable data is out there somewhere. The server-side application "dumbs down" the data so that humans can interpret it. Wouldn't it be nice if we could circumvent the flattening of the data for eyeballs and allow computers to talk to computers?

If I could somehow indicate from my computer program to the hotel site that a computer would be interpreting the information instead of a human, the hotel site could send the following back to my program, which would be much easier to process:

```
<avg-temperature deg="f">76</avg-temperature>
```

A program that provides this kind of computer-to-computer communication is called a Web service, and it is the next major innovation available in the infrastructure of the Web.

The existence of the Web, with millions of computers hooked to it, has encouraged companies all over the world to put their information online so that it can be accessible to customers and potential customers. A huge amount of data sits right behind server-side scripts, waiting to be accessed by Web browsers.

If your company has valuable information, wouldn't you benefit from the ability to repackage it and sell it in different ways? And if your company needs information, wouldn't it be cheaper to buy the information from someone on an as-needed basis than to build it yourself?

Think of Web services as applications that make it possible for you to program using data available on the Web, just as you can program now using data available internally. This ability to program the Web will be essential to how we use the Internet in the coming years.

THE IMPORTANCE OF AGGREGATION

Information aggregators have been around for centuries. My travel agent is a simple example, but there are many others. An independent insurance broker gathers information from many different insurance companies to find the best policy for his customers. A mortgage broker does the same for home loans. Just about any person whose job description includes the word "broker" is an information aggregator.

Like my travel agent, these aggregators can consider only a small number of alternatives at a time, simply because humans are relatively slow at collecting information. The advent of the Web and the possibility of Web services introduce innovative ways of aggregating information that no human could ever have managed.

One example of this innovative aggregation is reverse auctions. In this model, a buyer puts up a flag to indicate that he wants to buy a certain item. Vendors who can provide that item bid against each other until the price is the lowest possible. For large-ticket items, such as municipal salt contracts, this model is already up and running. However, if I wanted to buy a 10-pound box of nails, the cost of conducting a reverse auction would be much more than what I would save, as long as humans are involved.

If I could use computers to automate the process, however, the cost of the auction would be fractions of a penny. If I save a few cents on every 10-pound box of nails I buy, my total savings could be considerable. So how do we get the cost of bidding so low? By using open standards in an intelligent way.

LOOSELY COUPLED SERVICES

Computers communicate internally using a set of interfaces. These interfaces are usually defined by the operating system platform and by the languages in which programs are written. On modern object-oriented platforms, you can write programs that can be reused by other programs. One example is the Microsoft COM architecture. COM components are usually stored in dynamic-link library (DLL) files. Application programmers can use these components as building blocks. Think about the dialog box you see whenever you want to print a document from your word processor in Microsoft Windows. The programmer who wrote the word processor probably didn't write all the code for that dialog box. The dialog box is likely built from components that are made available by the Windows operating system and called by the word processor. In fact, that's why most dialog boxes have a consistent look in Windows.

Objects are pieces of code that perform certain tasks. Objects stand alone, so many different applications can share them. This application independence leads to lower development costs because programmers can leverage work that's already been done.

Objects usually have properties and methods. A property is some attribute of an object that you can interrogate or set to some value. For example, you might set a property of a font-selection dialog box to display only monospace fonts when the dialog box is opened.

A method is a function that an object performs when asked. A method might be *getStockPrice* or *multiplyTwoNumbers*. Depending on the method, an object might perform many different actions to produce a result. To get stock prices, for example, an object would probably connect to a database containing current stock information. The processing done by the object to create its result is none of my business; all I want is the result. This kind of black-box functionality is an important point to remember as processing moves toward platform independence.

Sometimes a method requires parameters. You don't want some arbitrary stock price; you want to indicate which company's stock information you're interested in. In such a case, you might pass the name of the stock as a parameter to the function. The method might also allow you to pass a date or time to get historical information.

On UNIX platforms, reusable objects take the form of shared objects that work in the same way as COM objects. Java platforms have Enterprise Java Beans (EJB). A Java program can call upon an EJB to perform certain services, and a Windows program can call upon a COM object to do certain things, but because the two programs speak different interface languages, they usually have trouble calling each other.

Systems that rely on proprietary objects are called tightly coupled because they rely on a well-defined but fragile interface. If any part of the communication between application and service object is disrupted, or if the call is not exactly right, "unpredictable results may occur" (to quote my IBM mainframe programmers' reference documents).

Another problem with tightly coupled systems is cross-machine communications. A Windows program that calls upon a COM object for certain services expects the COM object to be on the current machine—that is, the machine running the program that calls the object. For example, a Web server might have a service, available as a COM object, that connects to a local database to retrieve historical stock information for a company. That arrangement works fine as long as the object and the requesting program are on the same physical machine. However, if one machine provides the historical stock information and several Web servers are part of a load-balanced array, or "farm," the requesting program is not on the same machine. To deal with this problem, Microsoft developed the Distributed Component Object Model (DCOM). With DCOM, a user can access services on a machine over a network connection and get whatever information the service provides over the same connection. This kind of distributed system is also tightly coupled, but not as tightly coupled as normal COM, which requires both the object and the requesting program to be on the same machine. This distributed model is also available on other platforms, but getting service from one platform to another platform is still difficult. For example, a Windows program cannot make a DCOM call to an EJB running on a Linux box across town—although this is exactly the kind of transaction that needs to happen if Web services are to work. Companies all over the world have data that other companies could access easily. However, if a company had to call directly upon the objects that generate that data, that company would run into the cross-platform compatibility problem

I mentioned earlier. I can't directly invoke your EJB from my Microsoft Visual Basic application, and you can't directly invoke methods on my COM object from your Java program. To streamline communication between these object models, we need some way to decouple platform-specific requirements from the objects that create a view of data. The solution is the Simple Object Access Protocol, or SOAP. SOAP solves the problem of multiple platform incompatibilities in accessing data.

SOAP is a syntax that allows you to build applications for remotely invoking methods on objects. SOAP removes the requirement that two systems must run the same platform or be written in the same programming language. Instead of invoking methods through a proprietary binary protocol, a SOAP package uses an open standard syntax for making method calls. That syntax is XML. (Surprise!)

All information between the requesting application and the receiving object is sent as tagged data in an XML stream. This stream is a plain-text object that can be sent via HTTP through most existing firewalls. Figure 7-3 illustrates this process.

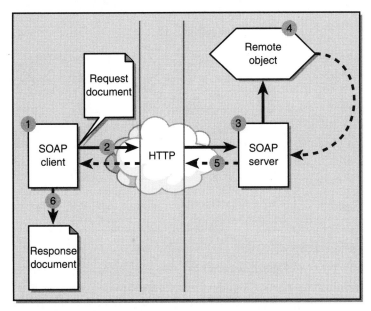

Figure 7-3. *SOAP provides a way of invoking object methods over a simple HTTP connection. The steps of this diagram are described in Table 7-1.*

As you can see in Figure 7-3, a SOAP client submits a request document over HTTP to a "listener" SOAP server at another site. This listening server captures the message, interprets the request, and invokes a method on an object in its domain. That object returns something useful to our application by responding through the SOAP server to our waiting client application. Table 7-1 explains the steps illustrated in Figure 7-3.

Step in Figure	Description
1	A program, acting as a SOAP client, creates an XML document that contains the information required to remotely invoke a method on an external system. Don't think that a SOAP client is a traditional client. For example, a SOAP client could be your Web server or some server-based application, but it could also be a part of a client on the desktop. A SOAP client is simply the thing that makes a request from a SOAP server. The SOAP client wraps the XML document inside a SOAP envelope and is turned into an HTTP *POST* request.
2	This package is sent over a standard HTTP connection.
3	A listening application—by definition, a SOAP server— receives the message. This application is usually a Web server, which is listening for SOAP requests in its normal stream of calls for HTML pages. The SOAP server parses the SOAP package and calls the appropriate object, passing as necessary the parameters that were included in the SOAP document.
4	The object performs the requested function and returns information to the SOAP server. The SOAP server packages the response in a SOAP envelope.
5	The response object is sent back to the requesting machine. Once again, the SOAP document is encapsulated in an HTTP response header.
6	The SOAP client waits for the response object. When the SOAP client receives the object, it strips the SOAP envelope and sends the response document to whatever application needs it.

Table 7-1. *A description of the steps illustrated in Figure 7-3.*

Since a SOAP document is being sent over HTTP (port 80), the document can go through almost any firewall—most firewalls are configured to allow such requests to move freely. Getting information between divergent platforms does not require any manipulation to the firewall infrastructure.

It is important to note that the object being invoked does not need any kind of modification. The SOAP server's job is to interpret the SOAP XML document that comes over the HTTP connection and turn it into a language the object understands. The SOAP server, then, acts as an interpreter, speaking both the SOAP language and the language of the object being called, and translating between the two. Therefore, the object can be written in any programming language on any platform. All communications are made by using documents written in XML syntax.

Chapter 8

Building a Web Service with SOAP

SOAP, the Simple Object Access Protocol, relies on two open standards: HTTP and XML. The SOAP XML syntax is straightforward, containing only a handful of elements and attributes. SOAP defines an envelope into which you can put data. The *SOAP:* namespace prefix defines the SOAP elements.

In this chapter, we will build an example that is broken into two parts. First we'll use JScript and the *XMLHTTP* object to create a SOAP client by hand. I want to start with the *XMLHTTP* object so that you can see exactly what goes on inside a SOAP client. The *XMLHTTP* object provides an interface between your application, which is a Web page containing JScript, and any other site over HTTP. We will use this page to post an XML document to a server. The big advantage to using HTTP is that posted data travels through firewalls without any modification. That means you can get information from your trading partners by using XML just as easily as through traditional HTML forms.

In the second part of our example, we will create a SOAP server and a Web service using a non-Microsoft product, OmniMark. OmniMark runs on Microsoft Windows platforms, but it also runs on many flavors of UNIX, including Linux. The point of including this product is to show you that a Web service is accessible through multiple platform/language combinations over the Web.

HTTP

To understand Web services using HTTP, you need to understand how HTTP works. HTTP is a simple protocol. It is plain-text–based, so it travels nicely over any transport medium you can think of. HTTP communication consists of a series of messages sent between a client and a server. These are classified as request and response messages. The HTTP standard defines several different request methods. The most common are *GET* and *POST*.

The *GET* Method

When the user types a URL into the address bar of a Web browser, a *GET* request is usually issued. If, for example, the user requests the file *http://www.myduckjokes.com/latest.htm*, the Web browser creates an HTTP packet—consisting of a request header—that is sent to the server at the IP address pointed to by the URL. The header looks something like this:

```
GET /latest.htm HTTP/1.1
Host: www.myduckjokes.com
Content-Type: text/html
{blank line}
```

An HTTP packet consists of the following parts:

- An initial line

- Zero or more header lines

- A blank line (for example, a solitary newline character)

- An optional message body (such as a file, query data, or query output)

The initial line indicates the purpose of the packet. In this case, the packet is a *GET* request instructing the server to access the file located at /latest.htm. The version of HTTP (1.1 in this example) finishes this line.

The next lines in the header indicate the parameters of the request. These consist of key-value pairs—that is, the name of the parameter starts a line, followed by a colon and space, followed by the value of the parameter. The parameter ends with a single newline character.

An HTTP request packet can contain dozens or even hundreds of parameters. It's in this packet that the browser can send the browser type, operating system type and version, and cookie information to a server. Obviously, the larger your HTTP packet is, the more time sending the request will take. The header ends with two newline characters in a row. All text after these newline characters is considered the body of the HTTP packet.

The packet is received by the HTTP server (also called a Web server), which tries to resolve the filename (/latest.htm). If possible, the HTTP server will find the page, perform any necessary processing, and return the resulting HTML as an HTTP response package. Listing 8-1 shows that the response package has an HTTP header, followed by two newline characters and then the payload. The payload is usually an HTML document.

HTTP Response

```
HTTP/1.1 200 OK
Date: Fri, 31 Dec 1999 23:59:59 GMT
Content-Type: text/html
Content-Length: 283

<HTML>
    <HEAD>
        <TITLE>Latest Duck-Bar Jokes</TITLE>
    </HEAD>
    <BODY>
        <H1>Latest Duck-Bar Jokes</H1>
        <P>A duck walks into a bar. The bartender says,
        "We don't serve ducks here." The duck says,
        "That's OK, I don't really like duck, anyway. How
        about a beer?"</P>
        <P></P>
    </BODY>
</HTML>
```

Listing 8-1. *An HTTP response packet.*

Notice that the response packet has information about itself in the first line of the header, followed by a series of key-value pairs that help the Web browser understand what to do with the packet.

The first line contains a status code. There are a number of these status codes. The most common is 200, which means "Package was delivered OK." Other common status codes are 404, which means that some resource wasn't found, and 500, which means that the server generated an error. The status code is meant to be readable by a computer; the message is meant to be readable by a human. Status codes are assigned to ranges of numbers:

- **1xx**   Indicates an informational message only

- **2xx**   Indicates success of some kind

- **3xx**   Redirects the client to another URL

■   **4xx**   Indicates an error on the client's part

■   **5xx**   Indicates an error on the server's part

All responses except those with 100-level status (but including error responses) must include the Date: header. All time values in HTTP use Greenwich Mean Time.

The *POST* Method

When the user hits a Submit button on a Web page, information is probably being posted to a Web server somewhere. HTML has elements that capture information from the user and send it to a Web server. In this example, we'll use two *INPUT* elements to retrieve data from a user, and we'll send that data to a server using the *POST* method. The file 1040.htm in Listing 8-2 shows a typical page that captures information from a user. You can find this file in the folder /Samples/Ch08 on the companion CD.

1040.htm

```
<HTML>
    <HEAD>
        <TITLE>1040 Super E-Z Form</H1>
    </HEAD>
    <BODY STYLE="font-family:Verdana;">
        <H1>1040 Super E-Z Form</H1>
        <FORM METHOD="POST" ACTION="/cgi-bin/processForm.pl">
            <TABLE>
                <TR>
                    <TD>Enter your social security number:</TD>
                    <TD><INPUT TYPE="TEXT" NAME="socSecNum"></TD>
                </TR>
                <TR>
                    <TD>How much did you make last year?</TD>
                    <TD><INPUT TYPE="TEXT" NAME="income"></TD>
                </TR>
                <TR>
                    <TD>Press "Calculate" for verdict</TD>
                    <TD><INPUT TYPE="SUBMIT" VALUE="Calculate"></TD>
                </TR>
            </TABLE>
        </FORM>
    </BODY>
</HTML>
```

Listing 8-2. *An HTML document containing a* FORM *element.*

Notice the *FORM* element. This element is used to combine user interface elements such as *INPUT* boxes, *TEXTAREA* fields, and *SUBMIT* buttons. In this example, *FORM* has two attributes, *METHOD* and *ACTION*. The *METHOD* attribute indicates that we are going to use the HTTP *POST* method to submit the data in the form to the Web server. The *ACTION* attribute contains the pathname of the script that's going to process this form data on the Web server. The .pl extension in the filename contained in the path indicates that we are going to execute a Perl script in the /cgi-bin directory. Perl script will interpret the name-value pairs in the posted HTTP package and (we hope) do something useful.

Loading the code in Listing 8-2 in a Web browser results in the view shown in Figure 8-1. The user has filled in the values.

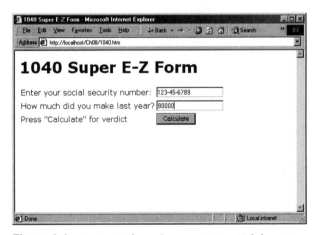

Figure 8-1. *An HTML form document in a Web browser.*

When the user clicks the Calculate button, the Web browser creates the HTTP packet shown in Listing 8-3.

HTTP Information

```
POST /cgi-bin/processForm.pl HTTP/1.1
Host: www.irs.gov
Content-Type: application/x-www-form-urlencoded
Content-Length: 35

socSecNum=123-45-6789&income=80000
```

Listing 8-3. *An HTTP package containing information captured from an HTML form.*

The Content-Type header tells the server that this packet is an encoded form object that the server will need to decode before routing it to the application. The body of the package contains the names of each of the input fields, along with the value the user typed in. An ampersand (&) separates each name-value pair.

When the server gets the package, it parses the values in the body and passes that information to the script. The script then takes over processing and is able to return a result through the HTTP server.

PORTS

Servers that communicate over IP listen to various IP ports to find out what to do. An FTP server constantly listens to port 21 (by default) for requests. The default port for HTTP is 80, meaning that a Web server listens to that port, waiting for requests to come along. You can change this port, but that's usually not a good idea, since applications assume they can send you an HTTP *GET* or *POST* request to port 80 and have your server process it in a known way.

Another form of HTTP, called HTTPS, provides secure encryption between a Web browser client and your Web server. A Web server that is HTTPS-compliant listens at port 443 by default. Web servers that have secure encryption capability will communicate with the Web browser by sending encryption codes when a user requests a secure connection. Every time the client and server exchange data, the sender encrypts the data and the receiver decrypts the data, all according to the encryption keys that they exchange.

Since HTTPS is more complex than HTTP, I don't want to spend more time on it. Just know that the client and server can negotiate encrypted packets in a manner that is transparent to the user and downstream processes.

Other services use other default ports. For example, the RealServer from RealNetworks uses ports 554 and 7070 (and port 80 if either of these is not available), and Telnet uses port 23. Network administrators can use firewalls and proxy servers to restrict access to certain information types by simply blocking packets targeted at particular ports.

FIREWALLS

I spent some time talking about the HTTP infrastructure because XML can be transferred through the same port. Most modern companies have a way for their employees to access Web pages. Since most public Web services listen to port 80, most firewalls allow data to flow freely through this port. Firewall software doesn't generally check for the type of data going through this port, because information providers add new data types all the time—keeping up would be an administrative nightmare. Using port 80 for getting information between businesses, then, is a no-brainer, because it doesn't involve complex administrative issues for network administrators.

The *POST* method provides an elegant way to ship data between clients and servers through the Web infrastructure. Because XML is based on the same encoding standards as HTML, you can easily use XML to pass information between two servers.

SOAP MESSAGE STRUCTURE

A SOAP document is an electronic envelope into which you place your payload. The payload consists of the tags that describe the method you want to invoke and the data that method invocation needs to do its job. Figure 8-2 shows the SOAP package.

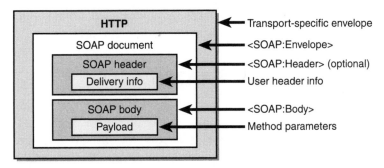

Figure 8-2. *A SOAP document is an envelope containing a payload sent to the SOAP server.*

A SOAP envelope document has two subelements, *SOAP:Header* and *SOAP:Body*. The *SOAP:Header* element contains information about the transaction. This information is user-defined, and its content depends on what you want to achieve. In the following example, the *SOAP:Header* element indicates a *Transaction* element that has a value of 5. The receiving application can use this value to do something useful. Notice that the *Transaction* element is in a user-defined namespace called *trans*.

```
<SOAP:Header>
   <trans:Transaction
     xmlns:trans="http://schemas.architag.com/transaction.xsd"
     SOAP:mustUnderstand="1">5</trans:Transaction>
</SOAP:Header>
```

A SOAP element can have the *SOAP:mustUnderstand* global attribute. This attribute indicates whether a header entry is mandatory or optional for the recipient to process. The value of this attribute is either *1* or *0*. It is designed to allow the specification to evolve over time. You could, for example, send a new SOAP document to a server that is written to an older specification. The *SOAP:Header* element is optional.

> **NOTE**   SOAP works well over HTTP, but the SOAP spec indicates that other transport protocols can be used.

The *SOAP:Header* element is the envelope's second subelement. For the SOAP request, the body contains tags defined by the method you are invoking. These tags contain information that the method needs to do its job. For the SOAP response document, the *SOAP:Body* element contains the data created as the result of the message. (I've just described what happens if the method succeeds. An optional *SOAP:Fault* element can indicate whether the SOAP server had a problem processing the request.)

SOAP also provides rich semantics for indicating encoding style, array structure, and data types. All this information is available from the SOAP spec.

THE XML NEWSFEED EXAMPLE

In the XML newsfeed example, we're dealing with a site that maintains a database of news articles that are of interest to the XML implementor. This site is available to the public at *http://architag.com/xmlnews.html*. Clicking on the URL invokes a Microsoft Active Server Pages (ASP) document, which connects to the database of news and creates HTML output that is sent to the user.

Suppose we wanted to have access to the information in the newsfeed database, but we wanted only the data, not the HTML that was created for consumption by a Web browser. In other words, we just want the raw news so that we can format it to suit our needs. To get to that data, we'll use SOAP.

The SOAP Client Application

First we're going to build a client that requests a Web service. We'll create this client as an HTML page that uses JScript in a browser. Figure 8-3, which is described in Table 8-1, shows how the client fits into our example. Figure 8-4 shows how the client looks in the browser. The HTML code in Listing 8-4 shows the body of the HTML document (getXMLNews.htm) we will use. The JScript follows in Listing 8-5. You can find the complete listings for this example on the companion CD at \Samples\Ch08\.

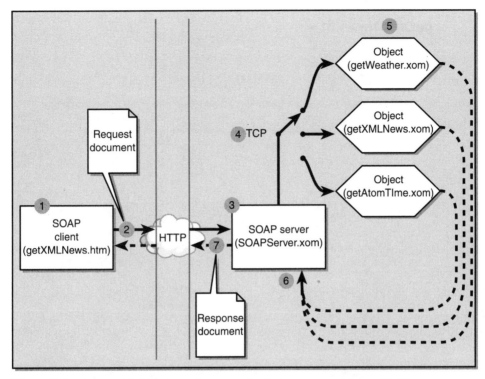

Figure 8-3. *Create a SOAP request document in the browser, post it to a SOAP server, process the request, and send back a SOAP response document. This process is described in Table 8-1.*

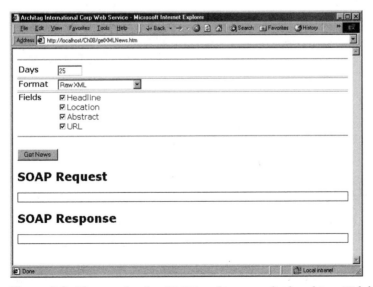

Figure 8-4. *The completed getXMLNews.htm page displayed in a Web browser.*

getXMLNews.htm

```
<HTML><HEAD>
</HEAD>
<BODY STYLE="font-family:Verdana;">
    <HR>
    <TABLE FRAME="VOID" BORDER="1" RULES="ROWS" WIDTH="100%">
        <TR>
            <TD WIDTH="80" VALIGN="TOP"><B>Days</B></TD>
            <TD VALIGN="TOP"><INPUT TYPE="TEXT" SIZE="5"
                ID="newsDays" VALUE="23"></TD>
        </TR>
        <TR>
            <TD WIDTH="80" VALIGN="TOP"><B>Format</B></TD>
            <TD VALIGN="TOP"><SELECT ID="newsFormat">
                <OPTION VALUE="XML">Raw XML</OPTION>
                <OPTION SELECTED VALUE="HTML3">HTML 3</OPTION>
                <OPTION VALUE="HTML4">HTML 4 - Netscape</OPTION>
                <OPTION VALUE="HTML4">HTML 4 - Explorer</OPTION>
                <OPTION VALUE="xHTML">xHTML</OPTION>
                <OPTION VALUE="Text">Text</OPTION>
                </SELECT>
            </TD>
        </TR>
        <TR>
            <TD WIDTH="80" VALIGN="TOP"><B>Fields</B></TD>
            <TD VALIGN="TOP">
                <INPUT CHECKED TYPE="CHECKBOX" NAME="newsFields"
                    ID="fldHeadline" VALUE="headline">Headline</INPUT>
                <BR><INPUT CHECKED TYPE="CHECKBOX" NAME="newsFields"
                    ID="fldLocation" VALUE="location">Location</INPUT>
                <BR><INPUT CHECKED TYPE="CHECKBOX" NAME="newsFields"
                    ID="fldAbstract" VALUE="abstract">Abstract</INPUT>
                <BR><INPUT CHECKED TYPE="CHECKBOX" NAME="newsFields"
                    ID="fldURL" VALUE="url">URL</INPUT>
                </TD>
        </TR>
    </TABLE>
    <HR>

    <BR><INPUT TYPE="BUTTON" VALUE="Get News"
        ONCLICK="ResultDiv.innerHTML=getXMLNews();">
    <H2>SOAP Request</H2>
    <DIV ID="SOAPDiv" STYLE="border:1pt black solid;"> </DIV>
    <H2>SOAP Response</H2>
    <DIV ID="ResultDiv" STYLE="border:1pt black solid;"> </DIV>
</BODY>
</HTML>
```

Listing 8-4. *The initial HTML code used to create a SOAP client interface as described in Step 1 of Table 8-1.*

Step	Description
1	First we create a SOAP client in the form of a Web page. A hard-coded HTML page is probably not what you would normally use, so consider this a learning tool. In actual practice, you would probably initiate a SOAP request from a server program that retrieves information from a number of different sources.
2	The SOAP document is sent over an HTTP connection as a *POST* command. In this example I use *localhost*, which points to the Web server on a local machine.
3	The SOAP server receives the request. The request is a CGI program written in OmniMark. The server reads the SOAP request and determines whether the method name is something it knows about. If the server recognizes the method,...
4	...the server opens a TCP connection to the appropriate service and sends the SOAP document to the service.
5	The service is another OmniMark program running in a console window, waiting for activity to happen at a particular port. The service does what it needs to do and returns a package to the server.
6	The server composes a SOAP response package, encapsulating the results from the service.
7	The response document is sent to the waiting client as an HTTP response package.

Table 8-1. *A description of the SOAP request process illustrated in Figure 8-3.*

To complete this page, we need to ask the Web service for a collection of items from an XML newsfeed. Later on, we'll write a Web service that responds to this request.

The getXMLNews.htm file lets users request information we have stored on a Web server. They can indicate the format they want this news in, and they can specify the number of days back to search the database. Our JScript will process the user request and indicate how far back from the current day we want to receive items, what the format of the information should be, and which fields we want to include in the response.

The Get News button will set in motion the following process:

1. Execute a JScript function that creates a SOAP document with a payload that contains a request that will be sent to a Web service.

2. This SOAP document is sent to the Web service via an HTTP *POST* command.

3. The Web service performs the following tasks, in the order indicated:

   ❑ Reads the SOAP document, extracting the payload

   ❑ Parses the request payload to determine the parameters of the method invocation

❑ Queries the database based on the parameters indicated

❑ Prepares a response packet

❑ Wraps the response packet as a SOAP response object

❑ Ships the response packet back to the browser as an HTTP response

4. The JScript function receives the response and transforms it with an XSLT style sheet.

Listing 8-5 shows the function for sending the *POST* command to our SOAP server. Table 8-2 offers a line-by-line description of the code in Listing 8-5. You can see the complete Web page in Figure 8-4.

getXMLNews# POST Function

```
1   <SCRIPT LANGUAGE="JScript">
2       var xmlhttp = new ActiveXObject("Microsoft.XMLHTTP");
3
4       var objStyle = new ActiveXObject("MSXML2.DOMDocument");
5       objStyle.async = false;
6       objStyle.load("ShowXML.xsl")
7
8       var SOAPRequest = new ActiveXObject("MSXML2.DOMDocument");
9       SOAPRequest.async = false;
10
11      var SOAPResponse = new ActiveXObject("MSXML2.DOMDocument");
12      SOAPResponse.async = false;
13
14      function getXMLNews()
15          {
16          xmlhttp.Open("POST",
17              "http://architag.com/scripts/SOAPServer.xar", false);
18          strXML =
19          "<SOAP:Envelope " +
20          "  xmlns:SOAP='urn:schemas-xmlsoap-org:soap.v1'>" +
21          "  <SOAP:Body>" +
22          "    <getXMLNewsRequest" +
23          "    xmlns='urn:schemas-architag-com:getXMLNews'>" +
24          "      <days>" + document.all.newsDays.value + "</days>" +
25          "      <format>" + document.all.newsFormat.value + "</format>" +
26          "      <fields>"
27          if (fldHeadline.checked) strXML += "headline "
28          if (fldLocation.checked) strXML += "location "
29          if (fldAbstract.checked) strXML += "abstract "
30          if (fldURL.checked) strXML += "url "
31          strXML += "                </fields>" +
```

Listing 8-5. *JScript used to post an XML document to a SOAP server.*

```
32          "          </getXMLNewsRequest>" +
33          "        </SOAP:Body>" +
34          "</SOAP:Envelope>"
35
36          SOAPRequest.loadXML(strXML)
37          SOAPDiv.innerHTML =
38              SOAPRequest.transformNode(objStyle.documentElement)
39          xmlhttp.setRequestHeader("SOAPMethodName", "getXMLNewsRequest")
40          xmlhttp.Send(SOAPRequest.xml);
41          SOAPResponse.loadXML(xmlhttp.responseXML.xml)
42          return SOAPResponse.transformNode(objStyle.documentElement)
43          }
44  </SCRIPT>
```

Line	Description
1	Beginning of the JScript block.
2	We use *ActiveXObject* to instantiate an *XMLHTTP* object.
4	We need to create several instances of the XML parser. First we create a copy that will hold our XSL style sheet.
5	The *async* property controls how the parser behaves as it loads the document. If we set the *async* property to *false*, the parser will wait until the document is loaded or until there is an error. If we set the *async* property to *true*, the parser will fire off an asynchronous process. Setting *async* to *true* is nice because we can load the document in the background. However, it complicates the program because we need to indicate the function that should execute when the load is finished. For now, let's simplify things and set the *async* property to *false*.
6	The *load* method loads an XML document from the URL indicated in the argument. In this case, the document is our XSL style sheet in the current directory.
8–9	A second instance of the XML processor will eventually hold our SOAP request document.
11–12	A third instance of the XML processor will hold the response document that comes back from the SOAP server.
14	The *getXMLNews* function will be called from the Web page.
16–17	The *Open* method of the *XMLHTTP* object creates a connection to the server. In this case, the server is an OmniMark program located on the Architag server in Colorado. The second argument is the *async* property, which works just like the *async* property on the XML parser object. We want to set this property to *false*, to force the program to wait until it receives the response.

Table 8-2. *Line-by-line description of the JScript code in Listing 8-5.* *(continued)*

Table 8-2. *continued*

Line	Description
18–34	The *strXML* = line builds the XML document as a serialized string, inserting values from the fields on the Web page. This process is known as "XML by concatenation." We could also build the XML document by inserting element and attribute nodes with the DOM API. That technique probably provides a more robust program, but I think the concatenation approach is easier to use when you are starting out.
36	Once we create the XML document, we load it into the XML processor. Now we have an object that we can manipulate.
37–38	This block of code generates part of the user interface. Using XSLT, we can transform the request document that we just loaded into an HTML string and display it on the page. In the HTML source, you'll see an HTML *DIV* element with an *ID* of *SOAPDiv*. This line sets the *innerHTML* property to a string of text. The *transformNode* method of the *SOAPRequest* object invokes the XSLT processor, which creates an HTML object. You can view this object on the page by setting the *innerHTML* property of the *DIV*.
39	The SOAP spec suggests that it's good practice to include the *SOAPMethodName* parameter as part of the HTTP request header. The value of this parameter should be the name of the method you are invoking.
40	The *Send* method sends the packet to the SOAP server. (The SOAP server was opened on line 16.) Remember that the *SOAPRequest* object is an in-memory, binary XML object. We need to re-serialize (turn the object into a sequential stream of XML characters) using the *.xml* property. The *Send* method first creates the HTTP header with the *SOAPMethodName* parameter, then creates a blank line (which separates the header from the body), and finally concatenates the XML document.
41	Now we wait. Since we set the *async* property to *false*, the process will wait on line 40 until the SOAP server returns an HTTP response packet. The packet comes in the form of a plain XML document (a serialized stream of Unicode characters). If we want to access this packet in our script, we must load this stream into the XML DOM as a tree object. The *LoadXML* method does this.
42	We want to process the return value as an HTML document. We can then return this document to the calling function. In this example, the function sets the *innerHTML* property of another *DIV*.

Implementing a SOAP Server in OmniMark

The SOAP server opened on line 16 in Listing 8-5 is an OmniMark program that calls another OmniMark program named SOAPServer.xom. SOAPServer.xom runs as an HTTP server. Let's take a look at OmniMark.

OmniMark is a fourth-generation, event-driven language that runs on most modern computer platforms. The language was first published in the early 1990s as a conversion tool. OmniMark has really grown up since then and is now a viable alternative to Perl for industrial-strength network programming applications.

OmniMark has an easy-to-learn syntax that resembles English. It also has built-in XML parsing and processing capabilities and by far the best pattern-matching processor available anywhere.

OmniMark is free. You'll find a copy on the CD included with this book. The CD also includes a terrific integrated development environment (IDE). This IDE is free for use at home and in school, but it will cost you a few hundred bucks if you want to use it at work. You'll find all this in the \OmniMark directory on the CD.

Since OmniMark is largely self-documenting, it is pretty easy to describe and learn. I've included my book *OmniMark at Work, Volume 1: Getting Started* on the companion CD. I wrote the book before the release of the current version of OmniMark, so the network programming concepts are fairly limited. However, the book does explain OmniMark's basic architecture, variable types, control structures, and techniques. A more recent description of OmniMark appears in Appendix A.

I want to show you two OmniMark programs here. The first is a CGI program named SOAPServer.xom that we call from our script. This program will parse the SOAP message and determine whether a service that can handle the request is loaded. The second program, SOAP.xin, runs continually as a service. This service listens at a known IP port and is activated when our CGI program sends the service a message on that port. The message sent by the CGI program is an XML stream. The service processes this request, formulates a response, and then sends the result back to the waiting CGI program.

In this example Web service, an XML document is passed between the OmniMark program acting as a SOAP server and the OmniMark process acting as the Web service. However, it is important to note that the programs that provide services in a Web service environment don't need to know anything about XML. The SOAP server's job is to translate the SOAP request into whatever language or form the service object requires. This means that 20-year-old COBOL programs can still work nicely as services. All the SOAP server needs to do is translate the SOAP request into the COBOL program's calling convention and turn the COBOL program's response into a SOAP response document.

SOAPServer.xom

We call the first program, SOAPServer.xom, as a CGI program in the same way we might call Perl programs. You can call the OmniMark program directly through a URL, or you can redirect it from an arguments file, as I have done in this example. The arguments file is SOAPServer.xar. I like this latter approach because it allows me to specify command-line arguments and have the OmniMark program execute in a location other than the scripts directory (perhaps from a hidden path or on another machine). Listing 8-6 shows the argument file.

OmniMark has a rich command-line interface. SOAPServer.xar contains the options passed to this interface. In line 1, the actual server program, SOAPServer.xom, is called as the source file (*-sb*). The *–i* directive in line 2 contains a path to common include files, and the *–x* directive in line 3 contains the path of the compiled libraries. Any errors reported by the program, or those sent to the #error stream, are sent to the file following the *–log* directive in line 4.

SOAPServer.xar

```
-sb SOAPServer.xom
-i "c:\program files\omnimark\xin\"
-x "c:\program files\omnimark\lib\=L.dll"
-log SOAPServer.log
```

Listing 8-6. *An argument file for calling an OmniMark SOAP server.*

Under some operating systems, OmniMark also supports the "hash-bang" directive as the first line in the file, somewhat like Perl does. The hash-bang directive looks like this:

```
#!/usr/bin/omnimark/bin/omnimark -sb helloworld.xom
```

Listing 8-7 contains the complete SOAPServer.xom CGI program. A line-by-line description of the program follows in Table 8-3.

SOAPServer.xom

```
1   include "SOAP.xin"
2
3   process
4       local stream methodName initial {""}
5       local stream SOAPResponse
6       local stream formVars variable initial-size 0
7       local stream remote-host initial {"localhost"}
8       local TCPConnection myConnection
9       local stream myRequest
10      local stream responseXML
11
12      cgiGetEnv into formVars
13      set methodName to UTIL_GetEnv ("HTTP_SOAPMETHODNAME")
14
15      open SOAPResponse as buffer
16      do scan #main-input
17          match any{formVars{"CONTENT_LENGTH"}}
```

Listing 8-7. *The OmniMark SOAP server as a CGI application.*

```
18                          => inputData
19                  do when methodName = ""
20                      put SOAPResponse "%n<SOAP:Fault>"
21                          || "%n  <faultcode>101</faultcode>"
22                          || "%n  <faultstring>no method specified"
23                          || "%n</faultstring>"
24                          || "%n</SOAP:Fault>"
25                  else
26                      do when portSOAP has key methodName
27                          set myConnection to TCPConnectionOpen
28                                  on remote-host
29                                  at portSOAP {methodName}
30                          open myRequest
31                              as TCPConnectionGetOutput myConnection
32                          put myRequest inputData || crlf
33                          close myRequest
34
35                          do when TCPConnectionIsConnected myConnection
36                              set responseXML to
37                                  TCPConnectionGetCharacters myConnection
38                              put SOAPResponse responseXML
39                          done
40                      else
41                          put SOAPResponse "<SOAP:Fault>"
42                              || "  <faultcode>101</faultcode>"
43                              || "  <faultstring>method not supported:"
44                              || " %g(methodName)</faultstring>"
45                              || "</SOAP:Fault>"
46                      done
47                  done
48          done
49      close SOAPResponse
50
51      output "Content-Type: text/xml" || crlf
52          || "Cache-control: private"
53          || crlf || crlf
54          || "<?xml version='1.0'?>"
55          || "%n<SOAP:Envelope "
56          || "%n   xmlns:SOAP='urn:schemas-xmlsoap-org:soap.v1'>"
57          || "%n   <SOAP:Body>"
58          || SOAPResponse
59          || "%n    </SOAP:Body>%n</SOAP:Envelope>%n"
60
61      catch #external-exception
62              identity catch-id
63              message catch-msg
64              location catch-loc
65          output 'An external exception occurred in SOAPServer.%n'
66              || '%g(catch-loc)%n'
67              || '%g(catch-id) : %g(catch-msg)%n'
```

Line	Description
1	The *include* directive does what you would expect: includes the code contained in SOAP.xin at this point in the program. SOAP.xin contains a common set of constants and functions used by this program and the Web services that this program calls.
3	OmniMark has two modes. It can act as a rules-based, event-driven environment in which some event (usually in the input stream) fires rules, where actions kick in. In this way, OmniMark resembles a fourth-generation object-oriented programming language. The OmniMark's other mode—called a process program—is like a third-generation language such as C. Our CGI program is this second type (a process program). In this mode, actions will be executed in the order in which they are written.
4–10	OmniMark has four basic types of variables: *counter* (integer data type), *stream* (string), *switch* (Boolean), and *pattern*. In addition to the four built-in variable types, OmniMark external functions can define their own data types, called opaque data types. We will use opaque data types when we connect to a database and retrieve records from queries.
	You must declare all variables except pattern variables as global or local. Global variables are available anywhere in the program. Local variables are available to any actions that are in the scope where you defined the local variable. (For more information about declaring variables, check out Chapter 5 of *OmniMark At Work*, available on the companion CD.) We'll use a debug stream to contain information that we might need if the program doesn't work exactly right.
	We must declare variables as the first elements inside of a scope. In this example, the scope is the process program. These variables will be active throughout the entire process program. If a local variable of the same name is declared in a subordinate scope, the inner local variable will override the outer local variable for the duration of the inner scope. The outer variable will take over once the scope in which the inner variable is declared ends.
	Welcome to hierarchical programming!
4	The *methodName* variable will contain the name of the method we are invoking.
6	Any OmniMark variable can exist as a "shelf." A shelf is a collection of like objects that can be accessed by their index offset (item 1, item 2, and so on) or by a descriptive key. A shelf is similar to an associative array in Perl.
	Here, we are creating a collection of streams under the name *formVars*. The keyword *variable* indicates that this collection is a shelf of like items, rather than a single variable.

Table 8-3. *A line-by-line description of the OmniMark SOAP server in Listing 8-7.*

Line	Description
8	The *TCPConnection* opaque variable type is defined by one of the external libraries included in SOAP.xin. We create a local name, *myConnection*, which will act as our handle to make TCP connections.
12	The *cgiGetEnv* function retrieves the values of all CGI-related environment variables. The function places those values on a keyed stream shelf of name-value pairs, in which the key of the item is the name of the environment variable and the item's value is the value of that variable. The *formVars* shelf now contains a collection of streams that are specified with associated keys. You can see some of these server variables in Table 8-4.
	To access any of these values, you need to indicate the member of the collection. For example, to access the *QUERY_STRING*, the OmniMark code is:
| | ```
set queryString to cgiGetEnv["QUERY_STRING"]
``` |
13	The *cgiGetEnv* function gets only predefined and expected server variables. HTTP 1.1 allows us to create our own environmental variables. The environmental variable we use for SOAP is the *SOAPMethodName* parameter. The *UTIL_GetEnv* function accesses any parameter from the HTTP header. To get the parameter we want, we need to add *HTTP_* to the beginning of the parameter's name and convert everything to uppercase.
15	You can use the *set* action to set a stream to some value, or you can open, append, and close a stream just as you would a file. In this example, we want to open the *SOAPResponse* stream in the same way we'd open an in-memory file so that we can occasionally put data into it.
16	The OmniMark CGI interface exposes the contents of the *POST* method as coming from the data source *#main-input*, which is a read-only stream.
	The *do scan* control structure exposes a string to a series of pattern-matching statements (*match*). If any of these patterns are found, the actions following the *match* statement are executed.
17	This line matches all the posted text. The *any* pattern declaration by itself will find a single character. If *any* is followed by an integer in curly brackets, it will find the number of characters indicated by that integer. In this case, we are interrogating the *CONTENT_LENGTH* environment variable sent in the HTTP header and grabbing exactly that number of characters into a pattern variable called *inputData*.

(continued)
```

Table 8-3. *continued*

Line	Description
19	The *do when* control block is like the *if* statement in most languages. In this case, if the *methodName* isn't set, we need to indicate an error because we can't figure out what method is requested.
20–24	SOAP defines an element for indicating that something went wrong with the SOAP request. The *faultcode* and *faultstring* elements are set to codes that might help the SOAP client make sense of the problem.
	The OmniMark concatenation characters | | will concatenate the string into a single unit. I use this to make the program more readable. The "*%n*" string inserts a newline character.
26	The *portSOAP* variable is a keyed array of items that was initialized in SOAP.xin. This array contains the names of the services offered, along with the port at which each service listens. The declaration looks like this:
| | ```
global stream portSOAP variable initial {
    "5432" with key "getWeather",
    "5433" with key "getXMLNewsRequest",
    "5434" with key "getAtomTimet"}
``` |
	If this stream shelf has an item with the key equal to the *methodName* of the request, we know to send the package to the port indicated in that member of the shelf.
27–31	Now we need to establish a connection to the port so that we can communicate with the service.
32	Once we've established the connection and opened the port, the *put* action sends data over the line. In this case, the OmniMark object is aware of XML and SOAP, so we send the entire SOAP document. However, we could use this same technique if the object knew nothing about XML or SOAP. The SOAP server's job is to make the translation between the SOAP request that comes in and whatever the object needs to service the request.
	At this point, the service that is listening at the port indicated will take over. Listing 8-9 shows the program, getXMLNews.xom. It will receive the package, do its magic, and then return a package to the server. In this case, it the getXMLNews program will give back an XML document that contains the data generated by the service.
35	A loop checks to assure that the connection is still active.
36–37	The server waits at this point until characters are sent back from the service. As characters are returned, the *responseXML* streams are captured.
40–45	If we don't recognize the *methodName*, we need to generate a *SOAP:Fault* package with useful information.
49	Like a file stream, an OmniMark stream must be closed before it is read back in. At this point, the *SOAPResponse* stream has the payload that we need to send back to the client.
```

Line	Description
51–59	The output action will send something to the output stream. This is a tricky concept in a hierarchical programming language. OmniMark allows you to redirect the output in many different ways. In this example, the output stream is the client that invoked the CGI program.
51–52	We need to set some HTTP header variables.
53	Two newline characters in a row separates the HTTP header from the body.
	Because we are creating an XML document, good form dictates that we include the XML declaration. The *SOAP:Envelope* root element follows. The two vertical bars indicate string concatenation.
61–67	OmniMark has a rich exception-handling interface. Actions in this *catch* directive will be executed in the event of a critical program error. Like virtually everything else in OmniMark, exception handling is, hierarchical in nature, allowing one nested routine to throw an exception to an outer routine.

Variable	Description
AUTH_TYPE	The authentication protocol currently being used. This variable is defined only if the server supports—and if access to the CGI program requires—authentication.
CONTENT_LENGTH	The length, in bytes, of the information the Web server sends to the CGI program as input. You'll use this variable most often when the CGI program uses the *POST* method to process input sent from an HTML form.
CONTENT_TYPE	The type of content the Web server sends to the CGI program as input.
HTTP_CONNECTION	The type of connection that the client and server use. For example, *HTTP_CONNECTION = Keep-Alive*.
HTTP_HOST	The IP address or host name of the accessed machine.
HTTP_USER_AGENT	The browser software and operating system that the client system is running.
QUERY_STRING	Contains the encoded data from a form submission when that form is submitted by the client by using the *GET* method. If a form is submitted using the *POST* method, this environment variable is not set, as the encoded data is passed to the CGI program through standard input (in OmniMark terms, through *#process-input*).

Table 8-4. *Server variables accessed by the* cgiGetEnv *command.*

getXMLNews.xom

Listings 8-8 and 8-9 show the service that waits for the *getXMLNewsRequest* method. The file is named getXMLNews.xom. Listing 8-8 shows the server loop, which listens to the appropriate port, reads data over TCP, and calls the function that provides the service. Table 8-5 breaks down this listing line by line. Listing 8-9 shows the service provider: a function that opens the database, retrieves the records, and builds the XML response payload. Table 8-6 offers a line-by-line description of Listing 8-9.

getXMLNews.xom

```
 1   include "SOAP.xin"
 2   declare catch server-die
 3
 4   process
 5       local TCPService myService
 6       local TCPConnection myConnection
 7       local stream caughtData
 8       local stream responseXML
 9
10       set myService to TCPServiceOpen
11           at portSOAP{"getXMLNewsRequest"}
12       put #error "getXMLNews listening on "
13           || portSOAP{"getXMLNewsRequest"} ||"%n"
14       throw server-die
15           unless TCPService-is-working myService
16
17       repeat
18           set daysWanted to 0
19
20           set myConnection
21               to TCPServiceAcceptConnection myService
22           throw server-die
23               unless TCPService-is-working myService
24           set caughtData to
25               TCPConnectionGetCharacters myConnection
26
27           put #error "getXMLNews caught and processed data on "
28               || portSOAP{"getXMLNewsRequest"}
29               || "%n----%n%g(caughtData)%n----%n"
30
31           clear fieldsWanted
32           using group processXML do
33               do xml-parse instance scan caughtData
34                   suppress
35               done
36           done
37
```

Listing 8-8. *The service that listens for* getXMLNewsRequest *methods.*

```
38          open responseXML as TCPConnectionGetOutput myConnection
39          put responseXML getXMLNews(daysWanted, formatType,
40              fieldsWanted) || crlf
41          close responseXML
42        catch #program-error
43            put #error "caught #program-error%n"
44
45        catch #external-exception
46                identity catch-id
47                message catch-msg
48                location catch-loc
49            output 'An external exception occurred.%n'
50            output '%g(catch-loc)%n'
51            output '%g(catch-id) : %g(catch-msg)%n'
52      again
53
54      catch server-die
55          open responseXML as
56              TCPConnectionGetOutput myConnection
57          put responseXML "<msg>getXMLNews Server killed</msg>"
58              || crlf
59          close responseXML
60          halt
61  ;-------------------------------------------------
62  group processXML
63  ;-------------------------------------------------
64  element #implied
65      suppress
66
67  element format
68      set formatType to "%c"
69
70  element days
71      set daysWanted to "%c"
72
73  element fields
74      repeat scan "%c"
75          match [any except " "]+ => field
76              set new fieldsWanted key field to field
77                  unless fieldsWanted has key field
78          match any
79      again
80
81  element die
82      do scan "%c"
83          match content-start POISON-PILL content-end
84              put #error "Shutting Down%13#%10#"
85              throw server-die
86  done
```

Line	Description
1	The *include* directive does what you would expect: includes the code contained in SOAP.xin at this point in the program. SOAP.xin contains a common set of constants and functions used by this file and the Web services that this program calls.
2	OmniMark's catch and throw capabilities give you the ability to declare your own rules that catch packages thrown under program control or as the result of an exceptional situation. In this case, we declare a catch that will be accessed if someone sends a poison pill to the server to shut it down.
4	We are running another process program.
5–6	We need to declare two variables for the TCP service and connection. These variables will be the conduit through which we communicate with the SOAP server.
10–11	The service is opened at the port indicated by the stream declared in SOAP.xin.
12–13	The *#error* stream is a write-only stream that is usually the command-line console from which the program was executed. This message will be displayed as the program starts.
14–15	If the TCP service has a problem, an exception is thrown to a catch that is defined elsewhere.
17	Unlike the CGI program you saw earlier in the chapter, this program stays in memory until it is killed by a poison pill or something grave happens with the TCP service manager. The *repeat...again* control structure is the loop that will be executed once for each message the program receives.
20–21	Each time through the loop, we need to establish a connection with the TCP service.
22–23	We need to check that the TCP service is healthy. If not, an exception is thrown.
24–25	This section of the loop is where the server spends most of its time waiting. The *TCPConnectionGetCharacters* function will catch messages sent to this program by the CGI program SOAPServer.xom.
27–29	Display the package on the console, just to provide some feedback for anyone who might be monitoring it.
31	The SOAP package indicates which fields the service requests. A shelf of streams contains those fields. Since we are in a server situation, we expect this program to be up and running for many, many requests. Therefore, we need to make sure we clean up after ourselves. By clearing this shelf, we set the number of items to zero so that later they can be initialized by another routine.

Table 8-5. *Line-by-line description of the service that listens for getXMLNewsRequest methods in Listing 8-8.*

Line	Description
32–36	OmniMark has XML processing available natively. Because we received an XML document, we need to look into that document to find out the parameters for our process. A group called *processXML* is elsewhere in the program. That group contains a set of rules that will process XML elements as they are encountered by some requesting process. This code processes the XML document in *caughtData* by invoking the XML parser and exposing the data to the element rules. Let's take a look at that now.
62	The *group* declaration creates a programming scope that we can call by name. This group contains a collection of element rules that are fired when the parser encounters certain elements in the input stream. The input stream, in this case, is the data sent here with the *do xml-parse* action on line 33.

The XML document we are processing looks like this:

```
<SOAP:Envelope
    xmlns:SOAP="urn:schemas-xmlsoap-org:soap.v1">
    <SOAP:Body>
        <getXMLNewsRequest
            xmlns="urn:schemas-architag-com:getXMLNews">
            <days>10</days>
            <format>XML</format>
            <fields>headline url abstract</fields>
        </getXMLNewsRequest>
    </SOAP:Body>
</SOAP:Envelope>
```

Line	Description
64–65	The *#implied* element rule will fire if no other element rule exists for a given event. This element rule will process all the elements in the SOAP namespace because we don't care about them at this point. All we really want are the number of days, the appropriate format for outputting, and the fields the user wants.
67–71	When the *format* element comes along, this element rule will fire, setting the format type to the appropriate value. The "*%c*" indicates the content of the element. Every element rule must process the contents exactly once with either the "*%c*" or *suppress*. (Note that the getXMLNews.xom program does not support any format type except raw XML.)
	The *days* element rule captures the *days* element and sets the appropriate variable.
73	This element rule will fire when the *fields* element comes along.

(continued)

Table 8-5. *continued*

Line	Description
74–79	The *repeat scan* control structure is similar to *do scan*, except it repeatedly processes the string until a character comes along that is not matched. The pattern following each *match* statement is evaluated to see whether it matches what is currently being scanned. As soon as a match is found in the loop, the actions underneath are processed and the process continues with the next character to be scanned.
	In this case, the contents are being scanned to see what fields are wanted. When a field is found, a new *fieldsWanted* item is created on the shelf.
81	This server program will run forever. You might need to kill the server for some reason. To kill the server, send the following code as one of the elements inside the SOAP request:
	`<die>poison-pill string</die>`
	This string is set in SOAP.xin. I recommend that you keep the string private, since anyone who can create a request package for your server can kill that request if he knows the poison pill string.
82–83	The poison pill string must be the only string inside the *die* element. Use the positional patterns, *content-start* and *content-end*, to achieve this.
84–85	If this string is found, an error will be sent to the console, and an exception thrown to the server-die catch,…
54–59	…which you'll find right here. This routine sends a single *msg* element, closes the connection, and exits the program gracefully.
38	Once we have all the data points we need, we can send the data back to the client, which should still be waiting for a response. The *responseXML* stream is used to establish a response stream. All we need to do is open the output connection, put data into it just as if it was a normal stream, and then close it. When the stream is closed, the data is sent back.
39–40	The *getXMLNews* function is described later. This function returns an XML document that contains the news, depending on the parameters selected.
42–43	OmniMark has rich exception-handling capabilities. Line 42 will catch any hard program errors. (These are run-time errors, such as those that result when trying to put data into an unopened stream or when accessing the value of an open stream.)
45–51	The exception handler in line 45 will catch external errors, such as trying to access a database that isn't open or trying to write to a read-only file.
52	This is the end of the repeat loop started in line 17.

getXMLNews return # function

```
1   macro outField token tagName is
2       do when fields has key tagName
3           put newsXML "%n          <%@(tagName)>"
4               || cleanString
5                   (dbFieldValue rsXMLNews key tagName)
6               || "</%@(tagName)>"
7       done
8   macro-end
9
10  define stream function getXMLNews (
11          value counter daysDesired,
12          value stream format,
13          read-only stream fields) as
14      local stream newsXML initial {""}
15      local dbDatabase dbXMLNews
16      local dbField rsXMLNews variable
17      local stream strSQL
18      local stream minusDate
19      local stream finalDate
20
21     set dbXMLNews to dbOpenODBC "XMLNews"
22     set minusDate to add-to-ymdhms now-as-ymdhms days -daysDesired
23     set finalDate to format-ymdhms "=xM/=xD/=xY" with -date minusDate
24      set strSQL to "SELECT * FROM News "
25          || "WHERE Date >= #%g(finalDate)# ORDER BY Date DESC"
26      dbQuery dbXMLNews sql strSQL record rsXMLNews
27
28      open newsXML as buffer
29      do when dbRecordExists rsXMLNews
30          put newsXML "%n<getXMLNewsResponse days='%d(daysWanted)'>"
31          repeat
32              exit unless dbRecordExists rsXMLNews
33              put newsXML "%n    <item date='"
34                  || dbFieldValue rsXMLNews key "date" || "'>"
35
36              outField "url"
37              outField "location"
38              outField "headline"
39              outField "abstract"
40
41              put newsXML "%n    </item>"
42              dbRecordMove rsXMLNews
43          again
44
```

Listing 8-9. *The OmniMark function that returns an XML document that will become the SOAP payload.*   *(continued)*

Listing 8-9. *continued*

```
45          put newsXML "%n</getXMLNewsResponse>"
46     else
47          put newsXML "%n<getXMLNewsResponse days='%d(daysWanted)'/>"
48     done
49
50     close newsXML
51     return newsXML
52
53     catch #external-exception
54            identity catch-id
55            message catch-msg
56            location catch-loc
57         output 'An external exception occurred.%n'
58         output '%g(catch-loc)%n'
59         output '%g(catch-id) : %g(catch-msg)%n'
```

Line	Description
10–13	OmniMark has two ways of creating callable sets of code. These lines contain a function definition. You can call functions from just about anywhere in an OmniMark program. This function, *getXMLNews*, returns a stream variable. The function is called with three arguments: a counter, a stream, and a shelf of streams.
14	The *newsXML* stream is where we build the XML document that we return as the SOAP payload.
15–16	The OmniMark Database library (OMDB) provides a set of objects and functions that simplify connecting to databases. Here we create two database objects: one for the ODBC database connection and one for a recordset that will be returned as the result of a SQL query.
21	The *dbOpenODBC* function opens an ODBC connection with the name *XMLNews* and returns a handle.
22–23	To build the SQL query, we need to calculate a date that is equal to a number of days prior to the current date. This offset is sent to us in the *daysDesired* argument to this function. The OmniMark date-time library has a number of functions that allow date mathematics. All dates are stored in a year-month-day-hour-minute-second format called *ymdhms*. First we determine the desired start day by subtracting *daysWanted* from the current day. Then we format that date into a form acceptable to the SQL processor. In this case, the date is in the form 4/26/2000.
24–25	We build the SQL query by plugging in the date calculated above. Then we send the query to the connected database with the *dbQuery* function. A recordset will be returned into *rsXMLNews*. This recordset is exposed as a shelf of an opaque data type defined by the OMDB functions.

Table 8-6. *Line-by-line description of server program in Listing 8-9.*

Line	Description
28	The *newsXML* stream is opened as a file-like buffer so that we can append to it.
29	The *dbRecordExists* function checks to see if the SQL query returned any records.
30	If the query did return any records, we need to start building the XML document with a root element of *getXMLNewsResponse*.
31–43	This *repeat...again* loop will execute once for each record returned from the query.
32	Once the last record is processed, the *dbRecordExists* function will return a *false*, at which time the *repeat...again* loop is exited.
34	We access the fields in the recordset object the same way we access keyed shelves—that is, we access their value by finding the item that has a certain key value. We use the *dbFieldValue* function to expose this information. This line will output the value of the field named *date* that was returned from the SQL recordset.
36–39	The *outField* macro will be called four times, passing the names of fields in the database.
1–8	Macros are simple yet powerful. A macro is really just a fancy string-replacement process done at pre-compile time. This macro will check to see whether the field indicated is one of the fields we asked for. If it is, the macro will create an element and put the value of the field inside.
42	The *dbRecordMove* function loads the next record into the *rsXMLNews* record set.
45	This line ends the *getXMLNewsResponse* document.
47	If no records return from the SQL query, we create an empty element, just so that we'll know nothing is there.
50–51	Close the stream and return it to the calling application.
53–59	This catch will execute if there is a problem with some external interface, usually caused by a file not found somewhere or some database trouble.

Testing the Service

Follow these steps to get our entire example running:

1. Start the getXMLNews service with the following command line:

```
omnimark -sb getXMLNews.xom -i "c:\omnimark\xin\"
-l "c:\omnimark\lib\=L.dll" -log getXMLNews.log
```

   The paths for the libraries (*-l*) and include files (*-i*) will vary depending on where you installed OmniMark.

2. Load the HTML driver program, getXMLNews.htm, into your Web browser.

3. Enter a value for the number of days, the format (remember that raw XML is the only format supported by this version), and the fields you want to see. Click Get News and watch the console run the service, as shown in Figure 8-5.

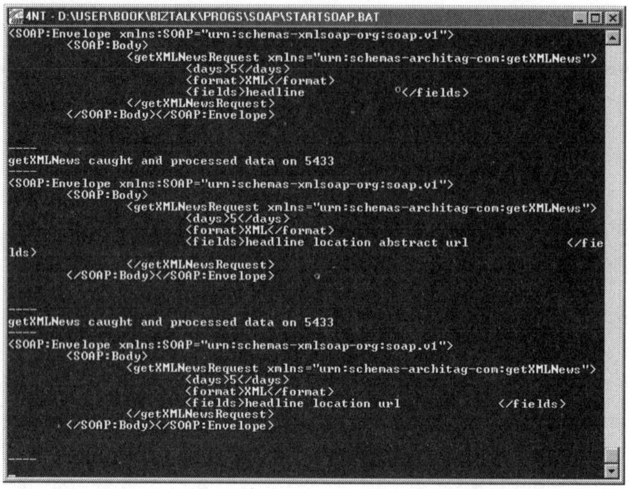

Figure 8-5. *The console showing output from getXMLNews.xom.*

Chapter 9

The BizTalk Framework

What happens if a hundred different companies all create their own schemas to describe an invoice? What are the chances that any of these schemas will be compatible? The schemas might contain the same elements, but each schema will use different element names. For example, all invoices will probably have invoice numbers, but the element names for invoice numbers might be called *InvNum*, *InvNo*, *InvoiceNo*, *InvoiceNum*, and so on. We could end up with a hundred different XML documents, all referencing the same data. Each document would have a different structure, making it difficult to share these documents among companies. If each of your business partners used its own schema, you would need to write a different program to work with each XML document. Clearly you wouldn't want to do that. You would want every partner to use the same structure.

The example I just described illustrates that we need a framework for developing industry schemas. This framework should specify a common set of elements for some objects but should also have enough flexibility to allow people to collaborate on the development of schemas. The BizTalk Framework tries to be just that.

The BizTalk Framework provides a set of rules and a set of starter tags for creating schemas for business-to-business (B2B) e-commerce. BizTalk was created to foster the use of XML by making it easier to build schemas that partners can share. A common set of rules for creating schemas will promote the creation of more schemas, which will make it easier for partners to agree upon which schema to use. The BizTalk Framework enables a broad audience to adopt a common approach to using XML.

To process BizTalk documents, you need a BizTalk Framework Compliant (BFC) server. The BizTalk Framework enables independent software vendors (ISVs) and developers to more easily map one business process to another, thereby allowing for faster adoption of electronic interchange in a wide variety of industries that are using XML. Further, by establishing a critical mass of schemas implemented in a consistent format, the BizTalk Framework provides a clear design target for tools and infrastructure ISVs building next generation products for e-commerce and application integration.

BizTalk comprises four facets of a single initiative:

- **The BizTalk Framework Independent Document Specification**   The BizTalk Framework is a set of tags that provides an addressing definition to get documents from one place to another and to invoke processing at each end. The BizTalk Framework works like a virtual envelope for sending business documents between trading partners. You can find a copy of this specification in Appendix B, and on the book's companion CD in the \References folder.

- **BizTalk.org**   BizTalk.org is a Web site that provides a place to learn about e-commerce technologies—XML in general and BizTalk in particular. This site has discussion groups offering peer support for developing (schemas) and help in integrating them into the BizTalk Framework. (I talk more about BizTalk.org in Appendix C.) BizTalk.org is also a repository for schemas, allowing you to post your schemas for others to access. This service is free.

- **BizTalk server**   To process your BizTalk documents, you'll need a BizTalk server, which is the software that reads BizTalk documents and then does something intelligent with them. The intelligent thing will depend on what systems you have in place and what needs to be done to process the documents. Consider other server software such as a mail server. Many different mail servers are available for companies to use. Mail servers run on any computer platform and range in price from free to expensive. Similarly, a BizTalk server can be written in any language to run on any computer platform. Several companies are working on servers that will process BizTalk documents and integrate with corporate back-end systems. You will see an example of a basic BizTalk server in Chapter 11.

- **Microsoft BizTalk Server 2000**   The Microsoft BizTalk Server 2000 runs on Microsoft Windows 2000 Server only. Because of the nature of the open specification BizTalk Framework, you can create BizTalk messages on a Linux system running a BizTalk server written in Java, and read the messages on a Windows 2000 Advanced Server using Microsoft BizTalk Server 2000. Microsoft BizTalk Server 2000 is more than just a piece of software that writes and reads BizTalk documents. The product contains a complete B2B integration environment that allows you to communicate with your business partners using XML.

THE BIZTALK DOCUMENT AND MESSAGE SPECIFICATION

The BizTalk Framework promotes the use of XML in B2B transactions by proposing a structure for creating XML documents. In this section, you will learn more about the BizTalk Framework.

Some people say that using XML to encode data is like using ASCII to produce text documents: the format is so flexible that no two uncoordinated efforts wind up being compatible. Let's say you use ASCII to encode your documents. I should be able to read them, right? Well, let's say that you write in French and read in English. Even though we are both using ASCII, we can't necessarily communicate. Using the same encoding technique just means that I can read your files on my machine. Full understanding doesn't take place until I can understand the framework in which you create your information. We have the same problem with XML. Just because you create an XML document doesn't mean that I can understand it. It just means that I can assure the document follows the rules of XML syntax and, if a schema is available, whether the document is valid according to the structure defined in the schema.

The problems with using XML to describe information range from deciding what to describe to deciding what to name each field. Once users get beyond these important issues, they need to tag their data so that another party or application can recognize what has been sent.

The BizTalk Framework provides a way for developers to write applications that can more easily process XML documents. The BizTalk Framework defines a set of tags and provides design guidelines and ideas for creating your own tag sets for exchanging information with your business partners. In other words, the BizTalk Framework defines a consistent way to use XML. As a result, you can easily determine what type of XML document you have received and what information the document contains.

The BizTalk Framework views XML documents as messages that businesses pass around. It is concerned partly with how these documents are created and partly with how they are routed. The BizTalk Framework provides the mechanisms to programmatically "mail" XML documents.

Many industries are working on schemas devoted to solving the information interchange problems in their particular industry. These schemas can't necessarily be shared across industries. A schema written to transmit medical records, for example, is not appropriate for financial transactions. An insurance claim schema would not be used for real estate transactions. These industry groups are concerned with defining the data structures, not necessarily with how the transactions get from one place to another.

BizTalk is driven by Microsoft and includes many organizations on its steering committee, including Ariba, Boeing, Compaq, J.D. Edwards, SAP, webMethods, UPS. Because many different industries are collaborating, BizTalk is a little different from efforts being made by particular industries or global organizations. BizTalk provides a framework for integration by specifying how to get information from one place to another.

As you will see, the actual information being sent can be any document using any schema. In this way, BizTalk becomes the wrapper for business documents, much like a paper envelope works now. Let's take a look at a typical business transaction the old way, and then see how we might use XML to do the same transaction.

THE BIZTALK FRAMEWORK IN B2B TRANSACTIONS

Let's look at a scenario of a business that will enable B2B transactions by using the BizTalk Framework to create XML documents.

We are a manufacturer of radio-controlled toy cars: *serious* toy cars. Our cars run on gasoline and have enough of a range to chase dogs and small children around the neighborhood. To make our toy cars, we buy parts, supplies, and services from a number of suppliers. These suppliers also have their own suppliers and other customers.

We want to use the Web to communicate with our suppliers and also to keep in touch with our customers, both retail stores and end-users. And of course we want to reuse as much of our existing processes as possible.

Preparing the Purchase Order

An event triggers the need for a business transaction. This event might be someone in an organization wanting to buy a product from a vendor. This particular event requires a purchase order to be sent to the organization.

Let's say my company wants to buy 10 small engines from your company. One of the procedures in my company is to create a purchase requisition form, which has fields that help the appropriate people process the request. This is an internal document designed to communicate between departments in my company.

After I fill out the purchase requisition, I give it to the person in my organization responsible for processing requisitions and creating purchase orders. Her name is Jean. Jean knows the business rules for processing these documents and will use these rules to deal with my request.

The first thing that Jean does is make sure I have the authority to spend the company's money. Jean looks at her list of budget approvers and notices that my name is on the list and that I have enough authority for this purchase.

Next Jean makes sure we don't already have a store of the products I requested in stock. Ordering parts that we already have in stock is a bad business idea, and this business rule has been put in place to prevent that possibility.

Once Jean is satisfied that my order is valid, she adds my purchase requisition to the pile of purchase requisitions in one corner of her desk. Other people in my company want to buy products from your company. As part of the agreement between your company and mine, we promise that, unless the order is an emergency requisition, no purchase order is made until there are at least three requisitions to order items from your company. It so happens that Jean notices two other purchase requisitions for items from your company, so it's time to create a purchase order with these three items.

Jean pulls up a form in her word processor and starts filling out the fields. The form has fields for address information, financial data, and shipping terms, and a place to put the part numbers, descriptions, and prices.

Jean completes the form and prints it. Then she pulls up a form for another document—a #10 paper envelope. She types my company's name and address in the upper left-hand corner and your company's name and address in the center of the envelope. She doesn't need to explicitly say that the address in the center of the envelope is the "To" address and the other is the "From" address. From centuries of convention, we all know that the address in the center of the envelope is the destination address and the address in the upper left-hand corner is the return address.

Above your company's address, Jean puts an important piece of information: *Attn: Purchase Order Processing Department*. Later we will see that this is an invocation of a method that causes your company to perform certain actions.

Jean prints the envelope, folds the purchase order document, puts it in the envelope, seals it, and adds proper postage. Then she walks down to the corner and puts the envelope in a blue box. Through the magic of the U.S. Postal Service, the envelope takes a mysterious journey that ends in your company's mailroom. This is an important part of the story.

If our two companies had to design a purchase order delivery system—that is, if we didn't have the infrastructure provided by the post office—we would have spent much of our time designing the delivery system, instead of dealing with the more direct business of ordering parts. We would need to develop an addressing structure, hire couriers or contract courier services, and worry about insurance, accidents, and a thousand other problems. Lucky for us, an infrastructure is already in place that we can use for a small fee.

It's also important to note that Jean had several options for delivering the message from my company to yours. She used the U.S. Postal Service, but she could also have used FedEx, Airborne Express, or even a local courier if our companies were within bicycling distance of each other. She also could have faxed the order, sent it by e-mail, or even posted it to a Web page interface.

A couple of days later, the envelope shows up at your company's mailroom. The mailroom clerk notices the *Attn: Purchase Order Processing Department* designation Jean placed at the top of the address block and routes the envelope internally to the person responsible for processing purchase orders, whose name is David.

Processing the Purchase Order

David looks at the envelope, notes who sent it, and then opens the envelope and takes the business document out. David is responsible for processing many different kinds of business documents. He deals with purchase orders, invoices, and Requests for Proposals (RFP), among others.

David notices that the document is a purchase order, so he goes into "purchase order process" mode. David is the keeper of your company's business rules for processing a purchase order. First David makes sure that your company and mine have a business arrangement for doing these transactions. This business arrangement probably states terms and conditions such as shipping times, return policies, and payment details. He then checks to make sure that my company has paid its bills and that no transactions between our companies are in dispute. Sending items to a company that is not paying is a bad business idea.

Once David is satisfied that your company has a current business arrangement with mine, he moves over to his purchase order processing system and transcribes the information from our purchase order to his system, using the business rules that your company has in place. One of your rules is to send a request to the warehouse to see whether the items requested in the purchase order are in stock.

David finds out that two of the three items are in stock and can ship immediately, but the third is out of stock and must be back-ordered. As part of our contractual arrangement, your company promises to send me a confirmation of the purchase order Jean sent to David. So David brings up a form in his word processor and fills out the information required. He notes that two of our items will ship today and the third needs to be back-ordered.

David prints the form, brings up an envelope form, and types two addresses. He refers to the envelope that Jean sent him and swaps the two address blocks, putting my company's address in the center and your company's address in the upper left-hand corner.

He takes out the envelope, folds and inserts the confirmation, seals the envelope, adds the proper postage, and drops it in a mailbox. A couple of days later, Jean gets the confirmation and processes it according to my company's business rules. One of those rules is to contact the three people in the company who made purchase requests and tell them the status of their orders. The one person who ordered parts that are back-ordered might want to have Jean send a cancellation order to your company and place a new order to another supplier of that particular part. This event would trigger certain other business rules on both sides of the transaction.

This is just one scenario. Jean has other ways to deal with purchase requisitions. For example, if an order is a rush, Jean might not need to combine it with two other items. Jean might also fax a rush order directly to David or even call him on the phone to confirm that he received the order. Sometimes Jean might decide to send a purchase order and supporting documents by overnight courier. These are transport issues, but Jean can make many other decisions to make her job more effective. She makes each one of these decisions based on business rules.

The point is that certain rules have been in place for the life of my company and other rules have been in place at your company. The advent of XML will not change the requirements either of our companies have for doing business. All we can expect XML and the BizTalk framework to do is to help us do business more effectively.

Interchange Evolution

My example company has developed a set of applications and business processes that allow it to do business. We select computer programs, interfaces, and employees to make everything work.

You also have selected a set of applications and business processes that work well for your business. However, our systems are probably completely incompatible. Our companies use paper as the universal interchange format for exchanging business information, but human interpretation is required to process the paperwork.

The interpreter needs to know the business rules and be able to perform the translation. In our case study, Jean and David fill that role for our respective companies.

The transaction I described does not happen in a vacuum. Before I sent any purchase orders, your company and my company formed a contractual arrangement for doing business. That contract set out specific terms for payment, shipping, dispute resolution, and other things businesses need to do business. Part of this contractual arrangement was the form in which our transactions take place. In the case of a purchase order, you told us what kind of information you needed to successfully process the order, and we told you in what format we would like to see the confirmation.

This type of transaction has been happening for centuries and works well, but an automated system that emulates it would be useful for making the transaction more efficient. The BizTalk Framework emulates this model for getting information from one place to the other.

Ordering by Using the BizTalk Framework

A BizTalk document is a SOAP 1.1 message in which the body of the message contains one or more business documents. The SOAP envelope is described in Chapter 8. Figure 9-1 illustrates the different parts of a BizTalk document.

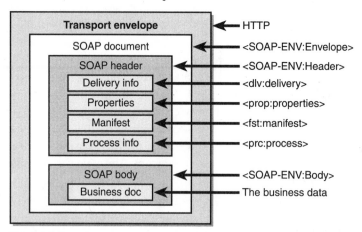

Figure 9-1. *A BizTalk document is a SOAP 1.1 message that has a number of elements designed to route and deliver business documents.*

A BizTalk document can be thought of as an extension of a SOAP document. The set of elements in a BizTalk document come from several namespaces, each one optimized for a particular purpose. The tags in these namespaces are called BizTags.

The entire document is contained in the SOAP *Envelope* element—that is, *Envelope* is the document's root element. As you might recall from Chapter 8 and as illustrated in Figure 9-1, a SOAP document consists of an optional *Header* element and a required *Body* element. In a BizTalk message, the *SOAP:Header* element is required because it contains some required BizTags. The *SOAP:Body* element contains the business data, which consists of one or more business documents.

Table 9-1 lists the BizTags in the BizTalk header's *SOAP:Header* element. Each one of these elements has its own namespace, which you can learn more about at the *schemas.biztalk.org* site.

BizTag Name	*Required*	*Namespace*
delivery	Yes	*http://schemas.biztalk.org/btf-2-0/delivery*
properties	Yes	*http://schemas.biztalk.org/btf-2-0/properties*
manifest	No	*http://schemas.biztalk.org/btf-2-0/manifest*
process	No	*http://schemas.biztalk.org/btf-2-0/process*

Table 9-1. *The elements contained in the BizTalk header's* SOAP:Header *element.*

The BizTalk document by itself can't really do anything until you send it somewhere. Transporting the document is the job of the transport envelope, which can be just about any electronic transfer protocol, such as HTTP, SMTP, or FTP. The BizTalk 2.0 specification describes only HTTP bindings.

Let's take a look at the BizTalk Framework tag set in action. Listing 9-1 shows a BizTalk document that provides the same data as the envelope and paper case study with Jean and David. Table 9-2, which follows the listing, describes this document line by line. Appendix B contains the BizTalk Framework 2.0 Document and Message Specification in its entirety.

NewPO.xml

```
1<?xml version="1.0"?>
2<SOAP-ENV:Envelope
3    xmlns:SOAP-ENV="http://schemas.xmlsoap.org/soap/envelope/"
4    xmlns:SOAP-ENC="http://schemas.xmlsoap.org/soap/encoding/"
5    xmlns:xsi="http://www.w3.org/1999/XMLSchema-instance">
6    <SOAP-ENV:Header>
7        <dlv:delivery SOAP-ENV:mustUnderstand="1"
8            xmlns:dlv="http://schemas.biztalk.org/btf-2-0/delivery"
9            xmlns:agr="http://www.trading-agreements.org/types/">
10            <dlv:to>
11 <dlv:address xsi:type="agr:department">Toy Car Parts</dlv:address>
12            </dlv:to>
13            <dlv:from>
14 <dlv:address xsi:type="agr:organization">Toi Carz</dlv:address>
15            </dlv:from>
16            <dlv:reliability>
17 <dlv:confirmTo>http://toicarz.com/biztalk/confirm.asp</dlv:confirmTo>
18 <dlv:receiptRequiredBy>2000-07-7T08:00:00+08:00</dlv:receiptRequiredBy>
19            </dlv:reliability>
20        </dlv:delivery>
21        <prop:properties SOAP-ENV:mustUnderstand="1"
22            xmlns:prop="http://schemas.biztalk.org/btf-2-0/properties">
23 <prop:identity>uuid:74b9f5d0 33fb 4a81 b02b 5b760641c1d6</prop:identity>
24            <prop:sentAt>2000-05-14T03:00:00+08:00</prop:sentAt>
25            <prop:expiresAt>2000-05-15T04:00:00+08:00</prop:expiresAt>
26            <prop:topic>http://toycarparts.com/BTServer.xar</prop:topic>
27        </prop:properties>
28 <fst:manifest xmlns:fst="http://schemas.biztalk.org/btf-2-0/manifest">
29            <fst:reference fst:uri="#PurchaseOrderBody">
30                <fst:description>Purchase Order</fst:description>
31            </fst:reference>
32            <fst:reference fst:uri="toicarz.sig">
33                <fst:description>Digital signature</fst:description>
34            </fst:reference>
35        </fst:manifest>
```

Listing 9-1. *A BizTalk document containing a purchase order.*   *(continued)*

NewPO.xml *continued*

```
36    </SOAP-ENV:Header>
37
38    <SOAP-ENV:Body>
39        <PurchaseOrder_1.0
40            xmlns="x-schema:http://toicarz.com/schemas/PurchaseOrder.xdr"
41            id="PurchaseOrderBody"
42            type="order"
43            PONumber="10-01-2118">
44            <Item number="122-11" quantity="100"/>
45            <Item number="237-82" quantity="10"/>
46            <Item number="811-91" quantity="25"/>
47        </PurchaseOrder_1.0>
48    </SOAP-ENV:Body>
49</SOAP-ENV:Envelope>
```

Line	Description
1	This is an XML document, so it begins with the XML declaration.
2	An XML document must have a single root element that starts at the top of the document and ends at the bottom. Since this is a SOAP envelope, the root element for this BizTalk 2.0 document is *SOAP-ENV:Envelope*.
3–5	This document uses three XML namespace declarations to indicate the schemas that will be used by the SOAP envelope.
6–39	The *SOAP-ENV:Header* BizTag contains identification and routing information for your BizTalk document.
7–20	The *dlv:delivery* BizTag contains information about the delivery and confirmation of the document.
7	The *mustUnderstand* attribute tells the receiving application that it must understand what it is getting. If it doesn't understand, it must return a SOAP fault element rather than try to fake the processing.
8	The delivery BizTags are found in the namespace indicated by this namespace declaration.
9	Another namespace that points to a set of trading partner agreements is declared.
10	The *dlv:to* BizTag indicates the name of the entity that will be receiving your document.
11	The *xsl:type* attribute indicates the data type according to the XML Schema Part 2: Datatypes Working Draft, which is published by the W3C.
12	The *to* data type is defined in the trading-partner agreement schema.
13–15	The *from* address takes the same form and contains the same attribute type as the *to* address.

Table 9-2. *Line-by-line description of the BizTalk document in Listing 9-1.*

Line	*Description*
16–19	The BizTalk server creating a message document can ask for confirmation that the message is received. This is done by adding an optional BizTag, *dlv:reliability*.
17	The *dlv:confirmTo* BizTag gives an address to which a receipt will be sent.
18	If the transmitting system does not get a receipt by the time indicated in the *dlv:receiptRequiredBy* BizTag , the transmitting system should resend the document.
21–27	The properties section defines certain properties of the BizTalk document.
22	The BizTags in the *prop:properties* element belong to the namespace indicated by the namespace declaration.
23	The *prop:identity* BizTag contains a Universally Unique Identifier (UUID). Most platforms have a way of generating this identifier.
24	The *prop:sentAt* BizTag contains a timestamp indicating the document was sent. This is a datetime.tz data type.
25	The *prop:expiresAt* BizTag contains the time the document expires. After this time, the associated BizTalk document is considered to be expired and must not be processed by the destination business entity.
26	The *prop:topic* BizTag contains the address of the BizTalk processor that will process the document.
28–35	The *fst:manifest* BizTag is optional. It contains a catalog indicating the contents of the BizTalk document.
29–31	The *fst:reference* BizTag occurs one or more times. It indicates the Uniform Resource Identifier (URI) and provides a description of what is in the BizTalk document. The first *fst:reference* element is a pointer to the document in the *Body* element of the SOAP *Envelope*.
32–34	This document also contains a digital signature file to guarantee the originator of the document. This will probably be included in the transport envelope as a MIME-encoded attachment.
38–48	The *SOAP-ENV:Body* element follows the *SOAP-ENV:Header* element. The *Body* element is analogous to the inside of the paper envelope in our case study. The *Body* element contains your business document and is defined using your schema.
40	Because your schema defines your document, you need to use a namespace declaration to indicate the location of the schema. In our case, we are using a schema called PurchaseOrder.xdr, which is located on our server. The receiving application will be able to find this schema if that application has access to the Web.
41–49	All that remains is the remainder of the purchase order itself and the closing tags to the *PurchaseOrder_1.0* element, the *SPOAP-ENV:Body* element, and the SOAP envelope, *SOAP-ENV:Envelope*.

The BizTalk document is actually two different documents. One document replaces the general-purpose paper envelope; the other document replaces the paper document inside that envelope. The innovation of namespaces and XML schemas allows us to create our virtual envelope and the virtual document inside.

NOTE   Remember that the document type definition schema syntax allows only a single document type in a document. A BizTalk document has at least two document types, which is allowed with the XML Data Reduced (XDR) schema syntax. This type of BizTalk transaction processing is not possible if you are using the document type definition (DTD) schema syntax.

When your company receives the XML document in Listing 9-1, a BizTalk server will read it and look for the information inside. First the BizTalk server will look at the *dlv:to* BizTag to determine which partner is to receive the document. Then the BizTalk server will probably parse the rest of the data items so that it can make an entry in an order-tracking database. Finally the server will take the actual order—the thing in the *SOAP-ENV:Body* element—and pass that order to an application that will process it. This processing depends entirely upon the systems each company has in place.

Delivery Receipt

Since we included the *dlv:reliability* BizTag, the receiving BizTalk server is required to send us a receipt. This receipt is shown in Listing 9-2.

Receipt.xml

```
<SOAP-ENV:Envelope
        xmlns:SOAP-ENV="http://schemas.xmlsoap.org/soap/envelope/">
  <SOAP-ENV:Header>
        <rct:receipt SOAP-ENV:mustUnderstand="1"
              xmlns:rct="http://schemas.biztalk.org/btf-2-0/receipt">
            <rct:receivedAt>2000-05-15T04:08:10-05:30</rct:receivedAt>
        </rct:receipt>
        <prop:properties SOAP-ENV:mustUnderstand="1"
            xmlns:prop="http://schemas.biztalk.org/btf-2-0/properties">
  <prop:identity>uuid:74b9f5d0-33fb-4a81-b02b-5b7606387dc1</
prop:identity>
            <prop:sentAt>2000-05-14T03:00:00+08:00</prop:sentAt>
            <prop:expiresAt>2000-05-15T04:00:00+08:00</prop:expiresAt>
            <prop:topic>http://toycarparts.com/POProc.asp</prop:topic>
        </prop:properties>
  </SOAP-ENV:Header>
  <SOAP-ENV:Body/>
</SOAP-ENV:Envelope>
```

Listing 9-2. *The receipt generated by the BizTalk server.*

The header of this document is similar to the header of the message that was sent. The only things that changed were the unique identifier in the *prop:identity* BizTag and the timestamps.

Notice in Listing 9-2 that the *SOAP-ENV:Body* element is empty. Although this element is required, it doesn't need any contents because the receipt document is just an indicator that the document was received properly.

The Order Confirmation

Once your back-end system confirms the order, you will create a BizTalk document that has the information we need to close out our order. Listing 9-3 shows the document; Table 9-3 describes it line by line.

Confirm.xml

```
1 <?xml version="1.0"?>
2 <SOAP-ENV:Envelope
3    xmlns:SOAP-ENV="http://schemas.xmlsoap.org/soap/envelope/"
4    xmlns:SOAP-ENC="http://schemas.xmlsoap.org/soap/encoding/"
5    xmlns:xsi="http://www.w3.org/1999/XMLSchema-instance">
6    <SOAP-ENV:Header>
7        <dlv:delivery SOAP-ENV:mustUnderstand="1"
8            xmlns:dlv="http://schemas.biztalk.org/btf-2-0/delivery"
9            xmlns:agr="http://www.trading-agreements.org/types/">
10           <dlv:to>
11 <dlv:address xsi:type="agr:department">Toi Carz</dlv:address>
12           </dlv:to>
13           <dlv:from>
14 <dlv:address xsi:type="agr:organization">Toy Car Parts</dlv:address>
15           </dlv:from>
16           <dlv:reliability>
17 <dlv:confirmTo>http://toycarparts.com/BTServer.xar</dlv:confirmTo>
18 <dlv:receiptRequiredBy>2000-07-7T08:00:00+08:00</dlv:receiptRequiredBy>
19           </dlv:reliability>
20       </dlv:delivery>
21       <prop:properties SOAP-ENV:mustUnderstand="1"
22           xmlns:prop="http://schemas.biztalk.org/btf-2-0/properties">
23 <prop:identity>uuid:74b9f5d0-33fb-4a81-b02b-5b7606434d3</prop:identity>
24           <prop:sentAt>2000-05-16T03:00:00+08:00</prop:sentAt>
25           <prop:expiresAt>2000-05-17T04:00:00+08:00</prop:expiresAt>
26           <prop:topic>http://toicarz.com/biztalk/confirm.asp</prop:topic>
27       </prop:properties>
```

Listing 9-3. *A BizTalk document that confirms a purchase order sent from one company to another.*   *(continued)*

Confirm.xml *continued*

```
28      </SOAP-ENV:Header>
29
30      <SOAP-ENV:Body>
31          <PurchaseOrder_1.0
32              xmlns="x-schema:http://toicarz.com/schemas/PurchaseOrder.xdr"
33              type="confirm"
34              PONumber="10-01-2118">
35              <Item number="122-11" quantity="100" shipped="100"/>
36              <Item number="237-82" quantity="10" shipped ="0"
37                  backordered="10"/>
38              <Item number="811-91" quantity="25" shipped="25"/>
39          </PurchaseOrder_1.0>
40      </SOAP-ENV:Body>
41 </SOAP-ENV:Envelope>
```

Line	Description
1	This is an XML document, so it begins with the XML declaration.
6–28	The structure of this *SOAP-ENV:Header* element is pretty much the same as the one that initiated the process, but this one contains information about the response document.
11, 14	The to and from addresses have been swapped.
30	The beginning SOAP document's *Body* element.
31–39	Notice that the confirmation document uses the same schema as the original purchase order in NewPO.xml. This isn't necessary; a confirmation document can have an entirely different schema for the *Body* element. In our case, we differentiate the function of the document by changing the *type* attribute in line 33 to *confirm*.
40–41	The closing tags to the *Body* element and the *Envelope*.

Table 9-3. *Description of the document in Listing 9-3.*

XML is a powerful syntax for communicating business transactions. As you have seen in this chapter, XML defines the entire transaction by using two independent schemas: the BizTalk message envelope and our purchase order.

Because BizTalk is rooted in XML, it is compatible with any business document specification, including those I mentioned earlier. BizTalk is an open specification that can be used by anyone who needs to do B2B e-commerce.

When your company's system receives this envelope at *http://toycarparts.com*, The BTServer.xar script will start processing the purchase order. This process replaces the work of David in our initial example. It will apply the same business rules that David used and send a confirmation in the form of a BizTalk document back to my company.

Potential for Automating Procurement

The scenario illustrated by the BizTalk request, confirmation, and response documents duplicates the manual processing that Jean and David have been performing for years. The big win in our scenario is that we have replaced humans with dependable computer processes, allowing us to do business faster and more efficiently. Don't worry about Jean and David, however. We promoted them because of their help in getting our BizTalk systems up and running. Jean and David are now vital resources for their organizations because of their knowledge of internal systems and the requirements for creating B2B applications in other areas of the company.

Of course, when computers replace people, errors replicate much faster, so debugging is of critical importance; no human cognitive processes are in place to make sure everything *looks* right.

No matter how great the system I've described here is, we are not taking full advantage of new technologies in the way we could be. The BizTalk server, acting as Jean's replacement, still gets catalogs from vendors. (Of course, these are also BizTalk messages that go through a different workflow in order to be added to our list of products that can be ordered.) These arrive at a leisurely pace, whenever the vendor gets a chance or has a product change. Assume that for most products ordered by my company, multiple vendors can provide suitable items.

At any given time, the system that our company uses to decide which vendor to place an order with doesn't know what each vendor has in stock and therefore runs the risk of finding out an item was back-ordered.

In the old system, Jean had time to consider only a small number of possible vendors when she was looking for the best combination of price and delivery for any given item. She could save money if she could look at several dozen different vendors, and she could save even more if she could look at thousands.

If each vendor with whom we do business exposed catalog and warehouse information to us in real time as Web services, we could ask each vendor whether a quantity of a particular part was in stock and how much it cost before we tried to place an order. We could use SOAP to request this information from thousands of potential vendors in a small amount of time. Once we determined our best combination of quality, availability, and price, we could create a formal purchase order, using BizTalk as the workflow package. We would potentially save a good deal of money by shopping around and placing our orders through BizTalk, and we would rarely get a notification that a part was back-ordered.

This scenario—which already describes what some companies are doing—turns the ordering process upside down. The process is called a reverse auction: vendors compete to provide their wares to a requesting organization by offering lower and lower prices in response to a bid from the purchaser. Real-time Web services can make reverse auctions a reality. As open standards that run on any platform, SOAP and BizTalk can help foster widespread acceptance of these practices.

Part III

The BizTalk Server

A BizTalk server is the piece of software that processes BizTalk documents. A BizTalk server can be as simple as a filter that reads a BizTalk document, looks for particular pieces of information, and passes that information to processes that can handle it. Or a BizTalk server can be as complex as an enterprise-level application that manages partner relationships, tracks critical-path workflow, maintains information about data transformation, and interfaces with legacy and new systems.

In Part III, you will learn about what you need to consider when developing your own BizTalk server or evaluating a commercial

BizTalk server for your organization. We will build two simple BizTalk servers, one that runs in a Windows DNA environment and one that runs on a non-Windows platform.

BizTalk System Requirements

A BizTalk server is the software that reads and processes BizTalk documents. Since the BizTalk Framework is a self-describing structure that uses XML syntax, an application that acts as a BizTalk server needs to understand XML—in other words, the server must have the ability to load an XML document and access its contents. That ability is really the only basic requirement of a BizTalk server. Of course, a server that can only load and access an XML document would not be of much use in an enterprise computing environment. The BizTalk Framework 2.0 Document and Message Specification calls the software that performs these basic tasks a BizTalk Framework Compliant server, or BFC server.

In this chapter, I mention many requirements that you might want to look for when you are selecting or building a BizTalk server for your environment. If you use my basic definition, you can see that a BizTalk server can be as simple as a filter that reads a BizTalk document, looks for particular pieces of information in the package, and sends that information—in pieces or as an entire document—to the appropriate application. Or a BizTalk server can be as sophisticated as a critical component in an integrated supply-chain management system. A BizTalk server can be the application around which an entire enterprise does business with its trading partners.

You can write a BizTalk server to run on any operating system platform and in any computer language that can invoke an XML processing application. A BizTalk server can run on any operating system, including Microsoft Windows and UNIX and can be written in platform-independent languages such as Java, Python, or OmniMark.

Your BizTalk server should be flexible enough to adapt to changing requirements in a dynamic business environment, have a sophisticated interface that allows it to coexist with and drive legacy applications, and be owned by your business users, who will operate it on a day-by-day basis. Your BizTalk server should allow for cross-platform and cross-language interactions, because not everyone uses the same systems. In this chapter, we'll review the necessary features of your BizTalk server. In Chapter 11, we'll look at examples of some of these features.

RELIABLE DELIVERY OVER ANY TRANSPORT

A BizTalk document sitting by itself is a thing of beauty. However, it's meant to be used—not just admired and appreciated. A BizTalk document needs to be transported so that it can achieve its purpose. Getting your BizTalk document from your company to your trading partner's company requires some sort of delivery system. Since you are dealing with electronic information, you can make this delivery by using any process that transfers bits from place to place.

HTTP is the easiest way to transport these bits. HTTP is everywhere, and virtually all firewalls in the world allow HTTP calls to pass through them without question. But not all your vendors will have the ability to receive requests through HTTP, and some might feel uncomfortable transferring plain text over HTTP. One alternative to HTTP is File Transport Protocol (FTP), which requires a user ID and password. This login layer reduces the risk of receiving bogus messages. If your trading partners don't have FTP servers, they are likely to have e-mail. Your BizTalk server should be able to send messages over the Simple Mail Transport Protocol (SMTP). An SMTP server is designed to forward e-mail messages around the Internet.

If your trading partners are living back in the twentieth century, they might not even have e-mail, so a more primitive means of transporting your BizTalk documents might be necessary. For maximum flexibility, your BizTalk server should have the ability to send messages to a fax machine or even be able to print out messages so that you can send them by postal courier. These protocols are designed to deliver documents for humans to read, so your BizTalk server should also have the ability to render your business documents in a way that is suitable for a human audience.

The main problem with HTTP, FTP, and SMTP is that they are unencrypted by default. This problem is made worse by the fact that these transport protocols usually rely on the Internet, which exposes your request to anyone who has the ability to sniff TCP packets. That brings us to the next requirement: security.

SECURITY

Sending BizTalk documents over HTTP presents a possible security risk. Since HTTP documents exist as clear text streams, it is possible for someone to read a message as it travels to its destination. The BizTalk Framework 2.0 specification provides for the ability to secure your BizTalk document using the S/MIME or PKCS security layers. You can, however, use other security layes if you wish.

An easy way to deal with the problem of open transactions is by using the HTTPS protocol. HTTPS ("S" stands for Secure) is used widely on the Web to protect transactions involving sensitive information such as account balances or credit card numbers. HTTPS relies on public key encryption to armor packets between the client and the server. When a client (usually a Web browser) requests a secure document, the Web server sends it an encryption key. During the rest of the session, the client uses that key to encrypt data. Only the server has the ability to decrypt the data. Public key encryption involves some complicated math concepts that I don't understand, but I do know that they have to do with finding factors by multiplying two very large prime numbers. Anyway, HTTPS works pretty well, depending on the length of the encryption key used. If you're concerned about security, you should upgrade your HTTPS servers to use the greatest key lengths available.

Your BizTalk server should have the ability to provide a secure transmission protocol that wraps around the document, keeping it safe from prying eyes. You'll also need to deal with the issue of unauthorized documents flowing to one of your trading partners. If one of your partners receives BizTalk requests as plain text over a public facility such as HTTP, the possibility exists that someone will send your partner a message that appears to be coming from you. This malicious behavior—known as spoofing—has been around since the earliest days of e-mail.

Your BizTalk server should allow you to attach some kind of digital signature to your message. Including a digital signature can be as easy as using the *attachment* element of the BizTalk document spec or can be more complex: you can attach the digital signature to the document in a way that depends on the transport-specific envelope.

ROUTING

The most important functionality of a BizTalk server is getting your documents from your system to someone else's system. This functionality might be as simple as posting a request to a Web server over HTTP, or it might require a complex set of routing steps to get around firewalls or other security measures. In addition, when you receive a response from your trading partner, you will probably need to route the response internally to the appropriate department.

Think about a municipal clerk. When you go to a municipal building, you submit forms at a window. You might have forms for paying a parking ticket or traffic ticket. You might have forms for building an extension onto your house. You might have an application for the state to recognize a marriage. The clerk behind the window routes your forms to the appropriate department in the building. This generalized clerical front-end saves you from having to decide which office door in the municipal building you should enter to deliver that form.

Your BizTalk server operates like that clerk: It must be able to recognize which kind of document is coming in and route that document to the appropriate party for processing. This routing usually involves kicking off a workflow process that is appropriate for each type of transaction.

WORKFLOW

When you receive a BizTalk document, certain things need to happen. First the document must be deconstructed into its various parts so that an application can find out what kind of document it is. For example, the application needs to access the information in the *address* and *state* fields so that it can find out where the document came from and what kind of process it needs to attach to the document. The *address* field is part of what determines the workflow that the BizTalk document will fire when it is received.

Once you know the document's identity and purpose, you can start the process of getting the document what it needs to achieve that purpose. This requires a workflow. To process a purchase order, for example, you might want to first find out whether the company requesting the products has a current relationship with your company and whether their account is in arrears. Then you might check to see whether the items requested are in stock or whether you need to purchase, build, or manufacture the items to fulfill the request.

Your BizTalk server should have some way of kicking off the appropriate workflow when a document comes in. An advanced BizTalk server will have some way to create and manage these workflows so that the application can easily access them and so that the users responsible for making the system work efficiently can maintain them.

SYNCHRONOUS AND ASYNCHRONOUS COMMUNICATION

In Chapter 9, you saw the structure of a BizTalk message. You send BizTalk messages to your trading partners in a number of ways. Once you create a BizTalk message, you must wrap it in some kind of transport-specific envelope so that it can get somewhere.

Your BizTalk server should have a way of sending messages synchronously. In synchronous communication, the server sends a document to another BizTalk server and waits for a response. This is a basic requirement and is the least complex way to send messages.

In a production environment, however, you might be sending dozens or even hundreds or thousands of BizTalk messages from your application. If your application had to worry about getting a response from each request, you might end up with bottlenecks. Therefore, you should also have an asynchronous method of sending messages.

QUEUING

Your BizTalk server should have a way of queuing messages so that it can move on to the next task. Remotely queuing messages is handy because it offloads the transmission details, but it requires a way to get status information back to the server. If, for example, a server sends a message to a queue and then moves on to the next task, the server has no idea whether the queuing mechanism was able to successfully deliver the package.

BATCH SUPPORT

BizTalk documents might be generated all day. Your relationship with some of your trading partners might require you to send them transactions only once a day during certain hours or only on particular days of the month. Your BizTalk server should have the ability to designate individual delivery of BizTalk documents, but it should also have the ability to send documents in a batch to a particular trading partner, if that is what the relationship requires.

DOCUMENT TRACKING AND ACTIVITY

In a queued environment, it is important to get information back to the server in case something goes wrong. For example, if the transfer of data is not completed, the server needs to know this so that it can try and resend the data or cancel the transaction. It is also desirable to have some way that operators can interrogate the status of a particular message or get statistics of the processes in general.

Your BizTalk server should have sophisticated transaction-tracking information, which might include the following features:

- Tracking documents individually or in batches
- Determining whether a document was delivered properly
- Querying the tracking database based on a document, a trading partner, or an activity
- Attaching time stamps for every activity a document takes
- Storing user-defined data, such as aggregate totals of purchase orders for easily reporting account activity on a partner-by-partner basis

All this data should be available at any time during the document's lifetime or afterward if you need to create post-transaction reports or support any possible post-transaction claims.

TRADING PARTNER MANAGEMENT

Every time you create a contractual relationship with a trading partner, you must be able to meet the requirements of that contract, including payment terms, discounts, delivery modes and requirements, and so on. All these factors constitute your relationship with your trading partner. Each relationship will be different.

Your BizTalk server should have the ability to track all aspects of this relationship as they pertain to generating and processing transactions between each partner and your company.

A BizTalk server should also be able to differentiate between business partners that you are currently trading with and those that you are considering trading with. For example, if you are negotiating with a potential partner, you might want to set up a *pro forma* relationship in your BizTalk server to test whether the parameters mandated by the trading partner agreement will fit into your system's workflow-management module.

SCALABILITY

Any system these days should be scalable. Your BizTalk server is no exception. Basing your system on a scalable transport protocol infrastructure such as HTTP is a good way to start. Placing business logic in a middle tier and accessing it internally by using an intranet and thin clients is another way to assure scalability from an internal user's perspective.

Your BizTalk server should also be able to handle the expected number of transactions in a given day, multiplied by a factor for growth. However, when you plan for growth, your focus shouldn't be on how many companies you're doing business with today but rather on the potential number of companies you'll be working with in the future. When you consider the explosive expansion of the Web in the short time it has been available, it's easy to imagine the potential for growth in the electronic transmission of B2B information. The low cost of using XML and BizTalk—compared to the high cost and complexity of traditional electronic data interchange (EDI) approaches—means that you will probably use electronic messaging that employs platform-independent standards such as XML and BizTalk with more of your current business partners. You might also be able to create relationships with even more business partners because of the low cost of electronic transactions.

DOCUMENT TRANSFORMATION

Each industry will probably have a set of schemas to use to communicate between members of the industry. For example, the insurance industry coalition named ACORD (*http://www.acord.com*) is developing a set of schemas for trading insurance-related documents such as policy applications and claim forms. The travel industry is working on standards for communicating hotel room availability and flight schedules. If you are involved with one of these industries, you should be able to easily read business documents directly from the body of the BizTalk envelope.

One of the themes of this book is doing business across industries. You might receive a purchase order from the automotive industry that has a structure defined by the members of that community. The structure of the purchase order might be completely different from the structure of a purchase order created by the trucking industry or the airline manufacturing industry. Each one of these purchase orders probably has the same basic information, just in a different structure. This approach is completely different from the traditional EDI approach, which required an invoice to have a single structure that you had to adhere to regardless of the information you and your trading partners might need in order to complete your transaction. Your BizTalk server should have the ability to access the information in each one of these documents. You can write programs to transform the automobile industry purchase order into the type of purchase order you use, or you could make it easy on yourself and use XSLT.

As you learned in Chapter 6, for document transformation, creating an XSLT style sheet is much more straightforward than writing a C program because XSLT works directly on the XML input, creating an XML output document that has the structure you need. Think of XSLT as a mapping function that maps certain elements in the input to elements in the output.

A BizTalk server should also be able to match each incoming document with the appropriate transformation map. You can specify this map as part of the trading partner agreement managed by the BizTalk server.

An advanced BizTalk server should also have the ability to create these XSLT transforms in an easy way and allow you to test and update them as needed.

THIRD-PARTY AND ISV EXTENSIBILITY

A BizTalk server does not run in a vacuum. Your BizTalk server should have the ability to receive plug-in extensions that make it easy to do business with industries or trading groups.

Third parties and independent software vendors (ISVs) who want to establish a reputation in the BizTalk server field might develop such interfaces. Your BizTalk server should have the ability to accept these interfaces, encouraging third parties to develop turnkey plug-ins.

Your server should accept any schema from any vendor and provide an interface that is sophisticated enough to allow the back-end processes that the BizTalk server communicates with to use information from all schemas.

EDI INTEROPERABILITY

Implementing a traditional EDI system requires a high level of customization and integration. Many companies have created EDI systems for doing business with their trading partners. These systems, while a pain to deploy and manage, are generally respected by companies that use them.

To a company that is happy with its existing (and working) EDI implementation, the prospect of dumping it and moving to XML and BizTalk might not be desirable. However, to close off the possibility of doing business with the many (usually large) companies that employ EDI is to close off a lot of potential business. For this reason, your BizTalk server should be able to create and accept EDI transactions. Doing so might be as simple as creating a map for transforming EDI documents to and from BizTalk documents or as complex as writing a subsystem that can understand EDI and communicate with your BizTalk document.

MULTIFACETED API

Remember that your BizTalk server is simply the mechanism that creates and tracks BizTalk documents. The BizTalk server's job is not to replace all the back-end processing that your company currently does. The BizTalk server you choose should have a multifaceted interface that allows you to send information to and get information from your BizTalk server.

The API should have the kind of hooks you need to communicate with back-end processes, including order fulfillment, accounting, production workflow, customer tracking, sales, and the hundred other systems that might require an interaction with your business partners.

FUTURE-PROOF FLEXIBILITY

Your system should be flexible enough to meet the diverse needs of your various trading relationships. It should also be able to adapt to changing conditions. For example, if a current customer communicates with you by sending EDI documents and suddenly wants to start using an industry-standard XML schema and BizTalk, you should be able to change your system to accommodate this request without having to reestablish a trading partner agreement. All the history with that customer remains intact; only the way you communicate changes.

Your system should also be capable of extending industry standard schemas. You might do business with 10 companies in a particular industry. Suppose an organization devoted to setting standards for that industry creates a set of schemas for industry members to share information. You might use this set of schemas to do business with all your customers who belong to that industry. However, what if you have a closer relationship with one of the members of this industry? You might want to share a little more with that member than with the others.

With XML, you can insert certain fields within the transaction documents you create for this particular customer without breaking the system. Likewise, if you include fields in the body of any BizTalk document that a particular trading partner doesn't need, that partner can just ignore them. Your BizTalk server should be able to manage this data and create customized views of data for each trading partner on a partner-by-partner basis.

Your system should be able to handle future business changes such as mergers and acquisitions. Your system should be flexible enough to maintain information about two customer companies that become one, or one company that splits into two. Your system should also be able to handle a merger or consolidation of your own company or, more likely, a change in organizational structure.

A FOCUS ON USER-DRIVEN BUSINESS

Because BizTalk is designed to maintain business relationships, your BizTalk server and its operation should be owned by business users, not IT staff. That means that every aspect of creating business relationships and document mapping should be accessible by business users, even though those users might not be programmers.

I'm not saying that your IT staff won't be involved in the installation and maintenance of a BizTalk system. Many integration aspects are necessary when implementing a BizTalk server or any piece of code that touches legacy applications. Your IT staff will certainly be involved in building the interfaces, or "tentacles," that integrate with legacy systems.

However, you don't want to have to contact the IT staff whenever you want to create a business relationship with a new customer. Business-process owners should be able to establish and maintain relationships, do outbound and inbound document transformations, make changes to data structures (as long as the changes don't affect the operation of existing systems), and generate reports regarding the status of the system and the health of business relationships.

Such a system must also be accessible to remote users in a secure way. You'll need to implement middle-tier technologies—along with request-time encryption—to make your system usable in this way.

Chapter 11

Building a BizTalk Server

My dad once told me that doing something difficult builds character. He said that if I worked to earn money, I would appreciate it more than if he just gave it to me. Of course, I realized that what he was saying was true, but I also think he just didn't want to give me the twenty bucks I asked for.

In this chapter, we will build character by building BizTalk servers the hard but rewarding way—by hand. To illustrate the process of building a BizTalk server, I find it helpful to work at the data level, developing programs that create BizTalk documents. These programs send the documents to a BizTalk server, where they are processed.

In our example, we will duplicate Jean and David's purchase order transaction from Chapter 9. This is a relatively simple example, but it illustrates all the concepts you need to know to start building your own BizTalk solution or to choose a vendor product. Plus, you will see how the BizTalk Framework can provide a data-level layer to facilitate communication through transactions.

Since the BizTalk Framework is an extension of SOAP, we will use SOAP to send data between the two companies as well as a great new tool named ROPE, the Remote Object Proxy Engine. ROPE, part of the Microsoft SOAP Toolkit for Visual Studio 6.0, provides a way of discovering Web services and accessing them using a simple COM interface.

The two companies we encountered in Chapter 9 are involved in this transaction: Toi Carz, Inc., (*www.toicarz.com*) and Toy Car Parts Corporation (*www.toycarparts.com*). As you'll recall, Toi Carz is a manufacturer, and Toy Car Parts is one of its suppliers. Toi Carz runs in a Microsoft Windows environment, making use of Active Server Pages (ASP) and Microsoft Visual Basic. Toy Car Parts has UNIX-based servers (Linux) and uses Apache as its Web server. It uses OmniMark to build three-tier Web applications.

In this example, I want to show how to send SOAP and BizTalk messages between two computers that are running different operating systems and programming languages. These examples will work in the environments I just listed, but for the purpose of demonstration and for ease of comprehension, I am running the Toy Car Parts system in a Microsoft Windows environment.

All examples in this chapter can be run on a single machine. I created them in this way for a couple of reasons. First, it greatly simplifies your work because you don't need to find two machines that are unoccupied. Second, I wrote most of this book on various planes flying high above and far away from any kind of network, so I designed the systems to be easily moved to two Windows systems. (God bless my IBM ThinkPad.) All you need to do is move these programs to different machines and change the URLs of each system. Changing the OmniMark programs so that they run on a UNIX system isn't simple, but it shouldn't be very difficult either. The biggest modification you'll make to the UNIX-side program will be in the form of database access. For the purposes of this example, I'm using the ODBC (Open Database Connectivity) layer in Windows. ODBC is supported in OmniMark, but OmniMark also supports OCI (Oracle Command Interface) for use on UNIX machines. The OCI interface is similar to ODBC, requiring only minor modifications to the code.

All code for the chapter is included on the companion CD in the \Samples\Ch11 folder. You can build a system that does what is described in this chapter by following the installation instructions in the Setup section later in the chapter. I'm assuming you are familiar with Visual Basic programming, so I don't spend much time covering the VB code.

I do, however, spend time talking about how the OmniMark programs work since OmniMark is new to many readers. If you want to get up to speed with OmniMark quickly, Appendix A is a good place to start, but you can probably get by with only the explanations of OmniMark I offer in this chapter. (I've also included an electronic copy of my book, *OmniMark at Work, Volume 1: Getting Started*, on the companion CD. This will save you 65 bucks, so next time we meet, you can buy me a beer.) OmniMark is a really great development language, and you won't be sorry if you spend a little time learning how it can help your network programming environment.

PROGRAM AND DATA FLOW

Let's take a look at how our example is going to work. Figures 11-1 and 11-2 show the process flow between the Toy Carz and Toy Car Parts. As you'll recall from Chapter 9, these two companies employ Jean and David, the clerks who created and processed business documents. We are going to replace their tasks with two computer systems.

Toi Carz

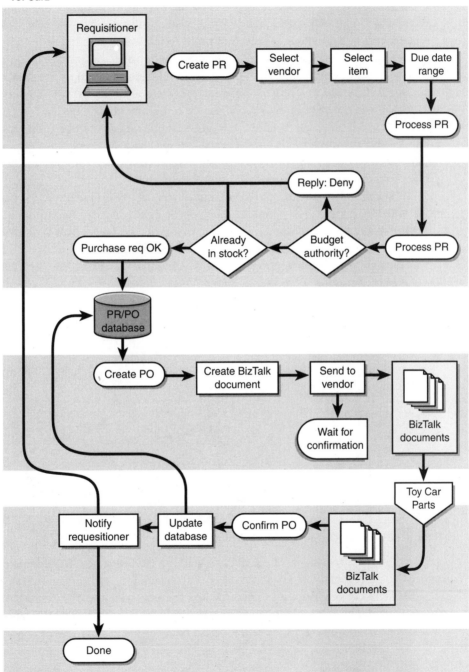

Figure 11-1. *Workflow illustrating the process put into motion when a purchase requisition is started.*

The process works like this: an event kicks off a process between the two companies. In Figure 11-1, an employee at Toi Carz wants to purchase something from Toy Car Parts. The employee creates a purchase requisition (PR), for which he will select an appropriate vendor, item, and preferred delivery date range.

This data is processed by an application that applies business rules in accordance with Toi Carz policies. First, the application checks an employee database to make sure the person entering the requisition has the authority to purchase the products requested. Then the application checks whether the items requested are already in stock. If so, the total number in the requisition will be adjusted accordingly. If the authority and stock queries pass, a purchase requisition is entered into a database. This database contains all purchase requisitions that have been run through the same process of verification.

At regular intervals, the purchase requisition database is scanned for the purpose of building purchase orders to send to Toi Carz vendors. That scanning process checks a vendor database for address information and builds BizTalk documents, each document containing a purchase order for the appropriate vendor. These BizTalk documents are sent to the vendors, one of which is Toy Car Parts. The Toy Car Parts program and data flow is shown in Figure 11-2.

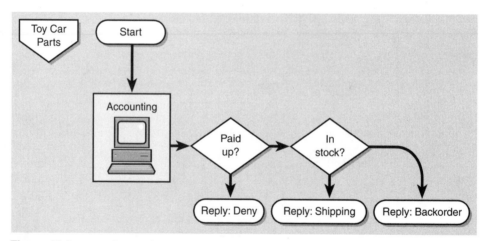

Figure 11-2. *Data flow within Toy Car Parts.*

When the program at Toy Car Parts gets the BizTalk document, the program parses the document to obtain the necessary information, including the purchase order payload. The customer record is interrogated to make sure the Toi Carz account is in good standing—that is, that Toy Car Parts has a current contractual relationship with Toi Carz and that Toi Carz is paying its bills.

Then the program checks to see whether the items are in stock. If the items are not in stock, a reply document is sent to Toi Carz informing the company that the item is on backorder. If the items are in stock, a record is placed in the orders database and the inventory is adjusted accordingly. Finally, a BizTalk document is sent back to Toi Carz containing a confirmation of the purchase order.

Let's look again at Figure 11-1. The BizTalk reply document created by Toy Car Parts is sent to Toi Carz. The BizTalk document is received by an ASP application, which captures the relevant information and does two things to complete the requisition process: it updates the outstanding purchase order database to indicate that the purchase order has been received and confirmed by the vendor, and it notifies each of the people who initiated the workflow.

ARCHITECTURE

The Toi Carz and Toy Car Parts systems use a number of programs to complete the requisition process. Tables 11-1 and 11-2 provide a description of the programs and their purpose. On the companion CD, two directories contain all the programs for Toi Carz (/Samples/Ch11/ToiCarz) and Toy Car Parts (/Samples/Ch11/ToyCarParts).

Program Name	Program Type	Description
prEnter.asp	ASP	This program creates a purchase requisition, connecting to the employee and vendor databases to display a list of all items available for ordering. It is processed by prProcess.asp.
prProcess.asp	ASP	This program processes a purchase requisition. It first checks to see whether an employee has sufficient authority to order the products, and then it assures that the items ordered are not already in stock.
poGen.exe	VB	This purchase order generation program reads the database containing purchase requisitions and generates purchase orders that are sent to the vendors. One of the vendors is Toy Car Parts, which will receive the purchase order. This program uses ROPE to package and send a SOAP document to a SOAP server.

Table 11-1. *Toi Carz programs used in the purchase requisition process.* *(continued)*

Table 11-1. *continued*

Program Name	Program Type	Description
poConfirm.asp	ASP	This program receives the BizTalk document that contains the purchase order confirmation. It updates the purchase order database, indicating that the purchase order has been processed, and then it informs the employees who made the purchase requisitions that their orders have been processed.

Program Name	Program Type	Description
PlaceOrder.htm	HTML page	Toy Car Parts has an existing legacy application that it uses internally for entering orders. When a purchase order is received, a clerk enters information into this form, which is an HTML document that captures order information.
PlaceOrder.xom	OmniMark	This program acts as a CGI script, which is called as the *ACTION* method in the *FORM* element in PlaceOrder.htm. PlaceOrder.xom contains business logic that makes sure the order conforms to internal checks and procedures. After conformity is confirmed, the program inserts the order into the order database. Toy Car Parts does not want to rewrite this system, which has been working fine for years. Its BizTalk server must be able to use this existing system.
BTServer.xom	OmniMark	This OmniMark program, written as a CGI script, first acts as a SOAP server, receiving a SOAP document sent from the ROPE interface in poGen.exe. Then the program turns into a BizTalk server, transforming the XML-based request into a document that pretends to be PlaceOrder.htm. BTServer.xom receives a response from PlaceOrder.xom and creates a BizTalk confirmation message, which BTServer.xom sends directly to Toi Carz as a POST message to an active server page, poConfirm.asp. This program processes the purchase order confirmation and closes the loop.

Table 11-2. *Toy Car Parts programs used in the purchase fulfillment process.*

The entire requisition process is shown in Figure 11-3.

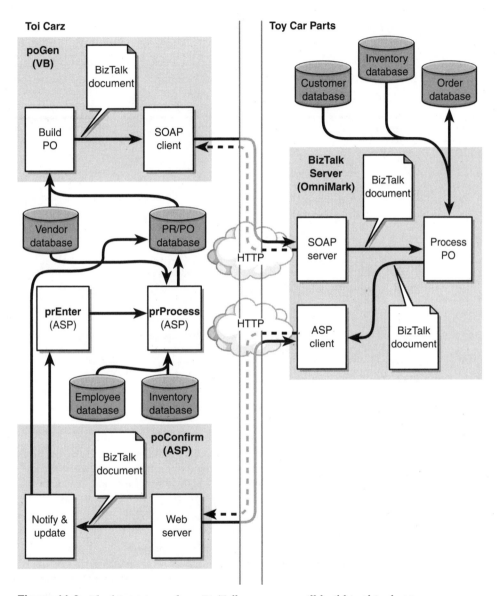

Figure 11-3. *The big picture: three BizTalk servers we will build in this chapter.*

DATABASES

Each company uses its own set of databases to keep track of things such as inventory, customers, and the status of orders. These databases are described in Tables 11-3 and 11-4. To use these databases in the BizTalk solution described in this chapter, you'll need to follow the instructions in the section titled "System Setup," later in this chapter. These are all Microsoft databases, so you can open them up to see the data structures and relationships.

Database	Description
Employees.mdb	A database of all employees and their budget authority level.
Inventory.mdb	The master inventory database containing information about all items that Toi Carz currently has in stock.
Vendors.mdb	A list of all products supplied by all vendors Toi Carz does business with. This database is updated whenever Toi Carz gets a new catalog from an existing vendor or a new vendor is signed up.
PurchaseOrders.mdb	A database with two tables: PORequests, which contains a list of all purchase requisitions submitted by Toi Carz employees; and POSent, which contains information on all purchase orders that have been generated and sent to vendors.

Table 11-3. *The Toi Carz databases.*

Database	Description
Customers.mdb	A list of all customers and their account status. Toy Car Parts will use this information to determine whether a customer is current in paying its bills before more product is sent to the customer.
Inventory.mdb	The master inventory database that contains all items in stock, their quantities, and their prices.
Orders.mdb	A database containing orders that were placed with the PlaceOrder system. This database integrates with Toy Car Parts systems that turn an order into a shipment and handle the proper accounting.

Table 11-4. *The Toy Car Parts databases.*

NOTE The PurchaseOrders.mdb database contains two tables linked from the Vendors.mdb database. These tables are named catalog and vendors. If you install the databases in a directory path other than the default (C:\TravisBook\Ch11\ToiCarz\), you'll need to update these links from within Access.

The purchase requisition system in our examples uses ODBC to simplify database connectivity across different database vendors. All the databases described in Tables 11-3 and 11-4 are simple Access database (.mdb) files, but they could very easily be Microsoft SQL Server or Oracle databases. Of course, changing the files to SQL or Oracle might require a change in some of the code.

SYSTEM SETUP

To make the purchase requisition system run, follow these steps:

1. Run the install program on the companion CD to copy the sample files from the CD to your hard drive. Alternatively, copy all the files on the companion CD from the directory \Samples\Ch11 to a convenient location on your hard disk. The default location this file structure is copied to is C:\TravisBook\Ch11 if you use the installer on the companion CD.

3. Create the ODBC data source names (DSNs) in Microsoft Windows 2000; the DSNs will act as handles for accessing the database files. From the start menu, select Settings and click Control Panel. In Control Panel, double-click Administrative Tools. In the Administrative Tools folder, you'll find the Data Sources (ODBC) icon. Double-click this icon to open the ODBC Data Source Administrator dialog box. In other versions of Windows, you can get to this tool by double-clicking the ODBC Data Sources icon in Control Panel.

3. You will create eight system DSN entries, which are listed in Table 11-5. Click on the System DSN tab. Click Add. Select Microsoft Access Driver (*.mdb) and then click Finish. Enter a Data Source Name from Table 11-5. Click the Select button and find the file, which was copied to your local drive in step 1. Click OK. Repeat this step for each of the databases listed in Table 11-5.

4. Create two Web shares. Use Windows Explorer to find the folder C:\TravisBook\Ch11. You should see the two company directories. Right-click on ToiCarz and select Sharing. Select the Web Sharing tab. Click Share

This Folder and accept the defaults in the Edit Alias dialog box. Repeat this step for the ToyCarParts directory, except click the Execute (Includes Scripts) option button. This will allow the OmniMark programs to execute in the ToyCarParts directory.

Data Source Name	Location
dbTC-Employees	C:\TravisBook\Ch11\ToiCarz\Employees.mdb
dbTC-Inventory	C:\TravisBook\Ch11\ToiCarz\Inventory.mdb
dbTC-PurchaseOrders	C:\TravisBook\Ch11\ToiCarz\PurchaseOrders.mdb
dbTC-Vendors	C:\TravisBook\Ch11\ToiCarz\Vendors.mdb
dbTCP-Customers	C:\TravisBook\Ch11\ToyCarParts\Customers.mdb
dbTCP-Inventory	C:\TravisBook\Ch11\ToyCarParts\Inventory.mdb
dbTCP-Orders	C:\TravisBook\Ch11\ToyCarParts\Orders.mdb

Table 11-5. *Information for creating DSN entries in step 3.*

ENTERING A PURCHASE REQUISITION

Two programs are used for entering a purchase requisition: prEnter.asp and prProcess.asp. The following sections describe these programs.

prEnter.asp

The prEnter.asp program is an ASP page that presents a view of the Vendors database, which contains catalogs for all approved vendors. Figure 11-4 shows this page with data selected.

This program reads the Employees and Vendors databases and populates drop-down list boxes. When a vendor is selected, the ASP page calls itself to update the items in the Item drop-down list box. This process is shown in Listing 11-1.

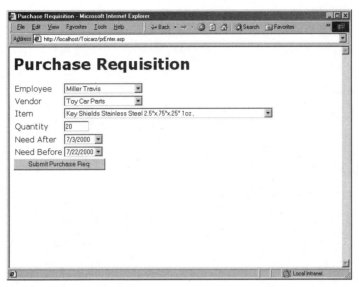

Figure 11-4. *The purchase requisition page, prEnter.asp, allows an employee to start the process of ordering goods.*

```
prEnter.asp

<%@language=vbscript%>
<%
Set oVendorConn = Server.CreateObject("ADODB.Connection")
oVendorConn.Open("dbTC-Vendors")

Function dateRange(fieldName, startDate, daysBackward, daysForward)
    If Request.Form(fieldName) = "" Then
        selectDate = FormatDateTime(startDate, vbShortDate)
    Else
        selectDate = Request.Form(fieldName)
    End If

    dateRange = vbCrLf & "<SELECT NAME='" & fieldName & "'>"
    For i = -daysBackward To daysForward
        thisDate = FormatDateTime(startDate + i, vbShortDate)
        dateRange = dateRange & vbCrLf & vbCrLf & "<OPTION "
        If thisDate = selectDate Then dateRange = dateRange & _
```

Listing 11-1. *prEnter.asp, a program for entering purchase requisitions.*   *(continued)*

Listing 11-1 *continued*

```
                "SELECTED"
            dateRange = dateRange & " VALUE='" & thisDate & "'>" _
                & thisDate & "</OPTION>"
        Next
        dateRange = dateRange & vbCrLf & "</SELECT>"
End Function
%>
<HTML>
    <HEAD>
        <TITLE>Purchase Requisition</TITLE>
        <SCRIPT>
        function loadItems()
            {
            document.all.vendorForm.action="prEnter.asp"
            document.all.vendorForm.submit()
            }
        </SCRIPT>
    </HEAD>
    <BODY STYLE="font-family:Verdana;">
    <H1>Purchase Requisition</H1>
    <FORM METHOD="POST" id="vendorForm" ACTION="prProcess.asp">
        <TABLE>
            <TR>
                <TD>Employee</TD>
                <TD>
                <SELECT NAME="requestorID">
                <OPTION VALUE="0">-- Select an Employee --</OPTION>"
                <%
                Set oConn = Server.CreateObject("ADODB.Connection")
                oConn.Open("dbTC-Employees")
                Set rsEmployee = oConn.Execute( _
                    "SELECT * FROM Employees ORDER BY LName")
                Do Until rsEmployee.EOF
                    Response.Write ("<OPTION ")
                    If Int(Request.Form("requestorID")) = _
                        Int(rsEmployee("empID")) Then
                        Response.Write (" SELECTED")
                    End If
                    Response.Write (" VALUE='" _
                        & rsEmployee("empID") & "'>"_
                        & rsEmployee("FName") & " " _
                        & rsEmployee("LName") _
                        & "</OPTION>")
                    rsEmployee.MoveNext
```

```
            Loop
            Set rsEmployee = Nothing
            oConn.Close
            Set oConn = Nothing
            %>
            </SELECT>
            </TD>
        </TR>
        <TR>
            <TD>Vendor</TD>
            <TD>
            <SELECT ID="vendorID" NAME="vendorID"
                ONCHANGE="javascript:loadItems();">
            <OPTION VALUE="0">-- Select a Vendor --</OPTION>
            <%
            Set rsVendor = oVendorConn.Execute( _
                "SELECT * FROM Vendors ORDER BY vendorName")
            Do Until rsVendor.EOF
                Response.Write ("<OPTION ")
                If Int(Request.Form("vendorID")) = _
                    Int(rsVendor("vendorID")) Then
                    Response.Write (" SELECTED")
                End If
                Response.Write (" VALUE='" _
                    & rsVendor("vendorID") & "'>" _
                    & rsVendor("vendorName") & "</OPTION>")
                rsVendor.MoveNext
            Loop
            Set rsVendor = Nothing
            %>
            </SELECT>
            </TD>
        </TR>
        <TR>
            <TD>Item</TD>
            <TD>
            <SELECT NAME="itemNum">
            <OPTION VALUE="0">-- Select an Item --</OPTION>
            <%
            If Request.Form("vendorID") <> 0 Then
                Set rsItem = oVendorConn.Execute( _
                    "SELECT * FROM catalog WHERE vendorID=" _
                    & Request.Form("vendorID") _
                    & " ORDER BY description")
```

(continued)

Listing 11-1 *continued*

```
                        Do Until rsItem.EOF
                            Response.Write(vbCrLf & "<OPTION ")
                        If Request.Form("itemNum") = rsItem("itemNum") Then
                                Response.Write(" SELECTED")
                            End If
                            Response.Write(" VALUE='" _
                                & rsItem("itemNum") & "'>" _
                                & rsItem("description") _
                                & ", " & rsItem("color") & "</OPTION>")
                            rsItem.MoveNext
                        Loop
                        set rsItem = Nothing
                    End If
                    %>
                    </SELECT>
                    </TD>
                </TR>
                <TR>
                    <TD>Quantity</TD>
                    <TD><INPUT NAME="itemQty" VALUE="1" SIZE="5">
                        </INPUT></TD>
                </TR>
                <TR>
                    <TD>Need After</TD>
                    <TD><%=dateRange("needAfter", Now(), 0, 30)%></TD>
                </TR>
                <TR>
                    <TD>Need Before</TD>
                    <TD><%=dateRange("needBefore", Now() + 21, 20, 30)%></
TD>
                </TR>
            </TABLE>
            <INPUT TYPE="SUBMIT" VALUE="Submit Purchase Req"></INPUT>
        </FORM>
        </BODY>
</HTML>
<%
oVendorConn.Close
Set oVendorConn = Nothing
%>
```

In the vendor pull-down box is an *ONCHANGE* event. Changing the value of this control executes the JScript function *loadItems*, which temporarily changes the *ACTION* method on the form, causing the page to reload itself. When the page calls itself, the page loads the Item dropdown box with all items from the selected vendor.

When the Submit button is clicked, prEnter.asp calls prProcess.asp, which verifies the requisition.

prProcess.asp

The prProcess.asp program contains business logic designed to verify that the requestor is authorized to purchase the desired items. The program also performs other checks, including determining whether the item is already in stock. Figure 11-5 shows the confirmation screen.

Figure 11-5. *ASP page confirming that a purchase requisition has been added to the purchase requisition database.*

Listing 11-2 shows prProcess.asp, which verifies that a purchase requisition is valid.

prProcess.asp

```
<%@ LANGUAGE = "VBScript" %>
<HTML><BODY STYLE="font-family:Verdana">
<%
' Open Employee database
Set oEmpConn = Server.CreateObject("ADODB.Connection")
oEmpConn.Open("dbTC-Employees")

' Open Vendor database
Set oVendorsConn = Server.CreateObject("ADODB.Connection")
oVendorsConn.Open("dbTC-Vendors")

' Open PO database
Set oPOConn = Server.CreateObject("ADODB.Connection")
oPOConn.Open("dbTC-PurchaseOrders")
```

Listing 11-2. *This program verifies that a purchase requisition is valid.* *(continued)*

Listing 11-2 *continued*

```
' Open Inventory database
Set oInventoryConn = Server.CreateObject("ADODB.Connection")
oInventoryConn.Open("dbTC-Inventory")

reqError = ""

' Do some error checking
Set itemRS = oVendorsConn.Execute("SELECT price FROM Catalog " _
    & "WHERE itemNum='" _
    & Request.Form("itemNum") _
    & "'")
If itemRS.EOF Then
    reqError = reqError _
        & "<BR>Cannot find item " _
        & Request.Form("itemNum")
End If

Set employeeRS = oEmpConn.Execute("SELECT purchaseLimit " _
    & "FROM Employees " _
    & "WHERE empID=" & Request.Form("requestorID"))
If employeeRS.EOF Then
    reqError = reqError _
        & "<BR>Cannot find employee " _
        & Request.Form("requestorID")
End If

' Check to see if our requestor has purchasing authority
qty = Request.Form("itemQty")
price = itemRS("price")
totalPrice = qty * price

If CDbl(totalPrice) > CDbl(employeeRS("purchaseLimit")) Then
    reqError = reqError _
        & "<BR>Your purchase authority of $" _
        & employeeRS("purchaseLimit") _
        & " is less than your request total of $" _
        & totalPrice _
        & ". Try again."
End If

' Check to see if the item is already in stock
Set inventoryRS = oInventoryConn.Execute( _
    "SELECT * FROM inventory " _
    & "WHERE vendorID=" & Request.Form("vendorID") _
    & " AND itemNum='" & Request.Form("itemNum") & "'")

qtyRequested = Request.Form("itemQty")
```

```
If Not inventoryRS.EOF Then
    qtyOnHand = inventoryRS("quantity")
    If CDbl(qtyOnHand) >= CDbl(qtyRequested) Then
        reqError = reqError _
            & "<BR>Inventory reports " _
            & qtyOnHand _
            & " units of item " _
            & Request.Form("itemNum") _
            & " already in stock. Requisition denied."
    Else
        reqMessage = reqMessage _
            & "<BR>Inventory reports " _
            & qtyOnHand _
            & " units of item " _
            & Request.Form("itemNum") _
            & " already in stock. Order quantity reduced to " _
            & qtyRequested - qtyOnHand _
            & " units."
        qtyRequested = qtyRequested - qtyOnHand
    End If
End If

If reqError <> "" Then
    Response.Write("<H1>Error</H1>")
    Response.Write(reqError)
Else
    Response.Write(reqMessage)
    Set rsOrder = Server.CreateObject("ADODB.Recordset")
    rsOrder.CursorType = 2
    rsOrder.LockType = 2

    rsOrder.Open "PORequests", oPOConn
    rsOrder.AddNew
    rsOrder("timeStamp")    = Now()
    rsOrder("requestorID") = Request.Form("requestorID")
    rsOrder("vendorID")     = Request.Form("vendorID")
    rsOrder("itemNum")      = Request.Form("itemNum")
    rsOrder("itemQty")      = qtyRequested
    rsOrder("needBefore")   = Request.Form("needBefore")
    rsOrder("needAfter")    = Request.Form("needAfter")
    rsOrder("itemPrice")    = price
    rsOrder.Update

    rsOrder.Close
    Set rsOrder = Nothing

    oPOConn.close
```

(continued)

Listing 11-2 *continued*

```
      Set oPOConn = Nothing
      Response.Write("<H1>Request added!</H1>")
      Response.Write("<P>Your request has been added to the " _
          & "purchase requisition database")
      Response.Write("<TABLE>")
      Response.Write("<TR><TD>Requestor ID</TD><TD>" _
          & Request.Form("requestorID") & "</TD></TR>")
      Response.Write("<TR><TD>Vendor ID</TD><TD>" _
          & Request.Form("vendorID") & "</TD></TR>")
      Response.Write("<TR><TD>Item Number</TD><TD>" _
          & Request.Form("itemNum") & "</TD></TR>")
      Response.Write("<TR><TD>Quantity</TD><TD>" _
          & qtyRequested & "</TD></TR>")
      Response.Write("<TR><TD>Need Before</TD><TD>" _
          & Request.Form("needBefore") & "</TD></TR>")
      Response.Write("<TR><TD>Need After</TD><TD>" _
          & Request.Form("needAfter") & "</TD></TR>")
  End If
  %>
  </BODY>
  </HTML>
```

ROPE and SDL

The program we will write in this section is poGen.exe, and we'll write it in Visual Basic. The poGen program uses a new Microsoft technology named ROPE (which you'll recall stands for Remote Object Proxy Engine). In Chapter 8, we built a SOAP client the hard way—that is, we concatenated strings to form the SOAP envelope, then sent that envelope, along with a payload inside, to a server that read the package and sent a response. Concatenating strings helped us understand SOAP packets and learn about how they work, but concatenation is not a very user-friendly way to write programs for a couple of reasons. First of all, programmers must know the SOAP syntax in order to make a remote procedure call. Second, they need to understand the rules of XML so that they create documents that are parser-friendly.

Wouldn't it be nice if there existed a service that stood between you and your creation of SOAP documents? This service could translate your server request into the required XML code and then return the expected data. In other words, wouldn't it be nice to have a proxy do your remote method-invocation bidding? That proxy is ROPE, which consists of a shared COM object (rope.dll) that comes with the SOAP Toolkit for Visual Studio 6.0, included on the companion CD. Figure 11-6 shows how ROPE works.

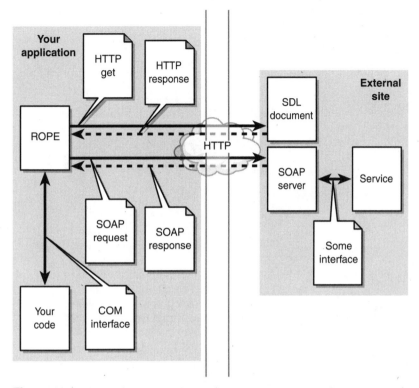

Figure 11-6. *ROPE translates requests for services into SOAP documents and communicates with remote objects.*

ROPE depends on the existence of an XML file tagged according to the Service Description Language (SDL). This tagged file describes all services that are available to a calling application. You can create an SDL document using the SOAP Toolkit Wizard that ships as part of the SOAP Toolkit. This wizard reads a COM object and creates the appropriate SDL. You can also write SDL documents by hand when you're dealing with non-COM applications as in Listing 11-3. The SDL specification is included with the SOAP Toolkit for Visual Studio 6.0. Listing 11-3 shows an example of the SDL document we are using.

> **NOTE** At the time of this writing, the SDL specification is still in flux. Most parties agree that an XML-based method-discovery system is needed, but the syntax might change by the publication date of this book. Check *http://architag.com/support* for update information.

Services.xml

```xml
<?xml version="1.0" ?>
<serviceDescription
    name="SoapService"
    xmlns="http://localhost/soapdemo/sdlschema.xml"
    xmlns:dt="http://www.w3.org/1999/XMLSchema"
    xmlns:ss ="#ServiceSchema">

    <import    namespace="#ServiceSchema" location ="#ServiceSchema"/>

    <soap xmlns="urn:schemas-xmlsoap-org:soap-sdl-2000-01-25">

        <interface name="BizTalkInterface"/>

        <service>
            <implements name="BizTalkInterface" />

            <!-- Send a BizTalk message for processing -->
            <requestResponse name="BizTalkMessage">
                <request ref="ss:BizTalkMessageRequest"/>
                <response ref="ss:BizTalkMessageResponse"/>
                <parameterorder>BizTalkDoc</parameterorder>
            </requestResponse>

            <!-- Check Inventory -->
            <requestResponse name="checkInventory">
                <request ref="ss:checkInventoryRequest"/>
                <response ref="ss:checkInventoryResponse"/>
                <parameterorder>itemNum quantity</parameterorder>
            </requestResponse>

            <!-- Check the server status ("are you OK?") -->
            <requestResponse name="RUOK">
                <request ref="ss:RUOKRequest"/>
                <response ref="ss:RUOKResponse"/>
            </requestResponse>

            <addresses>
                <location url="http://localhost/toycarparts/
```

Listing 11-3. *SDL defines Web services exposed to SOAP and ROPE.*

```
BTServer.xar"/>
            </addresses>
        </service>
    </soap>

    <ss:schema   id="ServiceSchema">
        <element name="BizTalkMessageRequest">
            <type>
                <element name="BizTalkDoc" type="dt:string"/>
            </type>
        </element>

        <element name="BizTalkMessageResponse">
            <type>
                <element name="DeliveryReceipt" type="dt:string"/>
            </type>
        </element>

        <element name="checkInventoryRequest">
            <type>
                <element name="itemNum" type="dt:string"/>
                <element name="quantity" type="dt:string"/>
            </type>
        </element>

        <element name="checkInventoryResponse">
            <type>
                <element name="itemPrice" type="dt:string"/>
                <element name="deliveryDate" type="dt:string"/>
            </type>
        </element>

        <element name="RUOKRequest">
            <type>
                <element name="Subsystem" type="dt:string"/>
            </type>
        </element>

        <element name="RUOKResponse">
            <type>
                <element name="Status" type="dt:string"/>
            </type>
        </element>

    </ss:schema>
</serviceDescription>
```

To provide a COM interface to your program, the ROPE object reads the SDL document to discover what services are available. These services are then exposed as SOAP-based Web services. In other words, to the ROPE programmer, the entire world looks like a COM object. This is very exciting stuff. You will see what the ROPE interface looks like in the *sendMsg* Visual Basic function in the next example.

The Purchase Order Generation Program

The purchase order generation program, poGen, reads the PORequests table in the PurchaseOrders database, collects requests by vendor, and creates a number of purchase orders that are shipped to various vendors based on their addresses in the Vendors database. It can be run daily or even every minute when there is a lot of internal purchase requisition traffic. The poGen user interface is shown in Figure 11-7. The important procedures in the poGen program are described in the following sections.

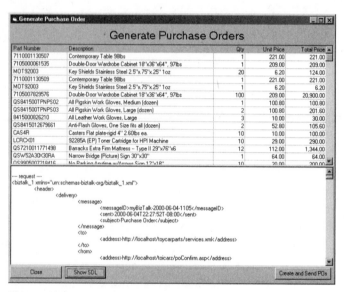

Figure 11-7. *The poGen program builds purchase orders and sends them, as BizTalk documents, to vendors.*

Form.Load subroutine

The *Form.Load* subroutine, shown in Listing 11-4, retrieves all purchase requisitions from the database and displays them in a window. This display is for demonstration purposes—a program that does what poGen does will probably not have any user interaction at all, just logging.

Form.Load

```
Private Sub Form_Load()
    Randomize
    strSQL = "SELECT PORequests.*, catalog.*, vendors.* " _
        & "FROM vendors INNER JOIN (PORequests " _
        & "INNER JOIN [catalog] ON [PORequests].[itemNum]=" _
        & "[catalog].[itemNum]) ON ([PORequests].[vendorID]=" _
        & "[vendors].[vendorID]) AND ([vendors].[vendorID]=" _
        & "[catalog].[vendorID]) ORDER BY [vendors].[vendorID]"
    Set odbPO = New ADODB.Connection
    odbPO.Open ("dbTC-PurchaseOrders")

    Set orsPO = odbPO.Execute(strSQL)
    Do Until orsPO.EOF
        gridPO.AddItem orsPO("itemNum") _
            & vbTab & orsPO("description") _
            & vbTab & orsPO("itemQty") _
            & vbTab & Format(orsPO("itemPrice"), _
                "#,##0.00") _
            & vbTab & Format(orsPO("itemPrice") _
                * orsPO("itemQty"), "#,##0.00")
        orsPO.MoveNext
    Loop
    orsPO.Close
    Set orsPO = Nothing
End Sub
```

Listing 11-4. *The* Form_Load *subroutine from the poGen program displays purchase requisitions.*

The poGen program uses the MSFlexGrid control to display columns of information. A query is made against the tables in the PurchaseOrder database and the grid control is filled.

createPO_Click subroutine

When the user clicks the Create And Send POs button, *the createPO_Click* subroutine collects all purchase requisitions for a given vendor and creates a single purchase order document for that vendor. Then it moves to the next vendor until all purchase requisitions are sent. This subroutine, *createPO_Click*, is shown in Listing 11-5.

createPO_Click

```
Private Sub createPO_Click()
    Dim txtBizTalk As String
    Dim txtSOAP As String
    Dim txtXML As String
    Dim oXMLDoc As New msxml2.DOMDocument
    Dim oParmsDoc As New msxml2.DOMDocument
    Dim orsRequisitions As New ADODB.Recordset
    Dim orsPOSent As New ADODB.Recordset
    Dim strSQL As String
    Dim currentDate As Date
    Dim strSendTo As String
    Dim strReplyTo As String
    Dim currentVendor As Integer
    Dim poNum
    Dim strParms As String

    txtResponse.Text = ""
    currentDate = Now()
    currentVendor = 0
    strSQL = "SELECT PORequests.*, vendors.*, PORequests.vendorID " _
        & "FROM vendors INNER JOIN " _
        & "PORequests ON vendors.vendorID = PORequests.vendorID " _
        & "ORDER BY PORequests.vendorID"
    orsRequisitions.CursorType = adOpenKeyset
    orsRequisitions.LockType = adLockOptimistic
    orsRequisitions.Open strSQL, odbPO, , , adCmdText

    orsPOSent.CursorType = adOpenKeyset
    orsPOSent.LockType = adLockOptimistic
    orsPOSent.Open "POSent", odbPO, , , adCmdTable

    Do Until orsRequisitions.EOF
        Screen.MousePointer = vbHourglass

        ' Generate a new purchase order number
        orsPOSent.AddNew
        orsPOSent("poDate") = currentDate
        orsPOSent("timeSent") = Now()
        orsPOSent.Update

        poNum = orsPOSent("poNum")

        ' Generate the purchase order number
        orsPOSent("messageID") = "uuid:" & genUUID()
        orsPOSent.Update
```

Listing 11-5. *The* createPO_Click *subroutine consolidates and sends purchase orders to vendors.*

```
        txtXML = "<purchaseOrder_Chapter11_1.0" _
            & vbCrLf & " xmlns = 'urn:purchaseOrder_Chapter12_1.0.xdr'" _
            & vbCrLf & " custID = '" & CUST_ID & "'" _
            & vbCrLf & " poNumber = '" & poNum & "'" _
            & vbCrLf & " poDate = '" & iso8601(currentDate) & "'>"
        currentVendor = orsRequisitions("vendorID")

nextItem:
        txtXML = txtXML & vbCrLf & "    <item" _
            & vbCrLf & " needAfter='" _
            & iso8601(orsRequisitions("needAfter")) & "'" _
            & vbCrLf & " needBefore='" _
            & iso8601(orsRequisitions("needBefore")) & "'" _
            & vbCrLf & " reqID='" & orsRequisitions("reqID") & "'" _
            & ">"

        txtXML = txtXML & vbCrLf & "    <number>" _
            & orsRequisitions("itemNum") & "</number>"
        txtXML = txtXML & vbCrLf & "    <price>" _
            & orsRequisitions("itemPrice") & "</price>"
        txtXML = txtXML & vbCrLf & "    <qty>" _
            & orsRequisitions("itemQty") & "</qty>"
        txtXML = txtXML & vbCrLf & "</item>"

        strParms = "<?xml version='1.0'?>" _
            & "<parms>" _
            & "    <toAddress type='agr:department'>" _
            & orsRequisitions("vendorToAddress") & "</toAddress>" _
            & "    <messageID>" & orsPOSent("messageID") _
            & "</messageID>" _
            & "    <sendTo>" & orsRequisitions("vendorToAddress") _
            & "</sendTo>" _
            & "    <confirmTo>" & orsRequisitions("vendorConfirmAddress") _
            & "</confirmTo>" _
            & "</parms>"
        orsRequisitions("poNum") = poNum
        orsRequisitions.Update
        orsRequisitions.MoveNext

        If orsRequisitions.EOF Then GoTo around
        If currentVendor = orsRequisitions("vendorID") Then
            GoTo nextItem
        End If

around:
        txtXML = txtXML & "</purchaseOrder_Chapter11_1.0>"
        oXMLDoc.loadXML (txtXML)
```

(continued)

Listing 11-5 *continued*

```
        If oXMLDoc.parseError.errorCode <> 0 Then
            MsgBox ("XML Error: " & oXMLDoc.parseError.reason _
                & " on line " & oXMLDoc.parseError.Line)
        End If

        oParmsDoc.loadXML (strParms)
        txtBizTalk = envelopeBizTalk(oXMLDoc, oParmsDoc)

        oXMLDoc.loadXML (txtBizTalk)
        If oXMLDoc.parseError.errorCode <> 0 Then
            MsgBox ("XML Error: " & oXMLDoc.parseError.reason _
                & " on line " & oXMLDoc.parseError.Line)
        End If

        sendMsg oXMLDoc
    Loop

out:
    orsPOSent.Close
    Set orsPOSent = Nothing
    orsRequisitions.Close
    Set orsRequisitions = Nothing
    Screen.MousePointer = vbDefault

End Sub
```

The subroutine builds the *PurchaseOrder_Chapter11_1.0* element as an XML string. This will be the payload placed into the BizTalk document shipped to the vendor.

sendMsg function

Interaction with the ROPE proxy is done in the sendMsg function. This function is shown in Listing 11-6.

```
sendMsg

Function sendMsg(oXMLDoc As msxml2.DOMDocument)
    Dim retryCount
    Dim sendTo As String

    ' Discover service call
    sendTo = oXMLDoc.selectSingleNode("//dlv:to/dlv:address").Text
```

Listing 11-6. *The* sendMsg *function creates a connection to an external Web service by reading the SDL file on the remote site and creating a COM interface.*

```
    Dim oROPE As New ROPE.Proxy
    Dim oPackager As New ROPE.SOAPPackager

    ' Call ROPE proxy
    Dim bRetVal As Boolean
    bRetVal = oROPE.LoadServicesDescription(icURI, sendTo)
    If (bRetVal = False) Then
        MsgBox "LoadServicesDescription = " _
            & bRetVal, , "LoadServicesDescription FAILED"
        End
    End If
    Dim sBuffer As String
    Dim sTransaction
    sTransaction = vbCrLf & "---- request ----" & vbCrLf & oXMLDoc.xml

    On Error GoTo badSOAP
    sBuffer = oROPE.BizTalkMessage(oXMLDoc.xml)
    sTransaction = sTransaction _
        & vbCrLf & "---- response ----" & vbCrLf & sBuffer
    sTransaction = sTransaction _
        & vbCrLf & vbCrLf & "------------------------" _
        & vbCrLf & vbCrLf
    txtResponse.Text = sTransaction & txtResponse.Text
    txtResponse.Refresh
    On Error GoTo 0
    Set oROPE = Nothing
    sendMsg = True
    Exit Function

badSOAP:
    Set oROPE = Nothing
    MsgBox ("SOAP server returned a fault")
    On Error GoTo 0
    sendMsg = False
    Exit Function

End Function
```

The main part of *sendMsg* is the instantiation and connection to the ROPE engine. Check out the following code:

```
bRetVal = oROPE.LoadServicesDescription(icURI, sendTo)
sBuffer = oROPE.BizTalkMessage(oXMLDoc.xml)
```

The first line creates a connection to the external service by loading the SDL document, providing a late-bound interface to the object. Late binding means that the methods of the object are not available at design time, only at run time. (You'll notice that the Microsoft IntelliSense processor does not expose the methods of the external object.)

Once the ROPE object has information from the SDL document, you can invoke methods by using a familiar COM interface. The previous two lines of code handle all the heavy lifting and deal with any external object that supports SOAP and SDL. If you want to see the methods discovered by the SDL query, click the Show SDL button.

PROCESSING A PURCHASE ORDER

Toy Car Parts has a legacy application that order entry clerks have been using to enter customer purchase orders. This application, PlaceOrder.htm, is an HTML document that calls a CGI program, written in OmniMark, to process the order. The interface for PlaceOrder.htm is shown in Figure 11-8.

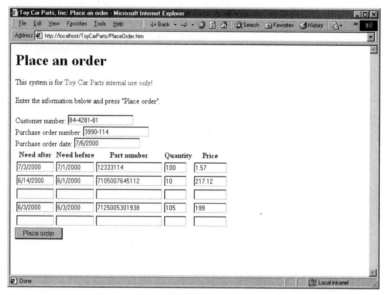

Figure 11-8. *The legacy order-processing application, PlaceOrder.htm*

PlaceOrder.htm is a simple HTML document with a form allowing the clerk to enter appropriate information for a purchase order. The data in the HTML form is sent to an OmniMark program that processes the order in accordance with business rules, updates the appropriate databases, and sends a response to the user. This response screen is shown in Figure 11-9.

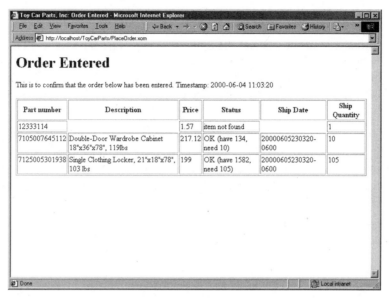

Figure 11-9. *The response generated by PlaceOrder.xom.*

A BizTalk-based automated purchase order processing system needs to perform the same tasks as the legacy application. We could write an application that processes a BizTalk-based document using the same rules as the legacy application, but that smells too much like work. We still want to have the manual legacy application available for entries that come in on paper purchase orders. If we wrote a BizTalk-smart application, we would need to maintain the same business rules in two places. It would be nice if we could somehow tie our automated system into the legacy application, using the BizTalk document as a surrogate human clerk.

So let's do that. Our BizTalk server must create the same kind of document that PlaceOrder.htm does and post that document to PlaceOrder.xom. This is not really that hard, and OmniMark makes it possible. What's a bit harder is interpreting the HTML response page that comes back from the application and doing something useful with it. We will generate and interpret the HTML response page with the BizTalk server.

Automating Purchase Order Processing

Continuing with our process flow scenario, a process at Toy Car Parts has received a request to invoke a method on a BizTalk server object. This method, which was discovered in the SDL request, is *BizTalkMessage*, and it is processed by a CGI application acting as the BizTalk server. The program BTServer.xom is written in OmniMark.

NOTE   The SOAP message created by poGen is not really what we need. At the time of this writing, the ROPE object is still being written. To use the late-bound method invocations, the SOAP document has to be fairly standardized. While these invocations work for most applications, the special requirements of a BizTalk message make the ROPE-generated SOAP envelope inadequate. Check *http://architag.com/support* to get a final version of this code. Ah, the joy of cutting-edge technology!

BizTalkMessage requires a single parameter, which is the BizTalk document. The ROPE object in the poGen program created the SOAP document. When it did, it created an HTTP header parameter that is defined by the SOAP specification, *SOAPAction*. This parameter indicates to the SOAP server which method it will invoke. OmniMark grabs this parameter using the *UTIL_GetEnv* function, shown here.

```
set SOAPAction to UTIL_GetEnv ("HTTP_SOAPACTION")
```

The *SOAPAction* parameter takes this form: *;http://localhost/toycarparts/ BTServer.xar#BizTalkMessage*. We need to isolate the action from the URL. The *SOAPAction* variable is checked using the code in Listing 11-7 to see whether it is one of the supported methods.

Checking SOAPAction

```
open SOAPResponse as buffer
do scan #main-input
  match any{formVars{"CONTENT_LENGTH"}}
       => inputData

    put Debug "%ninputData:%n%x(inputData)%n"
    set SOAPAction to UTIL_GetEnv ("HTTP_SOAPACTION")
    put Debug "%nSOAPAction (http):%g(SOAPAction)%n"
    ;http://localhost/toycarparts/BTServer.xar#BizTalkMessage
    do scan SOAPAction
        match [any except "#"]+ "#" any* => SOAPmethod
            set SOAPAction to SOAPMethod
    else
            set SOAPAction to ""
    done
    put Debug "%nSOAPAction (http):%g(SOAPAction)%n"

    do when SOAPAction = ""
        put SOAPResponse "%n<SOAP-ENV:Fault>"
            || "%n  <faultcode>101</faultcode>"
            || "%n  <faultstring>no method specified"
            || "%n</faultstring>"
            || "%n</SOAP-ENV:Fault>"
```

Listing 11-7. *Determining the method to invoke.*

```
else
    do scan SOAPAction
        match "BizTalkMessage"
            using group processPO do
                do xml-parse instance
                    scan inputData
                    suppress
                done
            done
            do when errorMsg = ""
                put SOAPResponse "%n     <BizTalkMessageResponse>"
                    || "%n        <DeliveryReceipt status='OK'>"
                    || "BizTalk Message received at "
                    || format-ymdhms
                        "=W, =xD =n =xY, =h:=m:=s =a.m. =t%n"
                        with-date now-as-ymdhms
                    || " From confirmation server: "
                    || escapeXML (fromPOConf)
                    || "</DeliveryReceipt>"
                    || "%n   </BizTalkMessageResponse>"
            else
                put SOAPResponse "%n     <BizTalkMessageResponse>"
                    || "%n        <DeliveryReceipt status='ERROR'>"
                    || "BizTalk Message Error: "
                    || errorMsg || ". Processed at "
                    || format-ymdhms
                        "=W, =xD =n =xY, =h:=m:=s =a.m. =t%n"
                        with-date now-as-ymdhms
                    || "</DeliveryReceipt>"
                    || "%n   </BizTalkMessageResponse>"
            done
        match "checkInventory"
            put SOAPResponse "%n     <checkInventoryResponse>"
                || "%n        <DeliveryReceipt status='OK'>"
                || "This method is not supported (2nd edition...). "
                || "Processed at "
                || format-ymdhms
                    "=W, =xD =n =xY, =h:=m:=s =a.m. =t%n"
                    with-date now-as-ymdhms
                || "</DeliveryReceipt>"
                || "%n   </checkInventoryResponse>"
        match "RUOK"
            put SOAPResponse "<RUOKResponse><status>"
                || "OK at "
                || format-ymdhms
                    "=W, =xD =n =xY, =h:=m:=s =a.m. =t%n"
                    with-date now-as-ymdhms
```

(continued)

Listing 11-7 *continued*

```
                   || "</status></RUOKResponse>"
         else
             put SOAPResponse "%n<SOAP-ENV:Fault>"
                   || "%n  <faultcode>100</faultcode>"
                   || "%n  <faultstring>method not supported:"
                   || "%n %g(SOAPAction)</faultstring>"
                   || "%n</SOAP-ENV:Fault>"
         done
     done
 done
 close SOAPResponse
```

The important part of this listing is invoked using the following six lines:

```
using group processPO do
    do xml-parse instance
        scan inputData
        suppress
    done
done
```

These code lines pass processing to a set of rules that are combined into an OmniMark group. The XML parser is invoked, and the XML document is passed there.

The processPO group starts dealing with the elements in the BizTalk document. The processPO group is shown in Listing 11-8.

processPO

```
;------------------------------------------------
group processPO
;------------------------------------------------
global stream txtSendTo
global stream txtReplyTo
global stream itemNum
global stream itemQty
global stream itemPrice
global stream poDate
global stream poNumber
global stream custID
global stream msgBody
global counter itemCounter
global stream needAfter
global stream needBefore
global stream promiseDate
global counter promiseQty
```

Listing 11-8. *The processPO group that contains rules to process XML elements in the BizTalk message.*

```
global stream rowData variable initial-size 0

element purchaseOrder_Chapter11_1.0
    local stream HTMLResponse
    local counter stepper
    local stream payload

    set poDate to attribute poDate
    set poNumber to attribute poNumber
    set custID to attribute custID
    set itemCounter to 0

    open msgBody as buffer
    put msgBody "CustNum=%g(custID)"
    put msgBody "&PONum=%g(poNumber)"
    put msgBody "&PODate=%g(poDate)"
    output "%c"
    close msgBody
    set HTMLResponse to postMsg (msgBody,
        "http://localhost/ToyCarParts/PlaceOrder.xar")

    clear rowData
    using group parseResponse do
        submit HTMLResponse
    done

    open payload as buffer

    put payload "<purchaseOrder_Confirm_Chapter11_1.0 "
        || "%n    xmlns='urn:purchaseOrder_Confirm_Chapter11_1.0'"
        || "%n    CustNum='%g(custID)'"
        || "%n    PONum='%g(poNumber)'>"

    repeat
        set itemNum to rowData item stepper
        increment stepper by 4
        set promiseDate to rowData item stepper
        increment stepper by 1
        set promiseQty to rowData item stepper

        do unless promiseDate = ""
            put payload "%n     <item reqID='"
            || "d" % (reqIDMapper item (stepper / 6)) || "'>"
            || "%n        <datePromised>" || promiseDate
            || "</datePromised>"
```

(continued)

Listing 11-8 *continued*

```
              || "%n          <qtyPromised>" || "d" % promiseQty
              || "</qtyPromised>"
              || "%n     </item>"
        done

        increment stepper by 1

        exit when stepper > number-of rowData
    again
    put payload "%n</purchaseOrder_Confirm_Chapter11_1.0>"
    close payload

    do
        local stream originalBizTalk

        set originalBizTalk to makeResponse(payload,
            txtReplyTo, txtSendTo)
        set fromPOConf to postMsg (originalBizTalk, txtReplyTo)
    done

element #implied
    suppress

element "dlv:address" when parent is "dlv:to"
    set txtSendTo to "%c"

element "dlv:address" when parent is "dlv:from"
    set txtReplyTo to "%c"

element item
    output "%c"
    increment itemCounter
    put msgBody "&After%d(itemCounter)=%v(needAfter)"
    put msgBody "&Before%d(itemCounter)=%v(needBefore)"
    put msgBody "&Part%d(itemCounter)=%g(itemNum)"
    put msgBody "&Qty%d(itemCounter)=%g(itemQty)"
    put msgBody "&Price%d(itemCounter)=%g(itemPrice)"
    set new reqIDMapper to attribute reqID

element number when parent is item
    set itemNum to "%c"

element price when parent is item
    set itemPrice to "%c"

element qty when parent is item
    set itemQty to "%c"
```

In Listing 11-8, the first element to be processed is *purchaseOrder_ Chapter11_1.0*. The main job of this element is to do enough processing to fool the legacy order processing program, ProcessOrder.xom, into thinking it is being called by PlaceOrder.htm. When *purchaseOrder_Chapter11_1.0* is encountered, ProcessOrder.xom starts building the body of an HTTP POST document. The HTTP POST method is covered in more detail in Chapter 8. The document is posted to the CGI program (PlaceOrder.xom) by the *postMsg* function, which is shown in Listing 11-9.

```
postMsg

define stream function postMsg (
    value stream payload,
    value stream url
    ) as
    local HttpRequest Request
    local HttpResponse Response
    local stream request-Headers variable
    local stream response-Headers variable

    HttpRequestSetFromURL Request from (url)
    set Request key "method" to "POST"
    set Request key "entity-body" to payload

    HttpRequestSend Request into Response

    HttpObjectGetHeaders Request into request-Headers
    HttpObjectGetHeaders Response into response-Headers

    do when not(HttpObjectIsInError Request)
        return Response key "entity-body"
    done
```

Listing 11-9. *The* postMsg *function performs an* HTTP POST *method to a CGI program.*

As shown in Listing 11-9, the *postMsg* function uses the OmniMark HTTP library of functions. The *HttpRequestSetFromURL* function initializes an HTTP packet. After that packet is set, we need to change the parameters to *POST* and put our payload inside the body of the document. Then we use the *HttpRequestSend* function to send the packet and place the response into another object. An example of the body of the *HTTP POST* package is shown here. (This code is one long line broken to fit on the book page.)

```
CustNum=84-4281-81&PONum=1182&PODate=2000-06-04&After1=2000-05-
24&Before1=2000-06-22&Part1=LSC91023&Qty1=1&Price1=340&After2=2000-05-
21&Before2=2000-06-11&Part2=LSC91012&Qty2=12&Price2=35
```

The only thing we are interested in is the body of the HTTP response document, which is returned to us after we post. This returned document is the HTML
created by the CGI program. An example is shown in Listing 11-10.

Return.htm

```
<HTML>
  <HEAD>
    <TITLE>Toy Car Parts, Inc: Order Entered</TITLE>
  </HEAD>
  <BODY>
    <H1>Order Entered</H1>
    <P>This is to confirm that the order below has been entered.
       Timestamp: 2000-06-04 11:54:52</P>
    <TABLE BORDER='1'>
      <THEAD>
        <TR>
          <TH>Part number</TH>
          <TH>Description</TH>
          <TH>Price</TH>
          <TH>Status</TH>
          <TH>Ship Date</TH>
          <TH>Ship Quantity</TH>
        </TR>
      </THEAD>
<TR>
    <TD VALIGN='TOP'>LSC91023</TD>
    <TD VALIGN='TOP'>"Marine Corps" Locker, 265lbs  </TD>
    <TD VALIGN='TOP'>340</TD>
    <TD VALIGN='TOP'>Manager approval (price too low)</TD>
    <TD VALIGN='TOP'>20000605235452-0600</TD>
    <TD VALIGN='TOP'>1</TD>
</TR>
<TR>
    <TD VALIGN='TOP'>LSC91012</TD>
    <TD VALIGN='TOP'>Single Clothing Locker, 21"x18"x78", 117lbs</TD>
    <TD VALIGN='TOP'>35</TD>
    <TD VALIGN='TOP'>Manager approval (price too low)</TD>
    <TD VALIGN='TOP'>20000605235452-0600</TD>
    <TD VALIGN='TOP'>12</TD>
</TR>
    </TABLE>
  </BODY>
</HTML>
```

Listing 11-10. *The HTML response document created by PlaceOrder.xom.*

Once the HTML document comes back, the rules in another group, parseResponse, are executed using the following code:

```
using group parseResponse do
    submit HTMLResponse
done
```

The parseResponse group contains a set of *find* rules that look for patterns in the text and set a keyed shelf (an associative array) of stream variables to values found in the table cells. The parseResponse group is shown in Listing 11-11.

```
parseResponse

;----------------------------
group parseResponse
;----------------------------
find ("<TD VALIGN='TOP'>" any** "</TD>" white-space*)+ => Cells
    repeat scan Cells
        match "<TD VALIGN='TOP'>" any** => Content "</TD>"
            set new rowData to Content
        match any
    again

find any
    ; suppress the rest
```

Listing 11-11. *The parseResponse group contains* find *rules to process the HTML document returned from PlaceOrder.xom.*

The rowData shelf contains all the content in the cells. Now it's time to finish the purchase order confirmation document that will be sent back to Toi Carz. The purchase order document should look something like this:

```
<purchaseOrder_Confirm_Chapter11_1.0
    xmlns='urn:purchaseOrder_Confirm_Chapter11_1.0'
    CustNum='84-4281-81'
    PONum='1189'>
    <item reqID='62'>
        <datePromised>20000606000352-0600</datePromised>
        <qtyPromised>1</qtyPromised>
    </item>
    <item reqID='70'>
        <datePromised>20000606000352-0600</datePromised>
        <qtyPromised>12</qtyPromised>
    </item>
</purchaseOrder_Confirm_Chapter11_1.0>
```

To achieve this document structure, we use the code shown in Listing 11-12.

Creating line items

```
put payload "<purchaseOrder_Confirm_Chapter11_1.0 "
    || "%n    xmlns='urn:purchaseOrder_Confirm_Chapter11_1.0'"
    || "%n    CustNum='%g(custID)'"
    || "%n    PONum='%g(poNumber)'>"

repeat
    set itemNum to rowData item stepper
    increment stepper by 4
    set promiseDate to rowData item stepper
    increment stepper by 1
    set promiseQty to rowData item stepper

    do unless promiseDate = ""
        put payload "%n    <item reqID='"
        || "d" % (reqIDMapper item (stepper / 6)) || "'>"
        || "%n        <datePromised>" || promiseDate
        || "</datePromised>"
        || "%n        <qtyPromised>" || "d" % promiseQty
        || "</qtyPromised>"
        || "%n    </item>"
    done

    increment stepper by 1

    exit when stepper > number-of rowData
again
put payload "%n</purchaseOrder_Confirm_Chapter11_1.0>"
close payload
```

Listing 11-12. *Creating line items for the purchase order confirmation program.*

The purchase order document is then wrapped inside a BizTalk document by using the *makeResponse* function, shown in Listing 11-13.

makeResponse

```
define stream function makeResponse(
  value stream strPayload,
  value stream strSendTo,
  value stream strReplyTo
  ) as
```

Listing 11-13. *The* makeResponse *function creates a BizTalk envelope and places a payload document inside.*

```
local stream response

set response to "<?xml version='1.0'?>"
|| "%n<SOAP-ENV:Envelope"
|| "%n  xmlns:SOAP-ENV='http://schemas.xmlsoap.org/soap/envelope/'"
|| "%n  xmlns:SOAP-ENC='http://schemas.xmlsoap.org/soap/encoding/'"
|| "%n  xmlns:xsi='http://www.w3.org/1999/XMLSchema-instance'>"
|| "%n  <SOAP-ENV:Header>"
|| "%n    <dlv:delivery SOAP-ENV:mustUnderstand='1'"
|| "%n xmlns:dlv='http://schemas.biztalk.org/btf-2-0/delivery'"
|| "%n       xmlns:agr='http://www.trading-agreements.org/types/'>"
|| "%n      <dlv:to>"
|| "%n        <dlv:address xsi:type='agr:department'>"
|| escapeXML(strSendTo) || "</dlv:address>"
|| "%n      </dlv:to>"
|| "%n      <dlv:from>"
|| "%n        <dlv:address xsi:type='agr:organization'>"
|| escapeXML(strReplyTo) || "</dlv:address>"
|| "%n      </dlv:from>"
|| "%n    </dlv:delivery>"
|| "%n    <prop:properties SOAP-ENV:mustUnderstand='1'"
|| "%n  xmlns:prop='http://schemas.biztalk.org/btf-2-0/properties'>"
|| "%n      <prop:identity>uuid:" || genUUID()
|| "</prop:identity>"
|| "%n      <prop:sentAt>"
|| iso8601(now-as-ymdhms) || "</prop:sentAt>"
|| "%n      <prop:expiresAt>"
|| iso8601(add-to-ymdhms now-as-ymdhms hours 2)
|| "</prop:expiresAt>"
|| "%n      <prop:topic>" || escapeXML(strReplyTo)
|| "</prop:topic>"
|| "%n    </prop:properties>"
|| "%n  </SOAP-ENV:Header>"
|| "%n  <SOAP-ENV:Body>"
|| "%n" || strPayload
|| "%n  </SOAP-ENV:Body>"
|| "%n</SOAP-ENV:Envelope>"
return response
```

In the next section we see the purchase order confirmation-processing program, which consists of an ASP page that processes an HTTP POST document containing a BizTalk message. It is called in the same way we called the order-processing program, PlaceOrder.xom.

PROCESSING THE PURCHASE ORDER CONFIRMATION

Back at Toi Carz, an ASP application named poConfirm.asp is waiting to receive confirmation of our purchase order. This program is acting as a BizTalk server in that it reads a BizTalk document and does processing based on the body element type and the contents of the payload. The purchase order confirmation program is shown in Listing 11-14.

```
poConfirm.asp

<%@language=vbscript%>
<%
Function ymdhms2mdy(ymdhms)
    strYear = mid(ymdhms, 1, 4)
    strMonth = mid(ymdhms, 5, 2)
    strDay = mid(ymdhms, 7, 2)
    ymdhms2mdy = strMonth & "/" & strDay & "/" & strYear
End Function

Function closeReq(reqID, datePromised, qtyPromised)
    Set dbPurchaseOrders = Server.CreateObject("ADODB.Connection")
    Set rsPORequests = Server.CreateObject ("ADODB.Recordset")
    rsPORequests.CursorType = 2
    rsPORequests.LockType = 2

    dbPurchaseOrders.Open "dbTC-PurchaseOrders"
    txtSQL = "SELECT PORequests.reqID, vendors.vendorName, " _
        & "PORequests.itemPrice, PORequests.needBefore, " _
        & "PORequests.needAfter, PORequests.itemQty, " _
        & "PORequests.qtyPromised, PORequests.datePromised, " _
        & "PORequests.itemNum, PORequests.requestorID, " _
        & "catalog.description, PORequests.itemPrice, " _
        & "PORequests.itemQty FROM [catalog] " _
        & "INNER JOIN (vendors INNER JOIN PORequests " _
        & "ON vendors.vendorID = PORequests.vendorID) " _
        & "ON catalog.itemNum = PORequests.itemNum " _
        & "WHERE (((PORequests.reqID)=" & reqID & "));"
    rsPORequests.Open txtSQL, dbPurchaseOrders
    rsPORequests("datePromised") = ymdhms2mdy(datePromised)
    rsPORequests("qtyPromised") = qtyPromised
    rsPORequests.Update

    Set dbEmployees = Server.CreateObject("ADODB.Connection")
    dbEmployees.Open "dbTC-Employees"
```

Listing 11-14. *The poConfirm.asp program processes the purchase order confirmation.*

```
    Set rsEmployees = dbEmployees.Execute( _
        "SELECT * FROM Employees where empID=" _
        & rsPORequests("requestorID"))

    If Not rsEmployees.EOF Then
        Set exchangeMail = CreateObject("CDONTS.NewMail")
        strFrom = "biztalk_robot@toicarz.com"
        strTarget = rsEmployees("EMail")
        strSubject = "Purchase requisition confirmation"
        strMsg = "The purchase requisition for your order has " _
                "been confirmed" _
            & vbCrLf & "  Item:          " & rsPORequests("itemNum") _
            & vbCrLf & "  Description:   " & rsPORequests("description") _
            & vbCrLf & "  Vendor:        " & rsPORequests("vendorName") _
            & vbCrLf & "  Qty Ordered:   " & rsPORequests("itemQty") _
            & vbCrLf & "  Qty Promised:  " & rsPORequests("qtyPromised") _
            & vbCrLf & "  Date Required: " & rsPORequests("needBefore") _
            & vbCrLf & "  Date Promised: " & rsPORequests("datePromised")

        Response.Write(vbCrLf & "Message to " _
            & rsEmployees("FName") & " " & rsEmployees("LName") _
            & " <" & rsEmployees("Email") & ">" _
            & vbCrLf & vbCrLf & strMsg)
        exchangeMail.Send strFrom, strTarget, strSubject, strMessage
        Set exchangeMail = Nothing
    End If

    rsPORequests.Close
    Set rsPORequest = Nothing
    dbEmployees.Close
    Set dbEmployees = Nothing
    dbPurchaseOrders.close
    Set dbPurchaseOrders = Nothing
End Function

Function closePO(poNum)
    Set dbPOSent = Server.CreateObject("ADODB.Connection")
    dbPOSent.Open "dbTC-PurchaseOrders"

    txtSQL = "UPDATE POSent SET confReceived=#" & CDate(date) _
        & "# WHERE poNum= " & poNum

    dbPOSent.Execute txtSQL', intrecs, adcmdtext

    dbPOSent.Close
    Set dbPOSent = Nothing
End Function
```

(continued)

Listing 11-14 *continued*

```
HTTPSize = Request.TotalBytes
HTTPBody = Request.BinaryRead(HTTPSize)
strXML = ""
For i = 1 To HTTPSize
    strXML = strXML & Chr(AscB(MidB(HTTPBody,i,1)))
Next

strXML = Replace (strXML, "%3C", "<")
strXML = Replace (strXML, "%3E", ">")
strXML = Replace (strXML, "%20", " ")
strXML = Replace (strXML, "%2F", "/")
strXML = Replace (strXML, "%3D", "=")
strXML = Replace (strXML, "%0A", vbCrLf)

Set oXMLDoc = Server.CreateObject("Microsoft.XMLDOM")
oXMLDoc.loadXML(strXML)

If oXMLDoc.parseError.errorcode <> 0 Then
    Response.Write("Error, Reason: " & oXMLDoc.parseError.reason _
        & ", Code: " & oXMLDoc.parseError.errorcode _
        & ", Line: " & oXMLDoc.parseError.line)
End If

poNum = oXMLDoc.selectSingleNode_
("//purchaseOrder_Confirm_Chapter11_1.0").attributes.getNamedItem_
("PONum").nodeValue

Set collItem = oXMLDoc.selectNodes("//item")
For i = 0 To collItem.length - 1
    reqID = collItem.item(i).attributes.getNamedItem("reqID").nodeValue
    datePromised = collItem.item(i).selectSingleNode("datePromised").text
    qtyPromised = collItem.item(i).selectSingleNode("qtyPromised").text
    Response.Write("reqID: " & reqID _
        & ", datePromised: " & datePromised _
        & ", qtyPromised: " & qtyPromised)
    closeReq reqID, datePromised, qtyPromised
Next

closePO(poNum)
%>
```

The poConfirm.asp program must perform three tasks. First it must close out each purchase requisition by updating the PORequests table with the delivery date and quantity promised by Toy Car Parts. It does this using the *closeReq* function. This function also performs the second task, notifying the person who placed the purchase requisition, by using the Collaboration Data Objects library CDONTS. CDONTS provides an interface for e-mail by using Microsoft Exchange Server.

The third task poConfirm.asp must perform is to close the purchase order by marking the record in the POSent table. It does this using the *closePO* function.

The program then sends a response to the OmniMark BizTalk server, which passes the message back to the purchase order generation program that started the process.

This is a very basic system showing the minimum requirements of a BizTalk server environment by using two different operating system/language platforms. It is, of course, more difficult to implement systems like this when many possible variables exist, but open standards such as BizTalk, SOAP, and XML make it much easier to build and deploy such systems.

One of the interesting challenges we overcame in building the system was getting use out of an existing application that has been working for years. The PlaceOrder system had been completely debugged and had worked well with our environment, so why should we change it? Because we were able to use state-of-the-art tools and open standards, we could breathe new life into a legacy application. The lesson here is that you don't necessarily need to discard working systems just because they aren't written using the newest tools and technologies.

Some really cool tools are coming along to help developers deploy systems that can communicate between you and your trading partners. The SOAP Toolkit for Visual Studio 6.0 is one such tool that allows developers to get beyond the XML syntax to deploy systems that leverage the entire Web. This is really powerful stuff! Other vendors have announced that they are supporting SOAP with tools similar to Microsoft's toolkit.

Other tools are being developed to work with BizTalk servers. In Chapter 12, I show you an early release of some tools built into the Microsoft BizTalk Server 2000 Technology Preview. These tools also allow the business programmer to get the most out of XML through useful utilities such as the BizTalk Editor, which allows you to create schemas, and the BizTalk Mapper, which creates transformations between different schemas. When Microsoft BizTalk Server 2000 is released, it will have other developer tools to help integrate business transactions into your enterprise systems.

Chapter 12

Microsoft BizTalk Server 2000

In Chapter 10, I mentioned factors that you might consider when writing or selecting a BizTalk Framework Compliant (BFC) server for your environment. Remember that the only real requirements of a BizTalk server are to understand the BizTalk framework tags and then do something intelligent with a document based on those tags. Microsoft BizTalk Server 2000 goes way beyond the basic XML processing capabilities I outlined in Chapter 10. This server combines several services that allow you to integrate business documents into your current system. The product also provides new components that you can use to manage your data and exchange information, as well as components for server management and maintenance. Microsoft has been behind the BizTalk initiative since its inception, and the product features what you need in a server designed—at the business-document level—to integrate your office with the offices of your trading partners.

BizTalk Server 2000 is a data-translation and application-integration server used to exchange business data. BizTalk Server 2000 uses XML to allow you to conduct your business partner relationships across industries and between business systems regardless of platform, operating system, or underlying technology. The server provides a standard gateway for sending and receiving documents across the Internet, and it offers a range of services that ensure data integrity, delivery, and security.

BizTalk Server 2000 functionality includes the ability to receive incoming documents, parse the documents to determine their specific format, extract key identifiers, identify specific processing rules, and deliver documents to their respective destinations. Also included are services for data mapping and services for ensuring data integrity, delivery, and security.

BizTalk Server 2000 provides tools for defining the structure of your business documents (schemas) and for transforming data between these documents by using XSLT. The BizTalk Server documents refer to this transformation as mapping.

The system uses XML for all data transfer but also accepts and creates other formats, most notably electronic data interchange (EDI). The tools in BizTalk Server 2000 offer the data translation necessary for an application-integration server.

This chapter uses two hands-on examples to examine a couple of the tools you can use to create and convert XML documents: the Microsoft BizTalk Editor and the Microsoft BizTalk Mapper.

THE BIZTALK EDITOR

In Chapter 4, I mentioned a tool for creating schemas, XML Authority. Why do you need another tool for creating schemas? While XML Authority is great for creating any kind of schema, the BizTalk Editor is optimized to create schemas that define business documents. Also, the schemas created by the BizTalk Editor contain extra information by way of some custom Microsoft and BizTalk namespaces that simplify mapping from one format to another. Using the BizTalk Editor, you can create schemas based on industry standards or you can create specifications unique to your organization.

Exercise: Creating a Purchase Order Schema

Let's use the BizTalk Editor to create a schema that can be used with BizTalk Server 2000. Let's create our favorite business document, the purchase order. This will be a standard purchase order schema that we might use to exchange business information with our partners. This example is created with tools from the BizTalk Server 2000 Tech Preview. You should have this or a subsequent version of BizTalk Server 2000 loaded on your system to complete the exercise.

1. First you need to load the BizTalk Editor. From the Start menu, select Programs, Microsoft BizTalk Server 2000, and then choose BizTalk Editor. You should see the screen shown in Figure 12-1.

    The example you see in Figure 12-1 is simple for the purpose of demonstrating the tools and how they work together. Most documents will be more complex than this—in some cases they will be much more complex. However, the concepts you'll learn here apply to all documents.

2. On the File menu, click New to create a new document. You will see the New Document Specification dialog box. Click Blank Specification, and then click OK.

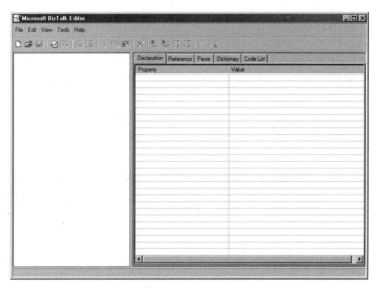

Figure 12-1. *The BizTalk Editor allows you to create specifications that describe the structure of a business document.*

3. In the panel on the left-hand side of the editor, you'll see a small icon with the label Blank Specification. This is a record that will act as the root of our document. Right-click on the record, and click Rename. Call the record *PurchaseOrder*. Press Enter.

Note that the BizTalk Editor does not use the familiar XML words element and attribute. Instead, it uses records and fields, which are more familiar to typical database programmers. A record is similar to a database record in that it can contain fields. A field is where the data is located. In the BizTalk Editor, a record can contain data and fields. In the declaration area, you must decide to make something an element or an attribute. By default, records are elements, and fields are attributes.

4. Right-click on the newly renamed record, and choose New Field. Call the field *PODate*.

5. Repeat step 4, and call this new field *CustomerNumber*.

6. Right-click on the *PurchaseOrder* record, and click New Record. You are going to create a container for other fields. Call the new record *Item*. Notice the pane on the right where this field is further defined. All the fields you've created are defined as *Type Attribute*, and the records are defined by default as *Type Element*. Click in the Content cell containing the value *Empty*. This turns the cell into a drop-down list box. Change the value in this cell by selecting *Text Only* from the drop-down list box. We'll use this record to hold the number of the item being ordered.

7. Right-click on the Item record, and select New Field. Name the field *Qty*. In the Declaration pane, click in the cell to the right of *Data Type* and select *Integer (int)* from the drop-down list.

8. Repeat step 7, and call this new field *Price* with a data type of *Fixed Point (14.4)*.

9. From the File menu, choose Save. Name the file *PurchaseOrder1.xml*, and put it in a convenient folder. The screen should look something like Figure 12-2.

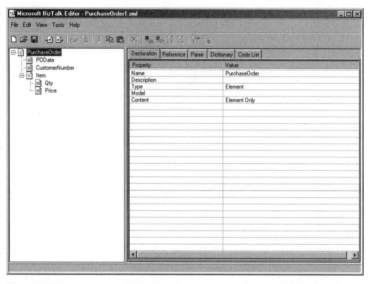

Figure 12-2. *Final purchase order structure in the BizTalk Editor.*

When you saved the document, the XML schema shown in Listing 12-1 was created. This schema, however, looks different from the basic schemas described in Chapter 4 because the BizTalk Server uses extra information that the basic schema syntax does not provide.

The PurchaseOrder1.xml document created in this example is specified in XML Data Reduced (XDR). However, when the W3C XML Schema Definition (XSD) syntax is finalized, Microsoft will support that syntax as well. Converting from one syntax to the other should be as easy as clicking Save As. You should also be able to use XSLT to make the syntax change.

In Listing 12-1, notice the *b:* namespace defined in the <Schema> start tag. This namespace contains a set of tags used by various parts of BizTalk Server 2000.

PurchaseOrder1.xml

```xml
<?xml version="1.0"?>
<Schema name="PurchaseOrder"
    b:root_reference="PurchaseOrder"
    b:standard="XML"
    xmlns="urn:schemas-microsoft-com:xml-data"
    xmlns:d="urn:schemas-microsoft-com:datatypes"
    xmlns:b="urn:schemas-microsoft-com:BizTalkServer">
    <b:SelectionFields/>

    <ElementType name="PurchaseOrder" content="eltOnly">
        <b:RecordInfo/>
        <AttributeType name="PODate">
            <b:FieldInfo/>
        </AttributeType>
        <AttributeType name="CustomerNumber">
            <b:FieldInfo/>
        </AttributeType>
        <attribute type="PODate"/>
        <attribute type="CustomerNumber"/>
        <element type="Item"/>
    </ElementType>

    <ElementType name="Item" content="textOnly" model="closed">
        <b:RecordInfo/>
        <AttributeType name="Qty" d:type="int">
            <b:FieldInfo/>
        </AttributeType>
        <AttributeType name="Price" d:type="fixed.14.4">
            <b:FieldInfo/>
        </AttributeType>
        <attribute type="Qty"/>
        <attribute type="Price"/>
    </ElementType>
</Schema>
```

Listing 12-1. *Schema created by the BizTalk Editor.*

THE BIZTALK MAPPER

In Chapter 6, you wrote an XSLT program to convert one XML document into another. This type of document conversion is a critical part of the BizTalk process if your business partners are using different schemas.

Although I like working directly with XSLT, not everyone does, and not all companies can afford to have an XSLT expert on staff. Using the BizTalk Mapper, you can map the records and fields of two different schemas. BizTalk Server 2000 uses these maps to process and translate data into formats that you can share within your own organization or with your partner organizations.

Exercise: Mapping Two Different Purchase Order Schemas

To explore how the BizTalk Mapper works, let's take the schema we just made and create a map from it to another schema that describes a purchase order.

1. Start the BizTalk Mapper from the Start menu by selecting Programs, Microsoft BizTalk Server 2000, and then clicking BizTalk Mapper.

2. You need to find the two schemas to map. From the File menu, select New. In the Select Source Specification Type dialog box, click Local Files to bring up the Select Source Specification dialog box and find the PurchaseOrder1.xml schema you created in the first example.

    The Select Destination Specification Type dialog box should now be visible. Repeat the process for the second schema, but find the purchase order that I created on the companion CD. It is in \Samples\Ch12\ PurchaseOrder2.xml. Your screen should look like Figure 12-3.

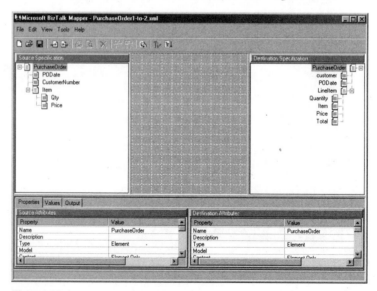

Figure 12-3. *Mapping two different purchase order schemas in BizTalk Mapper.*

You create a map by dragging from a field on the left to a matching field on the right. The process is about as simple as that, but this tool adds some other important functionality.

3. From the Tools menu, select Options to bring up the BizTalk Mapper Options dialog box. Select the Allow Record Links check box. Setting this option will allow you to map the textual contents of records rather than just fields. Click OK.

4. Drag and drop the *CustomerNumber* field in the Source Specification pane onto the *customer* field in the Destination Specification pane. You will see a line connecting the two, as Figure 12-4 illustrates.

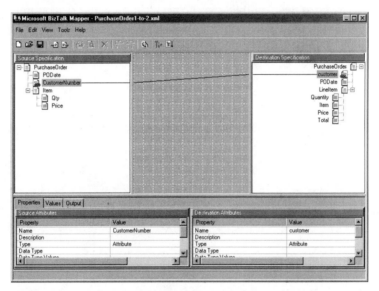

Figure 12-4. *You create maps by connecting the fields in the Source Specification pane to fields in the Destination Specification pane.*

5. Repeat step 4 three more times, mapping *Item* with *Item*, *Qty* with *Quantity*, and *Price* with *Price*. It's that easy!

6. Notice that the Destination Specification pane has a field that is not included in the Source Specification—*Total*, the total price for a line item. Without parallel fields, you can't directly map from the Source Specification document (window) to the Destination Specification document. So you'll have to do some computing. This is where the functoid comes in. From the View menu, select Functoid Palette. You'll see the Functoid Palette dialog box, as shown in Figure 12-5.

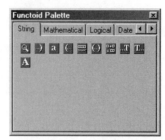

Figure 12-5. *Functoids provide many different computational aids for mapping fields between the source and destination files.*

7. The *Total* field in the Destination Specification is the product of the *Qty* and *Price* fields in the Source Specification pane, so you must do a little multiplication. Click on the Mathematical tab.

8. Select the functoid icon that looks like a multiplication symbol. Drag this functoid from the functoid palette into the grid between the Source Specification and the Destination Specification panels. Your screen should resemble Figure 12-6.

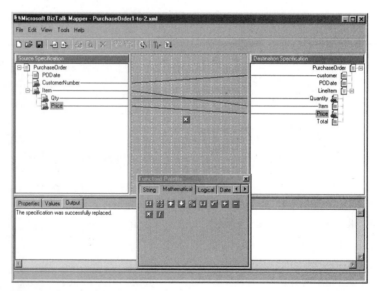

Figure 12-6. *The multiplication functoid allows you to multiply two numbers in the Source Specification and put the resulting product into a Destination Specification field.*

9. Drag a line from the *Qty* element in the Source Specification to the multiplication functoid.

10. Repeat step 9 with the *Price* element in the Source Specification.

11. Drag a line from the multiplication functoid to the *Total* field in the Destination Specification. You have just multiplied two numbers and output the product.

12. You still need to deal with the date. In the Source Specification document, the *date* field contains a date in a common U.S. form: month/day/year. In the Destination Specification, you must specify the date in ISO 8601 format: YYYY-MM-DD. No functoid exists to convert from one to the other, so you need to create a special script to do that. Click on the Advanced tab in the Functoid Palette dialog box. This tab contains a single functoid—the Custom Visual Basic Script functoid. Drag this functoid into the grid area.

13. Drag a line from the *PODate* field in the Source Specification to the scripting functoid, and then drag a line from the scripting functoid to the *PODate* element in the Destination Specification field.

14. Double-click on the scripting functoid, and click on the Script tab. You will see the default script shown in Figure 12-7.

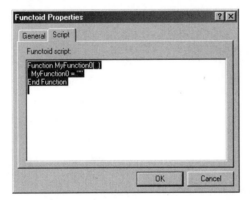

Figure 12-7. *The Custom Visual Basic Script functoid allows you to create scripts to assist in transforming a source document into a destination document.*

15. Delete the existing function, and replace it with the following script:

```
Function mdy2iso8601(dateIn)
    iFirst = instr(dateIn, "/")
    iSecond = instr(iFirst + 1, dateIn, "/")
    iMonth =  left(dateIn, iFirst - 1)
    iDay = mid(dateIn, iFirst + 1, iSecond - iFirst - 1)
    iYear = mid(dateIn, iSecond + 1, 4)
    mdy2iso8601 = iYear & "-" & right("0" & iMonth, 2) & _
                "-" & right("0" & iDay, 2)
End Function
```

The *mdy2iso8601* function converts a date in the source format (mm/dd/yyyy) into the equivalent that you need. Click OK to close the Functoid Properties dialog box. Your BizTalk Mapper screen should look like the screen in Figure 12-8.

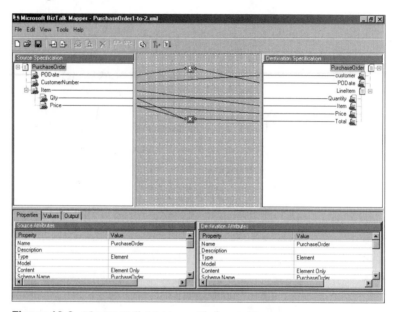

Figure 12-8. *The BizTalk Mapper with functoids.*

16. Now you need to test the script. Close the Functoid Palette dialog box. Click on the Values tab at the bottom of the BizTalk Mapper window. Make sure the *PODate* field of the Source Specification pane is highlighted, and then enter a Source test value in the form mm/dd/yyyy, such as 04/27/2000. You'll test this function in a later step. First you'll add more test data for some other fields.

17. Now you need to make sure the multiplication functoid works. Select the *Qty* field from the Source Specification pane. Enter a value in the field as an integer, such as 95.

18. Select the *Price* field from the Source Specification pane, and enter a decimal price such as 12.95.

19. Now you are ready to test. From the Tools menu, select Test Map. Notice that the Output tab is brought to the forefront, and the output of the process is displayed. The output should look like this:

```
<PurchaseOrder customer="CustomerNumber_1"
    PODate="2000-04-10">
<LineItem>
<Quantity>95</Quantity>
<Item>Item_1</Item>
<Price>12.95</Price>
<Total>1230.25</Total>
</LineItem>
</PurchaseOrder>
```

Notice that the *PODate* did change from one form to the other, and that the value inside the <Total> tags is the quantity multiplied by the price.

20. Now you need to create an XSLT style sheet that will do the transformation. Open the Tools menu, and then click Compile Map. Notice that the output is an XSLT program. It should look like the output in Listing 12-2.

   BizTalk Server 2000 will use the style sheet in Listing 12-2 when a document comes in from a trading partner who sends you XML documents by using the schema defined in PurchaseOrder1.xml.

21. Save the mapping specification by selecting File and then Save Compiled Map As. Name the file *PO1-2.xsl*. This is an XML document that the BizTalk Server uses to do mapping. You can use Microsoft Internet Explorer to view this file.

PO1-2.xsl

```
<xsl:stylesheet
    xmlns:xsl='http://www.w3.org/1999/XSL/Transform'
    xmlns:msxsl='urn:schemas-microsoft-com:xslt'
    xmlns:var='urn:var' xmlns:user='urn:user' version='1.0'>
    <xsl:output method='xml' indent='yes' omit-xml-declaration='yes'/>
    <xsl:template match='/'>
        <xsl:apply-templates select='PurchaseOrder'/>
    </xsl:template>
    <xsl:template match='PurchaseOrder'>
        <PurchaseOrder>
            <xsl:attribute name='customer'>
                <xsl:value-of select='@CustomerNumber'/>
            </xsl:attribute>
            <xsl:variable name='var:v1'
                select='user:mdy2iso8601(string(@PODate))'/>
            <xsl:attribute name='PODate'>
                <xsl:value-of select='$var:v1'/>
            </xsl:attribute>
```

Listing 12-2. *XSLT style sheet created by BizTalk Mapper.* (continued)

PO1-2.xsl *continued*

```
            <xsl:for-each select='Item'>
                <LineItem>
                    <Quantity>
                        <xsl:value-of select='@Qty'/>
                    </Quantity>
                    <Item>
                        <xsl:value-of select='./text()'/>
                    </Item>
                    <Price>
                        <xsl:value-of select='@Price'/>
                    </Price>
                    <xsl:variable name='var:v2'
            select='user:fctmathmultiply2(string(@Qty), string(@Price))'/>
                    <Total>
                        <xsl:value-of select='$var:v2'/>
                    </Total>
                </LineItem>
        </xsl:for-each>
        </PurchaseOrder>
    </xsl:template>

    <msxsl:script language='VBScript' implements-prefix='user'>
        <![CDATA[
        Function FctMathMultiply2( p_strParm0, p_strParm1 )
          If (  IsNumeric( p_strParm0 ) And _
             IsNumeric( p_strParm1 ) ) Then
                FctMathMultiply2 = CStr ( CDbl( p_strParm0 ) _
                * CDbl( p_strParm1 ) )
          Else
             FctMathMultiply2 = ""
          End If
        End Function

        Function mdy2iso8601(dateIn)
            iFirst = instr(dateIn, "/")
            iSecond = instr(iFirst + 1, dateIn, "/")
            iMonth =  left(dateIn, iFirst - 1)
            iDay = mid(dateIn, iFirst + 1, iSecond - iFirst - 1)
            iYear = mid(dateIn, iSecond + 1, 4)
            mdy2iso8601 = iYear & "-" & _
            right("0" & iMonth, 2) & _
            "-" & right("0" & iDay, 2)
        End Function
        ]]>
    </msxsl:script>
</xsl:stylesheet>
```

In addition to XML, the BizTalk Mapper can also read and write to other formats, including two widely used EDI specifications: ANSI X12 and EDIFACT. The BizTalk Mapper also allows mapping to Flat files, XML files defined with the document type definition (DTD) schema syntax, and XDR schemas. Even though the BizTalk Mapper can work with these diverse standards, it is optimized for use with the XML-based BizTalk Framework 2.0.

OTHER BIZTALK TOOLS

Microsoft BizTalk Server 2000 has several other features for managing partner relationships:

- **BizTalk Management Desk**   This is a graphical user interface (GUI) that you can use either on the server or remotely on a client to manage the exchange of data between trading partner organizations and applications.

- **BizTalk Server Administration Console**   This is a Microsoft Management Console (MMC) snap-in you can use to manage and maintain your server or server groups. The administration console documentation includes extensive troubleshooting information.

- **BizTalk Document Tracking**   This user interface tracks documents and monitors document activity as documents pass through the server. Document Tracking is essential for two major audiences: business analysts and system administrators. Business analysts rely on tracking documents and activities to monitor, analyze, and develop internal business strategies. By extracting and storing important user-defined data from within documents, system analysts can track and analyze detailed information about business operations. System administrators use tracking documents and activities to define the scope of data tracking, establish activity logging settings, purge settings, and perform troubleshooting analyses.

- **BizTalk Workflow Designer**   Workflows can be created through a wonderful interface that uses Microsoft Visio. This interface is a graphical representation of the flow of your business processes. A business analyst creates a workflow using a graphical drag-and-drop environment, and Microsoft BizTalk Server 2000 creates hooks into the appropriate processes to make the workflow do its work. This workflow is attached to the trading partner agreement and is executed whenever a document comes in from that partner.

BIZTALK SERVER 2000 DATA PROCESSING

BizTalk Server 2000 can do much more than move XML documents around the Internet. The product is designed to be a centerpiece for managing agreements between you and your trading partners. It does this by providing a rich set of tools for creating descriptions of your partnership arrangements.

In the following scenario, let's see how a BizTalk server can be used to integrate an order process between three companies. A description of the players follows.

- Toi Carz Corp. is a manufacturer that produces toy cars. Toi Carz is running Microsoft Commerce Server 2000 to manage its Internet presence. It is using Great Plains software as its accounting system. It is running BizTalk Server 2000 to manage its trading partner relationships.

- Toy Car Parts, Inc. is a distributor and importer of parts for toy cars and is one of Toi Carz' vendors. Because of acquisitions over the years, Toy Car Parts has an extensive set of legacy applications, some of which have been in use for decades. It is running an SAP R/3 system to manage its enterprise resource planning (ERP) environment. It is also running BizTalk Server 2000 to manage its trading partner relationships.

- Mehtap Enterprises is a manufacturer of motors for toy cars. Mehtap Enterprises is one of the manufacturers handled by Toy Car Parts, Inc. Mehtap Enterprises is an old brick-and-mortar manufacturer that installed an EDI system in the 1980s and hasn't upgraded since then. In order to deal with Mehtap Enterprises, we must be able to create and read certain EDI documents.

Placing an Order

In this example, an employee of Toi Carz will place an order for 10 Mehtap Enterprises engines. Its distributor, Toy Car Parts, Inc., has some inventory of these parts. The transaction is illustrated in Figure 12-9 and described in Table 12-1.

Figure Step	Description
1	An employee of Toi Carz places an order for products. The order is processed by Commerce Server 2000.
2	Commerce Server sends a request to BizTalk Server 2000.
3	BizTalk Server 2000 sends a message to the Great Plains accounting system,…
4	…which generates a purchase order in Great Plains format and sends it to BizTalk Server 2000.
5	BizTalk Server 2000 translates the Great Plains purchase order into a BizTalk document and sends the document to the BizTalk server at Toy Car Parts over the Internet using HTTP.

Table 12-1. *A description of Figure 12-9, which illustrates the flow of data between two companies using BizTalk servers.*

Figure Step	Description
6	Toy Car Parts uses SAP R/3. R/3 requires documents in IDoc format. BizTalk Server 2000 translates the BizTalk message into IDoc purchase order format and sends it to the SAP system.
7	The SAP system responds with an IDoc purchase order acknowledgment, which it sends back to the BizTalk server.
8	The Toy Car Parts BizTalk server transforms the acknowledgment into a BizTalk document and sends the document back to the Toi Carz BizTalk server.
9	The Toi Carz BizTalk server sends an acknowledgment (ack) over an internal system to Commerce Server 2000.
10	Commerce Server 2000 notifies the requestor that the distributor has received the order and that the distributor is currently processing the order.

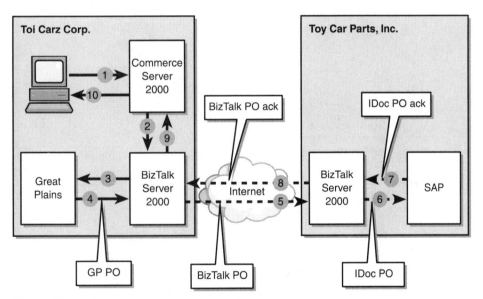

Figure 12-9. *Placing an order with a distributor.*

Checking Inventory and Ordering from the Manufacturer

Toy Car Parts needs to see if it has enough in stock to fulfill the order. Figure 12-10 shows how Toy Car Parts communicates with its suppliers. Table 12-2 describes the steps in Figure 12-10.

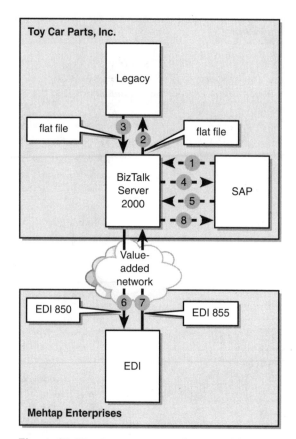

Figure 12-10. *Communication between the distributor and manufacturer.*

Figure Step	Description
1	The SAP system sends a request as an IDoc document to BizTalk Server 2000, asking the BizTalk server to request an inventory amount from the legacy inventory system.
2	BizTalk Server 2000 converts this IDoc file into a flat file, which is used to communicate with the legacy inventory system. It is important to note here that the SAP system doesn't "speak" flat file format, and the inventory system doesn't speak IDoc. BizTalk Server 2000 is providing the mapping between the two.
3	The legacy inventory system reports that only three parts are in stock.

Table 12-2. *A description of Figure 12-10.*

Figure Step	Description
4	Again, BizTalk Server 2000 translates the response, sending an IDoc document to the SAP system.
5	The SAP system knows that the request was for 10 units and knows that three are currently in stock, so it adjusts the order and creates an IDoc order for seven units. This order is sent to BizTalk Server 2000.
6	Since the manufacturer requires an EDI 850 order document, BizTalk Server 2000 converts the SAP IDoc request into an EDI 850 document and sends it over the value-added network, where the manufacturer, Mehtap Enterprises, is connected.
7	The EDI-based system at Mehtap Enterprises processes the request and sends back a response, as an EDI 855 Acknowledgment document. It is the job of the Mehtap Enterprises system to do whatever is necessary to fulfill the order. This is probably not an issue, since Mehtap Enterprises has been receiving orders as EDI 850 documents for decades. Mehtap Enterprises has no idea that we are speaking BizTalk, because BizTalk Server 2000 is doing all the transformation.
8	BizTalk Server 2000 converts the EDI 850 Acknowledgment into an IDoc and sends it to the SAP system.

Sending an Acknowledgment to the Requestor

The last step is to send an acknowledgment to Toi Carz to indicate that the order was placed and provide an approximate shipping date. This is done using an advance ship notice, or ASN. Figure 12-11 illustrates this process. Table 12-3 describes the steps illustrated in Figure 12-11.

You should take note of some important issues illustrated in this scenario. First, there is no need for any of the existing applications (in this case, Great Plains, SAP, legacy inventory, or manufacturer) to change the way they currently operate. The BizTalk server acts as a universal translator, reading requests from one place, interpreting those requests according to rules set up in the partnership agreement, and transforming them into the appropriate output.

Second, the Internet can be used to get transactions from one place to another. This means that any company that is hooked into the Internet can be part of our business, as long as we set up an agreement with it.

Third, value-added networks can be used instead of the Internet if those networks are already in place and working fine.

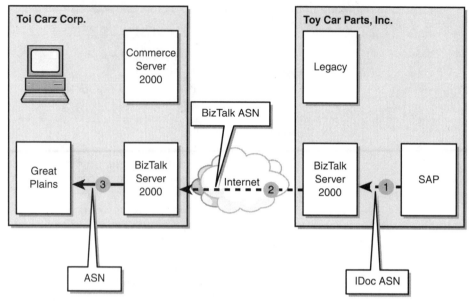

Figure 12-11. *Sending an advance ship notice back to the requesting organization.*

Figure Step	Description
1	The SAP system generates an ASN in IDoc format and sends it to BizTalk Server 2000.
2	BizTalk Server 2000 at Toy Car Parts converts this ASN into an XML document and sends it to the Toi Carz BizTalk server.
3	BizTalk Server 2000 at Toi Carz converts the XML document into an ASN that is compatible with the Great Plains software. From there, the Great Plains system is updated, and the Toi Carz personnel can query the database as they always have done.

Table 12-3. *Description of the steps in Figure 12-11.*

You should take note of some important issues illustrated in this scenario. First, there is no need for any of the existing applications (in this case, Great Plains, SAP, legacy inventory, or manufacturer) to change the way they currently operate. The BizTalk Server 2000 acts as a universal translator, reading requests from one place, interpreting those requests according to rules set up in the partnership agreement, and transforming them into the appropriate output.

Second, the Internet can be used to get transactions from one place to another. This means that any company that is hooked into the Internet can be part of our business, as long as we set up an agreement with it.

Third, value-added networks can be used instead of the Internet if those networks are already in place and working fine.

Part IV

References

These appendixes contain supplementary information that I felt was important but didn't quite fit as chapters of the book, so I have included them in this final section for your reference. Appendix A is designed to get you up to speed quickly with OmniMark, which plays a key role in the BFC server in Chapter 11. Appendix B, which contains the BizTalk Framework specification, and Appendix D, which contains the SOAP 1.1 specification, will be especially useful as you work your way through the code examples in Chapters 8 and 11. Appendix C lists a number of Web sites related to XML and BizTalk that I visit frequently.

Appendix A

OmniMark for the Impatient

OmniMark is used in this book as an example of a multiplatform programming language that has strong support for today's network programming environments. I have been using OmniMark for 10 years and find it to be stable, fast, and well supported. OmniMark started life as a tool for doing text conversion and has kept ahead of the hottest programming technologies since then.

Now OmniMark can provide a viable alternative to Perl for doing server-based programming. The OmniMark sales materials claim that OmniMark is "cheaper than Perl." This seems kind of silly, since Perl is free, right? Well, not exactly. If you've ever seen Perl code, you've probably noticed that it's visually noisy— because of the arcane regular expression syntax and its heavy use of brackets and other non-word syntax delimiters, Perl code can be difficult to understand.

If you are a Perl programmer, I want to ask you when you last fixed someone else's Perl program. Not easy, right? I've talked to many Perl programmers who would rather rewrite inherited code than fix it in place. Or how about that Perl program you wrote six months ago? Try to fix that today. I have found that the total cost of ownership (TCO) of Perl is quite high when you consider the maintenance issues.

Like Perl, OmniMark is a free product, but that's only part of its allure. OmniMark uses a pattern-matching syntax that is based on English grammar and is easy to learn and maintain. I've found that the total lifetime cost of an OmniMark program is much lower than the lifetime cost of a Perl program, because the OmniMark program can be maintained much more easily than a Perl program. Plus, OmniMark is much faster than Perl in a multiple-processor, multiple-server environment because it runs in a non-flushed mode on the server. A Perl program is typically invoked through a CGI interface. When the program is invoked, the Perl executable must be loaded each time, which opens the script for interpretation. Then everything is flushed, the process repeating for each call. New ISAPI filters and other methods allow Perl to execute in a non-flushed server mode, but in my experience, few programmers use them. This execution capability comes with OmniMark out of the box.

STREAMING PROGRAMMING LANGUAGE

A streaming programming language like OmniMark is designed to let the programmer process data streams directly and produce output stream immediately, minimizing the need to build intermediate data structures. Streaming languages are particularly useful in Internet or intranet environments, in which streaming data is ubiquitous.

Streaming languages have three principal advantages for network programming: efficiency, robustness, and productivity. Streaming languages are efficient because they minimize data copying and optimize data movement. They favor robustness because they reduce the use of variables and intermediate data structures, thus minimizing the places where errors can occur. Streaming languages enhance productivity because they foster a process-oriented programming style in which the program is a clear and direct description of the process being applied to the data.

As a streaming language, OmniMark handles input and output at the core of the language. OmniMark abstracts all data sources and data destinations so that all programming is done against generic OmniMark source objects and all output flows to generic OmniMark streams. Programmers attach sources and streams to data sources and destinations through either the core language or by OmniMark extension (OMX) components. The data processing and output creation are entirely independent of what kind of source or destination the data stream is attached to.

OmniMark maintains a current input and a current output. To process a source, you make that source the current input. To output to a destination, you make the stream attached to that destination the current output. This input-output model greatly simplifies processing, since you never need to specify what data an action operates on or what destination output goes to. You simply attach the appropriate streams and process the data as it flows. You can process data either by scanning or by parsing. Scanning employs OmniMark's sophisticated pattern-matching capabilities. Parsing employs OmniMark's integrated XML or SGML parser.

An OmniMark program consists of rules. A process rule initiates processing: you use a process rule to establish the current input and output and to initiate parsing or scanning. You use find rules for scanning. A find rule consists of a pattern to be matched in the data and a set of actions to be performed when that pattern is found. A variety of other scanning tools are also available for local scanning, the manipulation of variables, and dealing with various aspects of markup. Markup rules are used in parsing. Markup rules include element rules, which are fired when a parser encounters an element in XML or SGML data; data-content rules, which you use to process the data content of an element; and markup-error rules, which you use to catch and process errors in the markup.

The following simple OmniMark program counts the words in the text *"A duck walks into a bar"*:

```
global integer word-count initial {0}

process
   submit "A duck walks into a bar"
   output "d" % word-count || "%n"

find letter+
   increment word-count
```

The program consists of two rules and a global variable declaration. The process rule is fired when the program runs. The *submit* statement establishes the current input as the text *"A duck walks into a bar"* and initiates scanning.

The *find* rule is activated by the *submit* statement. It uses the pattern *letter+* to match any sequence of letters. In this pattern, the word *letter* is a character class representing all the uppercase and lowercase letters of the alphabet. The plus sign (+) is a repetition indicator. Together, they say "one or more letters."

Each time the *find* rule fires, it increments the global variable *word-count*. The *find* rule will fire once for each word (that is, each uninterrupted sequence of letters) in the current input. Once scanning is complete, execution moves on to the next statement in the process rule. This is the *output* statement that outputs the word count. Since the current output has not been established explicitly, output goes to the default current output, which is standard output, or standard out. If you run the program in the OmniMark Integrated Development Environment (IDE), the output will appear in the log window. If you run it on the command line, it will appear on the screen.

The *output* statement uses the format operator (%) to convert the value of the integer *word-count* to a string; it uses the concatenation operator (| |) to add a new line, represented by *"%n"*.

To try this program, type it into the OmniMark IDE and click Run. In this program, the order in which the rules appear doesn't matter, since each rule fires only when a specific event occurs. Thus we could just as easily write the program like this:

```
global integer wordcount initial {0}

find letter+
   increment wordcount

process
   submit "A duck walks into a bar"
   output "d" format wordcount || "%n"
```

This program runs the same way as the first program. This doesn't mean that the order of rules never matters in an OmniMark program. If one event causes more than one *find* rule to fire, the rule that occurs first will fire, and the one that occurs later will not. This allows you to put more specific rules before more general rules and have the general rules fire only if the specific rules do not. Take a look at this:

```
   global integer wordcount initial {0}

   process
      submit "A duck walks into a bar"
      output "d" format wordcount || "%n"

   find "duck"
      output "*"
```

(continued)

```
find letter+
  increment wordcount

find any
```

The preceding program prints *"5"*. The following program changes the order of the *find* rules and produces a different output:

```
global integer wordcount initial {0}

process
   submit "A duck walks into a bar"
   output "d" format wordcount || "%n"

find letter+
   increment wordcount

find "duck"
   output "*"

find any
```

This program prints *"6"*.

Why did I add *find any* as a new rule in both programs? Because it fixes an error in the first version of the program. The *find letter+* rule matches words. But what about the spaces between the words? If you actually ran the first program, you might have noticed that the result it printed was indented by four spaces. Those indents are the unmatched spaces from the input. Any input not matched by a *find* rule goes right through to current output. A *find any* rule at the end of a set of *find* rules is a sponge rule that soaks up any unmatched input. Of course, if you use the *find any* rule, it must always be the last *find* rule.

XML PROCESSING

OmniMark processes XML (and SGML) in a streaming manner. The XML data is streamed from its source into the parser. Structural features, such as elements, fire markup rules. Data content is streamed directly to current output unless intercepted or redirected by your program. The OmniMark actions *do xml-parse* and *do sgml-parse* direct the input to the markup processor. For example, the following code fragment sends a file named Myfile.xml to the XML parser of the markup processor:

```
do xml-parse instance
   scan file "Myfile.xml"
   output "%c"
done
```

When you process markup, you must deal with every level of nesting in the markup. Each element has content that can include other elements. When an element is encountered, you have to deal with three aspects: the start of the element, the content of the element, and the end of the element. To give you the opportunity to decide how and when to deal with the element content, markup processing stalls at each element. You need to explicitly get it going again.

How do you continue parsing? The OmniMark escape sequence *%c* causes parsing to continue. Think of it as equivalent to *continue xml-parse*. Since you will always want to continue parsing while generating output appropriate to the current element, the parse continuation operator takes the form of a text escape *%c* that you can drop into a text string. A *do xml-parse* simply sets up the parser in the appropriate initial state to process the input it receives. To actually start parsing, you must output the parse continuation operator *%c*:

```
do xml-parse document
   scan file "daffy.xml"
   output "Beginning %c End")
done
```

Each markup rule must output the parse continuation operator *%c* or its alternative, *suppress*, which continues parsing but suppresses the output of the parsed content. For obvious reasons, you cannot use *%c* or *suppress* more than once in a markup rule. Don't fall into the trap of thinking that *%c* stands for the content of an element. It does not. It is an instruction to continue parsing that content. Any output that appears with *%c* is either data content streamed directly to current output or output produced by the rules that fire while parsing element content.

CREATING INPUT SCOPES

To process any data in an OmniMark program, you must create an input scope with that data attached and then either scan or parse that data. You can create a current input scope using the statement *using input as* and naming a source:

```
process
   using input as file "daffy.txt"
      submit #current-input
```

The built-in variable *#current-input* stands for the source in the current input scope. Thus *submit #current-input* initiates scanning of the current input scope. You can shortcut the process by naming the source directly in the *submit* statement.

```
process
   submit file "daffy.txt"
```

In the preceding example, the *submit* statement both creates the current input scope and initiates scanning. The *#current-input* built-in variable is useful, however, when you want to continue scanning the current input scope in another scanning action. In the following example, a *do scan* statement in the *find* rule picks up the scanning of the current input scope at the current point, pulls out some data, and then allows the original scanning process to resume:

```
process
    submit file "sample.htm"

find ul "<table>"
    do scan #current-input
      match any++ => table-body ul "</table>"
        output table-body
    done
```

You also establish a current input scope when you use the *do xml-parse* statement. The *scan* parameter establishes the source:

```
do xml-parse document
    scan file "ducks.xml"
    output "%c"
done
```

CREATING OUTPUT SCOPES

All output from an OmniMark program goes to OmniMark's built-in current output. You do not usually need to explicitly state where you want output to go; everything goes to current output. You can change the destination of current output within a rule.

```
element duck
    local stream bar
    open bar as file "Bar.txt"
    using output as bar do
      output "quack quack quack %c"
    done
```

This rule temporarily changes the current output to the file Bar.txt. Any output that occurs in the *do...done* block following *using output as* goes to the new destination. Once the block is finished, current output reverts to its original destination. Note, however, that the *output* statement contains the parse continuation operator (*%c*). Thus the new output destination is in effect for all processing that occurs as part of the parsing of the *duck* element. This becomes the current output scope for all the *output* statements occurring in any of the markup rules fired as a result of parsing the *duck* element.

To understand how creating an output scope works, consider the XML file Duck.xml. This file contains a valid schema and the following markup:

```
<line>
A <player>Duck</player> goes up to the <player>bartender</player>
</line>
```

Now consider the following OmniMark program:

```
global stream words
global stream players

process
    open words as file "words.txt"
    open players as file "players.txt"
    using output as words
    do xml-parse instance
        scan file "duck.xml"
        output"%c"
    done

element line
    output "%c"

element player
    using output as players do
        output "%c "
    done
```

Running this program will leave you with two files: words.txt will contain "*A goes up to the*", and people.txt will contain *Duck bartender*. Look closely at this code to make sure you understand which output destination is in effect in the *element line* rule. Do you understand why the output ended up in the files it did? If you are comfortable with this, you know most of what you need to know about how OmniMark handles output. If you are still having trouble here, don't worry. This hierarchical programming model is new to most programmers. Because an XML document is a hierarchical object, this model is critical to processing XML documents. Just remember that output happens in a hierarchical scope. As you use OmniMark or any hierarchical programming language, you will start to see how the process works.

You can slightly shorten the last rule of the previous program by using *put* as shorthand for the *using output as* block:

```
element player
    put players "%c "
```

Here *put* establishes the stream *people* as the current output scope and outputs the string "*%c* " to the current output scope. Thus, this output scope will again be in effect for all rules fired as a result of "*%c*".

OmniMark's current output is a powerful mechanism that simplifies code by eliminating the need to always state where output is going. Once you've set the destination of the current output, all output goes to that destination unless you explicitly send it elsewhere. Note that this means that an *output* statement can execute in a different current output scope depending on the context in which it occurs. The ability to separate the creation of output from the establishment of output destination is a powerful and flexible feature of OmniMark programming.

Current output has the additional feature of being able to have more than one destination at a time. The following code will place *"A duck walks into a I've been barred!"* in both the file outfile.txt and in the variable *my-buffer*:

```
global stream my-file
global stream my-buffer

process
    open my-file as file "outfile.txt"
    output-to my-file
    submit "A duck walks into a bar"

find "bar"
    open my-buffer as buffer
    using output as my-buffer and #current-output
    do
        output "I've been barred!"
    done
```

The keyword *#current-output* stands for all destinations of current output. You can use *#current-output* to add a new destination to the output destinations currently active.

OMX COMPONENTS

OmniMark supports the use of files and constant expressions as input directly in the language. OMX components provide input from other sources and supply a variety of external functionality to OmniMark programs. Components are used to attach to external data sources and destinations, to create and manage connections to the source using the appropriate protocols, and to provide an interface to an OmniMark program that is either an OmniMark source or an OmniMark sink. You can then process the source or attach a stream to the sink and make the stream part of the current output scope.

The following two programs create a client-server environment where data is passed back and forth. The first program, server.xom, creates a TCP/IP connection and waits for something to happen on it. The second program, client.xom, creates a TCP/IP connection and attaches a source and a stream to the connection to read and write data to it:

```
include "omtcp.xin"

process
    ;establish the service
    local TCPService service initial {TCPServiceOpen at 5436}

    ;server loop
    repeat
        ;receive a connection from a client
        local TCPConnection connection initial
            {TCPServiceAcceptConnection service}

        ;receive the request string and print it out
        put #error TCPConnectionGetSource connection
            protocol IOProtocolMultiPacket || "%n"

        ;send a response
        set TCPConnectionGetOutput connection
            protocol IOProtocolMultiPacket
            to "<foo><bar>text</bar><baz bat='gruznatz'/></foo>"

        catch #program-error
    again
```

This is the client code:

```
include "omtcp.xin"
include "builtins.xin"

global stream server-host initial {"localhost"}
global integer server-port initial {5436}

declare catch connection-error

define switch function TCPconnection-is-working
        read-only TCPconnection connection
    as

    do when TCPConnectionIsInError connection
        local stream error-report variable
        TCPConnectionGetStatusReport connection into error-report
        log-message "TCP connection error:"
        repeat over error-report
            log-message error-report
        again
        return false
    else
        return true
    done
```

(continued)

```
process
    local TCPConnection connection
    local stream output-file
    local stream request

    ;open connection
    set connection to TCPConnectionOpen
        on server-host
        at server-port
    throw connection-error
        unless TCPconnection-is-working connection

    ;send the request
    set TCPConnectionGetOutput connection
        protocol IOProtocolMultiPacket
        to "<request><typelist/></request>"

    ;process the response
    do xml-parse instance
        scan TCPConnectionGetSource connection
            protocol IOProtocolMultiPacket
        put #error "%c"
    done

    catch connection-error
        put #error "Unable to connect%n"

element #implied
    put #error "%n[%q]%c[/%q]"
```

Run the server in one Command window, and then run the client in the other to observe the interaction. In these programs, the function *TCPConnectionOpen*—which you'll find in the omtcp library—creates a connection to a TCP/IP server and returns an OMX variable (connection) of type *TCPConnection*. This variable is a handle to the actual *TCPConnection* OMX, which manages the connection.

The function *TCPConnectionGetOutput* attaches an OmniMark stream (request) to the connection. You can then use this stream to send data to the server. The program generates the appropriate request by scanning the first item on the command line, represented by *args[1]*. The output generated by the *find* rules invoked by the *submit* statement will go straight to the server.

The function *TCPConnectionGetSource* returns an OmniMark source attached to the TCP/IP connection. This source is named in the *scan* parameter of *do xml-parse*, meaning that the data returned from the server is streamed directly into the XML parser.

VARIABLES AND DATA TYPES

OmniMark provides a variety of data types, both built-in and through OMX components. The *stream*, *switch* (Boolean), and *integer* variable types are built in. OmniMark has no string type, but *stream* variables handle string data. Additional numeric types *BCD* (binary coded decimal) and *float* are provided by OMX files. Numerous OMX variable types also represent many different external data sources.

Variables can be either global or local. Global variables exist for the lifetime of the program and are visible everywhere within a program. Local variables exist only within the rule or function in which they are declared.

Since you cannot use variables until you declare them, global variable declarations usually appear at the top of an OmniMark program, and local variables appear at the beginning of the rule or the function in which you plan to use them. You must indicate the scope of a variable (global or local) in the variable declaration.

A variable declaration that creates a global integer variable named *word-count* looks like this:

```
global integer word-count
```

To create a local stream variable named *quotation*, use the following variable declaration:

```
local stream quotation
```

To store a string in a stream variable, you can use the *set* keyword, as in the following example:

```
set quotation to "Do you have any grapes?"
```

You can set and change integer variable values the same way you set and change stream variables—using the *set* action—but you can also manipulate integer variables by using the *increment* and *decrement* actions. For example, to increase the value of the *count1* variable by 1, you need only use the following statement:

```
increment count1
```

You can increment or decrement the value of an integer variable by the value of another integer variable. For example, you could decrement the value of *count1* by the value of *count2* with the following code:

```
decrement count1 by count2
```

The program that follows makes use of a global switch variable to decide which *output* action should be executed.

```
global switch question

process
    set question to true
    do when question   ;checks if question is true
       output "to be"
    else
       output "not to be"
    done
```

Note that the output of this program will always be *"to be"*.

You can declare a variable with an initial value:

```
global integer count2 initial {3}
global stream quotation2 initial {"A mallard!"}
global switch status2 initial {true}
```

You can set a variable to the value of another variable. For example, the process rule in the following program will set the value of the global integer variable *var1* to the value of the local integer variable *var2* and give you the output *8*.

```
global integer var1

process
    local integer var2
    set var2 to 8
    set var1 to var2

process
    output "%d(var1)"
```

Finally, you can initialize a variable to a dynamic expression. For example, instead of writing this:

```
local TCPConnection connection

set connection to TCPConnectionOpen
    on server-host
    at server-port
```

you can initialize the variable dynamically:

```
local TCPConnection connection initial
 {TCPConnectionOpen
    on server-host
    at server-port
 }
```

I/O AND VARIABLES

OmniMark has three keywords that assign data to a destination: *set*, *output*, and *put*. *Set* is the only keyword that you can use with numeric data types. With stream variables, however, you can use all three. Stream variables serve as both output conduits and string variables. When used as string variables, stream variables are actually acting as conduits to buffers, which OmniMark treats as data sources and destinations like any other stream.

The *output* keyword sends data to a stream that has been opened with *open* and made part of the current output with *using output as*.

The *put* keyword works like the *using output as* control structure, allowing you to change the current output and create output in a single action.

The *set* keyword performs the functions of both *open* and *using output as*: it opens a stream, makes it current output, and outputs to it in a single operation. This means that, as far as streams are concerned, there aren't different keywords for dealing with variables and external data sources, but instead there are a selection of keywords that you can use as appropriate on either variables or external data sources. For example, you can use the *set* action to place a simple value into a file.

```
set file "duckbar.txt" to "A duck walks into a bar."
```

Likewise, you can use *open*, *put*, and *close* to set the value of a variable.

```
local stream Duck
open Duck as buffer
put Duck "A duck walks into a bar."
close Duck
```

The virtue of using the longer syntax is that you can write to the stream many times before closing it. This approach is much easier and more efficient than building up a string by a series of concatenations. Thus you can replace code like this:

```
set Duck to "A duck walks into a bar"
set Duck to Duck || "The bartender says, 'We don't serve ducks here'"
set Duck to Duck || "The duck says, 'That's OK, I don't like duck anyway.'"
set Duck to Duck || "'How about a beer?'"
```

with code like this:

```
open Duck as buffer
   using output as Duck do
      output "A duck walks into a bar"
      output "The bartender says, 'We don't serve ducks here'"
      output "The duck says, 'That's OK, I don't like duck anyway.'"
      output "'How about a beer?'"
   done
```

This is an enormously powerful feature of OmniMark that enables you to choose the type of data-assignment mechanism appropriate to the scale of the operation you want to perform. You can use *set* for any kind of small-scale assignment, whether to a file or a variable, without the bother of opening files or buffers. For large-scale operations, you can use *output* with any file or stream variable and perform multiple updates without the need to specify the destination or even worry about the kind of destination involved. Choosing the mechanism appropriate to the scale of the operation you are performing will greatly simplify your code.

You must close a stream before it can be read or output:

```
open Duck as buffer
put Duck "A duck walks into a bar."
close Duck
output Duck
```

You can use the action *reopen* to reopen a closed stream with its original content. However, if you use *open* to open the stream again, you'll lose the existing content:

```
open Duck1 as buffer
open Duck2 as buffer

put Duck1 "A duck walks into a bar."
put Duck2 " A duck walks into a bar."

close Duck1
close Duck2

reopen Duck1
open Duck2

put Duck1 "He walks up to the bartender"
put Duck2 "He walks up to the bartender"
```

The preceding code will leave the stream Duck1 containing both lines, but Duck2 will contain only *"He walks up to the bartender"*.

DATA STRUCTURES USING SHELVES

OmniMark provides a data structure named a shelf. You can refer to each item on a shelf either by position or by a textual key. Shelves can be either fixed or variable in size. All OmniMark variables are in fact shelves, though an ordinary variable is a fixed-size shelf with one item, so the fact that it is a shelf is not particularly significant.

A global stream shelf declaration that creates a shelf of variable size named *quotations* looks like this:

```
global stream quotations variable
```

The default size of a variable-size shelf is zero items. A local integer shelf declaration that creates an integer shelf named *totals* with a fixed size of *3* looks like this:

```
local integer totals size 3
```

If you want to create a shelf with initial values that are different from the defaults, add an *initial* keyword to the declaration, followed by the values you want on the shelf enclosed in brackets. For example:

```
global integer sizes size 4 initial {1, 2, 3, 4}
```

This declaration creates a global integer shelf named *sizes* that can hold four values with initial values of *1*, *2*, *3*, and *4*. You could also create a variable-size shelf that contains a number of initial values, like this:

```
global integer sizes variable initial {1, 2, 3, 4}
```

The only difference between these two shelves is that while the first is a fixed-size shelf holding four values, the second begins with four values and can expand or contract to hold as many values as required.

Additionally, you can create shelves of a particular size without having to assign initial values to the shelf items. Do this by using the *initial-size* keyword:

```
global integer sizes variable initial-size 4
```

This declaration creates an integer shelf that starts with four items and can expand or contract as required.

To add the string *"Now is the winter of our discontent"* in the variable stream shelf *quotations*, use the following action:

```
set new quotation to "Now is the winter of our discontent"
```

To access an item on a shelf, you must supply an indexer: either an item number or a key. Square brackets indicate item numbers; braces indicate keys.

```
set quotation[3] to "Words, words, words."
output quotation{"Hamlet"}
```

You can assign a key to an existing item:

```
set key of quotation[2] to "Richard iii"
```

You can set a key on a shelf item in the same action in which you create the new item. For example, to create a new item on the *quotes* shelf that has a value of *"Alas, poor Yorick."* with the key *"Hamlet"*, use the following action:

```
set new quotes{"Hamlet"} to "Alas, poor Yorick."
```

By default, new items are created at the end of a shelf. You can use the *before* or *after* keywords to create a new item somewhere else on a shelf. For example, to create a new item that will exist immediately before the second item on a shelf, use the following action:

```
set new quotes before [2] to "A horse!"
```

This action creates a new item containing the value *"A horse!"* between the first and second items on the *quotes* shelf. Since the item numbers are based on shelf position, this new item would become item 2, and the item that was number 2 would become number 3.

If you want to create a new item on a shelf just after an item that had the key *"Macbeth"*, use the action:

```
set new quotes{"Richard iii"} after {"Macbeth"} to "A horse!"
```

To help illustrate the concept of OmniMark shelves, the following program creates a stream shelf and sets the first item on that shelf to a value. Next the program gives that first item a key. Then three other items are created: one at the default end of the shelf, another before the second item on the shelf, and the third after a value with a set key.

```
process
    local stream quotes variable
    set new quotes{"Hamlet"} to "To be or not to be?"
    set new quotes{"Macbeth"} to "Is this a dagger?"
    set new quotes{"Richard iii"} before [2] to "A horse!"
    set new quotes{"Romeo"} after {"Richard iii"}
        to "Hark, what light through yonder window breaks?"

    repeat over quotes
        output key of quotes
            || " - "
            || quotes || "%n"
    again
```

This program has the following output:

```
Hamlet - To be or not to be?
Richard III - A horse!
Romeo - Hark, what light through yonder window breaks?
Macbeth - Is this a dagger?
```

REFERENTS

Referents are variables that can be output before their final values have been assigned. With referents, you can put placeholder variables in your output and then later assign or change their values. The following program illustrates the placeholder quality of referents:

```
process
    output "Goodbye, " || referent "world-type" || " world!"
    set referent "world-type" to "cruel"
```

The result of this program is to output the line *"Goodbye, cruel world!"*

The following example is more complex:

```
process
    local stream fowl
    set fowl to "Duck%n"
    set referent "water" to "Duck%n"
    output fowl
    output referent "water"
    set fowl to "bar%n"
    set referent "water" to "bar%n"
```

The output of this program is

```
Duck
bar
```

While the output value of stream *fowl* didn't change values after being output, the output value of referent *water* did. The final value of both variables did change to *water*, but only the output of the referent reflected this change.

Notice that while the stream *fowl* had to be declared before it was used, the referent *water* did not. All you need to do to create and use a referent is give it a name and set it to a value.

Another simple example of referents in action is in outputting page numbers that include *of n* values—for example, *page 1 of 8*. Until a document has been completely processed, you cannot know for certain how many pages it will have. With referents, however, you can simply put a placeholder where the page numbers will be in the output. After the document has been completely processed and the number of pages determined, the final values can be plugged into the referents.

The following program changes the number of a list of plays in a text file. Each time the program finds a number at the beginning of a line, it updates the referent *play-count* and outputs the current play number and the referent. Though the referent is updated and output each time the rule fires, all output copies of the referent are displayed with the referent's final value:

```
find line-start digit+ => play-number
    set referent "play-count" to play-number
    output "Play "
          || play-number
          || " of "
          || referent "play-count"

process
    submit file #args[1]
```

For the following input file:

```
1 Hamlet
2 Richard III
3 Macbeth
4 Romeo and Juliet
5 King Lear
```

the preceding program would produce the following output:

```
Play 1 of 5      Hamlet
Play 2 of 5      Richard III
Play 3 of 5      Macbeth
Play 4 of 5      Romeo and Juliet
Play 5 of 5      King Lear
```

By default, referents are resolved when the program ends. However, you can create a referents scope that will allow you to use *using nested-referents* to resolve referents earlier:

```
find line-start digit+ => play-number
   set referent "play-count" to play-number
   output "Play "
         || play-number
         || " of "
         || referent "play-count"

process
   using nested-referents
      submit file #args[1]
```

In this example, a referents scope is created that applies only to the *submit* action. Referents will be resolved as soon as the scanning initiated by *submit* is complete, rather than when the program ends.

CONDITIONAL CONSTRUCTS

Almost any statement in OmniMark can be made conditional simply by adding a *when* or *unless* keyword followed by a test. For example, any rule can have conditions added to it. The following rule will fire only when the value of *count1* equals *4*:

```
find "duck" when count1 = 4
   output "I found a duck%n"
```

The basic conditional construct is the *do when...done* block.

```
do when foo = 4
   output "Yes, the value of foo is four%n"
done
```

You can add an *else* option:

```
do when output-in-upper-case = true
   output "ug" % words || "%n"
else
   output words || "%n"
done
```

You can handle multiple cases using *else when*:

```
do when foo = 4
   output "Yes, the value of foo is four%n"
else when count1 = 5
   output "The value of foo is five%n"
else when count1 = 6
   output "The value of foo is six%n"
else
   output "The value of foo is not 4, 5, or 6%n"
done
```

You can construct complex conditional statements using *&* (and) and *|* (or):

```
do when (foo > 12 | foo < 56) & bar > 3
```

Another form of conditional construct is the *do select* construct:

```
do select foo
   case 1 to 5
      output "foo is small%n"
   case 50 to 100
      output "foo is large%n"
   else
      output "foo is medium sized%n"
done
```

You can also implement conditional logic by using the *do scan* construct, which uses scanning to evaluate data. Thus you can build your conditions based on pattern matching:

```
process
   do scan telephone-number
      match "(" digit{3} ")" digit{3} "-" digit{4}
         output "long distance call%n"
      match digit{3} "-" digit{4}
         output "local call%n"
      else
         output "unknown format%n"
   done
```

LOOPING CONSTRUCTS

OmniMark provides four types of looping constructs: *repeat*, *repeat for*, *repeat over*, and *repeat scan*.

A *repeat* loop will repeat the execution of the actions it contains until an explicit *exit* action is encountered in the loop.

```
process
   local integer foo
   repeat
     output "foo is " || "d" % foo || "%n"
     increment foo
     exit when foo = 4
   again
```

A *repeat for* loop repeats for each of the values of a control variable.

```
Process
   local integer foo
   repeat for integer foo from 1 to 7 by 2
       output "foo is " || "d" % foo || "%n"
   again
```

A *repeat over* loop repeats for each item on a shelf:

```
process
   local stream duckType variable
   set new duckType key "Sarkidiornis melanotos" to "Comb Duck"
   set new duckType key "Anas crecca" to "Green-winged Teal"
   set new duckType key "Melanitta perspicillata" to "Surf Scoter"
   repeat over duckType
       output key of duckType || "=" || duckType || "%n"
   again
```

Within a *repeat over* loop, you refer to the current item on the shelf by the name of the shelf alone, without an indexer.

You can use a *repeat scan* loop to scan data the same way you use *submit* and a set of find rules. The only differences are that a *repeat scan* is local to a single rule or function, and data not matched by a *repeat scan* does not stream through to current output. Instead, a *repeat scan* exits if it encounters any data it cannot match:

```
process
   local integer word-count
   repeat scan "Mary had a little lamb"
     match letter+
         increment word-count
     match any
   again
   output "d" % word-count
```

ARITHMETIC AND COMPARISON OPERATORS

OmniMark provides a full set of arithmetic and comparison operators. The arithmetic operators available in OmniMark are + (addition), − (subtraction), * (multiplication), / (division), and *modulo* (the remainder you get when you divide the number by the base value). Additional operators are available for some numeric types provided by OMX components.

OmniMark also provides a full set of comparison operators. Here are some examples:

```
process
   do when x = y
      output "equal%n"
   else when x > y
      output "greater%n"
   else when x < y
      output "lesser%n"
   done
```

The other available comparison operators are != (not equal), >= (greater than or equal to), and <= (less than or equal to).

PATTERN MATCHING

OmniMark allows you to use scanning to search for patterns in input data. For example, the following *find* rule will fire if the string *"Hamlet:"* is encountered in the input stream:

```
find "Hamlet:"
   output "<b>Hamlet</b>: "
```

Using this approach, however, requires you to write a separate *find* rule for each character name you want to enclose in HTML bold tags, as in the following example:

```
find "Hamlet:"
   output "<b>Hamlet</b>: "
find "Horatio:"
   output "<b>Horatio</b>: "
find "Bernardo:"
   output "<b>Bernardo</b>: "
```

This is where OmniMark patterns come in. OmniMark has rich, built-in pattern-matching capabilities that allow you to match strings through a more abstract string model rather than by matching a specific string, as in the following example. This *find* rule will match any string that contains any number of letters followed immediately by a colon:

```
find letter+ ":"
```

Unfortunately, the pattern described in this *find* rule isn't specific enough to flawlessly match only character names. It will match any string of letters followed by a colon that appears anywhere in the text, including words in the middle of sentences.

Words that appear in the middle of sentences rarely begin with an uppercase letter, whereas proper names usually do. This knowledge allows us to add further detail to our *find* rule. This *find* rule matches any string that begins with an uppercase letter (*uc*) followed by at least one other letter (*letter+*) and a colon (*:*):

```
find uc letter+ ":"
```

If we were actually trying to mark up an ASCII copy of *Hamlet*, however, our *find* rule would only match character names that contain a single word, such as Hamlet, Ophelia, or Horatio. Only the second part of two-part names would be matched. Names such as Queen Gertrude and Lord Polonius would be incorrectly marked up.

To match these more complex names as well as the single-word names, we'll have to further refine our *find* rule:

```
find uc letter+ (white-space+ uc letter+)? ":"
```

In this version of the *find* rule, the pattern can match a second word prior to the colon. The pattern *(white-space+ uc letter+)?* can match one or more white-space characters followed by an uppercase letter and one or more letters. These changes to the *find* rule allow it to match character names that consist of one or two words.

If you want to match a series of three numbers, use the following pattern:

```
find digit {3}
```

If you want to match either a four-digit or five-digit number, use the following pattern:

```
find digit {4 to 5}
```

To match a date that occurs in the yy/mm/dd format, use the following pattern:

```
find digit {2} "/" digit {2} "/" digit {2}
```

Match a Canadian postal code with the following pattern:

```
find letter digit letter space digit letter digit
```

The *letter* and *uc* keywords used to create the preceding patterns are named character classes. OmniMark provides a variety of built-in character classes:

- **letter** Matches a single letter character, uppercase or lowercase

- **uc** Matches a single uppercase letter

- **lc**   Matches a single lowercase letter
- **digit**   Matches a single digit (0 through 9)
- **space**   Matches a single space character
- **blank**   Matches a single space or tab character
- **white-space**   Matches a single space, tab, or newline character
- **any-text**   Matches any single character except for a newline character
- **any**   Matches any single character

You can also define your own customized character classes. For example, the following *find* rule would fire if any one of the four arithmetic operators was encountered by the *find* rule in the input data:

```
find ["+-*/"]
   output "found an arithmetic operator%n"
```

You can define character classes by exclusion using the *except* operator (\). The following *find* rule would match any character except for a right brace:

```
find [\ "}"]
```

You can use the *except* operator with a built-in character class. The following find rule matches any consonant:

```
find [letter \ "aeiouAEIOU"]
```

You can add string and built-in character classes together with the *or* operator to create new character classes. The following find rule matches any one of the arithmetic operators or a single digit:

```
find ["+-*/" | digit]
```

The following find rule matches any of the arithmetic operators or any digit except zero (*"0"*):

```
find ["+-*/" | digit \ "0"]
```

You can use the following occurrence operators to modify any pattern:

- **+**   One or more
- *****   Zero or more
- **?**   Zero or one
- ******   Zero or more upto
- **++**   One or more upto

As you saw earlier in this appendix, *letter+* matches one or more letters, *letter** matches zero or more letters, and *uc?* matches zero or one uppercase letter.

OmniMark pattern matching is greedy. The following rule will never fire:

```
find "<table>" any* "</table>"
```

This rule will never fire because *any** will match the entire input, including any occurrence of the string *"</table>"*. Because the *"</table>"* part of the pattern can never be matched, the whole pattern will always fail.

To write a pattern that matches characters up to a specific delimiter, use the ** or ++ occurrence indicators:

```
find "<table>" any** "</table>"
```

Here *any*** matches zero or more characters up to the string *"</table>"*.

The following rule will only fire if there is at least one character between *"<table>"* and *"</table>"* in the input:

```
find "<table>" any++ "</table>"
```

You can use *lookahead* in a pattern to see whether a pattern exists without consuming it:

```
find any++ lookahead "</table>"
```

This pattern will match any number of characters from the current point up to the occurrence of the string *"</table>"*, but will not consume *"</table>"*, leaving it in the input where other rules can match it. Note that at least one character must precede *"</table>"* or this rule will either fail or match all the way up to the next *"</table>"* in the data, if there is one.

The following rule eliminates this problem:

```
find any** lookahead "</table>"
```

However, this rule will fire twice if it fires at all: once when it matches all the characters up to *"</table>"* and again when it consumes zero characters followed by *"</table>"* (its location in the source following the first match). This rule could potentially go on matching zero characters followed by *"</table>"* forever, without ever moving forward. However, OmniMark does not permit two consecutive matches that consume zero data, so the rule will not fire again until more data has been consumed.

Both the * and ** occurrence operators can create patterns that match but which might not consume data. OmniMark will never permit two consecutive matches that do not consume data, but if you see rules or matches fire twice when you only expected them to fire once, it is probably because the second time is a zero-length match permitted by the use of * or **.

PATTERN VARIABLES

When you use patterns to match sections of input data, you must first capture the data in pattern variables for later use. You assign pattern variables by using the => symbol and reference them later. For example, in the first find rule in the following program the matched input data is assigned to the *found-text* pattern variable.

```
process
  . submit "A [mallard] duck walks into a bar."

find ("[" letter+ "]") => found-text
    output found-text

find any
```

This program outputs *[mallard]*.

What if you want to output only the word in the square brackets, but not the square brackets themselves? Try this:

```
process
    submit " A [mallard] duck walks into a bar."

find "[" letter+ => found-text "]"
    output found-text

find any
```

This program outputs *mallard*. Here, the pattern variable is attached only to the part of the pattern immediately preceding the pattern variable assignment. This is the default behavior of pattern variables. That's why the previous example wouldn't work correctly unless we surrounded the three elements of the pattern with parentheses to ensure that the text matched by the whole pattern was captured.

You can have more than one pattern variable in a pattern. You can even nest them. Consider this example:

```
process
    submit " A [mallard] duck walks into a bar."

find    ("[" => first-bracket
  letter+ => found-word
  "]" => second-bracket) => found-text

    output first-bracket
    output found-word
    output second-bracket
    output found-text

find any
```

The output of this program would be *[mallard][mallard]*. The first *"[mallard]"* is the result of the first three output actions; the second *"[mallard]"* is the result of the fourth output action.

FUNCTIONS

Like most languages, OmniMark supports functions. Unlike many languages, however, an OmniMark program is not simply a hierarchy of functions. Rules are the principal structural element of OmniMark programs; functions are supplementary structures. Functions cannot contain rules (though functions can invoke rules through *submit*, *do xml-parse*, and *do sgml-parse*). You can use functions to encapsulate code that you use commonly within different rule bodies. You can also use functions as pattern-matching functions or within patterns to dynamically define a pattern you want to match.

Functions isolate sections of code, but they don't isolate you from the current environment, in particular from the current output scope. Output in a function goes to the current output scope. If a function has a return value, that value goes to the calling action. If a function changes the destination of the current output scope (with *output-to*), this destination change carries over to the calling environment.

A function that returns a value is defined as follows:

```
define integer function add
   (value integer x,
    value integer y)
   as
   return x + y
```

The return type of the function is declared following the *define* keyword. The return type can be any OmniMark variable type or any OMX component type. The value is returned using the *return* keyword, which also exits the function.

Here is how you can call the *add* function.

```
process
   output "d" format add(2,3)
```

Functions can generate output. The following function outputs the value it generates rather than returning it to the calling action. Note that this function has no return type in the definition; no *return* is required.

```
define function output-sum
   (value integer x,
    value integer y
   )as
   output "d" format (x + y)
```

This function is called as if it were a regular OmniMark action.

```
process
   output-sum(2, 3)
```

You can also write functions that both return a value and do output.

```
define integer function add
   (value integer x,
    value integer y
   )as
   output "I will add %d(x) and %d(y)%n"
   return x + y

process
   local integer z
   set z to add(2,3)
   output "%d(z)%n"
```

While it is certainly possible to program this way, I recommend that you avoid writing functions that both do output and return a value. Not only do they make it hard to follow your code, but they can also have unexpected results. For example, if the return value is directed to current output, you might not get the function's return values nor output in the order you expect.

You can also write functions that neither return a value nor create output. The following function clears all the switches on a *switch* shelf that is passed to it as a modifiable argument:

```
define function clear-flags
   (modifiable switch the-flags
   ) as
   repeat over the-flags
      set the-flags to false
   again
```

Everything that you can do in the rule that calls a function you can do in the function itself. For example, a function can use the *%c* parse continuation operator when called from a markup rule. The most useful application of this feature is the ability to write a function that does generic processing on a class of markup element types.

The current input and output scopes apply to code within a function just as they apply to code in the rule (or function) that called the function.

CATCH AND THROW

You can use catch and throw to manage the execution flow in your OmniMark programs. It is probably easiest to think of catch and throw as an exception-handling mechanism. What is an exception? An exception is essentially an interruption to the normal flow of program processing. Some exceptions come whether you want them or not, in the form of run-time program errors or failure to communicate with the world outside your program. Other exceptions are used to solve programming problems.

A simple piece of code can usually handle 90 percent of all exceptions. The other 10 percent are exceptions that require significantly different processing. Dividing a problem up into normal cases and exceptions is a convenient way to simplify and organize your code. This does not mean that the exceptions are errors or even unexpected. Often the exceptional cases are what you are most interested in. Programming with exceptions is simply a technique for designing an algorithm to solve a particular problem.

You can use catch and throw in a program that nests deeply when you want to quickly get out of the nesting. OmniMark does not have a "goto" verb (thankfully), so getting out of a nested loop or other hierarchical area can be kind of tricky. With catch and throw, all you need to do is create a catch at the destination point and then throw to that point from somewhere inside the nested area. OmniMark is usually smart enough to take care of whatever housekeeping is required to exit the loop.

Catching Program Errors

The simplest use of catch and throw allows your program to recover when something goes wrong. Consider the following code, which contains the server loop of a simple server program:

```
include "omioprot.xin"
include "omtcp.xin"

process
   local TCPService my-service
   set my-service to TCPServiceOpen at 5432
   repeat
      local TCPConnection my-connection
      local stream   my-response
      set my-connection to TCPServiceAcceptConnection my-service
      open my-response as TCPConnectionGetOutput my-connection
      using output as my-response
      do
          submit TCPConnectionGetLine my-connection
      done
   again
```

Any error in the program or with the TCP connection will cause this program to terminate, since nothing exists to handle the error. You should always write a server program to stay running if at all possible, so we need to add something to allow the program to recover:

```
include "omioprot.xin"
include "omtcp.xin"

process
   local TCPService my-service
   set my-service to TCPServiceOpen at 5432
   repeat
     local TCPConnection my-connection
     local stream  my-response
     set my-connection to TCPServiceAcceptConnection my-service
     open my-response as TCPConnectionGetOutput my-connection
     using output as my-response
     do
        submit TCPConnectionGetLine my-connection
     done
     catch #program-error
   again
```

We have added only a single line, but this version of the program is much more robust. If any error occurs while in the *repeat* loop of any of the *find* rules invoked by *submit*, execution will transfer to the line *catch #program-error*. Along the way, OmniMark will clean up after itself. Local scopes will be terminated and resources released.

No attempt is made to salvage the work that was in progress when the error happened. That work and all its associated resources are thrown away. But the server will stay up and running, ready to receive the next request.

Of course, we'd like to know that the error occurred and why it occurred. The constant *#program-error* makes information available so that we can act on the error or at least report it. To ensure that errors get logged, we can rewrite the program like this:

```
include "builtins.xin"
include "omioprot.xin"
include "omtcp.xin"

process
   local TCPService my-service
   set my-service to TCPServiceOpen at 5432
   repeat
     local TCPConnection my-connection
     local stream  my-response
```

(continued)

```
      set my-connection to TCPServiceAcceptConnection my-service
      open my-response as TCPConnectionGetOutput my-connection
      using output as my-response
      do
          submit TCPConnectionGetLine my-connection
      done
      catch #program-error code c message m location l
       log-message ( "Error "
                            || "d" format c
                            || " "
                            || m
                            || " at "
                            || l
                            || " time "
                            || date "=Y/=M/=D =h:=m:=s"
                          )
  again
```

Notice that the catch line prevents everything that follows from being executed. The code inside a catch block is run only if the program encounters an error.

So far, we have seen nothing of the "throw" part of catch and throw. This is because OmniMark itself throws to *#program-error*. OmniMark can also throw to *#external-exception* if it has a problem communicating with the external world (such as being unable to open a file or communicate successfully with an OMX component). We didn't bother to catch *#external-exception* in the preceding code because the failure of a program to catch an external exception is itself a program error, which causes a throw to *#program-error*. In other circumstances we might want to use *#external-exception* explicitly. Suppose one of the *find* rules in our server program tried and failed to open a file:

```
find "open file " letter+ => fowl
    output file fowl
    catch #external-exception
    output "Unable to open file " || fowl || "."
```

The attempt to open the named file fails. This causes an external exception at the first *output* action. We catch the exception and provide alternate output. The program then continues as if nothing had happened.

Now our server is more robust since an error opening a file will not abort the processing of the current request. Instead, the client will receive the error message we output along with any other information the request generates.

Exception Handling

When it comes to throwing things, OmniMark does not get to have all the fun. You can create your own exceptions, throw your own throws, and define your own catches. The following program uses a programmer-defined exception to shut down the server by remote control:

```
include "builtins.xin"
include "omioprot.xin"
include "omtcp.xin"
declare catch nap-time

process
   local TCPService my-service
   set my-service to TCPServiceOpen at 5432
   repeat
      local TCPConnection my-connection
      local stream  my-response
      set my-connection to TCPServiceAcceptConnection my-service
      open my-response as TCPConnectionGetOutput my-connection
      using output as my-response
      do
          submit TCPConnectionGetLine my-connection
      done
      catch #program-error
   again
   catch nap-time

find "sleep"
   throw nap-time
```

Here we have a classic case of an exception. Every request to our server is a request for information—every request except one. The *"sleep"* request is an instruction to the server to shut itself down. This is the exceptional case and we handle it with an exception.

In the exceptional case in which we shut down the server, we need to jump out of the connection loop. We do this with a catch outside the loop. The catch is named *nap-time*. Catches are named so that we can have more than one and have each one catch something different. Like all names introduced into an OmniMark program, the name of a catch must be declared, which we do in the first line of the program. We place the catch outside the request-handling loop. Because OmniMark cleans up after itself while performing a throw, all resources belonging to the local scope inside the loop are properly closed down. Then, since we are outside the loop and at the end of the process rule, the program simply ends, shutting down the server.

The throw itself is simple. Having detected the exceptional case (the *sleep* request), we simply throw to the appropriate catch by name. OmniMark handles everything else.

Throwing Additional Information

When OmniMark throws to *#program-error* or *#external-exception*, it adds information in the form of three parameters: *code* (identity for *#external exception*), *message*, and *location*. You can also pass additional information with your throws by adding parameters to your catch declaration, following the form of a function definition. The following program adds the capability to log the reason for putting a server to sleep:

```
include "builtins.xin"
include "omioprot.xin"
include "omtcp.xin"
declare catch nap-time because value stream reason

process
    local TCPService my-service
    set my-service to TCPServiceOpen at 5432
    repeat
        local TCPConnection my-connection
        local stream  my-response
        set my-connection to TCPServiceAcceptConnection my-service
        open my-response as TCPConnectionGetOutput my-connection
        using output as my-response
        do
            submit TCPConnectionGetLine my-connection
        done
        catch #program-error
    again
    catch nap-time because r
        log-message ( "Shut down because "
                        || r
                        || " Time: "
                        || date "=Y/=M/=D =h:=m:=s"
                      )

find "sleep" white-space* any* => the-reason
    throw nap-time because the-reason
```

The *find* rule captures the rest of the *"sleep"* message and uses it as a parameter to the throw. The catch receives the data and uses it to create the appropriate log message.

Cleaning Up After Yourself

I said that OmniMark cleans up after itself, and it does: it cleans up everything it knows about. But this can still leave you with cleanup of your own to do. Or there might simply be statements that you always want to execute, even if an exception occurs. For this, OmniMark provides the *always* keyword. Let's suppose that our server does its own connection logging and uses OmniMark's logging facility for errors. We want the connection log file closed between requests to make it easy to cycle the log files, so we open and close the log file for each connection:

```
declare catch nap-time because value stream reason
include "builtins.xin"
include "omioprot.xin"
include "omtcp.xin"
global stream log-file-name initial {"nap-time.log"}
process
   local TCPService my-service
   local stream my-log
   set my-service to TCPServiceOpen at 5432
   repeat
      local TCPConnection my-connection
      local stream  my-response
      reopen my-log as file log-file-name
      set my-connection to TCPServiceAcceptConnection my-service
      put my-log TCPConnectionGetPeerIP my-connection
            || date "=Y/=M/=D =h:=m:=s"
      open my-response as TCPConnectionGetOutput my-connection
      using output as my-response
      do
          submit TCPConnectionGetLine my-connection
      done
      close my-log
      catch #program-error code c message m location l
         log-message ( "Error "
                    || "d" format c
                    || " "
                    || m
                    || " at "
                    || l
                    || " time "
                    || date "=Y/=M/=D =h:=m:=s"
                    )

   again
   catch nap-time because reason
      log-message ( "Shut down because "
                 || reason
                 || " Time: "
                 || date "=Y/=M/=D =h:=m:=s"
                 )
```

In this code, a problem processing the request would cause a throw to *#program-error*. This would mean that the line *close my-log* was never executed and the log file would remain open. (This is an exception OmniMark can't clean up itself, since the stream *my-log* belongs to a wider scope that is not being closed.) We want the line *close my-log* to be executed always, whether there is an error or not. To ensure this, we use *always*:

```
declare catch nap-time because value stream reason
include "builtins.xin"
include "omioprot.xin"
include "omtcp.xin"
global stream log-file-name initial {"nap-time.log"}
process
    local TCPService my-service
    local stream my-log
    set my-service to TCPServiceOpen at 5432
    repeat
        local TCPConnection my-connection
        local stream  my-response
        reopen my-log as file log-file-name
        set my-connection to TCPServiceAcceptConnection my-service
        put my-log TCPConnectionGetPeerIP my-connection
                || date "=Y/=M/=D =h:=m:=s"
        open my-response as TCPConnectionGetOutput my-connection
        using output as my-response
        do
            submit TCPConnectionGetLine my-connection
        done
        catch #program-error code c message m location l
            log-message ( "Error "
                        || "d" format c
                        || " "
                        || m
                        || " at "
                        || l
                        || " time "
                        || date "=Y/=M/=D =h:=m:=s"
                        )
        always
            close my-log

    again
    catch nap-time because reason
        log-message ( "Shut down because "
                    || reason
                    || " Time: "
                    || date "=Y/=M/=D =h:=m:=s"
                    )

find "sleep" white-space* any* => the-reason
    throw nap-time because the-reason
```

When a throw happens, OmniMark closes scopes one by one until it finds a scope that contains a catch for that throw. As it does so, OmniMark executes any code in an *always* block in each of those scopes, including the scope that contains the catch. So in this example, the *close* line will execute before the catch block is executed, no matter where or why an error occurs.

Programming with exceptions is a powerful technique that can make your programs both more reliable and easier to read and write. Here is our full server program with all our catch and throw functionality, plus logging of our external exception (but minus the *find* rules that do the rest of the work):

```
declare catch nap-time because value stream reason
include "builtins.xin"
include "omioprot.xin"
include "omtcp.xin"
global stream log-file-name initial {"nap-time.log"}
process
   local TCPService my-service
   local stream my-log
   set my-service to TCPServiceOpen at 5432
   repeat
      local TCPConnection my-connection
      local stream  my-response
      reopen my-log as file log-file-name
      set my-connection to TCPServiceAcceptConnection my-service
      put my-log TCPConnectionGetPeerIP my-connection
            || date "=Y/=M/=D =h:=m:=s"
      open my-response as TCPConnectionGetOutput my-connection
      using output as my-response
      do
         submit TCPConnectionGetLine my-connection
      done
      catch #program-error code c message m location l
         log-message ( "Error "
                    || "d" format c
                    || " "
                    || m
                    || " at "
                    || l
                    || " time "
                    || date "=Y/=M/=D =h:=m:=s"
                     )
      always
         close my-log

   again
   catch nap-time because reason
```

(continued)

```
log-message ( "Shut down because "
              || reason
              || " Time: "
              || date "=Y/=M/=D =h:=m:=s"
             )

find "sleep" white-space* any* => the-reason
   throw nap-time because the-reason

find "open file " letter+ => foo
   output file foo
   catch #external-exception identity i message m location l
   output "Unable to open file " || foo || "."
   log-message ( "Error "
                 || i
                 || " "
                 || m
                 || " at "
                 || l
                 || " time "
                 || date "=Y/=M/=D =h:=m:=s"
                )
```

RULE GROUPS

By default, all OmniMark rules are active all the time. You can change this by bundling your rules into groups:

```
group duck
   find "walks"
      output "#walks#"
   find "waddles"
      output "#waddles#"

group bar
   find "bartender"
      output "#bartender#"
   find "beer"
      output "#beer#"

group #implied
process-start
   using group duck
   do
      submit "A duck walks into a bar."
   done
```

```
using group bar
do
    submit "He says to the bartender, 'gimme a beer'."
done
```

In this program, only rules in the group *duck* are used to process *"A duck walks into a bar."* Only rules in the group *bar* are used to process *"He says to the bartender, 'gimme a beer'."*

Why *group #implied* before *process-start?* The process-start rule is a rule like any other, so it is affected by groups like any other rule. The *group #implied* statement stands for the default group. (In a program with no groups, all rules are in the default group.) Only the default group is active when a program starts. All other groups are inactive. So you have to have at least one rule in the default group to activate any of the other groups. If we didn't place the process-start rule into the default group, no rules would ever be active in this program.

Any rule that occurs before the first group statement in your program automatically belongs to the default group. However, if you use groups, you should place your global rules explicitly into *group #implied*. (Consider what would happen if you included a file that contained group statements at the top of your main program file and didn't explicitly assign your global rules to *group #implied*.)

All rules in the default group are global. You cannot disable the default group, so rules in the default group are always active. For this reason, you might want to keep the number of rules in the default group to a minimum. (Remember, however, that you must have at least one.)

Can you have more than one group active at a time? Certainly.

```
using group duck & bar & dick & harry
```

You can also add a group to the current set of active groups by using *#group* to represent all active groups.

```
using group duck & bar & #group
```

CONSTANTS AND MACROS

You can define macros by using the *macro* and *macro-end* keywords. Macros are useful for three purposes:

- defining constants

- defining complex patterns

- encapsulating code

The following macro defines a constant:

```
macro pi is
    3.1415926535897932384626ₐ
macro-end
```

You can use this macro in an equation, as in this program:

```
include "ombcd.xin"
macro pi is
 3.1415926535897932
macro-end

process
    local bcd area
    local bcd r initial {5.9}
    set area to pi * r * r
    output "d" % area
```

The following macro defines a pattern for a decimal number:

```
macro decimal-number is
    ("-"? digit+ ("." digit+)?)
macro-end
```

You can use this macro in a *find* rule:

```
find "[" decimal-number => number "]"
```

> Note: It is wise to surround any pattern defined in a macro with parentheses to ensure that the whole pattern is assigned to a pattern variable (if you use a pattern variable in the pattern).

The following macro encapsulates a block of code. In this case, the code is a catch block. You cannot encapsulate the code in a function, since a function would create a new scope, and a catch block must occur in the scope it is intended to catch for.

```
macro catch-and-report-program-errors is
    catch #program-error
        code c
        message m
        location l
    log-message (    "Error "
                  || "d" % c
                  || "%n"
                  || m || "%n"
                  || l || "%n"
                )
macro-end
```

You can use this macro where you would have placed a catch in your program.

```
include "ombcd.xin"
include "builtins.xin"
macro pi is
 3.1415926535897932
macro-end

macro catch-and-report-program-errors is
   catch #program-error
      code c
      message m
      location l
   log-message (    "Error "
               || "d" % c
               || "%n"
               || m || "%n"
               || l || "%n"
               )
macro-end


process
   local bcd area
   local bcd r initial {"5.9"}
   set area to pi * r * r
   output "d" % area
   catch-and-report-program-errors
```

FINANCIAL CALCULATIONS

You can perform financial calculations in OmniMark using the *BCD* data type to represent monetary values and fractional numbers such as tax rates. Unlike floating-point numbers, BCD numbers provide accurate fractions for financial calculations.

The following code sample shows basic financial calculations using BCD numbers. Note that the keyword *bcd* must precede literal BCD values.

```
include "ombcd.xin"

process
   local bcd price
   local bcd tax-rate
   local integer quantity
   local bcd total

   set price to 19.95
   set tax-rate to 0.07
   set quantity to 28
   set total to price * quantity * (1 + tax-rate)
   output "<$,NNZ.ZZ>" format total
```

The format string *"<$,NNZ.ZZ>"* uses the BCD template language to create an output string with a leading $, commas separating digits into groups of three, and two digits after the decimal point.

The following CGI program reads a decimal number from an HTML form and assigns the value to a BCD number:

```
include "ombcd.xin"
include "omcgi.xin"

declare #process-input has unbuffered
declare #process-output has binary-mode

process
    local stream form-data variable
    local bcd price
    local bcd tax-rate
    local integer quantity
    local bcd total

    CGIGetQuery into form-data

    set price to form-data{"price"}
    set quantity to form-data{"qty"}

    set tax-rate to  0.07
    set total to price * quantity * (1 + tax-rate)
    output "Content-type: text/html"
        || crlf
        || crlf
        || "<html><body>"
        || "<H1>Order confirmation</H1>"
        || "<p>Your total comes to: "
        || "<$,NNZ.ZZ>" format total
```

The following HTML document can be used to test the preceding CGI program:

```
<HTML>
    <HEAD>
        <TITLE>Place an order</TITLE>
    </HEAD>
    <BODY>
        <H1>Place an order</H1>
        <FORM METHOD="POST" ACTION="bcd.xom">
            Price: <INPUT TYPE="TEXT" NAME="price"></INPUT><BR>
            Quantity: <INPUT TYPE="TEXT" NAME="qty"></INPUT><BR>
            <INPUT TYPE="SUBMIT" VALUE="Calculate total with tax">
        </FORM>
    </BODY>
</HTML>
```

NETWORK PROGRAMMING

Network programming refers to all operations that happen behind the scenes and involve cooperation between multiple applications running on multiple machines across a network. Although the user never sees these programs, they do the real work on the Internet and in other networked environments.

The server is the workhorse of network programming. A server is a program that provides services to other programs. A server waits for a request from another program, decodes that request, and sends a response. Because servers run unattended for days and weeks, they must be robust.

The program requesting a service from a server is a client. A client issues a request and waits for a response from the server.

A middleware application is a program that acts as a go-between for two other programs. Generally, a middleware program adds value to the transaction. An active content server that receives requests from a Web server and queries a database to fill the request is acting as middleware. It manages the communication between the Web server and the database server and adds value by adding HTML tagging to the database results.

A middleware application acts as both a client and a server. You might encounter multitier architectures in which multiple middleware applications broker and add value to communication across a network. You can easily program servers and middleware applications in OmniMark by using the connectivity libraries.

When embarking on a network-programming project, you will need to know a little bit about protocols. A protocol is simply an agreement between a client and a server about how they will communicate. If you use a common published protocol or publish your own protocol, you can enable any number of clients to communicate with your server. On the other hand, if you keep your protocol private (or even encrypted), you can help to secure your server against intrusion.

You need to know about two important types of protocol: transport protocols and application protocols.

Transport protocols are used to actually get messages safely across the network from one machine to another. TCP/IP is the transport protocol used on the Internet and is supported by OmniMark's network libraries and the TCPService and TCPConnection OMX components.

An application protocol is an agreement about what constitutes a message and what the message means. While disk files contain end-of-file markers, a network message is just a stream of bytes over an open connection. You have to look at the data itself to determine whether you have found the whole message. The OmniMark I/O Protocol library supports all the common methods of delimiting a message.

Once you have a complete message, you must decode it to see what it means and then generate and send the appropriate response. OmniMark is an ideal language for decoding network protocols. Its streaming features enable you to easily interpret a message and quickly formulate a response.

A Simple Server

The following program is a simple OmniMark server that returns the first line of a nursery rhyme when it receives a message naming the principal character of that rhyme.

```
declare catch server-die
include "omioprot.xin"
include "omtcp.xin"
include "builtins.xin"

define switch function TCPservice-is-working
      read-only TCPService the-service
      as

   do when TCPServiceIsInError the-service
      local stream errorReport variable initial-size 0
      TCPServiceGetStatusReport the-service into errorReport
      log-message "TCPService Error:"
      repeat over errorReport
         log-message errorReport
      again
      return false
   else
      return true
   done


process
   local TCPService my-service
   set my-service to TCPServiceOpen at 5432
   throw server-die unless TCPService-is-working my-service
   repeat
      local TCPConnection my-connection
      local stream my-response
      set my-connection to TCPServiceAcceptConnection my-service
      throw server-die unless TCPService-is-working my-service
      open my-response as TCPConnectionGetOutput my-connection
      using output as my-response
         submit TCPConnectionGetLine my-connection
      catch #program-error
   again
   catch server-die

find "Mary%n"
```

```
   output "Mary had a little lamb%13#%10#"

find "Tom%n"
   output "Tom, Tom, the piper's son.%13#%10#"

find "Jack" | "Jill" "%n"
   output "Jack and Jill went up the hill.%13#%10#"

find "die%n"
   output "Argh! Splat!%13#%10#"
   throw server-die
```

A server operates rather like a telephone. First we place it in service by assigning it a telephone number. Then it must wait for a call. When a call comes, the server must answer the call, listen to the message, and make an appropriate response. The conversation can consist of a single exchange or multiple exchanges. When the conversation is over, the server hangs up and goes back to waiting for the next call.

We can break down the essential operation of a server into three phases:

- **Start up** Put the server in service
- **Request loop** Wait for calls, respond, and repeat
- **Shut down** Take the server out of service

Because a server runs for a long time and has to handle many requests, it has two overriding performance requirements:

- No matter what happens while servicing a request, the server must not crash. It must stay running.

- No matter what happens while servicing a request, the server must always return to a consistent ready state when the request is complete. (If the server were in a different state for each request, its responses would not be reliable.)

Let's look at how our sample server meets these requirements line by line.

```
process
   local TCPService my-service
   set my-service to TCPServiceOpen at 5432
```

This is the code that puts the server in service. It uses a TCPService OMX component to establish a service on port 5432 of the machine it is running on. The server's address will be the machine's network address combined with the port number. By using different ports, many different servers can run on the same machine concurrently.

```
repeat
      local TCPConnection my-connection
      ...
      set my-connection to TCPServiceAcceptConnection my-service
again
```

This is the code that listens for an incoming call. *TCPServiceAcceptConnection* waits for a client to connect. When the server receives a connection, it returns a TCPConnection OMX component, which represents the connection to the client. The *TCPConnection* variable *my-connection* is declared inside the *repeat* loop so that the variable will go out of scope at the end of the loop, providing automatic closure and cleanup of the connection.

```
repeat
      local TCPConnection my-connection
      ...
      set my-connection to TCPServiceAcceptConnection my-service
      ...
         submit TCPConnectionGetLine my-Conn
again
```

A *TCPConnection* OMX provides an OmniMark source so that the program can read data from the client. Reading data from a network connection, however, is different from reading from a file. While you can either read from or write to a file, a network connection is a two-way connection. OmniMark cannot detect the end of a message on a network connection the way it detects the end of a file. The connection stays open; there could always be more characters coming. For this reason, all network data communication requires a specific application protocol for determining the end of a message. OmniMark provides support for all the common application protocols used for this purpose through the I/O Protocol library. The TCP library uses the I/O Protocol library to support the common Internet protocols. This example uses a line-based protocol. In our request protocol, the end of a message is signaled by a line-end combination (ASCII 13, 10). The *TCPConnectionGetLine* function provides a source for line-end delimited data and closes that source when it detects a line end. We submit data from that source to our *find* rules, which will analyze the message and generate the appropriate response.

```
repeat
   ...
   local stream my-response
   ...
   open my-response as TCPConnectionGetOutput my-connection
   using output as my-response
      submit TCPConnectionGetLine my-connection
   ...
again
```

Our TCPConnection OMX represents a two-way network connection. Not only must we get a source from it to read data, but we must also attach an output stream to it so that we can send data over the connection to the client. We do this with the *TCPConnectionGetOutput* function.

Once we prefix our *submit* with *using output as my-response*, our *find* rules read from and write to the network connection.

```
find "Mary%n"
   output "Mary had a little lamb%13#%10#"

find "Tom%n"
   output "Tom, Tom, the piper's son.%13#%10#"
```

Ours is a line-based protocol, but line ends are different on different platforms (13, 10 on Windows, 10 on UNIX). OmniMark's *%n* is a normalized line end that will match either form. If you output *%n*, OmniMark will output the form appropriate to the platform the program is running on. Across a network—that includes machines from different platforms—we have to choose the appropriate form ourselves. Our protocol specifically requires 13, 10. But for matching purposes, we use *%n* so that even if the client forgets to send the appropriate line end sequence, we can still read the message. When we send, however, we explicitly send *"%13#%10#"* rather than *"%n"*. This reflects an important maxim of network programming that reflects the so-called Netiquette guidelines: Be liberal in what you accept, conservative in what you send.

This is the find rule that detects the poison-pill message:

```
find "die"
   output "Argh! Splat!%13#%10#"
   throw server-die
```

To ensure an orderly shutdown, we provide a means of terminating our server by sending it a message to shut itself down. (In a production system, you might want to pick a slightly less obvious message for the poison pill.)

Shutting down the server is an exception to normal processing. We accomplish it by initiating a throw to a catch named *server-die*.

```
process
   ...
   repeat
     ...
   again
   catch server-die
```

We catch the throw to *server-die* after the end of the server loop. OmniMark cleans up local scopes on the way, ensuring a clean and orderly shutdown. Since we are at the end of the process rule, the program exits normally.

Error and Recovery

A server needs to continue running despite any errors that occur in servicing a particular request. However, a server should shut down if it cannot run reliably. The following code provides for both situations:

```
define switch function TCPservice-is-working
       read-only TCPService the-service
       as

   do when TCPServiceIsInError the-service
      local stream errorReport variable initial-size 0
      TCPServiceGetStatusReport the-service into errorReport
      log-message "TCPService Error:"
      repeat over errorReport
         log-message errorReport
      again
      return false
   else
      return true
   done

process
   set my-service to TCPServiceOpen at 5432
   throw server-die unless TCPService-is-working my-service
   repeat
      ...
      set my-connection to TCPServiceAcceptConnection my-service
      throw server-die unless TCPService-is-working my-service
      ...
      catch #program-error
   again
```

If there is an error in processing a request, OmniMark initiates a throw to *#program-error*. We catch the throw at the end of the server loop, thereby providing for automatic cleanup of any resources used in servicing the request in progress, and assuring that the server returns to its stable ready state. (In this example, we've made no attempt to rescue the specific request in which the error occurred. In a production server you would want to provide such error recovery, but make sure you always have a fallback that aborts the current request and returns to a stable ready state.)

In the unlikely event that something goes wrong with the TCPService component, you can't do much except shut down the server. The current version of the TCP library does not support catch and throw, so you have to do an explicit test for errors in the service whenever you use the library. If you detect an error, log it and then throw to *server-die* to shut down the server.

This simple server program has everything you need for a robust and usable production server. You need to adapt the code to the protocol you are using, but apart from that, everything else is just regular OmniMark programming once input and output are bound to the connection.

A Simple Client

Any client program written in any language can use our server, as long as it knows the protocol. Here is a simple client written in OmniMark:

```
process
    local TCPConnection my-connection
    local stream my-request
    set my-connection to TCPConnectionOpen
                    on "localhost" at 5432
    open my-request as TCPConnectionGetOutput my-connection
    using output as my-request
        output #args[1] || "%13#%10#"
    close my-request

repeat
    output TCPConnectionGetCharacters my-Conn
    exit unless TCPConnectionIsConnected my-Conn
again
```

This client is called with the name of the nursery-rhyme character on the command line and prints out the line it receives from the server. Let's go through it line by line.

```
set my-connection to TCPConnectionOpen
                on "localhost" at 5432
```

Like the server program, the client uses a TCPConnection OMX component to create a connection. Unlike the server, the client does not require a TCPService component, as it is not establishing a service but simply making a connection to a service established elsewhere. The client takes a more active role than the server, however. While the server waits for a call, the client must take the initiative and make a call. It does this with the *TCPConnectionOpen* function. The *TCPConnectionOpen* function takes a network and port address for a server, and when the connection is made it returns a TCPConnection OMX, which we can write to and read from just as we did in the server program.

```
repeat
    output TCPConnectionGetCharacters my-Conn
    exit when TCPConnectionIsInError my-Conn
again
```

When we read the data returned from the server we actually have two choices. Since our protocol is line-based, we could use *TCPConnectionGetLine* to read the response. But we also know that the server will drop the connection as soon as it finishes sending data. (This behavior is part of our protocol as well.) So we choose to keep reading data until the connection is dropped. This way we will get at least partial data even if something goes wrong and the server never sends the end of line. Be conservative in what you send and liberal in what you accept.

Clients for Common Servers

Most of the client programs you write in OmniMark will probably be for well-known servers such as HTTP, FTP, or SMTP/POP. OmniMark's connectivity libraries provide direct support for these and other common protocols, greatly simplifying the task of retrieving data from these servers.

CGI PROGRAMMING IN OMNIMARK

You invoke an OmniMark program from the command line by using the following basic syntax, where Program.xom is the filename of the program to run:

```
omnimark -sb Program.xom
```

Contrast this to Perl's command-line interface. To run a Perl program you use the following syntax, where program.pl is the filename of the program to run:

```
perl program.pl
```

The free OmniMark C/VM (compiler/virtual machine) is analogous to the Perl or Python interpreter.

You can also pass OmniMark C/VM an argument file or an IDE project file. (I'll cover OmniMark argument files later in the chapter.)

Hash-Bang Notation

Hash-bang notation (sometimes known as she-bang or #!) is a way to allow a source file to specify a command line to use to run it.

Hash-bang notation is used primarily in UNIX-type operating systems. Microsoft Internet Information Services (IIS), for example, does not use this method. IIS runs CGI programs based on an associated file extension. Apache for Win32 uses hash-bang notation to configure programs to run as CGI programs.

Hash-bang notation is required for scripts run under the Apache Web server on any platform. When Apache processes a script, the Web server reads the first line of the program. If the first two characters of the first line of the program are #!, the Web server uses the rest of the first line (whatever follows #!) as the command line to use to run the script, placing the name of the script at the end of the command line.

For example, for the program Hello.xom:

```
#!C:\OmniMark\omnimark.exe -sb
process
```

```
output "Content-Type: text/html%13#%10#%13#%10#"
    || "Hello, OmniMark world!"
```

the Web server will run the following command:

```
C:\OmniMark\omnimark.exe -sb Hello.xom
```

For the corresponding Perl program Hello.pl :

```
#!C:\Perl\bin\Perl.exe
print "Content-Type: text/html\r\n\r\n";
print "Hello, Perl world!";
```

the Web server will run the following command:

```
C:\Perl\bin\Perl.exe Hello.pl
```

You'll find the comment character # in many of the UNIX-world scripting languages, such as Perl. Therefore, the #! line is ignored when the program is run. OmniMark behaves the same way. Even though OmniMark's comment character is a semicolon (;), OmniMark won't object to the #! if, and only if, it is in the very first line of the program.

> **NOTE** On UNIX-type systems, hash-bang programs must have the executable bit set to indicate to the Web server that the file can be executed; otherwise, the Web server will report an error when it is asked to invoke the CGI program. This bit is set using the *chmod* command.
>
> For example, to allow a UNIX Web server to run the Hello.xom program mentioned earlier, you have to make the program executable by entering:
>
> ```
> chmod a+x Hello.xom
> ```
>
> at the terminal prompt.

Configuring Web Servers for OmniMark CGI

This section describes how to configure IIS and Apache Web servers to run OmniMark CGI programs.

> **NOTE** You will need to log on to your machine with administrative rights to perform these steps.

Internet Information Services

To configure IIS on Microsoft Windows 2000 so that you can run OmniMark programs as CGIs, follow these steps:

1. Log on to your machine with administrative privileges.

2. Start the Microsoft Management Console by right-clicking the My Computer icon on the desktop and selecting Manage from the pop-up menu.

3. Expand Services and Applications and Internet Information Services in the Tree window of the console. Right-click on the Web site you want to add a CGI directory to, and select Virtual Directory under the New pop-up menu item. This will run the Virtual Directory Setup Wizard. Create a new virtual directory, and make sure that the executable flag is set. You'll use this directory to hold your OmniMark source files.

4. Right-click on the new CGI directory, and select Properties. A Properties dialog box will appear.

5. Click the Configuration button on the Virtual Directory tab. The Application Configuration dialog box will appear.

6. Click the Add button on the App Mappings tab. The Add/Edit Application Extensions Mapping dialog box will appear.

7. In the Executable text box, enter the command line to start the OmniMark C/VM, substituting %s for the filename of your script. Typically it will look like this:

```
C:\OmniMark\omnimark.exe -noexpand -sb %s
```

8. Type .xom in the Extension text box.

9. Ensure that Script Engine is checked, and click OK.

10. Repeat steps 7 through 9 for the extension .xop, using the following command line:

```
C:\OmniMark\omnimark.exe -noexpand -f %s
```

11. Repeat steps 7 through 9 for the extension .xar, using the following command line:

```
C:\OmniMark\omnimark.exe -noexpand -f %s
```

12. Repeat steps 7 through 9 for the extension .pmo, using the following command line:

```
C:\OmniMark\omnimark.exe -noexpand -s pmo.xom %s
```

13. Click OK to accept the settings.

14. In the Properties dialog box, make sure that Execute Permissions is set to Scripts and Executables, and click OK.

Personal Web Server on Windows 95/98

To configure Microsoft Personal Web Server (PWS) on Microsoft Windows 95/98 to run OmniMark programs as CGI, follow these steps:

1. As a safety measure, back up your registry.

2. Click Start, and select Run to open the Run dialog box. In the drop-down combo box, type *regedit* and click OK.

3. In the Registry Editor, navigate to HKEY_LOCAL_MACHINE\System\ CurrentControlSet\Services\w3svc\parameters\ ScriptMap.

4. From the Edit menu, select New and then click String Value. This will create a new string value icon and allow you to set its name.

5. Type *.xom* as the name of the entry.

6. Double-click on the new entry. The Edit String dialog box will appear.

7. In the Value data text box, type the command line for running .xom files, typically:

    ```
    C:\OmniMark\OmniMark.exe -noexpand -sb %s
    ```

8. Click OK.

9. Repeat steps 4 through 8 for the extension .xop, using the following command line:

    ```
    C:\OmniMark\OmniMark.exe -noexpand -f %s
    ```

10. Repeat steps 4 through 8 for the extension .xar, using the following command line:

    ```
    C:\OmniMark\OmniMark.exe -noexpand -f %s
    ```

11. Repeat steps 4 through 8 for the extension .pmo, using the following command line:

    ```
    C:\OmniMark\OmniMark.exe -noexpand -s pmo.xom %s
    ```

12. Close the Registry Editor.

Make sure you have a directory in your server configuration that is set up for running CGI programs. (See the PWS documentation for information on setting up and configuring such a directory.)

The Apache Web Server

The simplest way to make CGI scripts work in any version of Apache is to use the ScriptAlias directive in the Web server's configuration file. This directive maps a virtual directory to a physical directory and tells the Web server that any files in this directory will be run as CGI programs.

Notice that this directive only creates a virtual-to-physical directory mapping; it does not map file extensions to interpreters. Apache will use the hash-bang line at the top of each script to determine the appropriate command line to use.

Apache on Windows 2000

Add the following line to Apache's configuration file. This file is named httpd.conf in the directory in which you install Apache.

```
ScriptAlias /virtdir/ "C:/www/root/cgi-bin/"
```

In this line, *virtdir* is the name of the virtual directory you want to create and C:*/www/root/cgi-bin/* is the name of the physical directory that your CGI scripts reside in. Note the forward slashes on the physical path.

All our examples are going to assume that *virtdir* is *cgi-bin*, so the command should be this:

```
ScriptAlias /cgi-bin/ "C:/www/root/cgi-bin/"
```

Stop and restart the Apache server by selecting Start, Settings, Control Panel, and then Services to force the server to reread its configuration file.

Now a request to the Web server for *http://hostname/cgi-bin/Hello.xom* will cause the server to run the file C:\www\root\cgi-bin\Hello.xom.

Apache on UNIX/Linux

To configure Apache on UNIX or Linux machines to run OmniMark CGI programs, add the following line to Apache's configuration file.

```
ScriptAlias /virtdir/ "/www/root/cgi-bin/"
```

In this line, *virtdir* is the name of the virtual directory you want to create and */www/root/cgi-bin/* is the name of the physical directory your CGI scripts reside in. Notice the forward slashes on the physical path.

All our examples are going to assume that */virtdir* is /www/root/*cgi-bin,* so the command should be this:

```
ScriptAlias /cgi-bin/ "/www/root/cgi-bin/"
```

Stop and restart the Apache server by running the following line to force the server to reread its configuration file:

```
apachectl restart
```

Now a request to the Web server for *http://hostname/cgi-bin/Hello.xom* will cause the server to run OmniMark from the path specified at the top of the Hello.xom file with the source file as a parameter, as shown in the following code:

```
line:/usr/local/bin/omnimark -sb /www/root/cgi-bin/Hello.xom
```

Locating OmniMark's System Libraries

OmniMark uses system environment variables to find its system libraries and include files. On Windows platforms, the OmniMark installation program sets the environment variables. On UNIX-type systems, you will need to ensure that the following environment variables are set. Assuming the location of OmniMark is /usr/local/bin/omnimark, the following paths should be set up as environment variables:

```
OMNIMARK_INCLUDE /usr/local/bin/omnimark/xin/
OMNIMARK_XFLPATH /usr/local/bin/omnimark/lib/=L.so
```

Each UNIX system has its own procedure for setting environment variables.

NOTE These OmniMark system environment variables are separate and distinct from CGI environment variables.

Writing an OmniMark CGI Program

This section describes the basics of writing a CGI program in OmniMark, including how to work with forms and CGI environment variables.

OmniMark's CGI Library

The OmniMark library (omcgi.xin) provides helper functions for writing CGI programs. To take advantage of these functions, add the following code to every OmniMark CGI program:

```
include "omcgi.xin"
```

Retrieving Input from the Web Server

CGI programs retrieve their input—such as HTML form fields and values, script name, and the IP address of the client—from both environment variables that the Web server sets and from standard input.

The GET and POST Request Methods

HTTP defines several different types of client requests, named methods. The two most common methods are *GET* and *POST*. You might have seen or written HTML form markup that looks like this:

```
<form action="Commit.xom" method="post">...
```

When a browser makes a *GET* request, all request information is encoded in the URL itself. For instance, output from a form with two fields named *user* and *age* might look like this:

```
http://localhost/Commit.xom?user=Randall+McMurtry&age=29
```

The part of the URL to the right of the question mark is named the query string. It contains the information the client sends to the Web server for processing.

When the client makes a *POST* request, the query string is not appended to the end of the URL. Instead, it is sent in the body of the HTTP request.

Whichever method is used—*GET* or *POST*—you can use the *cgiGetQuery* function to access the form data in the same way.

Accessing *GET* and *POST* Information

The *cgiGetQuery* function (defined in omcgi.xin) determines which method (*GET* or *POST*) was used to send form data, decode the data, and copy the key/value pairs into a stream shelf that you provide.

For instance, the following CGI program displays the names and values of every form field in the request:

```
#!C:\Omnimark\omnimark -sb
declare #process-input has unbuffered
declare #process-output has binary-mode
include "omcgi.xin"

process
   local stream query variable

   cgiGetQuery into query
   output "Content-Type: text/html" || CRLF || CRLF
   repeat over query
     output key of query || ": " || query || "<br>"
   again
```

Assuming this program is named Commit.xom, run it with the following URL:

```
http://localhost/cgi-bin/Commit.xom?user=Randall+McMurtry&age=29
```

The browser will display the following information:

```
user: Randall McMurtry
age: 29
```

This type of code—which iterates over the values passed in the query string—is useful for CGI debugging.

Accessing CGI Environment Variables

The *cgiGetEnv* function (defined in omcgi.xin) copies the names/value pairs of a predefined set of CGI environment variables into a stream shelf that you supply. The set includes any environment variables that the Web server uses to pass information to the CGI program.

For instance, you can modify the Commit.xom program to display the unparsed query string before displaying the parsed values. The query string is passed to a CGI program through the *QUERY_STRING* environment variable:

```
#!/usr/local/bin/omnimark -sb

declare #process-input has unbuffered
declare #process-output has binary-mode
include "omcgi.xin"
```

```
process
   local stream query variable
   local stream env variable

   cgiGetQuery into query
   cgiGetEnv into env
   output "Content-Type: text/html" || CRLF || CRLF
   output "Raw query string: "
      || env key "QUERY_STRING" || "<br>"
            when env has key "QUERY_STRING"
   repeat over query
     output key of query || ": " || query || "<br>"
   again
```

Assuming this program is named Commit2.xom, run it with this URL:

```
http://localhost/cgi-bin/Commit2.xom?user=Randall+McMurtry&age=29
```

The browser will display the following information:

```
Raw query string: user=Randall+McMurtry&age=29
user: Randall McMurtry
age: 29
```

Notice the guard on the query string output statement in the OmniMark program. The Web server will create environment variables only when there is some appropriate data available. The following URL will result in the *QUERY_STRING* environment variable not being set:

```
http://localhost/cgi-bin/Commit2.xom
```

Sending Output to the Web Server

Returning output to the Web server is straightforward: a CGI program writes a simple header followed by some content information to standard output. OmniMark output statements write to standard output (*stream #process-output*) by default.

Forming the HTTP header

An HTTP header must be output before the HTTP body. These headers are processed by the Web server and help determine the content that is sent to the browser.

Most CGI programs send HTML to the browser, as shown in the following common form:

```
output
   "Content-Type: text/html"       ; <- header
   || CRLF || CRLF                 ; <- separator
   || "Hello, OmniMark world!"     ; <- body
```

Note that you must use the CRLF macro twice to create a blank line between the header and the body. Do not use OmniMark's *"%n"* to do this.

While a CGI program can send several other headers, only a few are generally used. For example, if you want to redirect the browser to another URL, you can use the following header instead of a Content-Type header:

```
output
   "Location: http://www.omnimark.com"
   || CRLF || CRLF        ; no body required
```

The Web server will interpret this directive and output the correct headers to the browser (for example: HTTP Status 302 -- Page moved). The browser will then be redirected to the desired page.

Copying binary files

Occasionally you will need to copy a binary file, such as a GIF, to the browser. To ensure that OmniMark does not affect any of the internals of the binary file, you must use OmniMark's binary-mode modifier:

```
#!/usr/local/bin/omnimark -sb
declare #process-input has unbuffered
declare #process-output has binary-mode
include "omcgi.xin"

   process
      output "Content-Type: image/gif"
             || CRLF || CRLF
             || binary-mode file "C:\TravisBook\AppxA\Duck.gif "
```

Notice that you must declare the output stream and the GIF file as binary.

Unbuffering standard input and output

OmniMark streams, including *#process-input* and *#process-output*, are normally buffered by OmniMark for efficiency. However, buffered input can cause problems with CGI programs. An OmniMark CGI program might wait indefinitely for the rest of its input data because of OmniMark stream buffering. For this reason, the following declaration must appear at the top of all OmniMark CGI programs that receive input from the browser:

```
declare #process-input has unbuffered
```

Optionally, you can also unbuffer *#process-output*:

```
declare #process-output has unbuffered
```

This declaration might make responses appear quicker to the browser, particularly for CGI programs that intersperse output with significant periods of processing.

Bulletproofing Your CGI Program

OmniMark provides the programmer with several techniques for writing reliable programs. In a CGI environment, perhaps the most important technique is catching errors that can abort processing.

Catching program errors

OmniMark will halt with interpreter error messages if an illegal action occurs. Examples of illegal actions are setting a keyed value for which no key exists, dividing by zero, accessing a file that doesn't exist, or even running out of disk space.

To ensure that OmniMark doesn't attempt to write interpreter errors back to the browser, use OmniMark's catch facility to catch *#program-error*:

```
#!/usr/local/bin/omnimark -sb
declare #process-output has unbuffered
declare #process-output has binary-mode
include "omcgi.xin"

process
   local stream query variable
   local stream env variable

   cgiGetQuery into query
   cgiGetEnv into env
   output "Content-Type: text/html" || CRLF || CRLF
   output "Raw query string: "
       || env key "QUERY_STRING" || "<br>"
   repeat over query
     output key of query || ": " || query || "<br>"
   again
   catch #program-error
     put #error "<br><b>An error occured in this CGI program.</b><br>"
```

Note that there is no guard on the use of the *env* shelf. Assuming this program is Commit3.xom, the following URL

```
/localhost/cgi-bin/Commit3.xom
```

will display the following output:

```
Raw query string: An error occured in this CGI program.
```

Preventing source-code snooping

OmniMark's macros can be expanded using the *-expand* command-line option. Anyone invoking an OmniMark CGI program with this option could cause the entire program to be sent back to the browser, even if the program has no macros. This presents an undesirable security problem. Always configure your Web server to invoke OmniMark with the *-noexpand* option, which will override any outside attempt to use the *-expand* option.

Pulling It All Together

Now you have all the pieces to write OmniMark CGI programs. In this section I've included two programs that illustrate the concepts discussed in this appendix.

Using a simple form

The first example displays a simple form that asks for your name and returns the number of vowels in your name.

To invoke this program, simply place it in your cgi-bin directory and enter the URL *localhost/cgi-bin/Vowel.xom*:

```
#!/usr/local/bin/omnimark -noexpand -sb
;
; URL localhost/cgi-bin/Vowel.xom
;
include "omcgi.xin"
declare #process-input has unbuffered
declare #process-output has unbuffered
declare #process-output has binary-mode

global stream query variable
global stream env variable

define stream function get-script-name
   as
   return env^"SCRIPT_NAME" when env has key "SCRIPT_NAME"
   return ""

 process

   cgiGetQuery into query
   cgiGetEnv into env

   output "Content-type: text/html" || CRLF || CRLF
      || "<html><head><title>OmniMark CGI Test</title></head><body>%n"
      || "<h1>OmniMark Vowel Counter</h1>%n"

   do when query has key "name"
      local counter vowels initial {0}
      do when length of query^"name" > 0
         repeat scan query^"name"
            match unanchored ul ["aeiou"]
               increment vowels
         again
         output "<p>" || query^"name" || ", you have %d(vowels) vowel"
         output "s" unless vowels = 1
         output " in your name.</p>%n"
      else
         output "<p><b>You didn't enter a name.</b></p>%n"
      done
   done
   output "<form action='"
      || get-script-name
```

```
     || "' method='get'>Your name: %n<input type='text' name='name'>%n"
     || "<input type='submit' value='Count Vowels'></form>"
     || "</body></html>%n"
```

Accessing external data sources

The second example is an OmniMark CGI program that gets the current time from the National Institute of Standards and Technologies atomic clock in Boulder, Colorado. The default refresh rate is 60 seconds; however, you can set it in the URL. For instance, *localhost/cgi-bin/atomclock?refresh=10* will set a 10-second refresh rate.

This program uses a local guard where the value of the refresh CGI query string is set. If the value isn't provided in the URL—or if it is non-numeric—the initial value will be used. The final *#program-error* trap will catch any other errors that are not anticipated but could still occur.

Finally, the *always* block ensures that the correct HTML ending sequence is issued regardless of what else occurs in the program.

```
#! /usr/local/bin/omnimark -noexpand -sb
;
; URL localhost/cgi-bin/atomclock?refresh=NN
;
declare #main-output has binary-mode
declare #main-output has unbuffered
include "omioprot.xin"
include "omtcp.xin"
include "omdate.xin"
include "omcgi.xin"

process
   local counter refresh-rate initial {60}
   local stream query variable
   output "Content-type: text/html" || CRLF ||*2
       || "<html><head><title>The Exact Local Time"
       || "</title></head>%n"
       || '<body bgcolor="ffffff" text="000000">%n'
   cgiGetQuery into query
   do        ; establish a guard for existance and type
      set refresh-rate to query^"refresh"
      catch #program-error
           ; just use the initial value
   done
   do scan TCPConnectionGetCharacters
          TCPConnectionOpen on "132.163.135.130" at 14
      match white-space* digit+ blank+ digit{2} => y "-"
           digit{2} => m "-" digit{2} => d blank+ digit{2} => h
           ":" digit{2} => min ":" digit{2} => s
        output  '<meta http-equiv="refresh" content="'
              || "d" % refresh-rate || '">%n'
```

(continued)

321

```
          || '<font face="Comic Sans MS">%n'
          || '<p align="center">The local time %n'
          || "according to the ATOMIC CLOCK in%n"
          || "<br>Boulder Colorado<br><br><b>%n"
          || format-ymdhms "=xh:=m:=s =a.m. on =W, =n =xD, =xY"
                 with-date ymdhms-adjust-time-zone
                 "20%x(y)%x(m)%x(d)%x(h)%x(min)%x(s)+0000"
                 to-be date "=t"
          || "%n</b></font><br><br></p>"
      else
          output "<h1>Date in unexpected format!</h1>%n"
      done
  catch #program-error message the-problem
      output "<p>" || the-problem || "</p>%n"
             || "<p><b>An error occurred in this CGI application.</b></p>%n"
  always
      output "</body></html>"
```

Using OmniMark's Argument and Project Files

The OmniMark C/VM supports several command-line options that you can examine by entering the following code from the command line:

```
omnimark -help
```

Often, Web servers only allow the substitution of a single option—the name of the program. You might want to include more options, the most important of which is a log file to capture compiler and interpreter errors. You can do this with an OmniMark arguments file or a project file. The two files accomplish the same thing; however, the project file is more up-to-date.

OmniMark's Argument File

By convention, an OmniMark argument file has the suffix .xar. So the program Hello.xom should have the argument file Hello.xar.

An argument file is a file containing the command-line arguments to be passed to an OmniMark program. Use the *–f* option to pass an argument file to OmniMark:

```
C:\omnimark\omnimark -noexpand -f Hello.xar
```

Assuming hello.xar contains the following two lines:

```
-sb hello.xom
-alog Hello.log
```

it is equivalent to the following command:

```
C:\omnimark\omnimark -noexpand -sb Hello.xom -alog Hello.log
```

OmniMark reads the argument file, ignores comments and extra white space, and treats the file's contents exactly like command-line options.

Hash-Bang Notation in Argument Files

UNIX-like systems do not have a file extension to key on for program invocation. They rely heavily on the hash-bang notation. You can place the hash-bang line at the top of the argument file:

```
#!/usr/local/bin/omnimark -f
-sb Hello.xom
-alog /www/root/log/Hello.log
```

> **NOTE** On a UNIX-type system, the .xar file must also be made executable.

Assuming the file Hello.xar is /www/root/cgi-bin/, the following URL will invoke hello.xom and append any log messages to Hello.log:

```
/localhost/cgi-bin/hello.xar
```

OmniMark's Project File

OmniMark has another, newer, variation on the arguments file named a project file. By convention, a project file has the suffix .xop. Thus the OmniMark program Hello.xom should have the project file Hello.xop.

A project file is an XML file that performs the same function as an arguments file and is invoked in exactly the same way. It, too, can have a hash-bang line as the first line (although XML doesn't strictly provide for this).

The OmniMark IDE generates project files directly, and the capabilities of project files will expand over the next few years.

> **NOTE** When you develop CGI programs with the IDE, be sure to add -*brief* under the Extra tab in Project Options. If you don't do this, OmniMark will emit its banner information before your program can output its HTTP headers, the Web server will become confused, and your CGI program will break.

Compiling CGI Programs

OmniMark offers a separate byte-code compiler available through the OmniMark Developers Network. For details, visit *http://www.omnimark.com*. Compiling CGI applications offers several key advantages:

- **Better response time**   Larger CGI applications can be more responsive because they don't need to be compiled each time they are executed.

- **Better source-code control**   You don't need to distribute source code across several machines or departments running the same CGI script.

- **Better application security**   OmniMark byte-code cannot be reverse-compiled. OmniMark's application strings do not show up in byte-code.

- **Better business security**   Your business logic will not be compromised if an outsider gains access to your Web server.

- **Better intellectual property protection**   CGI-based commercial applications can ship royalty-free in byte-code form, thereby protecting your intellectual property.

By convention, OmniMark byte-code files use the .xvc convention. Byte-code programs execute in a similar manner to source-code programs. The extension/executable pair that must be set up for the Web server should look like this:

```
.xvc = C:\OmniMark\omnivm -load %s
```

You don't need to use the *-noexpand* option. The VM does not have access to the macro source.

You can also use the VM with an arguments file. A VM arguments file uses the .xva convention. As with source code, the first line of a VM arguments file can be a hash-bang line.

The extension/executable pair that you must set up for the Web server should look like this:

```
.xva = C:\OmniMark\omnivm -f %s
```

FOR MORE INFORMATION ON OMNIMARK

This appendix has been a brief introduction to the OmniMark programming language. For more information about specifics in the language, check out my book, *OmniMark At Work, Volume 1: Getting Started*, which is included on the companion CD. Even though the book is a few years old and does not have much in the way of network programming concepts, *OmniMark At Work* is a good place to start to learn about the basics of the language, including data types, control structures, referents, structured text processing, and so on.

The OmniMark Technologies Web site *(http://www.omnimark.com)* also has a rich collection of articles, tips, and developer support. The site's OmniMark Developers Network is a subscription service that gets you access to the developers and provides very fast turnaround for problems. Support is also available by e-mail and mailing list.

If you are working in a network programming environment, you owe it to yourself to learn about how OmniMark can provide a viable alternative to Perl for cross-platform, high-performance, scalable Web architectures.

Appendix B

BizTalk Framework 2.0 Draft: Document and Message Specification

Microsoft Corporation
June 2000

DRAFT SPECIFICATION SUMMARY

This draft specification provides a general overview of the BizTalk Framework 2.0 conceptual architecture, including the BizTalk Document and BizTalk Message. It provides detailed specifications for the construction of BizTalk Documents and Messages, and their secure transport over a number of Internet-standard transport and transfer protocols.

CONTENTS

1. INTRODUCTION

The growing maturity of Internet-based secure transport protocols, combined with ubiquitous support for these protocols across networking, hardware, and software platforms, is enabling businesses to develop new ways to facilitate efficient and automated interactions. These interactions can occur between their own internal lines of business; productivity and knowledge management applications; the applications used by their customers and partners; and services provided by their commercial and corporate providers.

The challenges associated with enabling such efficient, automated interactions between applications across business boundaries, and in a cost effective manner, are similar to those associated with enabling them within an enterprise or departmental boundary. However, a new dimension of challenges in the areas of security and reliability must be addressed in order to communicate with other organizations.

These challenges of interaction across business boundaries include, but are not limited to, the following:

- Lack of a sufficiently-flexible and rich universal language to specify, package, publish, and exchange both structured and unstructured information across application or business boundaries.

- Lack of a flexible and rich universal language to specify, package, publish, and execute transformation rules to convert information from one format to the other as application and business boundaries are crossed.

- Lack of middleware-neutral, application-level communication protocols that enable automated interactions across application or business boundaries.

Extensible Markup Language (XML) and XML-based schema languages provide a strong set of technologies with a low barrier to entry. These languages enable one to describe and exchange structured information between collaborating applications or business partners in a platform- and middleware-neutral manner.

As a result, domain-specific standards bodies and industry initiatives have started to adopt XML and XML-based schema languages to specify both their vocabularies and content models. These schemas are becoming widely published and implemented to facilitate communication between both applications and businesses. Wide support of XML has also resulted in independent solution providers developing solutions that enable the exchange of XML-based information with other third-party or custom-developed applications. Several solution- or middleware/platform-specific approaches have been taken to address the lack of middleware-neutral, application-level communication protocols. However, no single proprietary solution or middleware platform meets all the needs of a complex deployment environment.

These proprietary initiatives have generally resulted in customers facing broad interoperability issues on their own. The BizTalk™ Framework addresses these interoperability challenges in a platform- and technology-neutral manner. It provides specifications for the design and development of XML-based messaging solutions for communication between applications and organizations. This specification builds upon standard and emerging Internet technologies such as Hypertext Transfer Protocol (HTTP), Multipurpose Internet Mail Extensions (MIME), Extensible Markup Language (XML), and Simple Object Access Protocol (SOAP). Subsequent versions of the BizTalk Framework will be enhanced to leverage additional XML and Internet-related, messaging-standards work as appropriate.

It is important to note that the BizTalk™ Framework does not attempt to address all aspects of business-to-business electronic commerce. For instance, it does not deal directly with legal issues, agreements regarding arbitration, and recovery from catastrophic failures, nor does it specify specific business processes such as those for purchasing or securities trading. The BizTalk™ Framework provides a set of basic mechanisms required for most business-to-business electronic exchanges. It is expected that other specifications and standards, consistent with the BizTalk™ Framework, will be developed for the application- and domain-specific aspects.

2. SPECIFICATION SCOPE AND EVOLUTION

This specification provides a general overview of the BizTalk Framework conceptual architecture, including the fundamental notions of BizTalk Document and BizTalk Message. It then provides detailed specifications for the construction of BizTalk Documents and Messages, and their secure transport over a number of Internet-standard transport and transfer protocols, as described below.

BizTalk Documents follow a number of rules for structure and content in order to provide rich functionality and predictable semantics. This specification describes the following aspects of BizTalk Documents and their semantics:

- Overall structure of BizTalk Documents.

- BizTalk headers for document routing, properties, catalog, and process management.

- Structure and handling of BizTalk Documents that require reliable delivery.

When implementing solutions using the BizTalk Framework, specific transport, encoding, and security mechanisms must be used to secure and deliver messages. This specification describes the following mechanisms and aspects of BizTalk Message encoding and transport:

- Transport bindings for Internet protocols (HTTP only; Simple Mail Transfer Protocol (SMTP), and File Transfer Protocol (FTP) to be added).

- MIME-based transfer encoding and attachment packaging.

- Signatures and encryption based on S/MIME and Public-Key Cryptography System (PKCS) (to be added).

This specification is intended to define messaging interaction between BizTalk Framework 2.0 Compliant servers, referred to as *BFC servers* in this specification.

2.1 Relationship to BizTalk Framework 1.0

The BizTalk Framework 2.0 specification is a major revision of the BizTalk Framework 1.0 specification. BizTalk Framework 2.0 includes the following new features:

- Transport bindings (HTTP only; SMTP, and FTP to be added).

- Reliable message delivery.

- MIME encoding for attachments.

- Security based on S/MIME and PKCS (to be added).

In addition, BizTalk Framework 2.0 has been influenced by many recent standards efforts including, but not limited to, the following:

- SOAP Version 1.1

- XML Schema Part 1: Structures

- XML Schema Part 2: Data types

- XML-Signature Syntax and Processing

The influence of SOAP 1.1 is most pervasive since BizTalk Framework 2.0 is an extension of SOAP 1.1, whereas BizTalk Framework 1.0 was "pre-SOAP." In addition, the opportunity for a major revision was used to rationalize the semantics, naming, and structure of many BizTags in the light of experience and the requirements of the new features in this specification.

One of the goals of BizTalk Framework 2.0 is to sufficiently explain wire-level behavior so that it's useful as the basis for interoperation among compliant servers. The semantics of many BizTags has been defined much more specifically than in BizTalk Framework 1.0. The structure and content of BizTalk Documents described in BizTalk Framework 1.0 have been preserved wherever possible, but precise semantics and consistency with standards have been given higher priority in order to provide a solid foundation for the future.

2.2 Versioning Model

BizTalk Framework 2.0 follows SOAP 1.1 in not defining a traditional versioning model based on major and minor version numbers. The version is implied by the namespace URIs used to qualify the BizTalk-specific header entries defined in this specification. Normal SOAP 1.1 rules for the **SOAP-ENV:mustUnderstand** attribute imply that if the header entries that are required to be understood carry the wrong namespace or are deemed ill-formed in some other fashion, the BFC server should respond with a **SOAP-ENV:mustUnderstand** fault.

In the context of the HTTP binding specified in section 10, this fault indication may be returned in the HTTP response. However, if the message is processed asynchronously, the HTTP response will be **202 accepted** and the fault should be returned asynchronously, whenever possible. See section 10 for further discussion of transport protocol binding.

3. DEPENDENCIES

3.1 Normative Specifications

Each BizTalk Framework document lists the existing or emerging Internet standards that it is built upon as normative references. Some of the content of the normative references may need to be reproduced for expository purposes in BizTalk Framework specifications. In all such cases, the normative references are authoritative. Every effort has been made to avoid discrepancies between the normative references and their usage in BizTalk Framework specifications. However, if a discrepancy is found, the normative reference provides the correct interpretation and the BizTalk Framework specification is in need of correction.

The following specifications are normative for this specification:

- Extensible Markup Language (XML) 1.0

- Simple Object Access Protocol (SOAP) Version 1.1

- Namespaces in XML

- Uniform Resource Identifiers (URI): Generic Syntax

- ISO 8601: Representations of dates and times

- Hypertext Transfer Protocol—HTTP/1.1

- XML Media Types

- MIME Part One: Format of Internet Message Bodies

- MIME Part Two: Media Types

- MIME Part Three: Message Header Extensions for Non-ASCII Text

- MIME Part Four: Registration Procedures

- Content-ID and Message-ID Uniform Resource Locators

3.2 Non-Normative Specifications

The following specifications have had an influence on this specification, but the relationship is not foundational and their content is not normative for this specification:

- XML-Data Reduced (XDR)

- XML Schema Part 1: Structures

- XML Schema Part 2: Data types

- XML-Signature Syntax and Processing

3.3 Use of XML Schema Data Types

This specification uses the type-qualification **xsi:type** attribute as well as a number of specific data types from the XML Schema specifications. These are listed below with explanations. This specification, however, does not mandate the use of a specific method for defining XML schemas.

The **xsi:type** attribute allows an element to explicitly assert its type in a specific XML document instance. This can be used to validate the structure of the element.

The data type **timeInstant** represents a specific instant of time. The value space of **timeInstant** is the space of combinations of date and time of day values as defined in section 5.4 of the ISO 8601 standard.

The **uriReference** data type represents a URI reference as defined in Section 4 of Request for Comments (RFC) 2396. A URI reference may be absolute or relative, and may have an optional fragment identifier.

A **complexType** is an element with content that is not a simple type, such as a string or a decimal number; the element contains subelements and/or attributes with their own content.

4. BIZTALK CONCEPTS

4.1 Terminology

This document uses a set of BizTalk-specific terms, as defined below:

- **BizTalk Framework Compliant (BFC) Server**   A BFC Server is represented by the set of services providing the message-processing functionality defined in the BizTalk Framework specifications.

- **Application** An Application is the line-of-business system where the business data or logic are stored and executed. An application also includes any additional adapters that may be required to emit or consume Business Documents (see below) and communicate with a BFC server.

- **Business Document** A Business Document is a well-formed XML document containing business-transaction data. This transaction data may represent a purchase order, invoice, sales forecast, or any other business information. One or more Business Documents form the body of a BizTalk Document (see below).

  The BizTalk Framework does not prescribe the content or structure (schema) of individual Business Documents. The details of the Business Document content and structure, or Schema, are defined and agreed upon by the solution implementers.

- **Schema** A Schema is the metadata used to describe the content and structure of a class of XML documents, in particular for a class of Business Documents. This formal description is used by application developers to create systems that process corresponding Business Documents, or by parsers that validate a Business Document's conformance to the Schema at run time.

  Organizations may publish their Schemas in the BizTalk Schemas Library, or through other means.

  NOTE Schemas for Business Documents do not contain any BizTags, as described in this specification. A schema contains only those tags required to support the business transaction, as agreed to by the cooperating business entities. General requirements and guidelines for Schema implementations are defined in the BizTalk Schema Guidelines.

- **BizTalk Document** A BizTalk Document is a SOAP 1.1 message in which the body of the message contains the Business Documents, and the header contains BizTalk-specific header entries for enhanced message-handling semantics.

- **BizTag** BizTags are the set of XML tags (both mandatory and optional) that are used to specify Business Document handling. More precisely, BizTags are elements and attributes defined in this specification and used to construct BizTalk-specific SOAP header entries in the BizTalk Document. They are processed by the BFC Server, or by other applications facilitating the document interchange.

- **BizTalk Message** A BizTalk Message is the unit of wire-level interchange between BFC Servers. BizTalk Messages are used to send BizTalk Documents, and any related files, between BFC Servers. A BizTalk Message must always contain a primary BizTalk Document that defines the semantics of the Message within the BizTalk Framework. It may in addition contain one or more attachments (see below), including well-formed XML documents, some of which may themselves be BizTalk Documents. BizTalk Documents carried as attachments are treated just like any other XML documents and have no special significance for the semantics of the BizTalk Message. The structure of a BizTalk Message is dependent on the transport being used to carry the message and often includes transport-specific headers.

- **Transport**   The actual interchange of BizTalk Messages between BFC servers presupposes a communication mechanism that is used to carry Messages physically from the source to the destination business entity. We use the term transport to refer to this mechanism. Transports used in this context will vary widely in their characteristics, ranging from simple datagram and file transfer protocols to transfer protocols such as HTTP and SMTP, and sophisticated, message-oriented middleware. This specification does not differentiate between transports based on their capabilities. Transport characteristics affect only the transport bindings specified in section 10.

- **Attachment**   Attachments are generally non-XML files or other related information that is not transmitted as a Business Document within the body of the BizTalk Document. These may be related images, large compressed files, or any other information format or content that is not an appropriate Business Document.

4.2   Logical Layering

The logical application model for the BizTalk Framework is implemented in layers. The layering described here is for illustrative and explanatory purposes. As the BizTalk Framework specification definitively specifies only the wire format for BizTalk Messages and the protocol for reliable messaging, alternative logical layering may be used, provided it supports equivalent functionality, without affecting compliance with this specification. These logical layers include the application (and appropriate adapters), the BFC Server, and transport. The application communicates with other applications by sending Business Documents back and forth through BFC Servers. Multiple BFC Servers communicate with one another over a variety of transport protocols, such as HTTP, SMTP, and Microsoft Message Queue (MSMQ). The BizTalk Framework does not prescribe what these transport protocols are, and is independent of the implementation details of each.

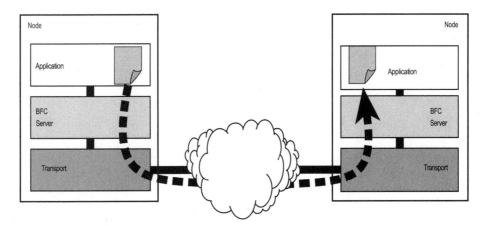

The application is responsible for generating the Business Documents and any attachments to be transmitted to its peer(s) and submitting them to the BFC Server. The responsibility for wrapping the Business Documents in a BizTalk Document may rest with either the application or the BFC server, depending on the implementation of the BFC server. The server processes the document and any attachments and constructs a BizTalk Message as appropriate for the transport protocol. The BFC Server uses information contained in the BizTags to determine the correct transport-specific destination address. The server then hands the message to the transport layer for transmission to the destination BFC Server. The interfaces between the business application, the BFC Server, and the transport layer are implementation specific.

5. BizTalk Document Structure

The following is an example of a simple BizTalk Document.

```
<SOAP-ENV:Envelope
            xmlns:SOAP-ENV="http://schemas.xmlsoap.org/soap/envelope/"
            xmlns:xsi="http://www.w3.org/1999/XMLSchema-instance">
    <SOAP-ENV:Header>
        <dlv:delivery SOAP-ENV:mustUnderstand="1"
            xmlns:dlv="http://schemas.biztalk.org/btf-2-0/delivery"
            xmlns:agr="http://www.trading-agreements.org/types/">
            <dlv:to>
                <dlv:address xsi:type="agr:department">
                    Book Order Department</dlv:address>
            </dlv:to>
            <dlv:from>
                <dlv:address xsi:type="agr:organization">
                    Booklovers Anonymous</dlv:address>
```

(continued)

```
            </dlv:from>
        </dlv:delivery>
        <prop:properties SOAP-ENV:mustUnderstand="1"
            xmlns:prop="http://schemas.biztalk.org/btf-2-0/properties">
            <prop:identity>
            uuid:74b9f5d0-33fb-4a81-b02b-5b760641c1d6</prop:identity>
            <prop:sentAt>2000-05-14T03:00:00+08:00</prop:sentAt>
            <prop:expiresAt>2000-05-15T04:00:00+08:00</prop:expiresAt>
            <prop:topic>http://electrocommerce.org/purchase_order/</
prop:topic>
        </prop:properties>
    </SOAP-ENV:Header>
    <SOAP-ENV:Body>
        <po:PurchaseOrder
            xmlns:po="http://electrocommerce.org/purchase_order/">
            <po:Title>Essential BizTalk</po:Title>
        </po:PurchaseOrder>
    </SOAP-ENV:Body>
</SOAP-ENV:Envelope>
```

This BizTalk Document consists of a standard SOAP 1.1 message that contains the following:

■ An application-specific Business Document (in this case a book purchase order), with its own application-defined XML namespace, carried in the body of the SOAP message.

■ BizTalk-specific <delivery> and <properties> SOAP header entries, constructed using BizTags defined in standard BizTag namespaces, with schema and semantics defined in this specification.

In general, the body of the SOAP message constituting a BizTalk Document contains several related Business Documents, and the header of the SOAP message contains several BizTalk-specific (and potentially other) header entries. The use of the **SOAP-ENV:mustUnderstand** attribute with a value of "1" implies (in accordance with the SOAP 1.1 specification) that the destination business entity receiving this Document must understand and correctly process the header entries so attributed, or if the header entry is not understood, the processing of the Document must be terminated with failure.

All BizTags are defined within standard BizTag namespaces with URIs derived by extension from the prefix http://schemas.biztalk.org/btf-2-0/. The scope of semantic significance for the BizTag namespaces is always confined to the header of the outermost BizTalk Document. If a BizTalk Document is carried whole in the body of another BizTalk Document, the BizTags in the inner document are "dormant" and ineffective—they are treated as business data for the purposes of processing the outer Document.

It is worth noting that the <to> and <from> routing tags, described in more detail below, often use business-entity names for source and destination addressing, rather than transport addresses such as HTTP URLs. The form and interpretation of the address content is indicated by the **xsi:type** attribute. The BizTalk Document structure and function are independent of the transports over which the Documents are carried.

6. BizTalk Document Body

The <Body> element of the SOAP message that constitutes a BizTalk Document contains the Business Documents being carried. In general, a BizTalk Document may carry a set of related Business Documents (for instance, a purchase order and a shipper's name and address for shipping that order).

Related Business Documents often have shared content. SOAP has a straightforward mechanism for encoding data targeted by multiple references; it uses XML ID attributes and relative URIs. Consider a simple elaboration of the purchase order example above in which both the purchase order and the shipping information reference information about the book. The <Body> element of the following BizTalk Document shows how this could be expressed using SOAP encoding rules.

```
<SOAP-ENV:Envelope
            xmlns:SOAP-ENV="http://schemas.xmlsoap.org/soap/envelope/"
            xmlns:SOAP-ENC="http://schemas.xmlsoap.org/soap/encoding/"
            xmlns:xsi="http://www.w3.org/1999/XMLSchema-instance">
   <SOAP-ENV:Header>
      <!-- headers omitted for brevity -->
   </SOAP-ENV:Header>
   <SOAP-ENV:Body>
     <po:PurchaseOrder
         xmlns:po="http://electrocommerce.org/purchase_order/">
         <po:item href="#theBook"/>
         <!-- and other purchasing information -->
     </po:PurchaseOrder>

     <ship:shippingInfo xmlns:ship="http://electrocommerce.org/
shippingInfo/">
         <ship:content href="#theBook"/>
         <!-- and other shipping information -->
     </ship:shippingInfo>

     <book xmlns="http://electrocommerce.org/bookInfo/"
         id="theBook"  SOAP-ENC:root="0">
         <Title>Essential BizTalk</Title>
         <!-- and other book information -->
     </book>
   </SOAP-ENV:Body>
</SOAP-ENV:Envelope>
```

This example also illustrates a problem that occurs when this technique is used. We would like the destination business entity to view this BizTalk Document as containing two Business Documents: the purchase order and the shipping information. However, the <Body> of the SOAP message contains three child elements. We need a way to distinguish the Business Documents from the elements that appear as direct children of <Body> because they are shared via multiple references.

SOAP provides the **SOAP-ENC:root** attribute as a method for signaling that an element is not an independent entity. Every immediate child of the <Body> element in a BizTalk Document is a contained Business Document *unless* that child carries the **SOAP-ENC:root** attribute with a value of "0".

7. BizTalk Document Header Entries

This section describes the four BizTalk-specific SOAP header entries that may occur in a BizTalk Document. They are concerned with Document routing and delivery, Document identification and other properties, a catalog of Document contents and attachments, and tracking of the business process context of which the Document is a part. The following table lists the four BizTags used to mark the header entries and their properties. Each header entry is described in more detail in the following sections, and schemas for the corresponding elements are provided in the appendix.

Tag Name	Mandatory	Kind	Type	Occurs
delivery	yes	element	complexType	once
Properties	yes	element	complexType	once
Manifest	no	element	complexType	once
Process	no	element	complexType	once

7.1   Document Routing and Delivery

Document routing is specified by a SOAP header entry marked by the <delivery> BizTag. This entry contains information about the source and destination of the BizTalk Document. There may also be a section that provides information required for reliable delivery. An extended version of the delivery header entry from the initial BizTalk Document example, including a reliability section, is shown below:

```
<dlv:delivery SOAP-ENV:mustUnderstand="1"
              xmlns:SOAP-ENV="http://schemas.xmlsoap.org/soap/envelope/"
              xmlns:xsi="http://www.w3.org/1999/XMLSchema-instance"
              xmlns:dlv="http://schemas.biztalk.org/btf-2-0/delivery"
              xmlns:agr="http://www.trading-agreements.org/types/">
```

```
<dlv:to>
   <dlv:address xsi:type="agr:department">
       Book Order Department</dlv:address>
</dlv:to>
<dlv:from>
   <dlv:address xsi:type="agr:organization">
       Booklovers Anonymous</dlv:address>
</dlv:from>
<dlv:reliability>
   <dlv:sendReceiptTo>
       www.we-love-books.org/po/confirmations
   </dlv:sendReceiptTo>
   <dlv:receiptRequiredBy>
       2000-05-14T08:00:00+08:00
   </dlv:receiptRequiredBy>
</dlv:reliability>
</dlv:delivery>
```

As noted in the context of the initial example, although the source and destination are specified as names of business entities marked by the <address> BizTag, the selection of transports and transport endpoints, over which the BizTalk Document is carried, often occurs separately between the business entities involved. It is entirely possible that multiple transports and transport endpoints are available for the communication and that they will change over time, without changing the names of the business entities (in <address>) and the structure of the BizTalk Documents exchanged between the entities. The exact routing logic used to deliver the BizTalk Document once it reaches the BFC server that is associated with the destination business entity is implementation dependent.

Understanding and processing the <delivery> header entry and all its contents at the recipient BFC server is always mandatory during successful processing of a BizTalk Document. The encoding of the <delivery> element must always contain the **SOAP-ENV:mustUnderstand="1"** attribute to reflect this. The following table lists the BizTags used to construct the subelements of the <delivery> header entry and their properties.

Tag Name	Mandatory	Kind	Type	Occurs
to	yes	element	complexType	once
from	yes	element	complexType	once
reliability	no	element	complexType	once

The <to> tag contains the specification of the destination business entity to which the BizTalk Document is to be delivered. This element contains exactly one occurrence of an <address> subelement.

The <from> tag contains the specification of the source business entity from which the BizTalk Document originates. This element contains exactly one occurrence of an <address> subelement.

The <address> tag contains the identification of a business entity in string form. The <address> element has a required **xsi:type** attribute. The value of the **xsi:type** attribute signifies the category of the address as well as the permissible structure of the string form of the address. Several categories, including organization name and URI reference, are used in examples in this specification.

The <reliability> tag is an optional element that contains the information necessary to perform reliable delivery of the enclosing BizTalk Document. If the <reliability> element is present, (the BFC server at) the destination business entity is required to send a receipt back to the given URL upon receiving and accepting the BizTalk Document. The Document-handling behavior related to this element and the structure and content of receipts is described in more detail in section 8. The <reliability> element contains two subelements listed in the table below.

Tag Name	Mandatory	Kind	Type	Occurs
sendReceiptTo	Yes	element	uriReference	Once
receiptRequiredBy	Yes	element	timeInstant	Once

The <sendReceiptTo> tag contains a URL that specifies the transport address (typically at the source business entity) to which a receipt for the BizTalk Document must be sent.

The <receiptRequiredBy> tag contains a time instant that specifies the absolute time by which a receipt for the delivery and acceptance of the BizTalk Document must be received by (the BFC server at) the source business entity. Failure to receive the receipt in time will typically initiate error-recovery behavior at the source. See the Explanatory Note associated with the <expiresAt> tag for a discussion of the merits and pitfalls of the use of absolute time instants in this context. See section 8 for details of the reliability protocol, including the semantics of this deadline.

7.2 Document Identification and Properties

Document identity information and other properties are specified by a SOAP header entry marked by the <properties> BizTag. The properties header entry from the initial BizTalk Document example is shown below.

```
<prop:properties SOAP-ENV:mustUnderstand="1"
    xmlns:SOAP-ENV="http://schemas.xmlsoap.org/soap/envelope/"
  xmlns:prop="http://schemas.biztalk.org/btf-2-0/properties">
      <prop:identity>
      uuid:74b9f5d0-33fb-4a81-b02b-5b760641c1d6
```

```
        </prop:identity>
        <prop:sentAt>2000-05-14T03:00:00+08:00</prop:sentAt>
        <prop:expiresAt>2000-05-15T04:00:00+08:00</prop:expiresAt>
        <prop:topic>
        http://electrocommerce.org/purchase_order/
        </prop:topic>
    </prop:properties>
```

Understanding and processing the <properties> header entry and all its contents at the recipient BFC server is always mandatory during successful processing of a BizTalk Document. The encoding of the <properties> element must always contain the **SOAP-ENV:mustUnderstand="1"**attribute to reflect this. The following table lists the BizTags used to construct the subelements of the <properties> header entry.

Tag Name	*Mandatory*	*Kind*	*Type*	*Occurs*
identity	yes	element	uriReference	once
sentAt	yes	element	timeInstant	once
expiresAt	yes	element	timeInstant	once
topic	yes	element	uriReference	once

The <identity> tag is a URI reference that uniquely identifies the BizTalk Document for purposes of logging, tracking, error handling, or other Document processing and correlation requirements. The <identity> tag must be universally unique. This could be accomplished, for instance, with Universally Unique Identifiers (UUIDs), as illustrated in the example above, or with cryptographic hash algorithms such as MD5 applied to the Business Document(s). The choice of <identity> tag form and the process of generating <identity> tag is implementation specific.

The <sentAt> tag is the sending timestamp of the Document. In the context of the transmission-retry behavior discussed in Section 8 section, this timestamp must always reflect the time at which the properties element was created.

The <topic> tag contains a URI reference that uniquely identifies the overall purpose of the BizTalk Document. The <topic> tag may be used for interest-based routing (publish/subscribe via topic-based addressing) and to verify the consistency of the BizTalk Document content with its intent. The latter use occurs in the HTTP binding as described in section 10. Although the process for creation of this element is implementation specific, it is recommended that the topic is either specified by the sending application or is inferred in a standard way by the BFC server from the Business Documents carried in the BizTalk Document, e.g. by using the namespace URI of the (first) Business Document as the topic.

The <expiresAt> tag is the expiration timestamp of the Document. Beyond the point in time stamped in this element, the associated BizTalk Document is considered to have expired and must not be processed by the destination business entity.

Care should be taken in specifying the expiration time, providing for a reasonable margin of error in time synchronization across distributed systems.

> **EXPLANATORY NOTE**   The business logic of the source business entity typically allocates a definite time interval for the performance of the business action represented by a BizTalk Document; it needs to be notified about failure to deliver the Document within the allocated time. There are two basic approaches to Document lifetime encoding: time to live (TTL) or maximum latency, and absolute expiration time. Both approaches have weaknesses. TTL is immune to time synchronization problems across machines, and is therefore best when low-latency messages are carried over fast transports. However, it effectively assumes instantaneous transport, which is an unreasonable assumption for some transports. Given the transport independence of the BizTalk Framework, use of TTL is problematic. The problem with using absolute expiration time (encoded as coordinated universal time) is the well-known clock-synchronization problem in distributed systems. However, the latency for messages that is expected in current usage of the BizTalk Framework tends to be high enough that synchronization is not expected to be a major issue. We therefore use absolute time encoding to specify lifetime. In future versions, the BizTalk Framework may support both kinds of lifetime encoding.

7.3   Document Catalog

Document catalog information is specified by an optional SOAP header entry marked by the <manifest> BizTag; it includes references to both the Business Documents carried within the primary BizTalk Document in the BizTalk Message, as well as any additional attachments, such as images or binary data, that may be considered a part of the BizTalk Message. Details of the structure of references to the attachments that are carried within the BizTalk Message are dependent on MIME encoding rules and are discussed in section 9. An example of the manifest header entry taken from section 9.1 is shown below:

```
<fst:manifest
    xmlns:fst="http://schemas.biztalk.org/btf-2-0/manifest">
        <fst:reference fst:uri="#insurance_claim_document_id">
            <fst:description>Insurance Claim</fst:description>
        </fst:reference>
        <fst:reference fst:uri="CID:claim.tiff@claiming-it.com">
            <fst:description>
            Facsimile of Signed Claim Document</fst:description>
        </fst:reference>
        <fst:reference fst:uri="CID:car.jpeg@claiming-it.com">
            <fst:description>Photo of Damaged Car
            </fst:description>
        </fst:reference>
</fst:manifest>
```

The purpose of the manifest is to provide a complete catalog of the BizTalk Message content for consistency checking, and for integrity and verification mechanisms such as digital signatures. To this end, an effort has been made to make the manifest structure as similar as possible to the structure used in XML digital signature work with the hope that the two will converge in future.

The <manifest> header entry is not mandatory. When present, the <manifest> header entry must catalog all the Business Documents carried in the BizTalk Document. In the primary BizTalk Document in a BizTalk Message, it must also catalog any attachments that are present in the enclosing BizTalk Message.

The <manifest> element is a sequence of <reference> elements, as shown in the table below.

Tag Name	Mandatory	Kind	Type	Occurs
reference	yes	element	complexType	one or more times

The <reference> tag contains a URI-valued attribute and a subelement containing freeform text as shown in the following table:

Tag Name	Mandatory	Kind	Type	Occurs
Uri	yes	attribute	uriReference	once
Description	no	element	string	once

The value of the **uri** attribute must be a URI reference that resolves to the resource denoted by the enclosing <reference> element. Typical values for this attribute are the following:

- Fragment identifiers of the form #id that resolve to Business Documents within the enclosing BizTalk Document, with an ID attribute value of id.

- Content-ID URLs of the form CID:content-id-value that resolves to attachments carried as MIME parts within the enclosing BizTalk Message, as described in section 9.2.

- URLs that resolve to resources, such as large files that are considered attachments, but whose content is not carried within the BizTalk Message itself.

- Note that this attribute is optional in XML digital signature but mandatory in this specification.

The <description> tag is a text description of the Business Document or attachment. The content is mixed (text with and without XML markup). It may be used as a supporting comment, or as a keyword for additional implementation-specific processing or reporting requirements.

7.4   Process Management

Process-management information is specified by an optional SOAP header entry marked by the <process> BizTag that includes information about the business process that provides the processing context for the BizTalk Document. An example of the process header entry is shown below:

```
<prc:process SOAP-ENV:mustUnderstand="1"
    xmlns:SOAP-ENV="http://schemas.xmlsoap.org/soap/envelope/"
    xmlns:prc="http://schemas.biztalk.org/btf-2-0/process">
    <prc:type>purchasing:Book_Purchase_Process</prc:type>
    <prc:instance>purchasing:Book_Purchase_Process#12345</prc:instance>
    <prc:handle>port:po_receiver</prc:handle>
</prc:process>
```

When present, understanding and processing of the <process> header entry and all its contents at the recipient BFC server is always mandatory during successful processing of a BizTalk Document. The encoding of the <process> element must always contain the **SOAP-ENV:mustUnderstand="1"** attribute to reflect this. The following table lists the BizTags used to construct the subelements of the <process> header entry and their properties:

Tag Name	Mandatory	Kind	Type	Occurs
Type	yes	element	uriReference	once
instance	yes	element	uriReference	once
handle	no	element	uriReference	once

The <type> tag contains a URI reference that signifies the type of business process involved, for example, the process of purchasing a book. This is a pattern of interchange of (typically) multiple BizTalk Documents that is agreed upon among two or more business partners. The pattern defines the "rules of the game" and is usually repeated many times.

The <instance> tag contains a URI reference that uniquely identifies a specific instance of the business process that this BizTalk Document is associated with (for example, an instance of the process of purchasing a book in which Booklovers Anonymous is in the process of purchasing a copy of Essential BizTalk). This is needed for correlation, as multiple instances of a given business process may be executing concurrently. A common way to construct this URI is to extend the URI for the process type with a fragment identifier signifying an instance—often a sequence number, as in the example above.

The <handle> tag is a URI reference that provides further information that may be required to identify a step or an entry point within the business process instance.

8. RELIABLE DELIVERY OF BIZTALK DOCUMENTS

BizTalk facilitates asynchronous document exchanges involved in e-commerce and Enterprise Application Integration, where specific delivery guarantees and error detection and reporting are necessary for integration of business functions across domain boundaries. High-performance-messaging middleware solutions for the Internet are emerging and should be used for this purpose when available. However, given the broad scope of deployment scenarios for BizTalk Framework-based application integration, and the continued use of transports with lower guarantees of service, it is important to provide a simple standard solution for reliable delivery of BizTalk Documents that can be easily implemented by BFC servers. This solution is described in the current section and is based on two simple notions:

- Document receipts.
- Idempotent delivery.

The overall purpose is to ensure a defined outcome for BizTalk Document delivery. The following points summarize the ideas on which the reliable delivery functionality described here is based:

- Receipts provide a way for (the BFC server at) the source business entity to assure itself that the BizTalk Document was received and accepted, using the identity for correlation.

- Given the possibility of multiple transmissions of the same BizTalk Document due to retry, (the BFC server at) the destination business entity may apply idempotent delivery rules to detect and eliminate duplicate Documents, again using the identity for correlation.

- If (the BFC server at) the source business entity does not receive a delivery receipt within the timeout period specified in the receiptRequiredBy element, a delivery failure report will be generated and corrective action taken.

- Note that there is a small but finite possibility that the Document will be delivered to the destination business entity and a delivery failure report will nevertheless be delivered to the source business entity, since all receipts may be lost due to transport failure.

The rest of this section describes the structure of a receipt document and the typical behavior of the source and destination business entities engaged in reliable delivery of BizTalk Documents. The details of actual behavior are implementation dependent and the description here is meant to serve as a guideline.

8.1   Structure and Content of Receipts

A BizTalk Framework Receipt is a SOAP 1.1 message that contains at least the <receipt> and <properties> header entries, and an empty body, as shown in the example below. A receipt is *not* a BizTalk Document. It is a SOAP message that acknowledges receipt of a BizTalk Document.

The content of the receipt unambiguously identifies the BizTalk Document being acknowledged, by including the universally unique identity of the Document. A timestamp for the time at which the Document was received at the destination is provided in the <receipt> header entry.

The following receipt corresponds to the initial example in this specification:

```
<SOAP-ENV:Envelope
              xmlns:SOAP-ENV="http://schemas.xmlsoap.org/soap/envelope/">
  <SOAP-ENV:Header>
      <rct:receipt SOAP-ENV:mustUnderstand="1"
          xmlns:rct="http://schemas.biztalk.org/btf-2-0/receipt">
          <rct:receivedAt>2000-05-15T04:08:10-05:30</rct:receivedAt>
      </rct:receipt>
      <prop:properties SOAP-ENV:mustUnderstand="1"
          xmlns:prop="http://schemas.biztalk.org/btf-2-0/properties">
          <prop:identity>
           uuid:74b9f5d0-33fb-4a81-b02b-5b760641c1d6</prop:identity>
          <prop:sentAt>2000-05-14T03:00:00+08:00</prop:sentAt>
          <prop:expiresAt>2000-05-15T04:00:00+08:00</prop:expiresAt>
          <prop:topic>http://electrocommerce.org/purchase_order/</
prop:topic>
      </prop:properties>
  </SOAP-ENV:Header>
  <SOAP-ENV:Body/>
</SOAP-ENV:Envelope>
```

In addition to the <receipt> header entry, a receipt must contain the <properties> header entry from the Document being acknowledged.

Understanding and processing of the <receipt> header entry and all its contents at the recipient BFC server is always mandatory during successful processing of a receipt. The encoding of the <receipt> element must always contain the **SOAP-ENV:mustUnderstand="1"** attribute to reflect this. The following table lists the BizTags used to construct the subelements of the <receipt> header entry and their properties:

Tag Name	Mandatory	Kind	Type	Occurs
receivedAt	yes	element	timeInstant	once

The <receivedAt> tag is the receiving timestamp for the Document acknowledged by this receipt. In the case of multiple copies of the BizTalk Document being received and accepted (see below for a discussion of the term "accepted"), the receiving timestamp may reflect either the time at which the first copy was received or the time at which the copy being acknowledged was received.

8.1.1   Behavior of the Source Business Entity

In accordance with common practice, it is assumed that the BizTalk Document being transmitted has been persisted in durable storage at the source business entity. It is strongly recommended that persistence in durable storage occur before a BizTalk Document is transmitted in the case of Documents that require reliable delivery with a defined outcome. However, this specification definitively specifies only wire-level behavior. Actual behavior at a business entity regarding storage and archival of business documents or the management of durable storage resources is implementation dependent and does not affect compliance with this specification.

The only special behavior required from a source business entity for reliable delivery of a BizTalk Document is to add a <reliability> element to the <delivery> header entry and to:

- Set the value of the <sendReceiptTo> subelement to an appropriate transport URL for receiving the receipt.

- Set the value of the <receiptRequiredBy> subelement to the required deadline for receiving the receipt.

The following description is a guideline for heuristic retry behavior that is likely to increase the probability of successful delivery in the presence of unreliable transports. The only required behavior in the context of retries is that the content of the BizTalk Document including header entries must not be altered in any way for a retry. In particular, the content of the <sentAt> property must remain the same, that is, what it was set to for the first transmission attempt.

The retry behavior of the source business entity is typically based on a parameter: the retry interval. This parameter may be fixed or may be configurable for each business relationship or even each transport used in the context of a given relationship. There is typically also a maximum retry count. The basic behavior pattern is very simple. Keep transmitting the document to the destination business entity at a frequency determined by the retry interval until one of the following occurs:

■   A receipt is received.

■   The receiptRequiredBy deadline expires.

■   The maximum retry count is exceeded.

At the end of this process, if a receipt has not been received, and the receipt-RequiredBy deadline expires, the delivery of the BizTalk Document is said to have failed. Normal operating procedure if this occurs is to notify the source application in an appropriate way, for instance by placing a copy of the Document in a dead-letter queue, but this is clearly implementation dependent.

It is worth noting that retries need not occur over the same transport that was used for the first transmission attempt. If multiple transport endpoints are available for transmission to the destination business entity as specified in the <to> address in the <delivery> header entry, new transport endpoints may be tried during retry attempts.

Actual implementations may use more elaborate algorithms for scalability and efficiency of resource use, as well as to account for peculiarities of the implementation context, such as intermittent connectivity.

8.1.2   Behavior of the Destination Business Entity

In accordance with common practice, it is assumed that, upon being accepted, each BizTalk Document will be persisted in durable storage at the destination business entity. It is strongly recommended that persistence in durable storage occur before a receipt is sent in the case of reliable delivery. In addition, idempotent delivery requires a minimum duration of archival for some information as noted below. However, this specification definitively specifies only wire-level behavior. Actual behavior at a business entity regarding storage and archival of business documents or the management of durable storage resources is implementation dependent and does not affect compliance with this specification.

The only special behavior required from a destination business entity for reliable delivery of BizTalk Documents is to transmit a receipt for each accepted Document in which the <reliability> element of the <delivery> header entry is present. The receipt must be sent to the transport address specified in the <sendReceiptTo> element. The term "accepted Document" in this case means the Document is recognized as being intended for the destination entity, including Documents that are copies or duplicates of previously received Documents (based on the identity). Documents that are received after the time instant specified in <expiresAt> is past are not accepted and must not be acknowledged with a receipt. Documents that are received after the time instant specified in <receiptRequiredBy> is past but before the time instant specified in <expiresAt> is past *are* accepted and *must* be acknowledged with a receipt. The structure of receipts and the required correlation between a Document and its receipt has been described above.

A destination business entity may in addition perform idempotent delivery of BizTalk Documents to the target applications at its own end. This may be a part of the business process agreed upon between the parties involved, or an independent configuration parameter at the destination that is either constant or configurable for each business or service relationship. Idempotent delivery implies that a BizTalk Document received at a destination business entity is delivered exactly once to its intended recipient application, even when it is received multiple times due to transport behavior or transmission retries at the source.

The guideline for duplicate removal to achieve idempotent delivery, when required, is to archive in durable store all BizTalk Documents accepted, at least until they expire (that is until the time instant specified in <expiresAt> is past). It is actually sufficient to archive only the identity of the BizTalk Document, given the requirement that the identity must be universally unique. Note that the duplicate removal process needs to be applied only after a Document is accepted.

8.2 Delivery and Processing Deadlines

It is important to understand the distinction between the two deadlines represented by the receiptRequiredBy and expiresAt elements. The content of receiptRequiredBy is the *delivery deadline* and the content of expiresAt is the *processing deadline*. The reason for making this distinction is that business actions often require a nontrivial amount of time for processing. If the action associated with a BizTalk Document is expected to take at most 4 hours to carry out, and must be completed within 12 hours of transmission of the Document, then the delivery deadline for this Document must be 8 hours rather than 12 hours. This flexibility is required in designing realistic business processes. The semantics of the two deadlines can be stated as follows:

- The delivery deadline concerns *acceptance* of the BizTalk Document by the destination business entity. The acceptance of a Document is defined in section 8.1.2. Acknowledgement of acceptance must be received by the source business entity by the delivery deadline.

- The processing deadline is the point in time beyond which the BizTalk Document, if unprocessed, is null and void. The Document must not be delivered to an application for normal processing or acknowledged in any way by the destination business entity after this point in time.

The following points clarify what happens as each deadline expires:

- When the delivery deadline expires:

- The sending BFC server should notify the sending application if a delivery receipt has not been received. This alerts the sending application to the possibility that the receiving application may not have received the Document, or if it did, may not have enough time to process it.

■ There is no essential significance for the receiving BFC server. The receiving server continues to accept and acknowledge Documents past this deadline. This means that receipts may be generated and received past this deadline. In fact, the receiver has no absolute need to know the delivery deadline. However, if the receiving server does not know when the delivery receipt is expected, it may choose to delay sending the receipt for internal optimization reasons, causing unnecessary complications at the sender; or, being aware of these consequences, it may give the receipt transmission the highest possible priority reducing its possibilities for internal optimization. The delivery deadline serves as a useful priority hint to the receiver for sending the delivery receipt, which is especially useful in intermittent connection scenarios.

■ When the processing deadline expires:

■ There is currently no special behavior recommended for the sending BFC server. In a future version of the BizTalk Framework, the notion of a processing acknowledgement may be added. If this concept were added, the sending BFC server should notify the sending application if a processing acknowledgement is not received before the processing deadline expires. This would alert the sending application to the likelihood that the receiving application has not processed the Document (even if a delivery receipt was received).

■ The receiving BFC server will reject all Documents that arrive past the processing deadline. They will not be acknowledged with any kind of receipt and will not be delivered to any application for normal processing.

9. BizTalk Documents with Attachments

Business processes often require Business Documents to be transmitted together with attachments of various sorts, ranging from facsimile images of legal documents to engineering drawings. The attachments are often in some binary format. This section specifies the following:

■ A standard way to associate a primary BizTalk Document with one or more attachments in a multipart MIME structure for transport.

■ The relationship between the MIME structure for attachments and the <manifest> header entry in the primary BizTalk Document.

Most Internet transports are capable of transporting MIME encoded content, although some special considerations are required for HTTP as described in the HTTP binding section.

9.1   Multipart MIME Structure

The compound content of a BizTalk Message, consisting of a primary BizTalk Document and one or more attachments, must be carried in a MIME structure that follows the rules for the multipart/related MIME media type as described in RFC 2387.

The following example shows a BizTalk Document with two attachments that constitutes an automobile insurance claim. The primary BizTalk Document contains the claim data, and is transmitted along with a facsimile image of the signed claim form (Claim.tiff) and a digital photo of the damaged car (Car.jpeg).

```
MIME-Version: 1.0
Content-Type: Multipart/Related;
        boundary=biztalk_2_0_related_boundary_example;
        type=text/xml;
        start="<claim.xml@claiming-it.com>"
Content-Description: This is the optional message description.

--biztalk_2_0_related_boundary_example
Content-Type: text/xml; charset=UTF-8
Content-Transfer-Encoding: 8bit
Content-ID: <claim.xml@claiming-it.com>

<?xml version='1.0' ?>
<SOAP-ENV:Envelope
                xmlns:SOAP-ENV="http://schemas.xmlsoap.org/soap/envelope/">
    <SOAP-ENV:Header>
        <!-- delivery and properties header entries omitted for brevity -->
        <manifest xmlns="http://schemas.biztalk.org/btf-2-0/manifest">
            <reference uri="#insurance_claim_document_id">
                <description>Insurance Claim</description>
            </reference>
            <reference uri="CID:claim.tiff@claiming-it.com">
                <description>Facsimile of Signed Claim Document
                </description>
            </reference>
            <reference uri="CID:car.jpeg@claiming-it.com">
                <description>Photo of Damaged Car</description>
            </reference>
        </manifest>
    </SOAP-ENV:Header>
    <SOAP-ENV:Body>
        <claim:Insurance_Claim_Auto id="insurance_claim_document_id"
                            xmlns:claim="http://schemas.risky-stuff.com/
Auto-Claim">
            <!-- ...claim details... -->
```

(continued)

```
        </claim:Insurance_Claim_Auto>
    </SOAP-ENV:Body>
</SOAP-ENV:Envelope>

--biztalk_2_0_related_boundary_example
Content-Type: image/tiff
Content-Transfer-Encoding: base64
Content-ID: <claim.tiff@claiming-it.com>

   ...Base64 encoded TIFF image...

--biztalk_2_0_related_boundary_example
Content-Type: image/jpeg
Content-Transfer-Encoding: binary
Content-ID: <car.jpeg@claiming-it.com>

   ...Raw JPEG image...

--biztalk_2_0_related_boundary_example--
```

The rules for the structure of the <attachment> elements describing the attachments in the <manifest> header entry of the primary BizTalk Document are explained in the next section. The rules for the use of the multipart/related media type are given in RFC 2387. The additional rules for the usage of the multipart/related media type in a BizTalk Message with attachments are as follows:

- The primary BizTalk Document is carried in the root part of the multipart/related structure.

- The media type for all BizTalk Documents is text/xml as described in RFC 2376.

- Every part, including the root part, must contain a Content-ID MIME header structured in accordance with RFC 2045.

- In addition to the required parameters for the multipart/related media type, the start parameter (optional in RFC 2387) must always be present.

9.2   Manifest Structure for Attachments

The relationship of the <reference> elements within the <manifest> header entry that denotes MIME part attachments is simple. The **uri** attribute of such <reference> element contains the location of the associated attachment in the form of the Content-ID URL based on the Content-ID of the MIME part that constitutes the attachment. The URL formed in accordance with RFC 2111 that defines Content-ID URLs.

10. TRANSPORT BINDING

10.1 HTTP Binding

This section describes the usage of the HTTP protocol for carrying BizTalk Documents, with or without attachments.

HTTP is a request/response protocol, whereas the BizTalk Framework architecture is based on asynchronous messaging. The HTTP resource being accessed as the target of a BizTalk Message is always assumed to be a message transfer agent, in the sense that the resource is not necessarily a SOAP processor as defined in the SOAP 1.1 specification, or a BFC Server as defined in this one. The meaning and contents of the HTTP response therefore only reflect the results of the attempted transfer of custody of the Message to the message transfer agent. Specifically, a successful response (2xx status code) does not necessarily imply the following:

■ The Message and its primary BizTalk Document have been accepted by the destination business entity in the sense of section 8.1.2.

   —or—

■ The integrity and namespace validity of the SOAP envelope have been verified.

This is because the message transfer agent is in general distinct from the destination business entity—for instance it may be an HTTP server forwarding messages to that entity through a message queuing arrangement.

The HTTP binding described here is a special case of the SOAP 1.1 HTTP binding and extends the latter in describing the use of the multipart/related MIME media type for carrying attachments with SOAP messages. All rules of the SOAP 1.1 HTTP binding apply to the simple case of plain BizTalk Documents (which are SOAP messages) being carried over HTTP. The rules for message structure differ from SOAP 1.1 for BizTalk Documents with attachments, as described below. Note that the HTTP binding described here does not use the SOAP remote procedure call (RPC) or synchronous request/response pattern. In particular, receipt messages generated as a part of the reliable delivery mechanism described in section 8 are always independent messages sent as HTTP requests. They are never delivered in the HTTP response corresponding to the HTTP request in which the BizTalk Document being acknowledged was carried.

The rules regarding HTTP status codes in the HTTP response apply regardless of the presence of attachments. Specifically, in the common asynchronous case where the HTTP (success) response is returned before the document has been processed, status code 202 accepted must be used. It is possible and permissible to delay the response until the document has been processed; in those cases, the HTTP response status code will provide more definitive information regarding the outcome, in accordance with SOAP 1.1 rules. Specifically, status code 200 may only be used after the receiver, or downstream processors to which processing may be delegated in full or in part, have fully examined the document, determined that all mandatory headers are in fact understood, and performed the actions indicated by the message contents.

10.1.1   Example of a Simple BizTalk Message

The following example shows the BizTalk Document from the initial example being carried as part of an HTTP message using the POST verb.

```
POST /bookPurchase HTTP/1.1
Host: www.we-have-books.com
Content-Type: text/xml; charset="utf-8"
Content-Length: nnnn
SOAPAction: http://electrocommerce.org/purchase_order/

<?xml version='1.0' ?>
<SOAP-ENV:Envelope
    xmlns:SOAP-ENV="http://schemas.xmlsoap.org/soap/envelope/"
    xmlns:xsi="http://www.w3.org/1999/XMLSchema-instance">
    <SOAP-ENV:Header>
        <dlv:delivery SOAP-ENV:mustUnderstand="1"
            xmlns:dlv="http://schemas.biztalk.org/btf-2-0/delivery"
            xmlns:agr="http://www.trading-agreements.org/types/">
            <dlv:to>
                <dlv:address xsi:type="agr:department">
                Book Order Department</dlv:address>
            </dlv:to>
            <dlv:from>
                <dlv:address xsi:type="agr:organization">
                Booklovers Anonymous</dlv:address>
            </dlv:from>
        </dlv:delivery>
        <prop:properties SOAP-ENV:mustUnderstand="1"
            xmlns:prop="http://schemas.biztalk.org/btf-2-0/properties">
            <prop:identity>uuid:74b9f5d0-33fb-4a81-b02b-5b760641c1d6
            </prop:identity>
            <prop:sentAt>2000-05-14T03:00:00+08:00</prop:sentAt>
            <prop:expiresAt>2000-05-15T04:00:00+08:00</prop:expiresAt>
            <prop:topic>http://electrocommerce.org/purchase_order/
            </prop:topic>
        </prop:properties>
    </SOAP-ENV:Header>
    <SOAP-ENV:Body>
```

```
        <po:PurchaseOrder xmlns:po="http://electrocommerce.org/
purchase_order/">
            <po:Title>Essential BizTalk</po:Title>
        </po:PurchaseOrder>
    </SOAP-ENV:Body>
</SOAP-ENV:Envelope>
```

This case falls squarely within the domain of the HTTP binding rules of SOAP 1.1 since the BizTalk Message payload consists of a single SOAP message.

The only rule in addition to SOAP 1.1 is the correlation for the SOAPAction HTTP header. The value of this header must be the URI reference contained in the mandatory <topic> element in the mandatory <properties> header entry.

10.1.2 Example of a BizTalk Message Including Attachments

```
POST /insuranceClaims HTTP/1.1
Host: www.risky-stuff.com
Content-Type: Multipart/Related;
        boundary=biztalk_2_0_related_boundary_example;
        type=text/xml;
        start="<claim.xml@claiming-it.com>"
Content-Length: nnnn
SOAPAction: http://schemas.risky-stuff.com/Auto-Claim
Content-Description: This is the optional message description.

--biztalk_2_0_related_boundary_example
Content-Type: text/xml; charset=UTF-8
Content-Transfer-Encoding: 8bit
Content-ID: <claim.xml@claiming-it.com>

<?xml version='1.0' ?>
<SOAP-ENV:Envelope
            xmlns:SOAP-ENV="http://schemas.xmlsoap.org/soap/envelope/"
            xmlns:xsi="http://www.w3.org/1999/XMLSchema-instance"
            xmlns:xsd="http://www.w3.org/1999/XMLSchema-datatypes">
    <SOAP-ENV:Header>
        <!-- manifest header entry omitted for brevity -->
        <delivery SOAP-ENV:mustUnderstand="1"
                xmlns="http://schemas.biztalk.org/btf-2-0/delivery">
          <to>
            <address xsi:type="xsd:uriReference">
             dept:insurance_claim_department</address>
          </to>
          <from>
            <address xsi:type="xsd:uriReference">
            agent:/WA/Issaquah#id=12345</address>
          </from>
        </delivery>
```

(continued)

```
            <prop:properties SOAP-ENV:mustUnderstand="1"
                xmlns:prop="http://schemas.biztalk.org/btf-2-0/properties">
                <!-- other elements omitted for brevity -->
                <topic>http://schemas.risky-stuff.com/Auto-Claim</topic>
            </prop:properties>
        </SOAP-ENV:Header>
        <SOAP-ENV:Body>
            <Insurance_Claim_Auto
                xmlns="http://schemas.risky-stuff.com/Auto-Claim"
                id="insurance_claim_document_id">
                <!-- ...claim details... -->
            </Insurance_Claim_Auto>
        </SOAP-ENV:Body>
</SOAP-ENV:Envelope>

--biztalk_2_0_related_boundary_example
Content-Type: image/tiff
Content-Transfer-Encoding: base64
Content-ID: <claim.tiff@claiming-it.com>

    ...Base 64 encoded TIFF image...

--biztalk_2_0_related_boundary_example
Content-Type: image/jpeg
Content-Transfer-Encoding: binary
Content-ID: <car.jpeg@claiming-it.com>

    ...Raw JPEG image...

--biztalk_2_0_related_boundary_example--
```

The basic approach to carrying multipart MIME structure in an HTTP message in this specification is to confine MIME-encoded content to the MIME parts, "lift" the multipart media type header to the HTTP level, and treat it as a native HTTP header. The rules for forming a BizTalk Message in the case of a BizTalk Document with attachments, encoded in a multipart/related MIME structure according to section 9.1, are as follows.

- The Content-Type: multipart/related MIME header must appear as an HTTP header. The rules for parameters of this header specified in section 9.1 apply here as well.

- No other headers with semantics defined by MIME specifications (such as Content-Transfer-Encoding) are permitted to appear as HTTP headers. Specifically, the MIME-Version: 1.0 header must not appear as an HTTP header. Note that HTTP itself uses many MIME-like headers with semantics defined by HTTP 1.1. These may, of course, appear freely.

■ The MIME parts containing the primary BizTalk Document and the attachments constitute the HTTP entity body and must appear exactly as described in section 9.1, including appropriate MIME headers.

11. BizTalk Document Schemas

11.1 XDR Schemas

11.1.1 Delivery header entry

```
<?xml version="1.0" ?>

<!--
    BizTalk Framework 2.0
    BizTalk Document Schema: delivery header entry
    Copyright 2000 Microsoft Corporation
-->

<Schema
    name="biztalk_2_0_delivery.xml"
    xmlns="urn:schemas-microsoft-com:xml-data"
    xmlns:dt="urn:schemas-microsoft-com:datatypes"
    xmlns:xsi="http://www.w3.org/1999/XMLSchema-instance">

    <!-- delivery header entry element -->
    <ElementType name="delivery" content="eltOnly">
        <element type="to" minOccurs="1" maxOccurs="1"/>
        <element type="from"  minOccurs="1" maxOccurs="1"/>
        <element type="reliability" minOccurs="0" maxOccurs="1"/>
    </ElementType>

    <ElementType name="to" content="eltOnly" >
        <element type="address" minOccurs="1" maxOccurs="1"/>
    </ElementType>

    <ElementType name="from" content="eltOnly">
        <element type="address" minOccurs="1" maxOccurs="1"/>
    </ElementType>

    <ElementType name="reliability" content="eltOnly">
        <element type="sendReceiptTo" minOccurs="1" maxOccurs="1"/>
        <element type="receiptRequiredBy" minOccurs="1" maxOccurs="1"/>
    </ElementType>

    <ElementType name="sendReceiptTo" content="textOnly" dt:type="uri"/>
    <ElementType name="receiptRequiredBy" content="textOnly" dt:type="dateTime.tz"/>
```

(continued)

```
<ElementType name="address" content="textOnly" dt:type="string">
    <attribute type="xsi:type" required="yes"/>
</ElementType>

</Schema>
```

11.1.2   Properties header entry

```
<?xml version="1.0" ?>

<!--
   BizTalk Framework 2.0
   BizTalk Document Schema: properties header entry
   Copyright 2000 Microsoft Corporation
-->

<Schema
   name="biztalk_2_0_properties.xml"
   xmlns="urn:schemas-microsoft-com:xml-data"
   xmlns:dt="urn:schemas-microsoft-com:datatypes"
   xmlns:xsi="http://www.w3.org/1999/XMLSchema-instance"
   xmlns:SOAP-ENV="http://schemas.xmlsoap.org/soap/envelope/">

   <ElementType name="properties" content="eltOnly">
       <attribute type ="SOAP-
ENV:mustUnderstand" default="1" required="yes"/>
       <element type="identity"    minOccurs="1" maxOccurs="1"/>
       <element type="sentAt"      minOccurs="1" maxOccurs="1"/>
       <element type="expiresAt"   minOccurs="1" maxOccurs="1"/>
       <element type="topic"       minOccurs="1" maxOccurs="1"/>
    </ElementType>

   <ElementType name="identity" content="textOnly" dt:type="uri"/>
   <ElementType name="sentAt" content="textOnly" dt:type="dateTime.tz"/>
   <ElementType name="expiresAt" content="textOnly" dt:type="dateTime.tz"/>
   <ElementType name="topic" content="textOnly" dt:type="uri"/>

</Schema>
```

11.1.3   Manifest header entry

```
<?xml version="1.0" ?>

<!--
   BizTalk Framework 2.0
   BizTalk Document Schema: manifest header entry
   Copyright 2000 Microsoft Corporation
-->
```

```
<Schema
    name="biztalk_2_0_manifest.xml"
    xmlns="urn:schemas-microsoft-com:xml-data"
    xmlns:dt="urn:schemas-microsoft-com:datatypes">

    <ElementType name="manifest" content="eltOnly">
        <element type="reference" minOccurs="1" maxOccurs="*"/>
    </ElementType>

    <ElementType name="reference" content="eltOnly">
        <attribute type="uri" required="yes"/>
        <element type="description" minOccurs="0" maxOccurs="1"/>
    </ElementType>

    <AttributeType name="uri" dt:type="uri"/>
    <ElementType name="description" content="mixed"/>

</Schema>
```

11.1.4   Process header entry

```
<?xml version="1.0" ?>

<!--
    BizTalk Framework 2.0
    BizTalk Document Schema: process header entry
    Copyright 2000 Microsoft Corporation
-->

<Schema
    name="biztalk_2_0_process.xml"
    xmlns="urn:schemas-microsoft-com:xml-data"
    xmlns:dt="urn:schemas-microsoft-com:datatypes"
    xmlns:SOAP-ENV="http://schemas.xmlsoap.org/soap/envelope/">

    <ElementType name="process" content="eltOnly">
        <attribute type="SOAP-ENV:mustUnderstand" default="1" required="yes"/
>
        <element type="type"           minOccurs="1" maxOccurs="1"/>
        <element type="instance"       minOccurs="1" maxOccurs="1"/>
        <element type="handle"         minOccurs="0" maxOccurs="1"/>
    </ElementType>

    <ElementType name="type" content="textOnly" dt:type="uri"/>
    <ElementType name="instance" content="textOnly" dt:type="uri"/>
    <ElementType name="handle" content="textOnly" dt:type="uri"/>

</Schema>
```

11.1.5   Receipt header entry

```
<?xml version="1.0" ?>

<!--
   BizTalk Framework 2.0
   BizTalk Document Schema: receipt header entry
   Copyright 2000 Microsoft Corporation
-->

<Schema
   name="biztalk_2_0_process_receipt_header.xml"
   xmlns="urn:schemas-microsoft-com:xml-data"
   xmlns:dt="urn:schemas-microsoft-com:datatypes"
   xmlns:SOAP-ENV="http://schemas.xmlsoap.org/soap/envelope/">

   <ElementType name="receipt" content="eltOnly">
      <attribute type="SOAP-ENV:mustUnderstand" default="1"
                 required="yes"/>
      <element type="receivedAt" minOccurs="1" maxOccurs="1"/>
   </ElementType>

   <ElementType name="receivedAt" content="textOnly"
                 dt:type="dateTime.tz"/>

</Schema>
```

11.1.6 SOAP 1.1 Envelope for BizTalk Document

```
<?xml version="1.0" ?>
<!--
   BizTalk Framework 2.0
   BizTalk Document Schema: envelope
   Copyright 2000 Microsoft Corporation

   This schema is based on the SOAP 1.1 schema
-->

<Schema
   name="biztalk_2_0_document_envelope.xml"
   xmlns="urn:schemas-microsoft-com:xml-data"
   xmlns:dt="urn:schemas-microsoft-com:datatypes">

  <!--
     SOAP envelope, header and body
  -->

  <ElementType name="Envelope" content="eltOnly">
     <element type="Header" minOccurs="1" maxOccurs="1"/>
     <element type="Body" minOccurs="1" maxOccurs="1"/>
  </ElementType>
```

```
<ElementType name="Header" content="eltOnly" model="open"
             xmlns:dlv="http://schemas.biztalk.org/btf-2-0/delivery"
             xmlns:prop="http://schemas.biztalk.org/btf-2-0/properties"
             xmlns:fst="http://schemas.biztalk.org/btf-2-0/manifest"
             xmlns:prc="http://schemas.biztalk.org/btf-2-0/process">
    <element type="dlv:delivery"        minOccurs="1" maxOccurs="1"/>
    <element type="prop:properties"     minOccurs="1" maxOccurs="1"/>
    <element type="fst:manifest"        minOccurs="0" maxOccurs="1"/>
    <element type="prc:process"         minOccurs="0" maxOccurs="1"/>
</ElementType>

<ElementType name="Body" content="eltOnly" model="open"/>

<!--
    Global Attributes.  The following attributes are intended
    to be usable via qualified attribute names on any Element type
    referencing them.
-->

<AttributeType name="mustUnderstand" default="0" dt:type="Boolean"/>
<AttributeType name="actor" dt:type="uri"/>

<!--
    'encodingStyle' indicates any canonicalization conventions followed
    in the contents of the containing element.  For example, the value
    'http://schemas.xmlsoap.org/soap/encoding/' indicates
    the pattern described in SOAP specification.
-->
<AttributeType name="encodingStyle" dt:type="string"/>

<!--
  SOAP fault reporting structure
-->

<ElementType name="Fault" content="eltOnly">
    <element type="faultcode" minOccurs="1" maxOccurs="1"/>
    <element type="faultstring" minOccurs="1" maxOccurs="1"/>
    <element type="faultactor" minOccurs="0" maxOccurs="1"/>
    <element type="detail" minOccurs="0" maxOccurs="1"/>
</ElementType>

<ElementType name="faultcode" content="textOnly" dt:type="string"/>
<ElementType name="faultstring" content="textOnly" dt:type="string"/>
<ElementType name="faultactor" content="textOnly" dt:type="uri"/>

<ElementType name="detail" content="eltOnly" model="open"/>

</Schema>
```

11.1.7 SOAP 1.1 Envelope for BizTalk Receipt

```
<?xml version="1.0" ?>
<!--
   BizTalk Framework 2.0
   BizTalk Document Schema: receipt
   Copyright 2000 Microsoft Corporation
-->

<Schema
   name="biztalk_2_0_receipt_envelope.xml"
   xmlns="urn:schemas-microsoft-com:xml-data"
   xmlns:dt="urn:schemas-microsoft-com:datatypes">

  <!--
     SOAP envelope, header and body
  -->

  <ElementType name="Envelope" content="eltOnly">
     <element type="Header" minOccurs="1" maxOccurs="1"/>
     <element type="Body" minOccurs="1" maxOccurs="1"/>
  </ElementType>

  <ElementType name="Header" content="eltOnly" model="open"
               xmlns:rct="http://schemas.biztalk.org/btf-2-0/receipt"
               xmlns:prop="http://schemas.biztalk.org/btf-2-0/properties"
               xmlns:fst="http://schemas.biztalk.org/btf-2-0/manifest"
               xmlns:prc="http://schemas.biztalk.org/btf-2-0/process">
     <element type="rct:receipt"      minOccurs="1" maxOccurs="1"/>
     <element type="prop:properties"  minOccurs="1" maxOccurs="1"/>
     <element type="fst:manifest"     minOccurs="0" maxOccurs="1"/>
     <element type="prc:process"      minOccurs="0" maxOccurs="1"/>
  </ElementType>

  <ElementType name="Body" content="empty" model="closed"/>

</Schema>
```

11.2 XSD Schemas

To be added

Microsoft hereby grants to all users of this BizTalk Framework specification, version 2.0 (the "Specification"), a perpetual, nonexclusive, royalty-free, worldwide right and license under any Microsoft copyrights in the Specification to copy, publish and distribute the Specification. Microsoft further agrees to grant to users a royalty-free license under applicable Microsoft intellectual property rights to implement and use the BizTalk Framework XML tags and schema guidelines included in the Specification for the purpose of creating computer programs that adhere to such guidelines—one condition of this license shall be the party's agreement not to assert patent rights against Microsoft and other companies for their implementation of the Specification. Microsoft expressly reserves all other rights it may have in the material and subject matter of this Specification. *Microsoft expressly disclaims any and all warranties regarding this Specification including any warranty that this Specification or implementations thereof does not violate the rights of others.*

Information in this document is subject to change without notice.

Appendix C

XML and BizTalk Web Sites

Many Web sites are devoted to the topics of XML, schemas, and BizTalk. Two sites dedicated to BizTalk are *http://biztalk.org*, which is maintained by the BizTalk steering committee, and the Microsoft BizTalk site, *http://www.microsoft.com/biztalk*. I am an admirer of—and frequent visitor to—these and several other sites that I'll describe in this chapter.

BizTalk.org

BizTalk.org is a place where you can find out about XML in general and BizTalk in particular. The site has several sections to help the new user learn about the technologies and best practices, communicate with other users who implement XML and BizTalk, and get hold of tools to help in his or her quest to create more sophisticated and efficient business-to-business (B2B) and business-to-consumer (B2C) applications.

If your boss comes to you tomorrow and says, "I want to be on line, I want to do B2B purchasing with such-and-such's system, and I want it tomorrow," BizTalk.org is the place to start. The site provides technical information to help you understand what schemas and applications a particular partner or industry group is using.

Peer-to-Peer Support

Many organizations involved in the standardization of business interchanges are more skilled in business-process modeling than in systems programming and XML. These groups can turn to the BizTalk.org Web site to discover the best practices for implementing their own schemas or to locate pre-existing XML schemas for use in their applications.

Probably the most important benefit of the BizTalk.org site is that it provides open access for anyone who wants to publish an XML schema or find published XML schemas. The mission of the site is to promote XML as a useful solution for businesses. To that end, BizTalk.org has two primary features. First there is the learning community, where people can find news and interact with their peers. This community takes the form of a set of open question-and-answer forums for issues related to schema development.

BizTalk.org's second major feature is a library of published schemas. These schemas are all prevalidated and stored within the library for anyone to access. A developer can be assured that the schemas found at BizTalk.org have been tested and are technically valid. Estimates indicate that up to 80 percent of the schemas available on the Web today have never been validated. Invalid schemas are worthless for validating XML documents—even documents created by the schema's publisher. Schemas submitted for publication on the BizTalk.org site go through a technical validation to ensure they do not contain errors. Samples provided with schemas are tested to ensure they are valid according to the schema they are matched up with.

The BizTalk.org schema hosting site provides around-the-clock access to schemas that have been published and authenticated. These schemas are available to anyone interested.

This schema-hosting site provides a neutral reference point and a resolvable URL for each published schema. Schemas hosted on BizTalk.org are version-controlled: once a schema is published, even the publisher cannot make changes to it. Version control is a critical service that any schema repository must be able to provide to be valuable. A business cannot rely on a repository that provides schemas that can change at any time.

MICROSOFT BIZTALK HOME PAGE

Microsoft's BizTalk site, *http://www.microsoft.com/biztalk*, is devoted to providing information about the BizTalk framework and Microsoft BizTalk Server 2000. During the development of BizTalk Server 2000, Microsoft's BizTalk site offered a preview version of the product so that people could get a feel for the product's features and usability. The site also offers successful case studies of XML in action by showing how companies use the BizTalk Framework to provide B2B transactions. Microsoft will use this site to introduce BizTalk Server 2000 and to provide support for it.

XML.COM

In 1998, Songline Studios, an affiliate of O'Reilly and Associates, joined Seybold Publications to create XML.com (*http://www.xml.com*), an advertisement-driven commercial site devoted to reporting on the state of the XML business. XML.com's editorial mission is to report fairly on events happening in XML, and they do an exceptional job in covering the state of standards developments and vendor implementations of XML.

XML.com is not simply a site that publishes technical information or press reports. Instead, the staff and contract writers contribute articles that cover conflicts in the industry or implementation-specific details where incompatibilities are likely to occur. For example, they reviewed how several popular parsers fared using the XML

Conformance Test Suite, a technical compatibility test designed by the Organization for the Advancement of Structured Information Systems (OASIS) and the U.S. National Institute of Standards and Technology (NIST). The test is designed to check a parser's adherence to the published W3C XML specification.

OASIS

OASIS is an XML industry group devoted to providing vendor-independent information about what is happening in the XML business. It is a consortium of companies interested in using XML to solve business problems. Most of these companies provide products that support XML to some extent or another, but OASIS also includes XML users.

The best resource on the OASIS site at *http://www.oasis-open.org*, is *The XML Cover Pages,* which (at the time of this book's publication) is maintained tirelessly by Robin Cover. Robin has reported on the SGML business for years, so was well positioned to cover the XML business since people first started talking about it.

The XML Cover Pages is updated daily—sometimes several times a day—and provides information not only on news releases from different companies, but also on much of the academic and standards work done around the XML standard.

XML.ORG

In May 1999, OASIS signed up eight companies that were building the XML market to sponsor a new site devoted to the XML industry: XML.ORG (*http://www.xml.org*). The site is designed to be an independent, reliable source of information for people whose information must be compatible between two vendors' systems.

The XML.ORG Steering Committee and the OASIS Board of Directors have been working on building a viable industry portal, complete with a place to register and store schemas. They are also dealing with some of the industry's most challenging issues, such as a comprehensive intellectual property (IP) policy.

No U.S. case law currently deals with the IP rights of schema owners. OASIS is being advised by the country's leading IP counsel and will likely develop the industry's best IP policy in this area. OASIS believes that having such policies in place before launching the registry and repository itself is critical.

OASIS formed the Registry and Repository Technical Committee, which has been working on standardizing a way to register schemas at any site and then store and access them easily. This is important work, because the XML industry needs reliable places to store schemas if namespaces are to succeed. Once the working group finishes the spec, it will build a reference application to demonstrate how the spec could work.

Because the OASIS process assimilates inputs from across an industry, the work tends to be more complex than it is with small, vendor-led groups. Although the industry standardization process can take longer, the results are more likely to be accepted by members than results offered by a single vendor that might have proprietary interests in mind.

<TAG> Newsletter

<TAG> Newsletter (http://tagnewsletter.com) has been published since 1987 as a technical newsletter for the information management business. I have been the editor of the newsletter since 1991. In 1992, *<TAG> Newsletter* became a monthly newsletter, and in 1999, we made it available online as a database-driven, interactive site that uses XML and XSL to create personalized information for our subscribers.

The mission of *<TAG>* is to provide XML implementers with the tools and information they need. *<TAG>* is mostly technical in nature, providing tutorials with code samples and technical tips. We also try to publish as many case studies and book reviews as possible to keep the publication well rounded.

In 1999, we re-engineered the site to provide our readers with a personalized view of the publication. We converted more than 1000 articles to XML and stored them in a database. Using the database, we are able to provide many different views of each article based on the profiles of each user. For example, a user visiting the site by using Netscape Navigator will get a page that has a different structure than a user accessing the site by using Microsoft Internet Explorer. The site does this by recognizing the difference between Web browsers and other access methods (offline subscriptions and cell phones, for example) and creates information responses tailored to those technologies.

One of the benefits of this personalized system is that it gives paid subscribers instant access to all articles on the site, up to and including the current edition. Nonsubscribers have access to everything on the site, but they only get the title, author, and abstract of articles that are less than a year old.

We perform personalization and browser-specific rendering using XML, XSLT, and middle-tier scripting in a holistic way. As we developed the site, we discovered some great ways to present our information assets. For example, when an article mentions an acronym, we tag it as such. This gives us the ability to render the acronym for the print publication as smaller capitals, but also allows us to "hide" the definition as a pop-up when we render for electronic delivery. In other places as well, we found information that could be rendered many ways for different outputs and readers. We wanted to share this information with our users, so we made a multipart case study/tutorial on the topic, starting in June 1999. Our goals were to create an intelligent content management and delivery environment and to spend as little money as possible on it. We achieved both. Our only expense was our time.

*XML*SOFTWARE

If you need to know what XML tools are available, you couldn't ask for a better site than *XML*SOFTWARE (*http://www.xmlsoftware.com*). This site, currently maintained by James Tauber and Linda van den Brink, is updated on a regular basis.

*XML*Software also offers e-mail notification when new items are added. The authors maintain other sites devoted to XML implementation and tools, including a schema repository. These other sites include *XML*INFO (*http://www.xmlinfo.com*) and SCHEMA.NET (*http://www.schema.net*). The*XML*Software site contains links to these sites.

Appendix D

Simple Object Access Protocol (SOAP) 1.1

W3C Note 08 May 2000

This version:
http://www.w3.org/TR/2000/NOTE-SOAP-20000508

Latest version:
http://www.w3.org/TR/SOAP

Authors (alphabetically):
Don Box, DevelopMentor
David Ehnebuske, IBM
Gopal Kakivaya, Microsoft
Andrew Layman, Microsoft
Noah Mendelsohn, Lotus Development Corp.
Henrik Frystyk Nielsen, Microsoft
Satish Thatte, Microsoft
Dave Winer, UserLand Software, Inc.

ABSTRACT

SOAP is a lightweight protocol for exchange of information in a decentralized, distributed environment. It is an XML based protocol that consists of three parts: an envelope that defines a framework for describing what is in a message and how to process it, a set of encoding rules for expressing instances of application-defined datatypes, and a convention for representing remote procedure calls and responses. SOAP can potentially be used in combination with a variety of other protocols; however, the only bindings defined in this document describe how to use SOAP in combination with HTTP and HTTP Extension Framework.

STATUS

This document is a submission to the World Wide Web Consortium (see Submission Request, W3C Staff Comment) to propose the formation of a working group in the area of XML-based protocols. Comments are welcome to the authors but you are encouraged to share your views on the W3C's public mailing list <xml-dist-app@w3.org> (see archives).

This document is a NOTE made available by the W3C for discussion only. Publication of this Note by W3C indicates no endorsement by W3C or the W3C Team, or any W3C Members. W3C has had no editorial control over the preparation of this Note. This document is a work in progress and may be updated, replaced, or rendered obsolete by other documents at any time.

A list of current W3C technical documents can be found at the Technical Reports page.

TABLE OF CONTENTS

1   INTRODUCTION

SOAP provides a simple and lightweight mechanism for exchanging structured and typed information between peers in a decentralized, distributed environment using XML. SOAP does not itself define any application semantics such as a programming model or implementation specific semantics; rather it defines a simple mechanism for expressing application semantics by providing a modular packaging model and encoding mechanisms for encoding data within modules. This allows SOAP to be used in a large variety of systems ranging from messaging systems to RPC.

SOAP consists of three parts:

- The SOAP envelope (see section 4) construct defines an overall frame-work for expressing **what** is in a message; **who** should deal with it, and **whether** it is optional or mandatory.

- The SOAP encoding rules (see section 5) defines a serialization mechanism that can be used to exchange instances of application-defined datatypes.

- The SOAP RPC representation (see section 7) defines a convention that can be used to represent remote procedure calls and responses.

Although these parts are described together as part of SOAP, they are functionally orthogonal. In particular, the envelope and the encoding rules are defined in different namespaces in order to promote simplicity through modularity.

In addition to the SOAP envelope, the SOAP encoding rules and the SOAP RPC conventions, this specification defines two protocol bindings that describe how a SOAP message can be carried in HTTP [5] messages either with or without the HTTP Extension Framework [6].

1.1   Design Goals

A major design goal for SOAP is simplicity and extensibility. This means that there are several features from traditional messaging systems and distributed object systems that are not part of the core SOAP specification. Such features include

- ■   Distributed garbage collection

- ■   Boxcarring or batching of messages

- ■   Objects-by-reference (which requires distributed garbage collection)

- ■   Activation (which requires objects-by-reference)

1.2   Notational Conventions

The keywords "MUST", "MUST NOT", "REQUIRED", "SHALL", "SHALL NOT", "SHOULD", "SHOULD NOT", "RECOMMENDED", "MAY", and "OPTIONAL" in this document are to be interpreted as described in RFC-2119 [2].

The namespace prefixes "*SOAP-ENV*" and "*SOAP-ENC*" used in this document are associated with the SOAP namespaces "*http://schemas.xmlsoap.org/soap/envelope/*" and "*http://schemas.xmlsoap.org/soap/encoding/*" respectively.

Throughout this document, the namespace prefix "xsi" is assumed to be associated with the URI "*http://www.w3.org/1999/XMLSchema-instance*" which is defined in the XML Schemas specification [11]. Similarly, the namespace prefix "xsd" is assumed to be associated with the URI "*http://www.w3.org/1999/XMLSchema*" which is defined in [10]. The namespace prefix "tns" is used to indicate whatever is the target namespace of the current document. All other namespace prefixes are samples only.

Namespace URIs of the general form "some-URI" represent some application-dependent or context-dependent URI [4].

This specification uses the augmented Backus-Naur Form (BNF) as described in RFC-2616 [5] for certain constructs.

1.3   Examples of SOAP Messages

In this example, a GetLastTradePrice SOAP request is sent to a StockQuote service. The request takes a string parameter, ticker symbol, and returns a float in the SOAP response. The SOAP Envelope element is the top element of the XML document representing the SOAP message. XML namespaces are used to disambiguate SOAP identifiers from application specific identifiers. The example illustrates the HTTP bindings defined in section 6. It is worth noting that the rules governing XML payload format in SOAP are entirely independent of the fact that the payload is carried in HTTP.

More examples are available in Appendix A.

Example 1

SOAP Message Embedded in HTTP Request

```
POST /StockQuote HTTP/1.1
Host: www.stockquoteserver.com
Content-Type: text/xml; charset="utf-8"
Content-Length: nnnn
SOAPAction: "Some-URI"

<SOAP-ENV:Envelope
  xmlns:SOAP-ENV="http://schemas.xmlsoap.org/soap/envelope/"
  SOAP-ENV:encodingStyle="http://schemas.xmlsoap.org/soap/encoding/">
  <SOAP-ENV:Body>
      <m:GetLastTradePrice xmlns:m="Some-URI">
          <symbol>DIS</symbol>
      </m:GetLastTradePrice>
  </SOAP-ENV:Body>
</SOAP-ENV:Envelope>
```

Following is the response message containing the HTTP message with the SOAP message as the payload:

Example 2

SOAP Message Embedded in HTTP Response

```
HTTP/1.1 200 OK
Content-Type: text/xml; charset="utf-8"
Content-Length: nnnn

<SOAP-ENV:Envelope
  xmlns:SOAP-ENV="http://schemas.xmlsoap.org/soap/envelope/"
  SOAP-ENV:encodingStyle="http://schemas.xmlsoap.org/soap/encoding/"/>
  <SOAP-ENV:Body>
      <m:GetLastTradePriceResponse xmlns:m="Some-URI">
          <Price>34.5</Price>
      </m:GetLastTradePriceResponse>
  </SOAP-ENV:Body>
</SOAP-ENV:Envelope>
```

2   THE SOAP MESSAGE EXCHANGE MODEL

SOAP messages are fundamentally one-way transmissions from a sender to a receiver, but as illustrated above, SOAP messages are often combined to implement patterns such as request/response.

SOAP implementations can be optimized to exploit the unique characteristics of particular network systems. For example, the HTTP binding described in section

6 provides for SOAP response messages to be delivered as HTTP responses, using the same connection as the inbound request.

Regardless of the protocol to which SOAP is bound, messages are routed along a so-called "message path", which allows for processing at one or more intermediate nodes in addition to the ultimate destination.

A SOAP application receiving a SOAP message MUST process that message by performing the following actions in the order listed below:

1. Identify all parts of the SOAP message intended for that application (see section 4.2.2)

2. Verify that all mandatory parts identified in step 1 are supported by the application for this message (see section 4.2.3) and process them accordingly. If this is not the case then discard the message (see section 4.4). The processor MAY ignore optional parts identified in step 1 without affecting the outcome of the processing.

3. If the SOAP application is not the ultimate destination of the message then remove all parts identified in step 1 before forwarding the message.

Processing a message or a part of a message requires that the SOAP processor understands, among other things, the exchange pattern being used (one way, request/response, multicast, etc.), the role of the recipient in that pattern, the employment (if any) of RPC mechanisms such as the one documented in section 7, the representation or encoding of data, as well as other semantics necessary for correct processing.

While attributes such as the SOAP encodingStyle attribute (see section 4.1.1) can be used to describe certain aspects of a message, this specification does not mandate a particular means by which the recipient makes such determinations in general. For example, certain applications will understand that a particular <getStockPrice> element signals an RPC request using the conventions of section 7, while another application may infer that all traffic directed to it is encoded as one way messages.

3 RELATION TO XML

All SOAP messages are encoded using XML (see [7] for more information on XML).

A SOAP application SHOULD include the proper SOAP namespace on all elements and attributes defined by SOAP in messages that it generates. A SOAP application MUST be able to process SOAP namespaces in messages that it receives. It MUST discard messages that have incorrect namespaces (see section 4.4) and it MAY process SOAP messages without SOAP namespaces as though they had the correct SOAP namespaces.

SOAP defines two namespaces (see [8] for more information on XML namespaces):

- The SOAP envelope has the namespace identifier "*http://schemas.xmlsoap.org/soap/envelope/*"

- The SOAP serialization has the namespace identifier "*http://schemas.xmlsoap.org/soap/encoding/*"

A SOAP message MUST NOT contain a Document Type Declaration. A SOAP message MUST NOT contain Processing Instructions. [7]

SOAP uses the local, unqualified "id" attribute of type "ID" to specify the unique identifier of an encoded element. SOAP uses the local, unqualified attribute "href" of type "uri-reference" to specify a reference to that value, in a manner conforming to the XML Specification [7], XML Schema Specification [11], and XML Linking Language Specification [9].

With the exception of the SOAP mustUnderstand attribute (see section 4.2.3) and the SOAP actor attribute (see section 4.2.2), it is generally permissible to have attributes and their values appear in XML instances or alternatively in schemas, with equal effect. That is, declaration in a DTD or schema with a default or fixed value is semantically equivalent to appearance in an instance.

4   SOAP ENVELOPE

A SOAP message is an XML document that consists of a mandatory SOAP envelope, an optional SOAP header, and a mandatory SOAP body. This XML document is referred to as a SOAP message for the rest of this specification. The namespace identifier for the elements and attributes defined in this section is "*http://schemas.xmlsoap.org/soap/envelope/*". A SOAP message contains the following:

1. The Envelope is the top element of the XML document representing the message.

2. The Header is a generic mechanism for adding features to a SOAP message in a decentralized manner without prior agreement between the communicating parties. SOAP defines a few attributes that can be used to indicate who should deal with a feature and whether it is optional or mandatory (see section 4.2).

3. The Body is a container for mandatory information intended for the ultimate recipient of the message (see section 4.3). SOAP defines one element for the body, which is the Fault element used for reporting errors.

The grammar rules are as follows:

1. **Envelope**

   ❑   The element name is "Envelope".

   ❑   The element MUST be present in a SOAP message.

   ❑   The element MAY contain namespace declarations as well as additional attributes. If present, such additional attributes MUST be namespace-qualified. Similarly, the element MAY contain additional sub elements. If present these elements MUST be namespace-qualified and MUST follow the SOAP Body element.

2. **Header** (see section 4.2)

   ❑   The element name is "Header".

   ❑   The element MAY be present in a SOAP message. If present, the element MUST be the first immediate child element of a SOAP Envelope element.

   ❑   The element MAY contain a set of header entries each being an immediate child element of the SOAP Header element. All immediate child elements of the SOAP Header element MUST be namespace-qualified.

3. **Body** (see section 4.3)

   ❑   The element name is "Body".

   ❑   The element MUST be present in a SOAP message and MUST be an immediate child element of a SOAP Envelope element. It MUST directly follow the SOAP Header element if present. Otherwise it MUST be the first immediate child element of the SOAP Envelope element.

   ❑   The element MAY contain a set of body entries each being an immediate child element of the SOAP Body element. Immediate child elements of the SOAP Body element MAY be namespace-qualified. SOAP defines the SOAP Fault element, which is used to indicate error messages (see section 4.4).

4.1.1   SOAP encodingStyle Attribute

The SOAP encodingStyle global attribute can be used to indicate the serialization rules used in a SOAP message. This attribute MAY appear on any element, and is scoped to that element's contents and all child elements not themselves containing such an attribute, much as an XML namespace declaration is scoped. There is no default encoding defined for a SOAP message.

The attribute value is an ordered list of one or more URIs identifying the serialization rule or rules that can be used to deserialize the SOAP message indicated in the order of most specific to least specific. Examples of values are

```
"http://schemas.xmlsoap.org/soap/encoding/"
"http://my.host/encoding/restricted http://my.host/encoding/"
""
```

The serialization rules defined by SOAP in section 5 are identified by the URI *"http://schemas.xmlsoap.org/soap/encoding/"*. Messages using this particular serialization SHOULD indicate this using the SOAP encodingStyle attribute. In addition, all URIs syntactically beginning with *"http://schemas.xmlsoap.org/soap/encoding/"* indicate conformance with the SOAP encoding rules defined in section 5 (though with potentially tighter rules added).

A value of the zero-length URI ("") explicitly indicates that no claims are made for the encoding style of contained elements. This can be used to turn off any claims from containing elements.

4.1.2 Envelope Versioning Model

SOAP does not define a traditional versioning model based on major and minor version numbers. A SOAP message MUST have an Envelope element associated with the *"http://schemas.xmlsoap.org/soap/envelope/"* namespace. If a message is received by a SOAP application in which the SOAP Envelope element is associated with a different namespace, the application MUST treat this as a version error and discard the message. If the message is received through a request/response protocol such as HTTP, the application MUST respond with a SOAP VersionMismatch faultcode message (see section 4.4) using the SOAP *"http://schemas.xmlsoap.org/soap/envelope/"* namespace.

4.2 SOAP Header

SOAP provides a flexible mechanism for extending a message in a decentralized and modular way without prior knowledge between the communicating parties. Typical examples of extensions that can be implemented as header entries are authentication, transaction management, payment etc.

The Header element is encoded as the first immediate child element of the SOAP Envelope XML element. All immediate child elements of the Header element are called header entries.

The encoding rules for header entries are as follows:

1. A header entry is identified by its fully qualified element name, which consists of the namespace URI and the local name. All immediate child elements of the SOAP Header element MUST be namespace-qualified.

2. The SOAP encodingStyle attribute MAY be used to indicate the encoding style used for the header entries (see section 4.1.1).

3. The SOAP mustUnderstand attribute (see section 4.2.3) and SOAP actor attribute (see section 4.2.2) MAY be used to indicate how to process the entry and by whom (see section 4.2.1).

4.2.1 Use of Header Attributes

The SOAP Header attributes defined in this section determine how a recipient of a SOAP message should process the message as described in section 2. A SOAP application generating a SOAP message SHOULD only use the SOAP Header attributes on immediate child elements of the SOAP Header element. The recipient of a SOAP message MUST ignore all SOAP Header attributes that are not applied to an immediate child element of the SOAP Header element.

An example is a header with an element identifier of "Transaction", a "mustUnderstand" value of "1", and a value of 5. This would be encoded as follows:

```
<SOAP-ENV:Header>
   <t:Transaction
      xmlns:t="some-URI" SOAP-ENV:mustUnderstand="1">
         5
   </t:Transaction>
</SOAP-ENV:Header>
```

4.2.2 SOAP actor Attribute

A SOAP message travels from the originator to the ultimate destination, potentially by passing through a set of SOAP intermediaries along the message path. A SOAP intermediary is an application that is capable of both receiving and forwarding SOAP messages. Both intermediaries as well as the ultimate destination are identified by a URI.

Not all parts of a SOAP message may be intended for the ultimate destination of the SOAP message but, instead, may be intended for one or more of the intermediaries on the message path. The role of a recipient of a header element is similar to that of accepting a contract in that it cannot be extended beyond the recipient. That is, a recipient receiving a header element MUST NOT forward that header element to the next application in the SOAP message path. The recipient MAY insert a similar header element but in that case, the contract is between that application and the recipient of that header element.

The SOAP actor global attribute can be used to indicate the recipient of a header element. The value of the SOAP actor attribute is a URI. The special URI "*http://schemas.xmlsoap.org/soap/actor/next*" indicates that the header element is intended for the very first SOAP application that processes the message. This is similar to the hop-by-hop scope model represented by the Connection header field in HTTP.

Omitting the SOAP actor attribute indicates that the recipient is the ultimate destination of the SOAP message.

This attribute MUST appear in the SOAP message instance in order to be effective (see section 3 and 4.2.1).

4.2.3   SOAP mustUnderstand Attribute

The SOAP mustUnderstand global attribute can be used to indicate whether a header entry is mandatory or optional for the recipient to process. The recipient of a header entry is defined by the SOAP actor attribute (see section 4.2.2). The value of the mustUnderstand attribute is either "1" or "0". The absence of the SOAP mustUnderstand attribute is semantically equivalent to its presence with the value "0".

If a header element is tagged with a SOAP mustUnderstand attribute with a value of "1", the recipient of that header entry either MUST obey the semantics (as conveyed by the fully qualified name of the element) and process correctly to those semantics, or MUST fail processing the message (see section 4.4).

The SOAP mustUnderstand attribute allows for robust evolution. Elements tagged with the SOAP mustUnderstand attribute with a value of "1" MUST be presumed to somehow modify the semantics of their parent or peer elements. Tagging elements in this manner assures that this change in semantics will not be silently (and, presumably, erroneously) ignored by those who may not fully understand it.

This attribute MUST appear in the instance in order to be effective (see section 3 and 4.2.1).

4.3   SOAP Body

The SOAP Body element provides a simple mechanism for exchanging mandatory information intended for the ultimate recipient of the message. Typical uses of the Body element include marshalling RPC calls and error reporting.

The Body element is encoded as an immediate child element of the SOAP Envelope XML element. If a Header element is present then the Body element MUST immediately follow the Header element, otherwise it MUST be the first immediate child element of the Envelope element.

All immediate child elements of the Body element are called body entries and each body entry is encoded as an independent element within the SOAP Body element.

The encoding rules for body entries are as follows:

1. A body entry is identified by its fully qualified element name, which consists of the namespace URI and the local name. Immediate child elements of the SOAP Body element MAY be namespace-qualified.

2. The SOAP encodingStyle attribute MAY be used to indicate the encoding style used for the body entries (see section 4.1.1).

SOAP defines one body entry, which is the Fault entry used for reporting errors (see section 4.4).

4.3.1 Relationship between SOAP Header and Body

While the Header and Body are defined as independent elements, they are in fact related. The relationship between a body entry and a header entry is as follows: A body entry is semantically equivalent to a header entry intended for the default actor and with a SOAP mustUnderstand attribute with a value of "1". The default actor is indicated by not using the actor attribute (see section 4.2.2).

4.4 SOAP Fault

The SOAP Fault element is used to carry error and/or status information within a SOAP message. If present, the SOAP Fault element MUST appear as a body entry and MUST NOT appear more than once within a Body element.

The SOAP Fault element defines the following four subelements:

- **faultcode**   The faultcode element is intended for use by software to provide an algorithmic mechanism for identifying the fault. The faultcode MUST be present in a SOAP Fault element and the faultcode value MUST be a qualified name as defined in [8], section 3. SOAP defines a small set of SOAP fault codes covering basic SOAP faults (see section 4.4.1)

- **faultstring**   The faultstring element is intended to provide a human readable explanation of the fault and is not intended for algorithmic processing. The faultstring element is similar to the 'Reason-Phrase' defined by HTTP (see [5], section 6.1). It MUST be present in a SOAP Fault element and SHOULD provide at least some information explaining the nature of the fault.

- **faultactor**   The faultactor element is intended to provide information about who caused the fault to happen within the message path (see section 2). It is similar to the SOAP actor attribute (see section 4.2.2) but instead of indicating the destination of the header entry, it indicates the source of the fault. The value of the faultactor attribute is a URI identifying the source. Applications that do not act as the ultimate destination of the SOAP message MUST include the faultactor element in a SOAP Fault element. The ultimate destination of a message MAY use the faultactor element to indicate explicitly that it generated the fault (see also the detail element below).

- **detail**   The detail element is intended for carrying application specific error information related to the Body element. It MUST be present if the contents of the Body element could not be successfully processed. It MUST NOT be used to carry information about error information belonging to header entries. Detailed error information belonging to header entries MUST be carried within header entries.

  The absence of the detail element in the Fault element indicates that the fault is not related to processing of the Body element. This can be used to distinguish whether the Body element was processed or not in case of a fault situation.

  All immediate child elements of the detail element are called detail entries and each detail entry is encoded as an independent element within the detail element.

  The encoding rules for detail entries are as follows (see also example 10):

  1. A detail entry is identified by its fully qualified element name, which consists of the namespace URI and the local name. Immediate child elements of the detail element MAY be namespace-qualified.

  2. The SOAP encodingStyle attribute MAY be used to indicate the encoding style used for the detail entries (see section 4.1.1).

  Other Fault subelements MAY be present, provided they are namespace-qualified.

4.4.1 SOAP Fault Codes

The faultcode values defined in this section MUST be used in the faultcode element when describing faults defined by this specification. The namespace identifier for these faultcode values is *"http://schemas.xmlsoap.org/soap/envelope/"*. Use of this space is recommended (but not required) in the specification of methods defined outside of the present specification.

The default SOAP faultcode values are defined in an extensible manner that allows for new SOAP faultcode values to be defined while maintaining backwards compatibility with existing faultcode values. The mechanism used is very similar to the 1xx, 2xx, 3xx etc basic status classes classes defined in HTTP (see [5] section 10). However, instead of integers, they are defined as XML qualified names (see [8] section 3). The character "." (dot) is used as a separator of faultcode values indicating that what is to the left of the dot is a more generic fault code value than the value to the right. Example

Client.Authentication

The set of faultcode values defined in this document is:

Name	*Meaning*
VersionMismatch	The processing party found an invalid namespace for the SOAP Envelope element (see section 4.1.2)
MustUnderstand	An immediate child element of the SOAP Header element that was either not understood or not obeyed by the processing party contained a SOAP mustUnderstand attribute with a value of "1" (see section 4.2.3)
Client	The Client class of errors indicate that the message was incorrectly formed or did not contain the appropriate information in order to succeed. For example, the message could lack the proper authentication or payment information. It is generally an indication that the message should not be resent without change. See also section 4.4 for a description of the SOAP Fault detail sub-element.
Server	The Server class of errors indicate that the message could not be processed for reasons not directly attributable to the contents of the message itself but rather to the processing of the message. For example, processing could include communicating with an upstream processor, which didn't respond. The message may succeed at a later point in time. See also section 4.4 for a description of the SOAP Fault detail sub-element.

5 SOAP ENCODING

The SOAP encoding style is based on a simple type system that is a generalization of the common features found in type systems in programming languages, databases and semi-structured data. A type either is a simple (scalar) type or is a compound type constructed as a composite of several parts, each with a type. This is described in more detail below. This section defines rules for serialization of a graph of typed objects. It operates on two levels. First, given a schema in any notation consistent with the type system described, a schema for an XML grammar may be constructed. Second, given a type-system schema and a particular graph of values conforming to that schema, an XML instance may be constructed. In reverse, given an XML instance produced in accordance with these rules, and given also the original schema, a copy of the original value graph may be constructed.

The namespace identifier for the elements and attributes defined in this section is "*http://schemas.xmlsoap.org/soap/encoding/*". The encoding samples shown assume all namespace declarations are at a higher element level.

Use of the data model and encoding style described in this section is encouraged but not required; other data models and encodings can be used in conjunction with SOAP (see section 4.1.1).

5.1 Rules for Encoding Types in XML

XML allows very flexible encoding of data. SOAP defines a narrower set of rules for encoding. This section defines the encoding rules at a high level, and the next section describes the encoding rules for specific types when they require more detail. The encodings described in this section can be used in conjunction with the mapping of RPC calls and responses specified in Section 7.

To describe encoding, the following terminology is used:

1. A "value" is a string, the name of a measurement (number, date, enumeration, etc.) or a composite of several such primitive values. All values are of specific types.

2. A "simple value" is one without named parts. Examples of simple values are particular strings, integers, enumerated values etc.

3. A "compound value" is an aggregate of relations to other values. Examples of Compound Values are particular purchase orders, stock reports, street addresses, etc.

4. Within a compound value, each related value is potentially distinguished by a role name, ordinal or both. This is called its "accessor." Examples of compound values include particular Purchase Orders, Stock Reports etc. Arrays are also compound values. It is possible to have compound values with several accessors each named the same, as for example, RDF does.

5. An "array" is a compound value in which ordinal position serves as the only distinction among member values.

6. A "struct" is a compound value in which accessor name is the only distinction among member values, and no accessor has the same name as any other.

7. A "simple type" is a class of simple values. Examples of simple types are the classes called "string," "integer," enumeration classes, etc.

8. A "compound type" is a class of compound values. An example of a compound type is the class of purchase order values sharing the same accessors (shipTo, totalCost, etc.) though with potentially different values (and perhaps further constrained by limits on certain values).

9. Within a compound type, if an accessor has a name that is distinct within that type but is not distinct with respect to other types, that is, the name plus the type together are needed to make a unique identification, the name is called "locally scoped." If however the name is based in part on a Uniform Resource Identifier, directly or indirectly, such that the name alone is sufficient to uniquely identify the accessor irrespective of the type within which it appears, the name is called "universally scoped."

10. Given the information in the schema relative to which a graph of values is serialized, it is possible to determine that some values can only be related by a single instance of an accessor. For others, it is not possible to make this determination. If only one accessor can reference it, a value is considered "single-reference". If referenced by more than one, actually or potentially, it is "multi-reference." Note that it is possible for a certain value to be considered "single-reference" relative to one schema and "multi-reference" relative to another.

11. Syntactically, an element may be "independent" or "embedded." An independent element is any element appearing at the top level of a serialization. All others are embedded elements.

Although it is possible to use the xsi:type attribute such that a graph of values is self-describing both in its structure and the types of its values, the serialization rules permit that the types of values MAY be determinate only by reference to a schema. Such schemas MAY be in the notation described by "XML Schema Part 1: Structures" [10] and "XML Schema Part 2: Datatypes" [11] or MAY be in any other notation. Note also that, while the serialization rules apply to compound types other than arrays and structs, many schemas will contain only struct and array types.

The rules for serialization are as follows:

1. All values are represented as element content. A multi-reference value MUST be represented as the content of an independent element. A single-reference value SHOULD not be (but MAY be).

2. For each element containing a value, the type of the value MUST be represented by at least one of the following conditions: (a) the containing element instance contains an xsi:type attribute, (b) the containing element instance is itself contained within an element containing a (possibly defaulted) SOAP-ENC:arrayType attribute or (c) or the name of the element bears a definite relation to the type, that type then determinable from a schema.

3. A simple value is represented as character data, that is, without any sub-elements. Every simple value must have a type that is either listed in the XML Schemas Specification, part 2 [11] or whose source type is listed therein (see also section 5.2).

4. A Compound Value is encoded as a sequence of elements, each accessor represented by an embedded element whose name corresponds to the name of the accessor. Accessors whose names are local to their containing types have unqualified element names; all others have qualified names (see also section 5.4).

5. A multi-reference simple or compound value is encoded as an independent element containing a local, unqualified attribute named "id" and of type "ID" per the XML Specification [7]. Each accessor to this value is an empty element having a local, unqualified attribute named "href" and of type "uri-reference" per the XML Schema Specification [11], with a "href" attribute value of a URI fragment identifier referencing the corresponding independent element.

6. Strings and byte arrays are represented as multi-reference simple types, but special rules allow them to be represented efficiently for common cases (see also section 5.2.1 and 5.2.3). An accessor to a string or byte-array value MAY have an attribute named "id" and of type "ID" per the XML Specification [7]. If so, all other accessors to the same value are encoded as empty elements having a local, unqualified attribute named "href" and of type "uri-reference" per the XML Schema Specification [11], with a "href" attribute value of a URI fragment identifier referencing the single element containing the value.

7. It is permissible to encode several references to a value as though these were references to several distinct values, but only when from context it is known that the meaning of the XML instance is unaltered.

8. Arrays are compound values (see also section 5.4.2). SOAP arrays are defined as having a type of "SOAP-ENC:Array" or a type derived there from.

SOAP arrays have one or more dimensions (rank) whose members are distinguished by ordinal position. An array value is represented as a series of elements reflecting the array, with members appearing in ascending ordinal sequence. For multi-dimensional arrays the dimension on the right side varies most rapidly. Each member element is named as an independent element (see rule 2).

SOAP arrays can be single-reference or multi-reference values, and consequently may be represented as the content of either an embedded or independent element.

SOAP arrays MUST contain a "SOAP-ENC:arrayType" attribute whose value specifies the type of the contained elements as well as the dimension(s) of the array. The value of the "SOAP-ENC:arrayType" attribute is defined as follows:

```
arrayTypeValue = atype asize
atype          = QName *( rank )
rank           = "[" *( "," ) "]"
asize          = "[" #length "]"
length         = 1*DIGIT
```

The "atype" construct is the type name of the contained elements expressed as a QName as would appear in the "type" attribute of an XML Schema element declaration and acts as a type constraint (meaning that all values of contained elements are asserted to conform to the indicated type; that is, the type cited in SOAP-ENC:arrayType must be the type or a supertype of every array member). In the case of arrays of arrays or "jagged arrays", the type component is encoded as the "innermost" type name followed by a rank construct for each level of nested arrays starting from 1. Multi-dimensional arrays are encoded using a comma for each dimension starting from 1.

The "asize" construct contains a comma separated list of zero, one, or more integers indicating the lengths of each dimension of the array. A value of zero integers indicates that no particular quantity is asserted but that the size may be determined by inspection of the actual members.

For example, an array with 5 members of type array of integers would have an arrayTypeValue value of "int[][5]" of which the atype value is "int[]" and the asize value is "[5]". Likewise, an array with 3 members of type two-dimensional arrays of integers would have an arrayTypeValue value of "int[,][3]" of which the atype value is "int[,]" and the asize value is "[3]".

A SOAP array member MAY contain a "SOAP-ENC:offset" attribute indicating the offset position of that item in the enclosing array. This can be used to indicate the offset position of a partially represented array (see section 5.4.2.1). Likewise, an array member MAY contain a "SOAP-ENC:position" attribute indicating the position of that item in the enclosing array. This can be used to describe members of sparse arrays (see section 5.4.2.2). The value of the "SOAP-ENC:offset" and the "SOAP-ENC:position" attribute is defined as follows:

```
arrayPoint = "[" #length "]"
```

with offsets and positions based at 0.

9. A NULL value or a default value MAY be represented by omission of the accessor element. A NULL value MAY also be indicated by an accessor element containing the attribute xsi:null with value '1' or possibly other application-dependent attributes and values.

Note that rule 2 allows independent elements and also elements representing the members of arrays to have names which are not identical to the type of the contained value.

5.2   Simple Types

For simple types, SOAP adopts all the types found in the section "Built-in datatypes" of the "XML Schema Part 2: Datatypes" Specification [11], both the value and lexical spaces. Examples include:

Type	*Example*
int	58502
float	314159265358979E+1
negativeInteger	−32768
string	Louis "Satchmo" Armstrong

The datatypes declared in the XML Schema specification may be used directly in element schemas. Types derived from these may also be used. An example of a schema fragment and corresponding instance data with elements of these types is:

```
<element name="age" type="int"/>
<element name="height" type="float"/>
<element name="displacement" type="negativeInteger"/>
<element name="color">
  <simpleType base="xsd:string">
    <enumeration value="Green"/>
    <enumeration value="Blue"/>
  </simpleType>
</element>

<age>45</age>
<height>5.9</height>
<displacement>-450</displacement>
<color>Blue</color>
```

All simple values MUST be encoded as the content of elements whose type is either defined in "XML Schema Part 2: Datatypes" Specification [11], or is based on a type found there by using the mechanisms provided in the XML Schema specification.

If a simple value is encoded as an independent element or member of a heterogenous array it is convenient to have an element declaration corresponding to the datatype. Because the "XML Schema Part 2: Datatypes" Specification [11] includes type definitions but does not include corresponding element declarations, the SOAP-ENC schema and namespace declares an element for every simple datatype. These MAY be used.

```
<SOAP-ENC:int id="int1">45</SOAP-ENC:int>
```

5.2.1 Strings

The datatype "string" is defined in "XML Schema Part 2: Datatypes" Specification [11]. Note that this is not identical to the type called "string" in many database or programming languages, and in particular may forbid some characters those languages would permit. (Those values must be represented by using some datatype other than xsd:string.)

A string MAY be encoded as a single-reference or a multi-reference value.

The containing element of the string value MAY have an "id" attribute. Additional accessor elements MAY then have matching "href" attributes.

For example, two accessors to the same string could appear, as follows:

```
<greeting id="String-0">Hello</greeting>
<salutation href="#String-0"/>
```

However, if the fact that both accessors reference the same instance of the string (or subtype of string) is immaterial, they may be encoded as two single-reference values as follows:

```
<greeting>Hello</greeting>
<salutation>Hello</salutation>
```

Schema fragments for these examples could appear similar to the following:

```
<element name="greeting" type="SOAP-ENC:string"/>
<element name="salutation" type="SOAP-ENC:string"/>
```

(In this example, the type SOAP-ENC:string is used as the element's type as a convenient way to declare an element whose datatype is "xsd:string" and which also allows an "id" and "href" attribute. See the SOAP Encoding schema for the exact definition. Schemas MAY use these declarations from the SOAP Encoding schema but are not required to.)

5.2.2 Enumerations

The "XML Schema Part 2: Datatypes" Specification [11] defines a mechanism called "enumeration." The SOAP data model adopts this mechanism directly. However, because programming and other languages often define enumeration somewhat differently, we spell-out the concept in more detail here and describe how a value that is a member of an enumerated list of possible values is to be encoded. Specifically, it is encoded as the name of the value.

"Enumeration" as a concept indicates a set of distinct names. A specific enumeration is a specific list of distinct values appropriate to the base type. For example the set of color names ("Green", "Blue", "Brown") could be defined as an enumeration based on the string built-in type. The values ("1", "3", "5") are a possible enumeration based on integer, and so on. "XML Schema Part 2: Datatypes" [11] supports enumerations for all of the simple types except for boolean. The language of "XML Schema Part 1: Structures" Specification [10] can be used to define enumeration types. If a schema is generated from another notation in which no specific base type is applicable, use "string". In the following schema example "EyeColor" is defined as a string with the possible values of "Green", "Blue", or "Brown" enumerated, and instance data is shown accordingly.

```
<element name="EyeColor" type="tns:EyeColor"/>
<simpleType name="EyeColor" base="xsd:string">
    <enumeration value="Green"/>
    <enumeration value="Blue"/>
    <enumeration value="Brown"/>
</simpleType>
```

```
<Person>
  <Name>Henry Ford</Name>
  <Age>32</Age>
  <EyeColor>Brown</EyeColor>
</Person>
```

5.2.3 Array of Bytes

An array of bytes MAY be encoded as a single-reference or a multi-reference value. The rules for an array of bytes are similar to those for a string.

In particular, the containing element of the array of bytes value MAY have an "id" attribute. Additional accessor elements MAY then have matching "href" attributes.

The recommended representation of an opaque array of bytes is the 'base64' encoding defined in XML Schemas [10][11], which uses the base64 encoding algorithm defined in 2045 [13]. However, the line length restrictions that normally apply to base64 data in MIME do not apply in SOAP. A "SOAP-ENC:base64" subtype is supplied for use with SOAP.

```
<picture xsi:type="SOAP-ENC:base64">
  aG93IG5vDyBicm73biBjb3cNCg==
</picture>
```

5.3 Polymorphic Accessor

Many languages allow accessors that can polymorphically access values of several types, each type being available at run time. A polymorphic accessor instance MUST contain an "xsi:type" attribute that describes the type of the actual value.

For example, a polymorphic accessor named "cost" with a value of type "xsd:float" would be encoded as follows:

```
<cost xsi:type="xsd:float">29.95</cost>
```

as contrasted with a cost accessor whose value's type is invariant, as follows:

```
<cost>29.95</cost>
```

5.4 Compound types

SOAP defines types corresponding to the following structural patterns often found in programming languages:

■   **Struct**   A "struct" is a compound value in which accessor name is the only distinction among member values, and no accessor has the same name as any other.

■   **Array**   An "array" is a compound value in which ordinal position serves as the only distinction among member values.

SOAP also permits serialization of data that is neither a Struct nor an Array, for example data such as is found in a Directed-Labeled-Graph Data Model in which a single node has many distinct accessors, some of which occur more than once. SOAP serialization does not require that the underlying data model make an ordering distinction among accessors, but if such an order exists, the accessors MUST be encoded in that sequence.

5.4.1   Compound Values, Structs and References to Values

The members of a Compound Value are encoded as accessor elements. When accessors are distinguished by their name (as for example in a struct), the accessor name is used as the element name. Accessors whose names are local to their containing types have unqualified element names; all others have qualified names.

The following is an example of a struct of type "Book":

```
<e:Book>
    <author>Henry Ford</author>
    <preface>Prefatory text</preface>
    <intro>This is a book.</intro>
</e:Book>
```

And this is a schema fragment describing the above structure:

```
<element name="Book">
<complexType>
  <element name="author" type="xsd:string"/>
  <element name="preface" type="xsd:string"/>
  <element name="intro" type="xsd:string"/>
</complexType>
</e:Book>
```

Below is an example of a type with both simple and complex members. It shows two levels of referencing. Note that the "href" attribute of the "Author" accessor element is a reference to the value whose "id" attribute matches. A similar construction appears for the "Address".

```
<e:Book>
    <title>My Life and Work</title>
    <author href="#Person-1"/>
</e:Book>
<e:Person id="Person-1">
    <name>Henry Ford</name>
    <address href="#Address-2"/>
</e:Person>
<e:Address id="Address-2">
    <email>mailto:henryford@hotmail.com</email>
    <web>http://www.henryford.com</web>
</e:Address>
```

The form above is appropriate when the "Person" value and the "Address" value are multi-reference. If these were instead both single-reference, they SHOULD be embedded, as follows:

```
<e:Book>
    <title>My Life and Work</title>
    <author>
        <name>Henry Ford</name>
        <address>
            <email>mailto:henryford@hotmail.com</email>
            <web>http://www.henryford.com</web>
        </address>
    </author>
</e:Book>
```

If instead there existed a restriction that no two persons can have the same address in a given instance and that an address can be either a Street-address or an Electronic-address, a Book with two authors would be encoded as follows:

```
<e:Book>
    <title>My Life and Work</title>
    <firstauthor href="#Person-1"/>
    <secondauthor href="#Person-2"/>
</e:Book>
<e:Person id="Person-1">
    <name>Henry Ford</name>
    <address xsi:type="m:Electronic-address">
        <email>mailto:henryford@hotmail.com</email>
        <web>http://www.henryford.com</web>
    </address>
</e:Person>
<e:Person id="Person-2">
    <name>Samuel Crowther</name>
    <address xsi:type="n:Street-address">
        <street>Martin Luther King Rd</street>
        <city>Raleigh</city>
        <state>North Carolina</state>
    </address>
</e:Person>
```

Serializations can contain references to values not in the same resource:

```
<e:Book>
    <title>Paradise Lost</title>
    <firstauthor href="http://www.dartmouth.edu/~milton/"/>
</e:Book>
```

And this is a schema fragment describing the above structures:

```
<element name="Book" type="tns:Book"/>
<complexType name="Book">
    <!-- Either the following group must occur or else the
        href attribute must appear, but not both. -->
    <sequence minOccurs="0" maxOccurs="1">
        <element name="title" type="xsd:string"/>
        <element name="firstauthor" type="tns:Person"/>
        <element name="secondauthor" type="tns:Person"/>
    </sequence>
    <attribute name="href" type="uriReference"/>
    <attribute name="id" type="ID"/>
    <anyAttribute namespace="##other"/>
</complexType>

<element name="Person" base="tns:Person"/>
<complexType name="Person">
    <!-- Either the following group must occur or else the
        href attribute must appear, but not both. -->
    <sequence minOccurs="0" maxOccurs="1">
        <element name="name" type="xsd:string"/>
        <element name="address" type="tns:Address"/>
    </sequence>
    <attribute name="href" type="uriReference"/>
    <attribute name="id" type="ID"/>
    <anyAttribute namespace="##other"/>
</complexType>

<element name="Address" base="tns:Address"/>
<complexType name="Address">
    <!-- Either the following group must occur or else the
        href attribute must appear, but not both. -->
    <sequence minOccurs="0" maxOccurs="1">
        <element name="street" type="xsd:string"/>
        <element name="city" type="xsd:string"/>
        <element name="state" type="xsd:string"/>
    </sequence>
    <attribute name="href" type="uriReference"/>
    <attribute name="id" type="ID"/>
    <anyAttribute namespace="##other"/>
</complexType>
```

5.4.2 Arrays

SOAP arrays are defined as having a type of "SOAP-ENC:Array" or a type derived there from (see also rule 8). Arrays are represented as element values, with no specific constraint on the name of the containing element (just as values generally do not constrain the name of their containing element).

Arrays can contain elements which themselves can be of any type, including nested arrays. New types formed by restrictions of SOAP-ENC:Array can also be created to represent, for example, arrays limited to integers or arrays of some user-defined enumeration.

The representation of the value of an array is an ordered sequence of elements constituting the items of the array. Within an array value, element names are not significant for distinguishing accessors. Elements may have any name. In practice, elements will frequently be named so that their declaration in a schema suggests or determines their type. As with compound types generally, if the value of an item in the array is a single-reference value, the item contains its value. Otherwise, the item references its value via an "href" attribute.

The following example is a schema fragment and an array containing integer array members.

```
<element name="myFavoriteNumbers"
        type="SOAP-ENC:Array"/>

<myFavoriteNumbers
  SOAP-ENC:arrayType="xsd:int[2]">
    <number>3</number>
    <number>4</number>
</myFavoriteNumbers>
```

In that example, the array "myFavoriteNumbers" contains several members each of which is a value of type SOAP-ENC:int. This can be determined by inspection of the SOAP-ENC:arrayType attribute. Note that the SOAP-ENC:Array type allows unqualified element names without restriction. These convey no type information, so when used they must either have an xsi:type attribute or the containing element must have a SOAP-ENC:arrayType attribute. Naturally, types derived from SOAP-ENC:Array may declare local elements, with type information.

As previously noted, the SOAP-ENC schema contains declarations of elements with names corresponding to each simple type in the "XML Schema Part 2: Datatypes" Specification [11]. It also contains a declaration for "Array". Using these, we might write

```
<SOAP-ENC:Array SOAP-ENC:arrayType="xsd:int[2]">
    <SOAP-ENC:int>3</SOAP-ENC:int>
    <SOAP-ENC:int>4</SOAP-ENC:int>
</SOAP-ENC:Array>
```

Arrays can contain instances of any subtype of the specified arrayType. That is, the members may be of any type that is substitutable for the type specified in the arrayType attribute, according to whatever substitutability rules are expressed in the schema. So, for example, an array of integers can contain any type derived from integer (for example "int" or any user-defined derivation of integer). Similarly, an array of "address" might contain a restricted or extended type such as "internationalAddress".

Because the supplied SOAP-ENC:Array type admits members of any type, arbitrary mixtures of types can be contained unless specifically limited by use of the arrayType attribute.

Types of member elements can be specified using the xsi:type attribute in the instance, or by declarations in the schema of the member elements, as the following two arrays demonstrate respectively.

```
<SOAP-ENC:Array SOAP-ENC:arrayType="xsd:ur-type[4]">
    <thing xsi:type="xsd:int">12345</thing>
    <thing xsi:type="xsd:decimal">6.789</thing>
    <thing xsi:type="xsd:string">
        Of Mans First Disobedience, and the Fruit
        Of that Forbidden Tree, whose mortal tast
        Brought Death into the World, and all our woe,
    </thing>
    <thing xsi:type="xsd:uriReference">
        http://www.dartmouth.edu/~milton/reading_room/
    </thing>
</SOAP-ENC:Array>
<SOAP-ENC:Array SOAP-ENC:arrayType="xsd:ur-type[4]">
    <SOAP-ENC:int>12345</SOAP-ENC:int>
    <SOAP-ENC:decimal>6.789</SOAP-ENC:decimal>
    <xsd:string>
        Of Mans First Disobedience, and the Fruit
        Of that Forbidden Tree, whose mortal tast
        Brought Death into the World, and all our woe,
    </xsd:string>
    <SOAP-ENC:uriReference>
        http://www.dartmouth.edu/~milton/reading_room/
    </SOAP-ENC:uriReference >
</SOAP-ENC:Array>
```

Array values may be structs or other compound values. For example an array of "xyz:Order" structs :

```
<SOAP-ENC:Array SOAP-ENC:arrayType="xyz:Order[2]">
    <Order>
        <Product>Apple</Product>
        <Price>1.56</Price>
    </Order>
    <Order>
        <Product>Peach</Product>
        <Price>1.48</Price>
    </Order>
</SOAP-ENC:Array>
```

Arrays may have other arrays as member values. The following is an example of an array of two arrays, each of which is an array of strings.

```
<SOAP-ENC:Array SOAP-ENC:arrayType="xsd:string[][2]">
   <item href="#array-1"/>
   <item href="#array-2"/>
</SOAP-ENC:Array>
<SOAP-ENC:Array id="array-1" SOAP-ENC:arrayType="xsd:string[2]">
   <item>r1c1</item>
   <item>r1c2</item>
   <item>r1c3</item>
</SOAP-ENC:Array>
<SOAP-ENC:Array id="array-2" SOAP-ENC:arrayType="xsd:string[2]">
   <item>r2c1</item>
   <item>r2c2</item>
</SOAP-ENC:Array>
```

The element containing an array value does not need to be named "SOAP-ENC:Array". It may have any name, provided that the type of the element is either SOAP-ENC:Array or is derived from SOAP-ENC:Array by restriction. For example, the following is a fragment of a schema and a conforming instance array.

```
<simpleType name="phoneNumber" base="string"/>

<element name="ArrayOfPhoneNumbers">
  <complexType base="SOAP-ENC:Array">
    <element name="phoneNumber" type="tns:phoneNumber"
             maxOccurs="unbounded"/>
  </complexType>
  <anyAttribute/>
</element>
<xyz:ArrayOfPhoneNumbers SOAP-ENC:arrayType="xyz:phoneNumber[2]">
   <phoneNumber>206-555-1212</phoneNumber>
   <phoneNumber>1-888-123-4567</phoneNumber>
</xyz:ArrayOfPhoneNumbers>
```

Arrays may be multi-dimensional. In this case, more than one size will appear within the asize part of the arrayType attribute:

```
<SOAP-ENC:Array SOAP-ENC:arrayType="xsd:string[2,3]">
   <item>r1c1</item>
   <item>r1c2</item>
   <item>r1c3</item>
   <item>r2c1</item>
   <item>r2c2</item>
   <item>r2c3</item>
</SOAP-ENC:Array>
```

While the examples above have shown arrays encoded as independent elements, array values MAY also appear embedded and SHOULD do so when they are known to be single reference.

The following is an example of a schema fragment and an array of phone numbers embedded in a struct of type "Person" and accessed through the accessor "phone-numbers":

```
<simpleType name="phoneNumber" base="string"/>

<element name="ArrayOfPhoneNumbers">
  <complexType base="SOAP-ENC:Array">
    <element name="phoneNumber" type="tns:phoneNumber"
             maxOccurs="unbounded"/>
  </complexType>
  <anyAttribute/>
</element>

<element name="Person">
  <complexType>
    <element name="name" type="string"/>
    <element name="phoneNumbers" type="tns:ArrayOfPhoneNumbers"/>
  </complexType>
</element>
<xyz:Person>
   <name>John Hancock</name>
   <phoneNumbers SOAP-ENC:arrayType="xyz:phoneNumber[2]">
      <phoneNumber>206-555-1212</phoneNumber>
      <phoneNumber>1-888-123-4567</phoneNumber>
   </phoneNumbers>
</xyz:Person>
```

Here is another example of a single-reference array value encoded as an embedded element whose containing element name is the accessor name:

```
<xyz:PurchaseOrder>
   <CustomerName>Henry Ford</CustomerName>
   <ShipTo>
      <Street>5th Ave</Street>
      <City>New York</City>
      <State>NY</State>
      <Zip>10010</Zip>
   </ShipTo>
   <PurchaseLineItems SOAP-ENC:arrayType="Order[2]">
      <Order>
         <Product>Apple</Product>
         <Price>1.56</Price>
      </Order>
```

```
      <Order>
         <Product>Peach</Product>
         <Price>1.48</Price>
      </Order>
   </PurchaseLineItems>
</xyz:PurchaseOrder>
```

5.4.2.1 Partially Transmitted Arrays

SOAP provides support for partially transmitted arrays, known as "varying" arrays in some contexts [12]. A partially transmitted array indicates in an "SOAP-ENC:offset" attribute the zero-origin offset of the first element transmitted. If omitted, the offset is taken as zero.

The following is an example of an array of size five that transmits only the third and fourth element counting from zero:

```
<SOAP-ENC:Array SOAP-ENC:arrayType="xsd:string[5]" SOAP-ENC:offset="[2]">
   <item>The third element</item>
   <item>The fourth element</item>
</SOAP-ENC:Array>
```

5.4.2.2 Sparse Arrays

SOAP provides support for sparse arrays. Each element representing a member value contains a "SOAP-ENC:position" attribute that indicates its position within the array. The following is an example of a sparse array of two-dimensional arrays of strings. The size is 4 but only position 2 is used:

```
<SOAP-ENC:Array SOAP-ENC:arrayType="xsd:string[,][4]">
   <SOAP-ENC:Array href="#array-1" SOAP-ENC:position="[2]"/>
</SOAP-ENC:Array>
<SOAP-ENC:Array id="array-1" SOAP-ENC:arrayType="xsd:string[10,10]">
   <item SOAP-ENC:position="[2,2]">Third row, third col</item>
   <item SOAP-ENC:position="[7,2]">Eighth row, third col</item>
</SOAP-ENC:Array>
```

If the only reference to array-1 occurs in the enclosing array, this example could also have been encoded as follows:

```
<SOAP-ENC:Array SOAP-ENC:arrayType="xsd:string[,][4]">
  <SOAP-ENC:Array SOAP-ENC:position="[2]" SOAP-
ENC:arrayType="xsd:string[10,10]>
   <item SOAP-ENC:position="[2,2]">Third row, third col</item>
   <item SOAP-ENC:position="[7,2]">Eighth row, third col</item>
  </SOAP-ENC:Array>
</SOAP-ENC:Array>
```

5.4.3 Generic Compound Types

The encoding rules just cited are not limited to those cases where the accessor names are known in advance. If accessor names are known only by inspection of the immediate values to be encoded, the same rules apply, namely that the accessor is encoded as an element whose name matches the name of the accessor, and the accessor either contains or references its value. Accessors containing values whose types cannot be determined in advance MUST always contain an appropriate xsi:type attribute giving the type of the value.

Similarly, the rules cited are sufficient to allow serialization of compound types having a mixture of accessors distinguished by name and accessors distinguished by both name and ordinal position. (That is, having some accessors repeated.) This does not require that any schema actually contain such types, but rather says that if a type-model schema does have such types, a corresponding XML syntactic schema and instance may be generated.

```
<xyz:PurchaseOrder>
    <CustomerName>Henry Ford</CustomerName>
    <ShipTo>
        <Street>5th Ave</Street>
        <City>New York</City>
        <State>NY</State>
        <Zip>10010</Zip>
    </ShipTo>
    <PurchaseLineItems>
        <Order>
            <Product>Apple</Product>
            <Price>1.56</Price>
        </Order>
        <Order>
            <Product>Peach</Product>
            <Price>1.48</Price>
        </Order>
    </PurchaseLineItems>
</xyz:PurchaseOrder>
```

Similarly, it is valid to serialize a compound value that structurally resembles an array but is not of type (or subtype) SOAP-ENC:Array. For example:

```
<PurchaseLineItems>
    <Order>
        <Product>Apple</Product>
        <Price>1.56</Price>
    </Order>
```

```
<Order>
    <Product>Peach</Product>
    <Price>1.48</Price>
</Order>
</PurchaseLineItems>
```

5.5 Default Values

An omitted accessor element implies either a default value or that no value is known. The specifics depend on the accessor, method, and its context. For example, an omitted accessor typically implies a Null value for polymorphic accessors (with the exact meaning of Null accessor-dependent). Likewise, an omitted Boolean accessor typically implies either a False value or that no value is known, and an omitted numeric accessor typically implies either that the value is zero or that no value is known.

5.6 SOAP root Attribute

The SOAP root attribute can be used to label serialization roots that are not true roots of an object graph so that the object graph can be deserialized. The attribute can have one of two values, either "1" or "0". True roots of an object graph have the implied attribute value of "1". Serialization roots that are not true roots can be labeled as serialization roots with an attribute value of "1" An element can explicitly be labeled as not being a serialization root with a value of "0".

The SOAP root attribute MAY appear on any subelement within the SOAP Header and SOAP Body elements. The attribute does not have a default value.

6 USING SOAP IN HTTP

This section describes how to use SOAP within HTTP with or without using the HTTP Extension Framework. Binding SOAP to HTTP provides the advantage of being able to use the formalism and decentralized flexibility of SOAP with the rich feature set of HTTP. Carrying SOAP in HTTP does not mean that SOAP overrides existing semantics of HTTP but rather that the semantics of SOAP over HTTP maps naturally to HTTP semantics.

SOAP naturally follows the HTTP request/response message model providing SOAP request parameters in a HTTP request and SOAP response parameters in a HTTP response. Note, however, that SOAP intermediaries are NOT the same as HTTP intermediaries. That is, an HTTP intermediary addressed with the HTTP Connection header field cannot be expected to inspect or process the SOAP entity body carried in the HTTP request.

HTTP applications MUST use the media type "text/xml" according to RFC 2376 [3] when including SOAP entity bodies in HTTP messages.

6.1 SOAP HTTP Request

Although SOAP might be used in combination with a variety of HTTP request methods, this binding only defines SOAP within HTTP POST requests (see section 7 for how to use SOAP for RPC and section 6.3 for how to use the HTTP Extension Framework).

6.1.1 The SOAPAction HTTP Header Field

The SOAPAction HTTP request header field can be used to indicate the intent of the SOAP HTTP request. The value is a URI identifying the intent. SOAP places no restrictions on the format or specificity of the URI or that it is resolvable. An HTTP client MUST use this header field when issuing a SOAP HTTP Request.

```
soapaction   = "SOAPAction" ":" [ <"> URI-reference <"> ]
URI-reference = <as defined in RFC 2396 [4]>
```

The presence and content of the SOAPAction header field can be used by servers such as firewalls to appropriately filter SOAP request messages in HTTP. The header field value of empty string ("") means that the intent of the SOAP message is provided by the HTTP Request-URI. No value means that there is no indication of the intent of the message.

Examples:

```
SOAPAction: "http://electrocommerce.org/abc#MyMessage"
SOAPAction: "myapp.sdl"
SOAPAction: ""
SOAPAction:
```

6.2 SOAP HTTP Response

SOAP HTTP follows the semantics of the HTTP Status codes for communicating status information in HTTP. For example, a 2xx status code indicates that the client's request including the SOAP component was successfully received, understood, and accepted etc.

In case of a SOAP error while processing the request, the SOAP HTTP server MUST issue an HTTP 500 "Internal Server Error" response and include a SOAP message in the response containing a SOAP Fault element (see section 4.4) indicating the SOAP processing error.

6.3 The HTTP Extension Framework

A SOAP message MAY be used together with the HTTP Extension Framework [6] in order to identify the presence and intent of a SOAP HTTP request.

Whether to use the Extension Framework or plain HTTP is a question of policy and capability of the communicating parties. Clients can force the use of the HTTP Extension Framework by using a mandatory extension declaration and the "M-" HTTP method name prefix. Servers can force the use of the HTTP Extension Framework by using the 510 "Not Extended" HTTP status code. That is, using one extra round trip, either party can detect the policy of the other party and act accordingly.

The extension identifier used to identify SOAP using the Extension Framework is *http://schemas.xmlsoap.org/soap/envelope/*.

6.4 SOAP HTTP Examples

Example 3

SOAP HTTP Using POST

```
POST /StockQuote HTTP/1.1
Content-Type: text/xml; charset="utf-8"
Content-Length: nnnn
SOAPAction: "http://electrocommerce.org/abc#MyMessage"

<SOAP-ENV:Envelope...


HTTP/1.1 200 OK
Content-Type: text/xml; charset="utf-8"
Content-Length: nnnn

<SOAP-ENV:Envelope...
```

Example 4

SOAP Using HTTP Extension Framework

```
M-POST /StockQuote HTTP/1.1
Man: "http://schemas.xmlsoap.org/soap/envelope/"; ns=NNNN
Content-Type: text/xml; charset="utf-8"
Content-Length: nnnn
NNNN-SOAPAction: "http://electrocommerce.org/abc#MyMessage"

<SOAP-ENV:Envelope...
```

(continued)

```
HTTP/1.1 200 OK
Ext:
Content-Type: text/xml; charset="utf-8"
Content-Length: nnnn

<SOAP-ENV:Envelope...
```

7 USING SOAP FOR RPC

One of the design goals of SOAP is to encapsulate and exchange RPC calls using the extensibility and flexibility of XML. This section defines a uniform representation of remote procedure calls and responses.

Although it is anticipated that this representation is likely to be used in combination with the encoding style defined in section 5 other representations are possible. The SOAP encodingStyle attribute (see section 4.3.2) can be used to indicate the encoding style of the method call and or the response using the representation described in this section.

Using SOAP for RPC is orthogonal to the SOAP protocol binding (see section 6). In the case of using HTTP as the protocol binding, an RPC call maps naturally to an HTTP request and an RPC response maps to an HTTP response. However, using SOAP for RPC is not limited to the HTTP protocol binding.

To make a method call, the following information is needed:

- The URI of the target object

- A method name

- An optional method signature

- The parameters to the method

- Optional header data

SOAP relies on the protocol binding to provide a mechanism for carrying the URI. For example, for HTTP the request URI indicates the resource that the invocation is being made against. Other than it be a valid URI, SOAP places no restriction on the form of an address (see [4] for more information on URIs).

7.1 RPC and SOAP Body

RPC method calls and responses are both carried in the SOAP Body element (see section 4.3) using the following representation:

- A method invocation is modelled as a struct.

- The method invocation is viewed as a single struct containing an accessor for each [in] or [in/out] parameter. The struct is both named and typed identically to the method name.

- Each [in] or [in/out] parameter is viewed as an accessor, with a name corresponding to the name of the parameter and type corresponding to the type of the parameter. These appear in the same order as in the method signature.

- A method response is modelled as a struct.

- The method response is viewed as a single struct containing an accessor for the return value and each [out] or [in/out] parameter. The first accessor is the return value followed by the parameters in the same order as in the method signature.

- Each parameter accessor has a name corresponding to the name of the parameter and type corresponding to the type of the parameter. The name of the return value accessor is not significant. Likewise, the name of the struct is not significant. However, a convention is to name it after the method name with the string "Response" appended.

- A method fault is encoded using the SOAP Fault element (see section 4.4). If a protocol binding adds additional rules for fault expression, those also MUST be followed.

As noted above, method and response structs can be encoded according to the rules in section 5, or other encodings can be specified using the encodingStyle attribute (see section 4.1.1).

Applications MAY process requests with missing parameters but also MAY return a fault.

Because a result indicates success and a fault indicates failure, it is an error for the method response to contain both a result and a fault.

7.2 RPC and SOAP Header

Additional information relevant to the encoding of a method request but not part of the formal method signature MAY be expressed in the RPC encoding. If so, it MUST be expressed as a subelement of the SOAP Header element.

An example of the use of the header element is the passing of a transaction ID along with a message. Since the transaction ID is not part of the signature and is typically held in an infrastructure component rather than application code, there is no direct way to pass the necessary information with the call. By adding an entry to the headers and giving it a fixed name, the transaction manager on the receiving side can extract the transaction ID and use it without affecting the coding of remote procedure calls.

8   SECURITY CONSIDERATIONS

Not described in this document are methods for integrity and privacy protection. Such issues will be addressed more fully in a future version(s) of this document.

9   REFERENCES

[1] S. Bradner, "The Internet Standards Process -- Revision 3", RFC2026, Harvard University, October 1996

[2] S. Bradner, "Key words for use in RFCs to Indicate Requirement Levels", RFC 2119, Harvard University, March 1997

[3] E. Whitehead, M. Murata, "XML Media Types", RFC2376, UC Irvine, Fuji Xerox Info. Systems, July 1998

[4] T. Berners-Lee, R. Fielding, L. Masinter, "Uniform Resource Identifiers (URI): Generic Syntax", RFC 2396, MIT/LCS, U.C. Irvine, Xerox Corporation, August 1998.

[5] R. Fielding, J. Gettys, J. C. Mogul, H. Frystyk, T. Berners-Lee, "Hypertext Transfer Protocol -- HTTP/1.1", RFC 2616, U.C. Irvine, DEC W3C/MIT, DEC, W3C/MIT, W3C/MIT, January 1997

[6] H. Nielsen, P. Leach, S. Lawrence, "An HTTP Extension Framework", RFC 2774, Microsoft, Microsoft, Agranat Systems

[7] W3C Recommendation "The XML Specification"

[8] W3C Recommendation "Namespaces in XML"

[9] W3C Working Draft "XML Linking Language". This is work in progress.

[10] W3C Working Draft "XML Schema Part 1: Structures". This is work in progress.

[11] W3C Working Draft "XML Schema Part 2: Datatypes". This is work in progress.

[12] Transfer Syntax NDR, in "DCE 1.1: Remote Procedure Call"

[13] N. Freed, N. Borenstein, "Multipurpose Internet Mail Extensions (MIME) Part One: Format of Internet Message Bodies", RFC2045, Innosoft, First Virtual, November 1996

A   SOAP ENVELOPE EXAMPLES

A.1   Sample Encoding of Call Requests

Example 5

Similar to Example 1 but with a Mandatory Header

```
POST /StockQuote HTTP/1.1
Host: www.stockquoteserver.com
Content-Type: text/xml; charset="utf-8"
Content-Length: nnnn
SOAPAction: "Some-URI"

<SOAP-ENV:Envelope
  xmlns:SOAP-ENV="http://schemas.xmlsoap.org/soap/envelope/"
  SOAP-ENV:encodingStyle="http://schemas.xmlsoap.org/soap/encoding/"/>
  <SOAP-ENV:Header>
      <t:Transaction
          xmlns:t="some-URI"
          SOAP-ENV:mustUnderstand="1">
              5
      </t:Transaction>
  </SOAP-ENV:Header>
  <SOAP-ENV:Body>
      <m:GetLastTradePrice xmlns:m="Some-URI">
          <symbol>DEF</symbol>
      </m:GetLastTradePrice>
  </SOAP-ENV:Body>
</SOAP-ENV:Envelope>
```

Example 6

Similar to Example 1 but with multiple request parameters

```
POST /StockQuote HTTP/1.1
Host: www.stockquoteserver.com
Content-Type: text/xml; charset="utf-8"
Content-Length: nnnn
SOAPAction: "Some-URI"

<SOAP-ENV:Envelope
  xmlns:SOAP-ENV="http://schemas.xmlsoap.org/soap/envelope/"
  SOAP-ENV:encodingStyle="http://schemas.xmlsoap.org/soap/encoding/"/>
```

(continued)

```
    <SOAP-ENV:Body>
        <m:GetLastTradePriceDetailed
          xmlns:m="Some-URI">
            <Symbol>DEF</Symbol>
            <Company>DEF Corp</Company>
            <Price>34.1</Price>
        </m:GetLastTradePriceDetailed>
    </SOAP-ENV:Body>
</SOAP-ENV:Envelope>
```

A.2   Sample Encoding of Response

Example 7

Similar to Example 2 but with a Mandatory Header

```
HTTP/1.1 200 OK
Content-Type: text/xml; charset="utf-8"
Content-Length: nnnn

<SOAP-ENV:Envelope
  xmlns:SOAP-ENV="http://schemas.xmlsoap.org/soap/envelope/"
  SOAP-ENV:encodingStyle="http://schemas.xmlsoap.org/soap/encoding/"/>
  <SOAP-ENV:Header>
      <t:Transaction
        xmlns:t="some-URI"
        xsi:type="xsd:int" mustUnderstand="1">
          5
      </t:Transaction>
  </SOAP-ENV:Header>
  <SOAP-ENV:Body>
      <m:GetLastTradePriceResponse
        xmlns:m="Some-URI">
          <Price>34.5</Price>
      </m:GetLastTradePriceResponse>
  </SOAP-ENV:Body>
</SOAP-ENV:Envelope>
```

Example 8

Similar to Example 2 but with a Struct

```
HTTP/1.1 200 OK
Content-Type: text/xml; charset="utf-8"
Content-Length: nnnn

<SOAP-ENV:Envelope
  xmlns:SOAP-ENV="http://schemas.xmlsoap.org/soap/envelope/"
  SOAP-ENV:encodingStyle="http://schemas.xmlsoap.org/soap/encoding/"/>
```

```
    <SOAP-ENV:Body>
        <m:GetLastTradePriceResponse
          xmlns:m="Some-URI">
            <PriceAndVolume>
                <LastTradePrice>
                    34.5
                </LastTradePrice>
                <DayVolume>
                    10000
                </DayVolume>
            </PriceAndVolume>
        </m:GetLastTradePriceResponse>
    </SOAP-ENV:Body>
</SOAP-ENV:Envelope>
```

Example 9
Similar to Example 2 but Failing to honor Mandatory Header

```
HTTP/1.1 500 Internal Server Error
Content-Type: text/xml; charset="utf-8"
Content-Length: nnnn

<SOAP-ENV:Envelope
  xmlns:SOAP-ENV="http://schemas.xmlsoap.org/soap/envelope/">
  <SOAP-ENV:Body>
      <SOAP-ENV:Fault>
          <faultcode>SOAP-ENV:MustUnderstand</faultcode>
          <faultstring>SOAP Must Understand Error</faultstring>
      </SOAP-ENV:Fault>
  </SOAP-ENV:Body>
</SOAP-ENV:Envelope>
```

Example 10
Similar to Example 2 but Failing to handle Body

```
HTTP/1.1 500 Internal Server Error
Content-Type: text/xml; charset="utf-8"
Content-Length: nnnn

<SOAP-ENV:Envelope
  xmlns:SOAP-ENV="http://schemas.xmlsoap.org/soap/envelope/">
  <SOAP-ENV:Body>
      <SOAP-ENV:Fault>
          <faultcode>SOAP-ENV:Server</faultcode>
          <faultstring>Server Error</faultstring>
```

(continued)

```
            <detail>
                <e:myfaultdetails xmlns:e="Some-URI">
                    <message>
                        My application didn't work
                    </message>
                    <errorcode>
                        1001
                    </errorcode>
                </e:myfaultdetails>
            </detail>
        </SOAP-ENV:Fault>
    </SOAP-ENV:Body>
</SOAP-ENV:Envelope>
```

Index

Note: Page numbers in italics refer to code listings, figures, or tables.

Symbols and Numbers

A

B

BRIAN TRAVIS

 Brian Travis is Founder and Chief Technical Officer of Architag International Corporation (*http://www.architag.com*), a consulting and training company based in Colorado.

Brian is an expert in real-world XML implementations. Since founding Architag (then known as Information Architects) in 1993, he has created intelligent content management systems and e-business solutions for clients around the world.

Brian is also a noted instructor and lecturer in XML and related standards. In his role as principal instructor for Architag University, he teaches clients about XML in the United States, Europe, and Asia. Brian speaks and leads tutorials and seminars for the largest internet and e-commerce conferences in the world, including Internet World, Web Design and Development, Microsoft TechEd, and COMDEX.

Brian has written books on intelligent content management and is the editor of *<TAG> Newsletter*, a publication that is devoted to structured information systems and has a worldwide readership. His current work-in-progress is "1,001 Duck-Bar Jokes," which will be published when that magical number in the title is reached. He currently has 26.

Brian lives in United Airlines seat 2C, but he pays taxes in Colorado, where he is the only one in the neighborhood with a T1 line going to his La-Z-Boy.

His passion, however, is soaking in the spa, basking in the moonlight.

The manuscript for this book was prepared using Microsoft Word 2000. Pages were composed by Microsoft Press using Adobe PageMaker 6.52 for Windows, with text in Garamond and display type in Helvetica Black. Composed pages were delivered to the printer as electronic prepress files.

Cover Graphic Designer

Girvin | Branding & Design

Cover Illustrator

Glenn Mitsui

Interior Graphic Artist

Michael Kloepfer

Principal Compositor

Daniel Latimer

Principal Proofreader/Copy Editor

Patricia Masserman

Indexer

Julie Kawabata

MICROSOFT LICENSE AGREEMENT
Book Companion CD

IMPORTANT—READ CAREFULLY: This Microsoft End-User License Agreement ("EULA") is a legal agreement between you (either an individual or an entity) and Microsoft Corporation for the Microsoft product identified above, which includes computer software and may include associated media, printed materials, and "online" or electronic documentation ("SOFTWARE PRODUCT"). Any component included within the SOFTWARE PRODUCT that is accompanied by a separate End-User License Agreement shall be governed by such agreement and not the terms set forth below. By installing, copying, or otherwise using the SOFTWARE PRODUCT, you agree to be bound by the terms of this EULA. If you do not agree to the terms of this EULA, you are not authorized to install, copy, or otherwise use the SOFTWARE PRODUCT; you may, however, return the SOFTWARE PRODUCT, along with all printed materials and other items that form a part of the Microsoft product that includes the SOFTWARE PRODUCT, to the place you obtained them for a full refund.

SOFTWARE PRODUCT LICENSE

The SOFTWARE PRODUCT is protected by United States copyright laws and international copyright treaties, as well as other intellectual property laws and treaties. The SOFTWARE PRODUCT is licensed, not sold.

1. **GRANT OF LICENSE.** This EULA grants you the following rights:

    a. **Software Product.** You may install and use one copy of the SOFTWARE PRODUCT on a single computer. The primary user of the computer on which the SOFTWARE PRODUCT is installed may make a second copy for his or her exclusive use on a portable computer.

    b. **Storage/Network Use.** You may also store or install a copy of the SOFTWARE PRODUCT on a storage device, such as a network server, used only to install or run the SOFTWARE PRODUCT on your other computers over an internal network; however, you must acquire and dedicate a license for each separate computer on which the SOFTWARE PRODUCT is installed or run from the storage device. A license for the SOFTWARE PRODUCT may not be shared or used concurrently on different computers.

    c. **License Pak.** If you have acquired this EULA in a Microsoft License Pak, you may make the number of additional copies of the computer software portion of the SOFTWARE PRODUCT authorized on the printed copy of this EULA, and you may use each copy in the manner specified above. You are also entitled to make a corresponding number of secondary copies for portable computer use as specified above.

    d. **Sample Code.** Solely with respect to portions, if any, of the SOFTWARE PRODUCT that are identified within the SOFTWARE PRODUCT as sample code (the "SAMPLE CODE"):

    i. **Use and Modification.** Microsoft grants you the right to use and modify the source code version of the SAMPLE CODE, *provided* you comply with subsection (d)(iii) below. You may not distribute the SAMPLE CODE, or any modified version of the SAMPLE CODE, in source code form.

    ii. **Redistributable Files.** Provided you comply with subsection (d)(iii) below, Microsoft grants you a nonexclusive, royalty-free right to reproduce and distribute the object code version of the SAMPLE CODE and of any modified SAMPLE CODE, other than SAMPLE CODE, or any modified version thereof, designated as not redistributable in the Readme file that forms a part of the SOFTWARE PRODUCT (the "Non-Redistributable Sample Code"). All SAMPLE CODE other than the Non-Redistributable Sample Code is collectively referred to as the "REDISTRIBUTABLES."

    iii. **Redistribution Requirements.** If you redistribute the REDISTRIBUTABLES, you agree to: (i) distribute the REDISTRIBUTABLES in object code form only in conjunction with and as a part of your software application product; (ii) not use Microsoft's name, logo, or trademarks to market your software application product; (iii) include a valid copyright notice on your software application product; (iv) indemnify, hold harmless, and defend Microsoft from and against any claims or lawsuits, including attorney's fees, that arise or result from the use or distribution of your software application product; and (v) not permit further distribution of the REDISTRIBUTABLES by your end user. Contact Microsoft for the applicable royalties due and other licensing terms for all other uses and/or distribution of the REDISTRIBUTABLES.

2. **DESCRIPTION OF OTHER RIGHTS AND LIMITATIONS.**

    - **Limitations on Reverse Engineering, Decompilation, and Disassembly.** You may not reverse engineer, decompile, or disassemble the SOFTWARE PRODUCT, except and only to the extent that such activity is expressly permitted by applicable law notwithstanding this limitation.

    - **Separation of Components.** The SOFTWARE PRODUCT is licensed as a single product. Its component parts may not be separated for use on more than one computer.

    - **Rental.** You may not rent, lease, or lend the SOFTWARE PRODUCT.

    - **Support Services.** Microsoft may, but is not obligated to, provide you with support services related to the SOFTWARE PRODUCT ("Support Services"). Use of Support Services is governed by the Microsoft policies and programs described in the user manual, in "online" documentation, and/or in other Microsoft-provided materials. Any supplemental software code provided to you as part of the Support Services shall be considered part of the SOFTWARE PRODUCT and subject to the terms and conditions of this EULA. With respect to technical information you provide to Microsoft as part of the Support Services, Microsoft may use such information for its business purposes, including for product support and development. Microsoft will not utilize such technical information in a form that personally identifies you.

- **Software Transfer.** You may permanently transfer all of your rights under this EULA, provided you retain no copies, you transfer all of the SOFTWARE PRODUCT (including all component parts, the media and printed materials, any upgrades, this EULA, and, if applicable, the Certificate of Authenticity), **and** the recipient agrees to the terms of this EULA.

- **Termination.** Without prejudice to any other rights, Microsoft may terminate this EULA if you fail to comply with the terms and conditions of this EULA. In such event, you must destroy all copies of the SOFTWARE PRODUCT and all of its component parts.

3. **COPYRIGHT.** All title and copyrights in and to the SOFTWARE PRODUCT (including but not limited to any images, photographs, animations, video, audio, music, text, SAMPLE CODE, REDISTRIBUTABLES, and "applets" incorporated into the SOFTWARE PRODUCT) and any copies of the SOFTWARE PRODUCT are owned by Microsoft or its suppliers. The SOFTWARE PRODUCT is protected by copyright laws and international treaty provisions. Therefore, you must treat the SOFTWARE PRODUCT like any other copyrighted material **except** that you may install the SOFTWARE PRODUCT on a single computer provided you keep the original solely for backup or archival purposes. You may not copy the printed materials accompanying the SOFTWARE PRODUCT.

4. **U.S. GOVERNMENT RESTRICTED RIGHTS.** The SOFTWARE PRODUCT and documentation are provided with RESTRICTED RIGHTS. Use, duplication, or disclosure by the Government is subject to restrictions as set forth in subparagraph (c)(1)(ii) of the Rights in Technical Data and Computer Software clause at DFARS 252.227-7013 or subparagraphs (c)(1) and (2) of the Commercial Computer Software—Restricted Rights at 48 CFR 52.227-19, as applicable. Manufacturer is Microsoft Corporation/One Microsoft Way/Redmond, WA 98052-6399.

5. **EXPORT RESTRICTIONS.** You agree that you will not export or re-export the SOFTWARE PRODUCT, any part thereof, or any process or service that is the direct product of the SOFTWARE PRODUCT (the foregoing collectively referred to as the "Restricted Components"), to any country, person, entity, or end user subject to U.S. export restrictions. You specifically agree not to export or re-export any of the Restricted Components (i) to any country to which the U.S. has embargoed or restricted the export of goods or services, which currently include, but are not necessarily limited to, Cuba, Iran, Iraq, Libya, North Korea, Sudan, and Syria, or to any national of any such country, wherever located, who intends to transmit or transport the Restricted Components back to such country; (ii) to any end user who you know or have reason to know will utilize the Restricted Components in the design, development, or production of nuclear, chemical, or biological weapons; or (iii) to any end user who has been prohibited from participating in U.S. export transactions by any federal agency of the U.S. government. You warrant and represent that neither the BXA nor any other U.S. federal agency has suspended, revoked, or denied your export privileges.

DISCLAIMER OF WARRANTY

NO WARRANTIES OR CONDITIONS. MICROSOFT EXPRESSLY DISCLAIMS ANY WARRANTY OR CONDITION FOR THE SOFTWARE PRODUCT. THE SOFTWARE PRODUCT AND ANY RELATED DOCUMENTATION ARE PROVIDED "AS IS" WITHOUT WARRANTY OR CONDITION OF ANY KIND, EITHER EXPRESS OR IMPLIED, INCLUDING, WITHOUT LIMITATION, THE IMPLIED WARRANTIES OF MERCHANTABILITY, FITNESS FOR A PARTICULAR PURPOSE, OR NONINFRINGEMENT. THE ENTIRE RISK ARISING OUT OF USE OR PERFORMANCE OF THE SOFTWARE PRODUCT REMAINS WITH YOU.

LIMITATION OF LIABILITY. TO THE MAXIMUM EXTENT PERMITTED BY APPLICABLE LAW, IN NO EVENT SHALL MICROSOFT OR ITS SUPPLIERS BE LIABLE FOR ANY SPECIAL, INCIDENTAL, INDIRECT, OR CONSEQUENTIAL DAMAGES WHATSOEVER (INCLUDING, WITHOUT LIMITATION, DAMAGES FOR LOSS OF BUSINESS PROFITS, BUSINESS INTERRUPTION, LOSS OF BUSINESS INFORMATION, OR ANY OTHER PECUNIARY LOSS) ARISING OUT OF THE USE OF OR INABILITY TO USE THE SOFTWARE PRODUCT OR THE PROVISION OF OR FAILURE TO PROVIDE SUPPORT SERVICES, EVEN IF MICROSOFT HAS BEEN ADVISED OF THE POSSIBILITY OF SUCH DAMAGES. IN ANY CASE, MICROSOFT'S ENTIRE LIABILITY UNDER ANY PROVISION OF THIS EULA SHALL BE LIMITED TO THE GREATER OF THE AMOUNT ACTUALLY PAID BY YOU FOR THE SOFTWARE PRODUCT OR US$5.00; PROVIDED, HOWEVER, IF YOU HAVE ENTERED INTO A MICROSOFT SUPPORT SERVICES AGREEMENT, MICROSOFT'S ENTIRE LIABILITY REGARDING SUPPORT SERVICES SHALL BE GOVERNED BY THE TERMS OF THAT AGREEMENT. BECAUSE SOME STATES AND JURISDICTIONS DO NOT ALLOW THE EXCLUSION OR LIMITATION OF LIABILITY, THE ABOVE LIMITATION MAY NOT APPLY TO YOU.

MISCELLANEOUS

This EULA is governed by the laws of the State of Washington USA, except and only to the extent that applicable law mandates governing law of a different jurisdiction.

Should you have any questions concerning this EULA, or if you desire to contact Microsoft for any reason, please contact the Microsoft subsidiary serving your country, or write: Microsoft Sales Information Center/One Microsoft Way/Redmond, WA 98052-6399.

PN 097-0002296